Prentice Hall Style Manual

PRENTICE HALL
STYLE
MANUAL

MARY A. DE VRIES

PRENTICE HALL
Englewood Cliffs, New Jersey 07632

Prentice-Hall International (UK) Limited, *London*
Prentice-Hall of Australia Pty. Limited, *Sydney*
Prentice-Hall Canada, Inc., *Toronto*
Prentice-Hall Hispanoamericana, S.A., *Mexico*
Prentice-Hall of India Private Limited, *New Delhi*
Prentice-Hall of Japan, Inc., *Tokyo*
Simon & Schuster Asia Pte. Ltd., *Singapore*
Editora Prentice-Hall do Brasil, Ltda., *Rio de Janeiro*

© 1992 *by*

Mary A. De Vries

10 9 8 7 6 5 4 3 2

Library of Congress Cataloging-in-Publication Data

De Vries, Mary Ann.
Prentice Hall style manual / Mary A. De Vries
    p. cm.
Includes index
ISBN 0-13-720293-8
    1. English language—Business English—Handbooks, manuals, etc.
2. Commercial correspondence—Handbooks, manuals, etc. 3. English
language—Style—Handbooks, manuals, etc. 4. Business writing—
Handbooks, manuals, etc. I. Prentice-Hall, inc. II. Title.
III. Title: Style Manual.
PE1479.B87D4   1992
808'.027'02465—dc20   91-40079
                                      CIP

ISBN 0-13-720293-8

Printed in the United States of America

Preface

The foundation for this book is based on two premises: First, stylebooks traditionally have dealt with style (punctuation, capitalization, and so on) at the expense of the closely related matter of format (arrangement of elements on a page). Second, most stylebooks are oriented toward a specific discipline, such as biology, or have a strong scholarly or publishing bent.

People in various businesses and professions have additional needs. They must style and format a great variety of material not just books and articles. They regularly work with letters, reports, schedules, itineraries, meeting materials, and countless other items. To help secretaries, administrators, managers, and many others in their business and professional work—as well as the writers and editors of books, articles, and the like—the *Prentice Hall Style Manual* was developed as a two-part work, both a style manual and a formatting guide.

Before personal computers (PCs) became popular and desktop publishing was available, written material was prepared by typewriter either in manuscript form, to be sent to a typesetter, or as finished copy, such as a letter. So the need for styling and formatting has always existed; computer technology has simply stretched the horizons and brought the need for understanding and expertise in this area to an individual level. With a PC one can now be a "typesetter" as well as a writer or preparer of manuscripts.

Stylebooks, however, have not provided the full range of information that people in business and professional occupations require. An accountant once told me about the problems she had in explaining to her staff how to prepare various financial statements—margins, spacing, indentions, position of headings, arrangement of footnotes, and so on. She expressed her dismay at the lack of a book that one could open to a specific model and say, "Here, do it just like this." In fact, she said the best of all worlds would be a book that not only has models of all sorts of material but also covers the essential points of style. Although I spoke with her several years ago, she was already describing the *Prentice Hall Style Manual*. Because she echoed the request of so many others, the book eventually became a reality and is designed to reflect precisely those needs that she expressed.

It is amazing—or perhaps it isn't—that so many questions arise when we have to write something and prepare a draft or the final copy for it.

- Should I capitalize every word in a table heading? (Chapters 10 and 21)

- How much space should I leave before and after a footnote? (Chapters 9 and 21)

- What is the proper punctuation in the address of an OCR-format envelope? (Chapters 12 and 15)

- When is a quotation indented as a block (extract), and should it be single- or double-spaced? (Chapters 2 and 21)

- Should I indent carryover lines in a column list and, if so, how many spaces? (Chapters 10 and 21)

- Should terms like *free-trade zone* be capitalized? (Chapters 1 and 3)

- In a letter, if I refer to the company president by title, without his or her name, should I capitalize the word *president?* (Chapters 1 and 3)

- Since the trend is to write abbreviations without periods, should I also omit the periods in academic degrees such as *Ph.D.*? (Chapters 1 and 6)

- Should the subject line in a letter be centered or positioned flush left? (Chapters 12 and 15)

- When can a foreign term be written without accents and in roman type (no italics)? (Chapters 1 and 8)

Part I, "Style Guide," answers questions about writing style (e.g, capitalization) and type style (e.g., italics versus roman). Almost every rule or suggested style in part I has examples to illustrate its practical application. These essential points of style are presented in the first thirteen chapters.

1. Elements of Style
2. Punctuation
3. Capitalization
4. Spelling
5. Word Division
6. Abbreviations
7. Numbers and Symbols
8. Foreign Terms
9. References
10. Tables
11. Forms of Address
12. Letters
13. Memos

In addition to the hundreds of examples and illustrations of style in part I, about two hundred complete models of formats are provided in part II, "Model Formats." These samples of actual documents and other written material are arranged in 125 categories such as "proposals" and "announcements." (See the alphabetical list of models following the Contents.) The model formats are collected in seven chapters

(Chapters 15 through 21) preceded by an introductory discussion (Chapter 14) about preparing material by typewriter or computer.

14. Formatting
15. Correspondence
16. Filing
17. Law
18. Statistics and Finance
19. Meetings
20. Record Keeping
21. Reports

Most of the models in part II were prepared on a Zenith Data Systems 286 Personal Computer using Microsoft Word Version 4.0 and were printed on an Apple LaserWriter® II NTX laser printer. Some were prepared in full or in part with an IBM Selectric typewriter using Adjutant and Light Italic typefaces. Those who prepare material with more (or less) advanced equipment and software might have different results and could experience more (or less) versatility in formatting. Nevertheless, the models in part II are realistic representations of existing documents and other literature prepared in a widely accepted format. In most cases the format can be imitated completely or can be modified in full or in part to suit personal preferences or to adapt the format to specific company requirements.

Since some items (such as a report) might be prepared first as a double-spaced draft and then in a single-spaced final format, many of the format categories include examples of both double-spaced and single-spaced pages. Other items (such as a letter) are always single-spaced, and some (such as a news release) are always double-spaced. For rules concerning such specifications, read the relevant chapter in part I. Chapter 9, for instance, provides the rules and guidelines for writing various types of references, and chapter 21 provides numerous models of actual notes, bibliographies, and other references. Similarly, chapter 10 gives rules and examples for writing, capitalizing, and punctuating the major elements in tabular material, and chapter 21 provides the models of various statistical and textual tables, lists, and outlines.

To illustrate the points of style discussed in part I, fictional text was created for the models in part II. In some cases the text was adapted from ideas or sample material supplied by individuals and organizations. I am especially grateful to Jean McCormack for her help in locating authentic samples of many of the items. I also want to acknowledge the substantial contribution of the U.S. Small Business Administration, whose Business Development Publications were the inspiration and source of numerous topics depicted in the models. Finally, I greatly appreciate the opportunity to reproduce some of the signs and symbols and the foreign-language material in chapters 7 and 8 from the U.S. Government Printing Office *Style Manual.*

Contents

Models

Part I

STYLE GUIDE

Chapter 1

ELEMENTS OF STYLE

If you are writing something such as a thank-you letter, a poem, a speech, or a report, *style* to you may mean only the way in which you express yourself (language, tone, and so on), whether you are formal and businesslike or informal and chatty. For those who publish what you write, as well as for many writers themselves, *style* encompasses much more, including the so-called mechanics of communication such as punctuation, capitalization, spelling, word division, abbreviations, numbers and symbols, and foreign terms. All of these elements characterize a person's distinctive treatment of words and terms and are essential components of style. Consider these statements by Lee, Marsha, and Jeremy.

Lee: The Board of Trustees elected a new President at its Annual Meeting, June 7, 1991—its first meeting of the new fiscal year.

Marsha: The Board of Trustees elected a new president at its annual meeting—June 7, 1991, the first meeting of the new fiscal year.

Jeremy: The board of trustees elected a new president at its annual meeting, June 7, 1991, the first meeting of the new fiscal year.

Which sentence is styled correctly? All of them are correct. In some points of style there is no right or wrong. The choice is a matter of preference; however, some styles, though technically correct, may be awkward or out of date. In the above examples, Lee used an older style, in which general titles (common nouns) are capitalized; Marsha used a mixture; and Jeremy used the newer style, in which common nouns are not capitalized. In regard to punctuation, both Lee and Marsha used a dash, although in different places, whereas Jeremy used only commas. Many authorities would prefer Jeremy's choice, believing that a dash is unnecessary in such a case and that a comma is all that is needed.

CHOICE OF WRITING STYLE

What style should I use? That's a perplexing question to many persons. At work, though, you may not have to make a decision; your employer may already have a preferred style that you should use with all company literature and communications. At school, educators should use the preferred style of the institution, and students should ask their instructors if any such preferences apply to their assignments. Although you have greater latitude in personal and social messages, certain items such as wedding invitations must follow a prescribed style to be socially proper. Literary writers can often determine which style to follow by checking previously published material in magazines, journals, books, and so on, especially samples produced by publications or book publishers to which they intend to submit their manuscripts.

Punctuation

Many choices concerning punctuation will be left to your discretion, even when you are expected generally to follow an employer's or someone else's style. An organization may, however, be concerned about something such as overpunctuation—too many commas, quotation marks, and the like. Or it may prefer to have terms you define italicized (or underlined in manuscript) rather than enclosed in quotation marks.

A "boreen" is a narrow country lane.

A *boreen* is a narrow country lane.

But in other matters the decision may be up to you and will depend on your preference. Perhaps, for instance, you prefer to set off parenthetical thoughts with dashes rather than enclose them in parentheses.

His tools—drill, stapler, saw, and so on—are in perfect working condition.

His tools (drill, stapler, saw, and so on) are in perfect working condition.

Rules, with examples, are provided in chapter 2 for the fourteen principal marks of punctuation: apostrophe, brackets, colon, comma, dash, ellipsis points, exclamation point, hyphen, parentheses, period, question mark, quotation marks, semicolon, and virgule.

Capitalization

Should you write *Communist* or *communist?* The *Pope* or the *pope?* The *Earth* or the *earth?* The *University* or the *university?* Individuals and organizations vary in their preferences concerning capitalization, but the trend is toward lowercase (small) letters for common nouns and uppercase (capital) letters for proper nouns.

The program honored veterans of the *Vietnam War.*

The program honored veterans of the *war in Vietnam.*

This modern practice may sound simple and easy to follow, but it is complicated by exceptions to the rules. A title such as *senator*, for example, is not capitalized when standing alone, but the title *Speaker of the House* should be capitalized in all cases to avoid confusion with references to another type of *speaker* (anyone), such as the person presently talking or someone addressing an assembly. Other exceptions are also recognized by style authorities, for instance:

Stone Age, nuclear age

Gothic, baroque

Milky Way, aurora borealis

Bushman, aborigine

Tropic of Cancer, equator

The rules (and exceptions) that apply to capitalization style, with examples, are given in chapter 3 in these categories: education; geography; government and politics; history; holidays, time, and seasons; the judiciary; military service; proper nouns; religion; science; and titles and headings.

Spelling

Although there are some choices in questions of spelling (*zeros* or *zeroes*), the greatest concern is accuracy. Spelling is the bane of even some of the most successful writers. Computer spell-checkers have solved this problem to a point, but if you write *affect* when you mean *effect,* the computer will not recognize your error. Also, some words you use may not be in the spell-checker's dictionary, and the computer will ask you to confirm or correct the questionable word. In addition, the more words you misspell, the longer the spell-checking process will take, which is a nuisance if you are in a hurry. Even with the extensive benefits of advanced technology, then, we still need to improve the accuracy of our spelling.

Some authorities believe there are so many spelling rules and so many complicated exceptions to the rules that the rules are almost useless. Rather than memorize the rules and the exceptions, these authorities would urge you to commit as many words as possible to memory and check a modern dictionary when your memory fails you. Others believe that however numerous and complicated the rules may be, they are invaluable and great timesavers. This book recognizes the validity of both views and in chapter 4 offers essential rules of spelling, with exceptions, for those who want to use them advantageously.

Spelling plural forms of words, for instance, isn't as simple as it seems. You have to decide when to add *s* or *es*, when to change the last letter of a word before adding *s*, or when to change the form of the word entirely.

ring, rings

dish, dishes

self, selves

child, children

Compounds can be tricky too. Should you use a hyphen? Write the compound as two words? Write the compound as one word without a hyphen? Not only do different rules apply, but also contemporary practice sometimes differs from traditional usage.

backup, start-up

time-sharing, profit sharing

secretary-treasurer, attorney general

Prefixes and suffixes are perhaps the most complicated. Generally, you should not use a hyphen after a prefix or before a suffix.

interoffice

parapsychology

catlike

statewide

But how do you know when to double a final consonant or change the final letter before adding a suffix or other word ending?

try, trying

infer, inferred

two, twofold

fly, flier

whole, wholly

Detailed explanations of these and other spelling rules, with numerous examples, are given in chapter 4.

Word Division

If you use a computer, the wordwrap feature of your program may eliminate your worries about choosing the proper place to divide a word at the end of a line. In that case, the computer simply moves to the next line any word that is too long. But if you want to intervene or if you are using another means of production where word division is a common occurrence (although authorities recommend that you try to avoid it), you need to observe certain rules and standard practices.

Careful writers and correspondents are distressed by the illogical and incorrect way that words are sometimes divided. Incorrect word division makes reading difficult; it can confuse a reader and slow the pace of reading. Making mistakes also draws attention to the writer's ignorance in this matter. Notice how clumsy these improper divisions appear (the correct division is in parentheses).

eyesi-ght (eye-sight)

fac-esaving (face-saving)

nonv-ector (non-vector)

treb-le (tre-ble)

Chapter 5 groups the rules of word division into six categories: syllables and letters, prefixes and suffixes, compounds, abbreviations, names, and numbers.

Abbreviations

Before deciding what style to use for your abbreviations, you need to ask whether you should even use abbreviations. Generally, in formal writing you shouldn't (except for something such as *R.s.v.p.* on an invitation). In informal writing, certain abbreviations are acceptable if you follow the applicable rules. It is acceptable, for instance, to use the abbreviated form of an organization's name, provided that you spell it out in full the first time mentioned and put the initials in parentheses after the name. But other abbreviations such as *apt.* for *apartment* are a sign of laziness even in informal writing. Such abbreviations should be used only in note taking. Those who monitor language usage have noticed a substantial increase in the use of technical abbreviations (such as *v* for *volt*) in scientific writing but a decrease in the use of general abbreviations (such as *amt.* for *amount*) in other writing.

The main concerns in regard to the style of abbreviations are when to use small or capital letters, when to use periods or other punctuation, and where or whether to add spaces between letters in abbreviations. The trend is toward less punctuation and fewer capital letters.

acct.	account
assn.	association
kg	kilogram
mpg	miles per gallon
CORE	Congress of Racial Equality
USGPO	United States Government Printing Office
B.S.	bachelor of science
Ph.D.	doctor of philosophy
AZ	Arizona
VI	Virgin Islands

Refer to chapter 6 for rules on the proper abbreviation style and for lists of abbreviations in these categories: general abbreviations, technical abbreviations, organizations, academic degrees, and postal abbreviations.

Numbers and Symbols

How to style numbers and symbols depends on the type of writing you are doing. If you are writing a scientific treatise, for instance, you will probably spell out numbers *one* through *nine* (or *ten*) and use numerals for everything else. But if you are writing a letter to a business colleague, you will probably spell out numbers *one* through *ninety-nine* and all large round numbers such as *five hundred*. In scientific usage you will probably use numerals for all measurements (*5 km*), but in general writing you will probably spell out such references (*five kilometers*). The same reasoning applies to signs and symbols such as *$* and *%*.

Authorities in different fields, therefore, have different requirements. If your place of employment does not have a company style manual, you will need to determine more than just the type of material you are composing; you will also need to decide how to style specific numerical or symbolic references to organizations (*First Baptist Church*), assemblies (*Sixth Annual Conference*), streets (*Third Avenue*), and other formal designations. Also, what about plurals of numbers (*tens, 297s*)? Time (*2 a.m.*)? Names (*Henry VIII*)? Craft (*Mariner II*)? Deciding how to write inclusive numbers can be difficult. Do you write *108-9* or *108-109? 1987-88* or *1987-1988?* Does A.D. precede or follow the year (*A.D. 275*)? What about B.C. (*275 B.C.*)?

Business report writers, students, researchers, and many others are concerned about the proper style for numbers in outlines and other lists. In scientific usage, there are endless signs and symbols to deal with as well. All of these problems are discussed in detail in chapter 7.

Foreign Terms

Some people rarely use foreign terms in their messages. But as communication among countries increases, we find ourselves including *glasnost* and other foreign terms more frequently. The main decisions to make concerning foreign terms are how to capitalize them, how to punctuate them, how to divide them at the end of a line, whether to italicize them (or underline them in manuscript), and whether to use diacritical marks and which ones.

Some foreign words have become completely anglicized. Those words do not require diacritical marks (see chapter 8 for a complete list).

a la carte

canape

coup d'etat

soiree

Other foreign terms require diacritical marks.

attaché

chargé

entrepôt

père

Most authorities agree that familiar foreign words need not be italicized. If you don't know how familiar the term is (this keeps changing too), use roman (nonitalic) type.

Chapter 8 includes the alphabets of familiar foreign languages and includes rules on special characters and syllabication.

References

Notes, reference lists, bibliographies, and the like are used to give credit to a source of information and to refer readers to further information. The appropriate style depends on the discipline involved. A poet, a psychologist, and a physicist would each likely style reference sources differently. Many of the various disciplines, in fact, have style manuals with guidelines concerning their preferred reference style.

This book provides guidelines and examples for general usage in the absence of particular requirements for a specific discipline. The following footnote style is also suitable for end-of-page notes or end-of-chapter and end-of-book lists. Words underlined in manuscript would be set in italics in printed material.

1. This point is elaborated in Max R. Holloman, *The New Science* (New York: Pen and Book Associates, 1990), 109-10.

Source notes are used with tables and other illustrations.

Source: Judith Hillyer, "Portable Offices," *Office Showroom* 7 (1991): 7-8.

Credit lines are source notes that specify permission granted by the source to use the material cited.

Courtesy of The Penworth Corporation, Jackson, Mississippi.

Reference lists are alphabetical lists of sources consulted by the author of the material being written. One popular style is the name-date system.

Apman, Joel T. 1979. *Society in Transition.* Chicago: Morris Publications.

Bibliographies also are alphabetical lists of works that an author has consulted.

Benston, Louis. "Econometrics." *Watson's Journal,* Winter 1990, 17-19.

The rules and examples in chapter 9 illustrate the variety of styles used for notes, reference lists, and bibliographies and indicate the proper style for various types of published material from books to articles to congressional reports to academic papers.

Tables

Textual and statistical tabular material presents a styling challenge. Many writers are surprised by the variety of styles that can be adopted. The complexity of the material has a lot to do with the style chosen and the placement of the various elements: table number, title, crossheads and stub (left-hand column), body, and footnotes and source notes. Whatever style is chosen, though, a prime objective must be to provide a clear and simple construction.

Numerous questions arise when compiling data in tabular form. As well as selecting proper headings, should you use rules and where should you place them? Should you repeat in each row the *$, %,* or other sign used in the first row? Should you indent runover (carryover) lines and, if so, how many spaces? Should you use a dash or the abbreviation *N/A* (not applicable) in a blank space? What is the rule for using letters (*a, b, c*) as opposed to numbers (*1, 2, 3*) for table notes? After the table body, does the source note precede any footnotes? Does a general note precede numbered or lettered footnotes? Are tables in a book numbered consecutively (*1, 2, 3, 4, . . .*) or with double digits by chapter (*1.1, 1.2, 1.3, . . . 2.1, 2.2, 2.3, . . .*)? Should you capitalize each word in a crosshead? In the stub?

Refer to chapter 10 for guidelines concerning the many decisions that must be made in choosing a table style and arranging the various elements properly.

Forms of Address

One sure sign of the way that things change over time is the change in address style, or the titles used in referring to people. In the 1970s and even the 1980s, some people were still nervous about using the title *Ms.* Today many people are nervous about using *Miss* or *Mrs.* At one time it would have been considered a terrible blunder to use the title *esquire* with a woman's name. Now it is considered bad manners not to use it in the same situations in which it would be used with a man's name. In matters of forms of address, therefore, it is not so much a matter of choosing a style as one of knowing what is the latest acceptable style.

Titles are not the only problem. What about academic degrees? Some people have more than one degree. In such cases, if all degrees are listed, the rule is to list the one pertaining to the person's profession first.

Mary Benchley [a scientist], Sc.D., Ph.D.

Donald Farnsworth [a medical doctor], M.D., LL.D.

Sometimes a person's name or gender is unknown. The old style of always using *Mr.* or *Gentlemen* in such cases is now considered rude; instead, you should omit the title for a person and add *Ladies* for a corporation of both men and women.

Dear L. B. Jones:

Ladies and Gentlemen:

Specific rules apply in the case of retired officials. Retired military officers retain their titles, for example, but retired politicians do not. Special rules apply in social situations, too, with variations for single, married, and divorced women. In companies, single-gender designations such as *Messrs.* or *Mesdames* are used only when a firm consists solely of men or women. All of these intricacies are explained in detail in chapter 11.

Letters and Memos

You have several choices in letter and memo style. Letters are usually prepared in one of five principal formats: full block, block, modified block, simplified, and official/personal. Memos take many forms, such as the note format or speed-message format.

In a business letter, you will be concerned with the position and style (punctuation, capitalization, and so on) of these key elements: attention line, body, copy notation, complimentary close, continuation-page heading, dateline, enclosure notation, envelope, identification line, inside address, mail notation, personal or confidential notation, postscript, reference line, salutation, signature, and subject line. The memo has guide headings, a body, miscellaneous notations, and an envelope.

Since the appearance of your letter or memo creates the first impression of you on a reader, it is important to style your message attractively and make it consistent with accepted format specifications. Computers have the advantage of being able to store these format specifications for future recall.

Chapter 12 provides rules, with examples, for writing the sixteen key elements in a letter, as well as the envelope. Chapter 13 offers rules and examples for styling the key elements of a memo.

CHOICE OF TYPE STYLE

In general writing by typewriter or computer, most decisions about type style concern choice between italic and roman and small letters and capital letters. You may wonder how to style titles and subheadings, for example, or whether to italicize (underline in manuscript) a word being defined or put it in quotation marks. Unless you are involved in publishing, you won't be concerned about matters such as type size (such as 10-point Helvetica) and leading (points of space between lines). Rather, you will use the type supplied with your typewriter or computer. But depending on your word processing program, you may be able to make choices involving superscripts such as this^2 and subscripts, such as this$_2$. You will also be able to underline words, like this, or possibly use an italic face like *this*, or a boldface like **this**.

Italics can be designated in one of two ways. If your equipment has an italic face, you can simply type or print out the material in that typeface. But if you are preparing material that will be copyedited and then typeset and printed by traditional means, the preferred practice is to underline words that you want italicized (use a single underline). Boldface (such as **style**) is indicated by drawing a single wavy line under the material like this. Small capitals (such as THIS) are designated by drawing two lines under the material like this. Decisions about the use of bold or small caps for material such as chapter titles or text subheads are usually made by the publisher, not the writer, however. (See chapter 3 for guidelines concerning the capitalization of words, terms, titles, and other elements.)

In printed material, the punctuation that follows a word is usually in the same typeface as the word itself, for example, **New York:**. But parentheses and brackets should remain roman, for example, (**New York:**). For more about punctuation, see chapter 2.

If your equipment cannot print subscripts and superscripts, you can instruct a typesetter to use lowered and raised numbers as follows:

Everyone knows the basic abbreviation for water: H 2 O.

Macauley then prepared a more formal document. 3

When preparing material that will not be published, some writers type note numbers with diagonals or parentheses.

The poem was the last he wrote./5/

The poem was the last he wrote.(5)

Note that in American-style writing, the punctuation is placed inside the note number.

The poem was the last he wrote.[5]

Use of Italics

In ordinary writing, the choice of type style is often confined to a decision of when to use italics. But first the question of whether it is appropriate to do anything must be asked. Some writers overuse italics, just as they overuse quotation marks, which then lose their effectiveness and create a cluttered page that distracts readers and impedes their reading. Such overuse tends to come from a desire to emphasize words repeatedly. But a sentence that can't convey its message without the use of italics is often ineffectively written. Although the use of italics (or quotation marks) in such cases is inexcusable, in other cases the use is proper and even required for adherence to accepted conventions.

Definitions. It is proper to italicize (underline in manuscript) terms being defined.

A *stylebook* is a work that describes an accepted style of written or printed material.

Some writers also italicize special or technical terms that are being discussed on first use.

The question of *insurgence,* as discussed in this section, has led scholars to formulate two main theories.

In certain disciplines, such as theology and philosophy, writers may enclose special terms in single quotation marks instead of using italics. In such cases, punctuation follows the closing quote.

This logic belies the concept of 'rebirth'.

Words Used as Words. A word referred to as a word is italicized (underlined in manuscript), and the same style may be used for letters referred to as letters.

The word *handsaw* is self-explanatory.

The *e* is silent in *dupe*.

But words preceded by the expression *so called* should not be italicized or enclosed in quotation marks.

The so-called army of migrant workers invaded the small farming community.

Legal Cases. All words, except the abbreviation *v*. (*versus*), in legal cases should be italicized (underlined in manuscript). The letter *v* may be in either an italic or roman typeface.

The Wright Corporation v. Henderson and Association

The Wright Corporation v. *Henderson and Association*

the *Wright* case

In *Wright,* the decision was unanimous.

Wright Corporation's case is a recent example.

In footnotes to works of law, the case name often is not italicized.

9. The Wright Corporation v. Henderson and Associates, 521 U.S. 722, 311 (1990).

For detailed information on legal citations, refer to *A Uniform System of Citation,* published by the Harvard Law Review Association, Cambridge, Massachusetts.

Craft and Vessels. Formal names of air, sea, and space vessels and craft, such as ships and submarines, airplanes, and spacecraft, as well as satellites, programs, and related names and titles, should be italicized (underlined in manuscript), except for any abbreviation such as USS that precedes the name of a vessel or craft. Informal references to vessels or craft, to their class or make, or to related programs should not be italicized. Names of missiles and rockets also are not italicized.

the *Peggy Lee*

SS *Windstar*

     Apollo II
     Concorde
     Amtrak
     Star Wars program
     ICBM

Biological Terms. The rules for scientific terminology, such as biological terms, are complex and may differ among disciplines. The following guidelines may be followed in the absence of specific requirements in your field. For detailed instructions, refer to the *CBE Style Manual* prepared by the Council of Biology Editors.

In descending order, the basic groups are the phylum or division, class, order, family, genus, and species. Of these groups, the genus and species names are both italicized (underlined in manuscript), but the genus name is capitalized whereas the species name is not. Also, genus names should be spelled out in full the first time but may be abbreviated thereafter (*H. sapiens*). Races, varieties, and subspecies are also italicized but a designation such as "var." (*varietas*) is not. Above the genus level, names are capitalized but not italicized. Vernacular or common names (such as "fruit fly") are not italicized and are not capitalized unless a proper noun is included.

     Home (genus)
     alba (species)
     var. *hirta* (variety)
     Virginia creeper (common name)

Foreign Terms. Unfamiliar foreign terms such as *snedig* (Dutch: shrewd) should be italicized (underlined in manuscript). (But see chapter 8 for a list of anglicized foreign words that need not be accented or italicized.) Full sentences should not be italicized. Also, proper names (people, companies, places, and so on) and abbreviations for Latin words used in notes and bibliographies should be in roman type. The word *sic,* meaning "thus" or "in this manner," should be italicized, however. (It is used to point out an error in the original copy.)

     morfil
     alfil
     cafe
     matinee
     ibid.
     et al.
     "The professer's [*sic*] contract was renewed."

Quotations. Quoted material, except for a blocked quotation (extract), is always enclosed in quotation marks. If italics appeared in the original copy, they should be duplicated in the quotation. If you want to use italics to emphasize something in a quote, put the words *italics mine, italics added, emphasis mine,* or *emphasis added* in parentheses after the quotation or in brackets after the italicized words within the quotation. If italics are in the original copy and you believe it is necessary to explain (usually it isn't) that you did not add those italics, the correct phrase is *italics in original* or *John Doe's italics.*

"Winston regarded the policy as a *disgrace,* not an honor" (italics mine).

"Winston regarded the policy as a *disgrace* [italics added], not an honor."

"Winston regarded the policy as a *disgrace,* not an honor" (italics in original).

Legend Guide Words. Legends that identify people, places, or things in illustrations must often use words such as *left* or *above* to orient the reader. Sometimes letters or symbols are used to point out the same letters or symbols that appear on the face of the illustration. Guide words, letters, or symbols are often shown in italics (underlined in manuscript), with the name of the subject following.

Top, Dean Mason, Harold Blum, Lois Shoemaker; *bottom,* Roy Ellsworth, Jane Forrest, Rene Jamison, Tom Paulette.

Tables. Some parts of tables are frequently italicized (or underlined in manuscript). Subheadings in the stub (the lefthand column), for example, may be italic. The word *source* or *note* following the table body is commonly also italic. Within the table body, some text words may be italicized according to the same rules that apply to any other text. (See examples in chapter 10.)

Note: The figures in this table have been rounded for convenience.

Mathematics. Mathematical copy often makes extensive use of italics, although some publishers set all math letter symbols roman. If you use numerous equations in a manuscript, you would not likely designate italics by underlining every letter. But an occasional math letter symbol in a manuscript should be underlined. Do not, however, designate italics for abbreviations such as "tan" (tangent).

Therefore, $X = XM - YZ$.

Therefore, $\cos x (\sin x - 5) = 3$.

When you state theorems, rules, corollaries, and the like, specify italics for the descriptive heading.

Definition 2.6. Operators consist of verbs and conjunctions.

For a detailed guide to preparing mathematical copy, refer to *Mathematics into Type,* published by the American Mathematical Society in Providence, Rhode Island.

Notes and Bibliographies. Titles of books and periodicals in notes and reference lists are italicized (or underlined in manuscript), as are titles of long poems, plays, and other independent works reproduced in another volume. An introductory article (*a, an, the*) in a newspaper or journal title (*The New York Times*) is usually omitted in notes and bibliographies. An introductory heading such as *note* or *source* is commonly italicized. But chapter or article titles are set roman and in quotation marks.

Evans, Karl. *The Revival.* New York: Haliman Publishers, 1959.

Source: Joanne Byrd, "Notes from a Psychic," *New Bedford Times,* June 1989.

4. Walter Morley, *A Play for Jessica,* in *Collected Plays,* ed. Mary Reuter (Nashville: Playwright Press, 1988).

Cross-references. Some writers use italics (or underlining in manuscript) for cross-reference words such as *see* and *see also* in both notes and text discussion. These words are also sometimes italicized in indexes.

See chapter 7.

4. *See also* John Hartmann, *Writer's Notebook* (Los Angeles: Workshop Press, 1985).

Subheads. If you are preparing a manuscript with more than three levels of heads, you may want to italicize some of them (or underline them in manuscript) to help distinguish among the levels.

The Alphabetical Reference List. This list consists of sources without expository comments. . . .

Continuation Lines. Words that indicate something will be continued on a succeeding page or is being continued from a preceding page are *continuation lines.* These words are usually italicized (or underlined in manuscript) and enclosed in parentheses or brackets. The enclosing punctuation, however, is not italicized.

(To be continued)

[Continued from page 532]

(Continued)

[Continued on page 19]

Books and Other Publications. Titles of books, periodicals, newspapers, booklets, and pamphlets should be italicized (or underlined in manuscript) in the text as well as in notes and bibliographies. The word *magazine,* however, is italicized only if it is a part of the periodical's formal name. Parts of publications such as chapter titles, short stories, or essays, should be in roman type and enclosed in quotation marks. Titles such as *preface* and *index* are neither italicized nor enclosed in quotation marks. Series and edition titles also are set in roman type without quotes. Theses, papers, and other unpublished works are set roman but enclosed in quotation marks. Titles of long poems published separately are italicized, but short poems are set in roman type and enclosed in quotation marks. Titles of plays are always italicized, whether as a title in a collection or as a separate work. Parts of poetry and plays, however, such as "stanza 2" or "scene

1" are not italicized, but stage directions in a play are usually enclosed in parentheses or brackets and italicized (*reaching for the door*).

The Practical Writer's Guide (book)

New York Times Magazine (periodical)

Time magazine (periodical)

New York Times (newspaper)

Irrigation Systems (booklet)

The Divine Comedy (long poem)

Yesterday's Hope (play)

Writers usually do not italicize the article "the" preceding a periodical or newspaper title. Also, the articles *a, an,* and *the* may be omitted from titles in text discussion when their use would be awkward.

He follows the *New York Times* avidly.

The Shipmates by O'Donnell is the first book on the list.

The first book on the list (O'Donnell's *Shipmates*) is unavailable.

When making a publication's name plural or possessive, italicize only the title, not the apostrophe or the s.

The *Wall Street Journal*s are ready for delivery.

Have you seen *Fortune*'s latest issue?

Do not use the word *on* before a formal title.

I ordered a book on finance.

I ordered the book *Financial Success.*

Films and Television Programs. Titles of motion pictures are italicized (or underlined in manuscript), whereas titles of radio and television programs are in roman type and enclosed in quotation marks.

Being There (movie)

"Day's End" (radio program)

"Designing Women" (television program)

Musical Works. Long compositions such as operas, symphonies, oratorios, and motets are italicized (or underlined in manuscript); short compositions and songs are set in roman type and enclosed in quotation marks. A descriptive word or phrase for a composition is italicized if the piece is long and quoted if it is short. A title that identifies the work only by its form with no descriptive phrase or title is set in roman type without quotes. The abbreviations "op." (opus) and "no." (number) are not italicized.

Beethoven's *Emperor* Concerto

Piano Concerto no. 5

the *Messiah* (long composition)

William Tell Overture

"Star-Spangled Banner" (song)

Sonata in E-flat

Artwork. Titles of works of art such as paintings, sculptures, and statues are always italicized (or underlined in manuscript), but general references or traditional titles such as the Mona Lisa are not.

The Thinker (sculpture)

The Last Supper (painting)

Final Days (statue)

For examples of the proper style for other material such as trademarks, mottoes, and computer terminology, see chapter 3.

USING A CONSISTENT STYLE

Your writing and type styles may be determined by someone else such as your employer. Depending on your profession, you may be required to follow the style of the American Psychological Association, the Modern Language Association, the Council of Biology Editors, the American Mathematical Society, or some other organization. Perhaps your organization has its own in-house style guide or requires that personnel or members use another published stylebook. Whether or not someone else decides which style to use in your written material, however, there is another requirement that largely depends on you—consistency in whatever style you employ.

Readers are annoyed and confused by inconsistency in points of style (spelling, punctuation, capitalization, and so on) and format (arrangement of elements on a page). Consider some of the pitfalls that most writers encounter.

- Do you write *non-essential* on one page and *nonavailable* on another page? Or first *salable* and then *saleable?*

- Do you sometimes capitalize *Board of Trustees* and sometimes write *board of trustees?*

- Do you spell out *for example* part of the time and use the abbreviation *e.g.* the rest of the time?

- Do you sometimes center first-level heads and use all capital letters and other times use both capital and small letters flush left?

- Do you call some tabular material a *table* and other tabular material a *figure?*

- Do you refer to *J. B. Burns* on page 60 and *John Burns* on page 70?

- Do you abbreviate states traditionally (*Mass.*) in your notes and use two-letter postal abbreviations (*MA*) in your bibliography entries?

- Do you underline some terms being defined and put quotes around others?

- Do you use contractions (*don't*) heavily in chapter 1 and always spell out the words (*do not*) in chapter 2?

- Do you introduce extracts (blocked quotations) with a colon part of the time and with a comma the rest of the time?

- Are your titles and headings worded one way within the body of your work and another way on the contents page?

- Do you sometimes write *UK* and sometimes *U.K.?*

- Do you write *$100* part of the time and *one hundred dollars* the rest of the time?

- Do you use an accent with *cliché* on page 10 and omit the accent on page 11?

- Do you format your footnotes indented-paragraph style in chapter 1 and flush-left style in chapter 2?

- Do you write your name as *C. J. Parker* in the signature line of a letter and then sign it *Charlie Parker?*

- Do you sometimes refer to *2 o'clock in the afternoon* and other times use *2:00 p.m.?*

- Do you indent your blocked quotations one-half inch part of the time and one inch the rest of the time?

- Do you refer to yourself as *the author* in the beginning and then start writing *I* later in your work?

These questions suggest the many places and ways in which inconsistency can occur. Not only must writers be constantly on guard but they must also review their work—sometimes over and over—for consistency in all matters of style.

Chapter 2

PUNCTUATION

The main function of punctuation is to make what is written clear and readable. If the reader might misread a statement or stumble over the wording, it may be that necessary punctuation is lacking or misplaced. Rewording the sentence may help, but only up to a point without corresponding improvement in punctuation.

Although some marks of punctuation are required according to accepted conventions (complete sentences must have a period or other concluding punctuation), other uses depend on the style of the writer. Some persons punctuate wherever it is technically correct to use a mark (*close punctuation*); others use punctuation only when it is necessary for clarity and readability (*open punctuation*). Close punctuation is preferred by traditionalists, and open punctuation is practiced by contemporary writers who prefer a modern style.

The trend is clearly toward the use of only essential punctuation. Previously, for example, it was considered proper to insert a comma wherever one paused in a sentence.

It is exciting, but not very practical.

Today, many authorities shun this practice and refer to such marks as misplaced, unnecessary, or incorrect punctuation. If, however, there were two independent clauses (two subjects and two predicates) in the above example, the comma would be technically correct.

It is exciting, but it is not very practical.

Even in this case, however, some writers who use the open style would consider the two clauses to be so simple and brief that the comma could best be omitted.

It is exciting but it is not very practical.

The second "it is," though, would probably be deleted by a careful writer or editor as being wordy and unnecessary. We would then be left with the version used by writers who prefer the modern, open style.

It is exciting but not very practical.

Punctuation, then, is one of the many style considerations, but it is so critical to meaning that even authorities who promote open punctuation show great respect for its proper use.

Writers not only choose between open and close punctuation; they also make choices about individual marks of punctuation. For example:

The winter was harsh—reminiscent of the 1970 deep freeze; it covered the earth with a thick glaze of ice and snow.

The winter was harsh—reminiscent of the 1970 deep freeze—and covered the earth with a thick glaze of ice and snow.

The winter was harsh, reminiscent of the 1970 deep freeze. It covered the earth with a thick glaze of ice and snow.

The winter was harsh (reminiscent of the 1970 deep freeze) and covered the earth with a thick glaze of ice and snow.

All of the above examples are technically correct; the choice depends on the writer. In these subtle ways writers consciously or subconsciously use punctuation to mark their style.

In deciding how to use punctuation properly and effectively, two questions arise that perplex many people. One is whether the punctuation after a word in italics or boldface should also be in italics or boldface. Usually, it is, although parentheses and brackets should remain in roman type.

U.S. News and World Report:

(Continued on page 5)

The other question concerns spacing around punctuation. For example, do you put one or two spaces after a period or a colon? The answer depends on how you are preparing your material. A compositor would leave only one space after such punctuation, whereas a writer preparing a manuscript by conventional means (typewritten or computer printout) would leave two spaces. A writer preparing a manuscript for submission by diskette, however, might be asked to leave only one space. The traditional rules for spacing, still observed in handwritten and typewritten material, are as follows:

- *Place one space* after (1) a comma, (2) a semicolon, (3) a period after an abbreviation, (4) a period in the initials of a person's name, and (5) an exclamation point within a sentence.

- *Place two spaces* after (1) a colon, (2) a sentence, and (3) a period that follows a number or letter introducing an item in a list.

- *Do not space* (1) before or after a dash or hyphen, (2) before or after an apostrophe unless it begins or ends a word, (3) between quotation marks and the matter enclosed, (4) between parentheses or brackets and the matter enclosed, (5) between any word and the punctuation that follows, or (6) between periods within abbreviations (*N.Y.*).

Unless your computer preparation or publishing requirements dictate otherwise, the above rules are still valid and should be followed regardless of whether you are preparing material by hand, typewriter, or computer.

In the case of occasional foreign passages used in English text, writers generally punctuate the foreign material according to English-language rules of punctuation. For complete foreign works, the punctuation should follow the rules for the language in question. (See chapter 8 for a discussion of foreign expressions and a list of seven familiar foreign alphabets.)

PRINCIPAL MARKS OF PUNCTUATION

The principal marks of punctuation are apostrophe, brackets, colon, comma, dash, ellipsis points, exclamation point, hyphen, parentheses, period, question mark, quotation marks, semicolon, and virgule.

Apostrophe (')

The apostrophe has four key functions: (1) to indicate the possessive case of nouns and indefinite pronouns, (2) to form contractions and show omitted characters, (3) to form plurals, and (4) to denote other forms of words, abbreviations, and numbers.

Possession. An apostrophe, with or without an *s,* is added to a word to show possession. Notice that only an apostrophe is added when an additional *s* would make the word hard to pronounce.

Mrs. Jones's [*or* Jones'] students

Mr. Burns's [*or* Burns'] car

the Harrises' party

three weeks' vacation

Jesus' sermons

Moses' journey

for appearance' sake

for goodness' sake

the doctor's prescription

her boss's instructions

the witness's testimony

the boys' locker room

the boy's hat

Gomez's editorial

Saint Louis's townhouses

Los Angeles' smog

everyone's vote

anybody's opinion

Contractions and Omission of Letters. An apostrophe is inserted in the position where letters, numbers, or other characters have been omitted.

I've (I have)

doesn't (does not)

class of '70 (1970)

take 'em (them)

goin' (going)

rock 'n' roll (rock and roll)

Old Kentuck' (Kentucky)

Plurals. An apostrophe is used to form the plural of some words or other elements that are referred to as words or elements. Note, however, that the apostrophe is used only when needed for clarity.

The two *x's* are variables.

He got four *A's* this semester.

All I heard was a lot of *buts* and *ifs*.

How many *Ph.D's* are on the faculty?

Other Forms. The apostrophe is used to denote the inflected form of certain verbs composed of figures or letters. It may also be used with figures or letters when *-er* is added but should be omitted when not needed for clarity.

He *OK'd* the order.

She *deep-6'd* the letter.

The rumor is that he's a *CIA'er*.

Brackets [ ]

Brackets are used for many of the same purposes as parentheses, particularly to enclose parenthetical material. They are essential for enclosing your own comments and corrections within quoted material. Sometimes parenthetical material falls within other parenthetical material, in which case both brackets and parentheses are used, one within the other. Brackets may also be used for continuation lines.

Parenthetical Insert. Use both brackets and parentheses when parenthetical inserts appear within other parenthetical comments or to enclose mathematical elements within other expressions.

The company (Norden and Reames Associates [NRA]) was incorporated last year.

The number of weapons (intercontinental ballistic missiles [ICBMs]) that are stockpiled changes every year.

$a - 9[(x + z)y]$

$[x - y + z(mv)]$

Quoted Material. Place inside brackets any inserted material that is not part of a direct quotation. This includes comments, corrections, and spelling changes. If the first letter at the beginning of a quote is changed, it may be enclosed in brackets as the last example shows, although this is not a requirement except in quotations from legal or scholarly material.

"The article appeared in Wednesday's paper [*New York Times*] in the business section."

"I don't believe that the legislation are [*sic*] dead."

"The play was produced by Professor M[orris] and his colleagues."

"The charges [against her] have been dropped."

My report draws on the manager's remark that we are "hav[ing] a serious backlog problem."

He replied, "[T]his is a mockery of justice."

Continuation Line. A continuation line may be enclosed within brackets or parentheses. Often the words (not the brackets) are italicized (underlined in manuscript); sometimes the continuation line is set in a smaller type without brackets or parentheses.

[*Continued on page 191*]

[*To be concluded*]

(*Continued from page 163*)

Colon (:)

The colon is used to emphasize a comment or to introduce material such as a formal list, series, or quoted passage. The colon is also used in salutations and identification lines of letters, dialogue, footnotes, expressions of clock time, and ratios. Place the colon outside of quotation marks and parentheses.

Emphasis. When emphasis in a sentence is marked by an interruption or pause, a colon may be used. Often, however, a semicolon is sufficient, or individual sentences are used. When a full sentence follows the colon, the first word may or may not be capitalized, depending on the preferred style.

According to the *Gazette*, "The concert has billed top entertainers": this may account for the run on tickets.

According to the *Gazette,* "The concert has billed top entertainers"; this may account for the run on tickets.

Many students were entirely unprepared for the test: four in my class, for example, were no-shows.

Many students were entirely unprepared for the test. Four in my class, for example, were no-shows.

Introduction of Material. Although a colon is properly used to introduce formal lists, particularly after words such as *the following* or *as follows,* it should be omitted if the list is the direct object of a preposition or verb or follows a form of the verb *to be.* In most cases, a simple listing requires no introduction.

Three states received federal aid: West Virginia, South Carolina, and Ohio.

The three states that received federal aid are West Virginia, South Carolina, and Ohio.

The contents include (1) grammar, (2) spelling, (3) composition, and (4) manuscript preparation.

Correspondence and Dialogue. A colon follows names in dialogue and letter salutations and separates initials in identification lines of letters. It sometimes follows reference lines in correspondence as well as guidewords (e.g., *To, From*) in memos.

JENNIFER: What was the question?

Dear Bill:

HA:bm

Your reference: MCZX32.1

To:

Notes. Colons are used after cities or states and after dates in notes, bibliographies, and reference lists.

3. Bertrand Walters, *The Last Store on the Block* (Boston: People's Press, 1988).

Hart, Timothy. "Unusual Times." *New Life Journal* 2 (1990): 16-19.

(Donaldson 1991: 64)

Time and Ratios. A colon follows the hour in numerical time expressions and separates the elements of ratios.

6:30 a.m.

5:1 ratio

Comma (,)

Like the period, the comma is a heavily used mark of punctuation. It has many functions, among them its use between sentences, clauses, phrases, and words in a series. It is also used to set off introductory or nonrestrictive phrases and clauses and to separate other elements such as interjections, adjectives, and appositives. The comma is also used to show the omission of words and to introduce quoted material.

Sentences, Clauses, Phrases, and Words in a Series. The comma is used to separate compound sentences and set off nonrestrictive clauses, introductory phrases (except very short ones), and words in a series. A general rule is that nonrestrictive, nonessential expressions *are* set off by commas; restrictive, essential expressions *are not* enclosed in commas. The comma should be omitted immediately preceding a verb unless the comma is used to separate a question from the main clause. In addition, writers who observe the practice of open punctuation often omit the comma in some of these cases unless essential for clarity and ease in reading.

> A comma is frequently necessary to separate complex compound sentences, but it is often omitted by writers who espouse open punctuation unless punctuation is needed for clarity and readability.
>
> The award-winning researcher at Hillsdale Labs, *home of the famous Hillsdale Think Tank,* will publish his findings in July.
>
> Ms. Hendricks, *upon hearing the news,* caught the next plane to Los Angeles.
>
> The man *who is coming through the door* is the new president.
>
> *When you consider the consequences of consumer borrowing,* other alternatives become more attractive.
>
> *Whether or not you agree with it,* the bill becomes law tomorrow.
>
> She *wondered, is this* the reason for Jim's dismissal?
>
> *Thus* we have to approach the problem from a new perspective.
>
> *In 1987* we bought a motor home.
>
> The *stove, refrigerator, and dishwasher* are being sold with the house.

Interjections and Other Elements. The comma is used to set off a variety of elements such as interjections (*Oh*), transition words (*however*), appositives, and two or more adjectives when each one modifies the noun without the other. Do not, however, set off an appositive that is essential to the meaning of the sentence (often answering the question *which one*). A comma is also used to avoid confusion with adjacent numbers or similar words and to separate items in addresses. But short antithetical phrases should not be interrupted with a comma.

> *Oh,* I don't know.
>
> *Sir,* will you please take your seat?
>
> It's clear, *therefore,* that prices will rise.
>
> He originated the rumor, *namely,* that the factory is scheduled to close this summer.
>
> The treasurer, *Phil Ormsley,* will report next.
>
> My oldest brother, *Richard,* is the president.
>
> My brother *Tim* [which brother?] is the treasurer.

The *cold, clear* water is refreshing.

The *apathetic governmental* staff needs strong motivation.

In *1989, 32,484* people signed the petition.

The date is *January 7, 1991*.

If that's what the trouble *is, is* it any wonder he is discouraged?

Send it to *Prentice Hall Building, Englewood Cliffs, NJ 07632*.

The *more the merrier*.

Omission of Words. A comma should be inserted in the place where words are omitted.

The first meeting will be in Akron, Ohio; the *second, in* Jackson, Mississippi.

The truth *is, we* aren't sure.

Quotations. Commas are used to introduce quoted material unless the quote is restrictive and essential to the meaning of the sentence and the comma would interrupt the natural flow. Use a colon rather than a comma to introduce a long, formal quotation.

Nancy smiled and said, "I couldn't be more pleased."

"No doubt," said Henry, "we will hear from him again.

The newsletter predicts "a severe drought" this year.

The legal report indicates that "capital punishment is likely to return in many states."

Dash (—)

In ordinary typewritten or computer-prepared copy, the dash is written as two hyphens, with no space between them. In printed material, the two typed hyphens are set as a solid rule called the *em dash* (—). (An *em* is the square of any size of type.) An *en dash* (–), typed as one hyphen, is one-half the size of an em dash. Writers, however, need not concern themselves with the selection of em and en dashes since such decisions are made by the editors preparing a manuscript for production.

The em dash in typeset material is used any time that a writer would use an ordinary dash consisting of two hyphens. The en dash is set instead of a hyphen mainly to show inclusive numbers or equal elements. It also is used instead of a hyphen in compound adjectives that have two words or a hyphenated word as one of their parts. An en dash should never be substituted, however, for the words *from, to,* or *between*.

Wright—he's the best person for the job.

See pages 168–69, 107–8.

It occurred in the 1970–80 decade.

The magazine's date is June–July 1989.

The owner–manager is Bill Timmons.

The style is pre–World War II vintage.

Read *from* page 168 *to* 169.

It happened *between* 1970 *and* 1980.

A 3-em dash (three joined em dashes) is used to designate succeeding authors in bibliographies. In the example below, the second book was also written by Dawn Worley.

Worley, Dawn. *Sociology Redefined.* New York: Sociology Printers, 1982.

_____. *The New Social Science.* Sacramento, Calif.: Sacramento Academic Press, 1984.

The dash may be used with other punctuation marks in certain instances. It may follow an abbreviation that ends in a period, or it may follow parenthetical, quoted, or similar material that is enclosed in parentheses or with a question mark or exclamation point. But do not use a dash with a comma or semicolon.

The vase is dated 810 B.C.—a century before the other artifacts in our collection.

The chemical reaction was severe (*see* page 40)—too severe in my judgment.

The weather station recorded record-breaking temperatures—118 degrees!—in Phoenix and Yuma, Arizona, yesterday.

The dash is largely used to set off parenthetical material or to show interruption or a shift in thought. Although a colon is usually preferred to introduce lists, a dash is sometimes used. Similarly, although a comma or semicolon usually precedes expressions such as *that is, namely, therefore,* or *however,* a dash may be used when strong emphasis is desired. As a general rule, one should avoid the dash unless a sudden or strong departure or emphasis is needed. In general commentary, a comma or other routine punctuation is preferred.

Interruption or Sudden Change. The dash is inserted before or after comments that mark an abrupt shift in thought or interruption.

The academic community—should we include secondary schools?—is scrambling for outside funding.

Mark programmed the computer to reject any unrelated data—how he defined *unrelated,* I don't know.

Hendricks, Lewis, Morgan—I want all of you to work on the construction bids.

The book was written in 1983—published in 1985—by Benjamin Goldberg.

Lists. The dash may be used to introduce in-text lists when the items of the list describe or define the preceding item. It is also used, but less frequently, in place of numbers, letters, or bullets in stacked lists.

We are working hard to reduce employee problems—absenteeism, tardiness, alcoholism, poor motivation, and so on.

The floor was littered with trash—cigarettes, newspapers, candy wrappers, and beer cans.

Tomorrow we will discuss these topics:

—Client files

—Forms location

—Document system

—Litigation control

Strong Emphasis. When a comma or semicolon does not provide the emphasis desired, a dash may be used before certain expressions.

The Wilsons—that is, the children and their mother—are moving to Hartford next week.

"Yes, I have an opinion about his speech—it's rubbish!"

Quotations. A dash is commonly used before the name of an author in an epigraph or other displayed quotation. A dash is also used in quotations to show an incomplete remark.

Life is not what I expected—it's far better.

—Jonathan Creole, 1932

"He may have said that but—"

Ellipsis Points (. . .)

Ellipsis points, or dots, are written as a series of three periods and indicate the omission of material from a quotation. When the three periods follow the end of a sentence where a period already exists, the series appears as four dots, with a space around each of the three that are ellipsis points. (An alternative style always uses three dots and omits the period at the end of a sentence.)

"Call the department . . . and schedule another meeting. . . . Be sure to include the branch manager."

It is not necessary to put ellipsis points at the beginning or end of either a full quote or an incomplete sentence.

According to the speaker, "Systems design is a priority in aerospace companies."

The speaker pointed out that "systems design is a priority" in aerospace firms.

The same rule applies to an extract (blocked quotation): if the opening word continues a thought in the preceding introductory text, ellipsis points are not needed.

The mayor reported that the council is divided over the water issue.

Four members, in fact, voiced angry rebuttals to the proposal that population trends required the purchase of an additional water supply before the end of the decade. Three members vowed to issue their own proposal before the end of the month.

When an extract ends with a complete sentence, as in the above example, ellipsis points are not needed at the end even though further material (additional sentences) may be omitted. If you believe it is crucial, however, to emphasize that preceding and concluding material has been omitted—because this is not obvious to the reader or the reader absolutely must be reminded that this is the case—use three dots before the quote and four, including the period, after the last sentence.

Ellipsis points are essential in certain cases: to show the omission of words within a sentence, to show the omission of material between sentences or paragraphs, and to show an incomplete sentence. Sometimes ellipsis points are used in nonquoted material to show incomplete thoughts or long pauses in thought or to show an abrupt change in pace or emphasize a thought (much in the same way a dash is used).

Omission Within a Sentence.   Three periods are used to show that something has been omitted from within a quoted sentence. If the periods fall next to other punctuation, such as a comma or a semicolon, the other marks are usually retained only if they are an aid to readability.

> "For employees . . . on a wage basis, . . . hours worked is a key factor in computing earnings and deductions."

> According to the U.S. Postal Service:

>> Printed matter is paper . . . not having the character of . . . personal correspondence . . . ; it is reproduced by any process other than handwriting or typewriting.

If a full nonrestrictive clause or phrase is omitted, you can usually omit the commas, dashes, or other marks enclosing it. In the first example below, the words "such as France" can be omitted without retaining the commas around them.

> "To countries other than Canada, such as France, the AO rate applies."

> "To countries other than Canada . . . the AO rate applies."

Omission Between Sentences and Paragraphs.   When the material omitted falls between two sentences in the same or different paragraphs, retain the ending punctuation of the first sentence (period, exclamation point, or question mark) even if the last words of the sentence are omitted. Then add the three ellipsis points after that ending punctuation, with a space around each one. Even if the first part of the second sentence is missing, follow the same procedure.

In the following example, the last part of the first sentence is missing, but the period appears anyway. The first words of the second sentence are missing, so the word *you* begins with a small letter.

> "Minutes are kept chronologically in a minute book. . . . you can easily locate them by date."

Some writers, however, prefer that the second sentence begin with a capital letter.

If the quote is taken from scholarly material or legal text, the *y* in the word *you*, if changed to a capital letter, should appear in brackets.

> "Minutes are kept chronologically in a minute book. . . . [Y]ou can easily locate them by date."

With quotes from recent (modern) works, the brackets around the *y* would usually be omitted.

> "Minutes are kept chronologically in a minute book. . . . You can easily locate them by date."

When a quote is incorporated into a nonquoted sentence so that the two form a complete thought, the first word need not be capitalized even if it is capitalized in the original quotation.

> Remember that "minutes are kept chronologically in a minute book. . . . you can easily locate them by date."

The procedure for using a period followed by three dots to show material omitted between two sentences assumes that both sentences quoted are grammatically complete even if words are missing; that is, both have a subject and a predicate and each makes sense standing alone. See the next section for the procedure with incomplete sentences.

Incomplete Sentence. Three dots alone, without a period, at the end of a quote are used to show that the end of the sentence has been omitted, leaving an incomplete sentence (a sentence fragment).

> "The economic seminar is scheduled for . . ."

> "Certain situations are emotional, although . . ."

Other Uses of Ellipsis Points. Less frequently, ellipsis points are used in place of a dash or other punctuation in certain situations. They may be used to show long pauses in thought or to show incomplete thoughts, and they may be used instead of a dash to show an abrupt change or special emphasis (the dash is usually preferred for this).

> I wonder if . . . what do you think?

> The report made it clear . . . or did it?

> Think about it . . . a trillion dollar deficit!

Exclamation Point (!)

The exclamation point is used to show sudden or strong feeling or to express irony. Since emotion should be obvious in a well-written passage, the need for the exclamation point is slight in most cases, and writers tend to overuse it.

When it is part of the parenthetical or quoted copy, the exclamation point is placed inside other punctuation such as parentheses or quotation marks. When it is not part of the parenthetical or quoted copy, the exclamation point is placed outside.

Look at this (I can't believe it!).

"I can hardly believe what he said (or meant)!"

"Let the games begin!"

According to the report, the device was a "total failure"!

A comma should not be used with an exclamation point unless the exclamation is part of a title and must be retained. A dash may follow an exclamation point if the exclamation point belongs with the material being set off by the dash.

"We saw the play *Really, Mother!*," she said.

Here are the contracts—finally!—all signed and sealed.

Sudden or Strong Feeling. The exclamation point may be used to indicate especially strong feeling or emphasis. It is sometimes used in place of a question mark when an indication of tone is especially important.

Be careful!

How could you do that!

Oh, what a day!

What a beauty!

Irony. When a comment is made satirically or has an ironic bent, the exclamation point may be used to make this clear. It may show, for instance, that the writer really means the opposite of what he or she is saying.

Oh, lovely! We're out of gas.

Aren't you in a good mood!

Oh, to be young and carefree!

Don't knock yourself out!

Hyphen (-)

The hyphen is used mainly to divide words at the end of a line, to connect compounds and certain prefixes or suffixes, and to show inclusive numbers (for this, however, see the discussion of the en dash under "Dash," on page 27). The hyphen may also be used to show pronunciation or to indicate letter-by-letter spelling.

Word Division. The hyphen is used to break a word at the end of a line.

After a thorough search, he found a willing *substitute.*

To settle the dispute, they are undertaking *arbitra-
tion.*

For numerous examples and guidelines on the proper division of words, see chapter 5.

Compounds. The different parts of some compound terms are connected by hyphens. (See the discussion of compounds in chapters 4 and 5.) Although many compounds are written closed (no space or hyphen between the parts) and some are open (a space between the parts), others are hyphenated. Hyphens are used in both noun compounds (*vice-consul*) and adjective compounds (*problem-solving effort*).

Nouns:	secretary-treasurer
	owner-operator
	father-in-law
	great-grandmother
	ex-senator
Adjectives:	well-known poet
	high-technology office
	open-ended discussion
	quasi-public corporation
	low-interest-rate loan

Prefixes and Suffixes. In contemporary writing, most prefixes and suffixes are written closed (no hyphen or space between the parts of the compound). But sometimes a hyphen is needed, such as before a proper noun, to clarify meaning or to avoid the difficulty of reading double letters.

re-creation (created again), recreation (leisure time)

pro-American, prorevolutionary

anti-intelligence, antisocial

bell-like, catlike

Note that publishers often use an en dash (see "Dash," on page 27) when one part of the compound has two words or is hyphenated.

post–World War I

pre–Civil War

Pronunciation and Spelling. The hyphen is used to indicate pronunciation of letters and syllables. Dictionaries and spelling books, in particular, employ the hyphen for this purpose.

ma-lev-o-lent

mal-fea-sance

pres-ent

pre-sent

The hyphen is also used to convey to readers the idea that a word is to be read (spelled out) letter by letter.

> I want you all to study: s-t-u-d-y.
>
> I said no! N-o!

Parentheses ( )

Parentheses are used to enclose and insert material that is incidental or supplementary to the text. Such parenthetical material may be inserted within a sentence, at the end of it, or between sentences. The text or sentence containing the insertion should be able to stand on its own if read without the parenthetical comments. Parentheses are also used around letters and numbers of enumerations in the text and in equations, as well as to enclose cross-references. In notes they are used to enclose publishing data, and in scripts they are used to enclose stage directions. Brackets, however, not parentheses, should be used for inserting comments within quoted material.

Parenthetical Comments. A variety of material can be enclosed in parentheses, for example, definitions or translations, explanations, abbreviations, additional facts, and incidental comments.

> Only two divisions in the company (sales and accounting) stayed within budget.
>
> The sodality (brotherhood) was formed in 1939.
>
> Once the prototype has been tested (the first tests of a year ago failed), it will be scheduled for preproduction review.
>
> The statistics came directly from the Office of Management and Budget (OMB).
>
> The company suffered its greatest losses in the 1980s (especially in 1982 and 1983).
>
> I saw it in the Flagstaff (Ariz.) museum.
>
> The convention is scheduled for San Diego (a great place to be in the winter).

Miscellaneous Data. Parentheses are regularly used to enclose numbers or letters of in-text lists; to enclose cross-references appearing in the text; to enclose data in footnotes, source notes, and other reference material; to insert stage directions in stage, screen, and other scripts; and to enclose letters and numbers in mathematical material.

> The investment firm is holding a seminar on the merits of (a) stocks, (b) bonds, (c) Treasury bills, and (d) mutual funds.
>
> One author documented why the insurance industry needs a massive overhaul (see appendix 5.A).
>
> Bronson, Melanie. "The Ring of Fire." *Literary Journal* 7 (March 1981): 17–32.
>
> FATHER (*motioning to the door*): I want you to leave this house.
>
> $a(x + y) \times b (x - y) = 7$

Period (.)

The period is probably the most familiar punctuation mark and the one least in danger of being overused (like the exclamation point) or used incorrectly (like the dash or comma). In addition to its obvious use as a mark to end a sentence, it has several other uses, such as in abbreviations (see chapter 6) and after initials and letters or numbers in list enumerations. (See also "Ellipsis Points," on page 29, for other uses of the period.)

In American-style punctuation, the period is placed inside closing quotation marks (in British style it appears outside). With parentheses, it goes inside the closing parenthesis when terminating a complete sentence and outside if only a fragment appears within the parentheses.

Terminal Punctuation. When a period is called for as opposed to a question mark or other concluding punctuation, place it after the last word of a full sentence or a sentence fragment that appears in the running text. Omit it after list items that are not full sentences (unless one item in the list is a complete sentence; then put a period after each item). Also omit the period after headlines, chapter titles, and the like.

The incorporators held their first meeting in January 1989.

"Is it possible that he overlooked the theft? Not likely."

The check was made out for five hundred dollars ($500).

The check was made out for five hundred dollars. (This is the limit for single-signature checks.)

The following supplies should be taken on a business trip:

1. Stationery

2. Envelopes

3. File folders

4. Business cards

5. Checkbook

HARTSHORNE FALLS DECLARED DISASTER AREA

Abbreviations and Initials. The period is used in some abbreviations, such as academic degrees, although the trend is to omit it with other abbreviations. Do not add space around periods in an abbreviation. In names, put a space between initials. (Some writers put a space between two initials but no space between three or more initials).

John Jones, Ph.D., M.A., B.F.A.

He arrived at 3:30 p.m.

The lessons begin with events of 1000 B.C.

asap (as soon as possible)

5. Ibid., p. 6.

R. F. Fitzgerald

R. F. N. Fitzgerald

Question Mark (?)

The question mark is another familiar mark of punctuation and is used to indicate a direct question or expression of doubt. It is placed inside of quotation marks only if it is part of the material being quoted. The most common mistake that writers make in using the question mark is placing it after a remark that is really a statement or request.

Direct Question. Put a question mark after every direct question, whether the question is within or at the end of a sentence. But use a period when a question is not intended.

Have you seen today's paper?

"Are these figures correct?" she asked.

She asked, are these figures correct?

The question isn't *who* but *how many*.

He asked, is it true that "retail sales have declined for three straight quarters"?

The question raised in the *Sun* is, "Why have retail sales declined for three straight quarters?"

Should we schedule the meetings weekly? Monthly?

The mechanical device (a household robot?) is activated by voice command.

Will you please hand me the tape.

Ms. Rogers asked whether we had received the updated policy manual.

Doubt. A question mark is used to signal readers that the writer is doubtful about certain facts or figures. In such cases, place the question mark immediately after the material in question.

The case was decided favorably (unanimously?) for the defendant on November 17.

I noticed in the *Digest* of February 24(?), 1989, that earth temperatures are not rising as much as expected.

Quotation Marks (")

Quotation marks are used to indicate both exact quotations and nonquoted words that an author wants to emphasize for another reason. Since one must not use the words of another person without giving due credit, the rules concerning the use of quotation marks are very important. (For details on the style for indicating omitted words in a quoted passage, see "Ellipsis Points," on page 29.)

In American-style punctuation, the period and comma are placed inside the quotation marks, and the colon and semicolon are placed outside. (Foreign-language phrases or sentences quoted in an English-language text are treated the same as English comments in regard to the use of quotation marks.)

> "Let us begin."

> The text advised that "one should use nongender-specific words to ensure nondiscriminatory writing": *people, civilization,* or *humankind* instead of *mankind; salesperson* instead of *salesman;* and so forth.

Place the dash, exclamation point, and question mark inside the quotation marks when they are part of only the quoted portion of the sentence and outside when they pertain to the entire sentence.

> How do you explain his comment that "all life forms are doomed to eventual extinction"?

> "No," he shouted, "I will not be a party to that!"

> Organized thoughts—which, according to Edward Maybell, "are a rarity, indeed"—are essential to success.

Writers who quote from other works may make a few stylistic changes without violating the rule to quote exactly. They may, for example, correct a simple typographical error without calling attention to it, but they should not change an author's intentional peculiarities of style or spelling. They may also change the first letter of a quoted passage to a capital or a small letter as desired to fit more logically into the writer's own text.

Note numbers may (and should) be omitted in a quotation since they would make no sense to readers unless an author's entire work were reprinted. Final punctuation marks may also be changed or omitted to suit a writer's text. In addition, publishers sometimes make type changes, perhaps changing a word in capitals to small capitals or a word in small capitals to italics.

Extract. When a prose quotation runs to eight or more lines, it should usually be set as an extract (an indented, blocked quotation). In an extract, the opening and closing quotation marks are omitted (unless the extract consists of speech or dialogue, which is always enclosed in quotation marks). The fact that the words are indented in a block format tells readers that it is a direct quote. Single quotation marks within the original passage are then changed to double quotation marks within the extract. Extracts should always have a note number or a name-date reference at the end (see chapter 9).

> If the first sentence of the extract is not the first sentence of the paragraph from which the passage is taken, do not indent the opening line and do not use ellipsis points.[4]

> According to W. B. Goldman, "If quotes from succeeding paragraphs in the extract also do not begin with the first sentence in each paragraph, start them flush left as well." But put a space between each paragraph of the quote for clarity. (Henderson 1988: 3)

Poetry of more than two lines should be displayed. Each line should be reproduced like the original in terms of indention, spacing between lines, and the like.

No motion has she now, no force;

She neither hears nor sees;

Rolled round in earth's diurnal course;

With rocks, and stones, and trees.

—William Wordsworth, *A Slumber Did My Spirit Seal* (1799)

In-Text Quote. Many quotes are not indented and blocked in extract fashion. In such cases opening and closing quotation marks are used, and any quote within the quote would be enclosed in single quotation marks.

Despite widespread criticism for its possible racial slurs, "'The book is an essential guide to one of today's most necessary skills,' according to Peter Rawlston, and I wholeheartedly agree" (Dougherty 1990: 176).

Nonquoted Use. Quotation marks are sometimes used to enclose words that are being defined or referred to as words, although italics are preferred for this. They may also enclose special terms or the translation of a foreign term. Some disciplines such as philosophy and theology enclose special terms in single quotation marks, in which case a terminal period goes outside the mark. Sentences within sentences may also be enclosed in quotation marks. But paraphrases and indirect quotations should not be enclosed in quotation marks.

The robots "conversed" by means of coded signals.

The Spanish term *erguir* means "to raise."

He contested the association of the 'righteous' with the 'divine'.

As Hobbes said, "Words are wise men's counters."

Fletcher said that beggars can't be choosers.

Semicolon (;)

Like a period and sometimes a comma, the semicolon is used between two sentences. Although it is not employed frequently, there are times when a comma between compound sentences seems too mild, and yet a period makes too abrupt a break. When the semicolon is used between compound sentences, the conjunction between them is usually dropped. Occasionally, the semicolon is used in place of a comma, and the conjunction remains if the sentence is very long and complex. (For a sentence with a brief, simple structure, the conjunction should be omitted.)

A semicolon is used to separate items in a series when those items already have other punctuation. It also precedes introductory or transitional words such as *for example* and *however* if a complete sentence follows. Semicolons are used in certain citations too. When using it with quotation marks, place the semicolon outside the marks.

Between Sentences or Clauses. The semicolon may be used instead of a period or comma between sentences that are closely related but could each stand alone. Usually, if a conjunction such as *and* is retained, a comma is preferred.

> *Adopting* a report is a more common motion than *accepting* a report; it is used regardless of the type of report.

> *Adopting* a report is a more common motion than *accepting* a report, and it is used regardless of the type of report.

> The firm has offered microfilm services on a wide scale since 1975, according to the *Bulletin*, the company's in-house magazine for management personnel; and it intends to expand its services to the West Coast by July of this year.

Series. The semicolon is used to separate items in a series when the items already have other punctuation.

> The frames are distributed by Altier, Inc., Lincoln, Nebraska; Numerics Unlimited, St. Louis, Missouri; and Magic Squares, Des Moines, Iowa.

> The third prize offered optical items such as designer eyewear, bifocals, and prescription sunglasses; the second prize offered window supplies such as mirrors, shower stalls, and medicine cabinets; and the third prize offered electronic equipment, antiques, and fine art.

Introductory and Transitional Words. The semicolon is used before conjunctive adverbs and other words used transitionally when a complete sentence follows the transitional word(s). If an incomplete sentence follows, a comma precedes the word. A comma is always used before *so* and *yet*.

> The system contracts involved more uncertainty for the suppliers; *therefore,* they provided for higher rates.

> In 1985 the company had a turnover of 425 jobs; *moreover,* there were 6,745 absences and sick leaves.

> The team won four victories in a row; *that is,* there were four wins on the home court.

> A writer makes many decisions concerning format, *so* these guidelines are especially helpful.

Citations. Notes in a series, name-date citations, and the like are separated by a semicolon.

> (Jason 1990; Morris 1981)

> 1. Terry Ferguson, *Landslide* (New York: Nature Press, 1989); Harrison, *The Waste Disposal Nightmare;* and Jennifer Carter, "Nuclear Waste," *Science Magazine* 4 (1984): 16-32.

Virgule (/)

The virgule, also well known as the diagonal, solidus, or slash, has a variety of functions. It is most often used between inclusive numbers and between words of equal weight, replacing a hyphen or en dash; to designate the word *per* or *to* in measures and ratios; in mathematical copy; and to indicate separate lines such as in poetry.

Between Numbers and Words. Use no space on either side when writing the virgule between inclusive numbers and nouns of equal weight.

the 1989/1990 decade

the April/May 1991 issue

a scientist/educator

the Missouri/Arkansas border

Per or To. The virgule takes the place of the word *per* or *to* in measures and ratios. Again, use no space on either side of the virgule.

10,000 manuscripts/month

50 lbs./in.

a 40/60 ratio

a 50/50 chance

Mathematical Copy. The virgule is used in slashing fractions in mathematical material. It is especially common in superscripts and subscripts. No space is added on either side of the virgule.

$y^{(a+b)/(x+m)}$

$\exp((a - b)/(c + d))$

Separate Lines. The virgule is used in a text paragraph, as opposed to a displayed quote, to show where a new line of poetry begins. It can also be used for any other situation in which you want to designate a new line. Typesetters usually put a thin space around each side of the virgule in these cases.

Sir John Davies wrote in 1596: "What can we know? or what can we discern, / When error chokes the windows of the mind?"

Divide a name at the end of a line as follows: Roger C. / Douglas.

Chapter 3

CAPITALIZATION

The capitalization of names, titles, and various terminology is of concern to all writers who want to use an accepted modern style. There is no universally accepted style for capitalization, however. Certain disciplines, particularly in scientific areas, tend to capitalize more, whereas others tend to capitalize less. Although this is not a matter of right or wrong, the trend in most contemporary writing is toward the use of capital letters only when essential, for example, in an official name or title.

George Washington University

Prentice Hall Style Manual

The decision of whether to capitalize something is not really that simple, however. The long list of rules in this chapter, with the numerous exceptions, testifies to the extensive considerations that apply to decisions of what to capitalize and when. This book provides a general style suitable to most social, business, and professional pursuits. But if your employer requires another style, you must follow it.

Since style is always to some extent a matter of personal taste, you may have preferences that lead you to deviate from the style presented here. Writers who lend strength to the idea of personal preferences should also place a great deal of emphasis on the matter of consistency. If there are crimes of the pen in capitalization, they occur more in the consistent use of a style than in any choice concerning capitalization of particular terms.

The points of style given in this chapter are arranged in eleven major categories: education; geography; government and politics; history; holidays, time, and seasons; the judiciary; military service; proper nouns; religion; science; and titles and headings. For rules concerning the capitalization of abbreviations, see chapter 6; for numbers, chapter 7; for foreign terms, chapter 8; and for notes and bibliographies, chapter 9.

EDUCATION

Titles

Capitalize titles such as *president*, *dean*, and *professor* when they precede a name, when part of a fellowship or professorship title that includes a proper noun, in inside addresses of letters, and in formal listings such as an address list. Use small (lowercase) letters when titles follow a name in ordinary text or in informal references to a position such as "the professor of economics."

> Last month Dean James Ardas, College of Arts and Sciences, resigned.
>
> James Ardas, dean, College of Arts and Sciences, resigned last month.
>
> The conference was opened by Professor Lois Hewlitt.
>
> The conference was opened by Lois Hewlitt, professor of business law.
>
> the Dean J. Foster Adams Fellowship
>
> Dr. William Proust
> Jonas Henry Professor Emeritus
> Midland Agricultural College
> Columbus, GA 31907
>
> The senior professor of agricultural science, Dr. Proust, was recently appointed Jonas Henry Professor Emeritus at Midland Agricultural College.

Degrees, Honorary Positions, and Awards

Capitalize both abbreviations of degrees and the full titles in addresses or formal listings and usually when they follow a name. Lowercase the full titles when they are used alone or in general references such as "the master's degree."

> Mary Seymour, Sc.D.
> Jacksonville University
> Jacksonville, FL 32207
>
> Mary Seymour, Doctor of Science (*or* doctor of science), Jacksonville University, Jacksonville, FL 32207, has joined the faculty.
>
> Ned Jenkins, Master of Science (*or* master of science), will teach the course.
>
> Ned Jenkins, M.S. in business administration, will teach the course.
>
> Mary Seymour has a doctor of science degree.
>
> Bertrand Newton, Fellow of the Royal Order, attended Hill University.
>
> Bertrand Newton was a fellow at Hill University.
>
> The Warren Shields Scholarship was recently established.
>
> A scholarship was recently established in memory of Warren Shields.

Institutions

Capitalize the official name of a school, division, or department. Lowercase general references such as "the university."

John Quincy Adams High School, the high school

the University of Virginia, the university in Richmond, Virginia

Princeton and Yale universities

the School of Medicine, the medical school

the Department of English, the English department

the Department of Social Studies, the social studies department

the Board of Trustees of Mason College, the board of trustees, the board

Classes

Capitalize the official names of classes. Lowercase general references to members of the class.

He is a member of the Senior Class.

He is a senior.

Courses and Programs

Capitalize the official name of a course or program. Lowercase general or informal references.

He took Classical Greek 101.

He studied classical Greek.

She enrolled in the Metropolitan Areas Development Program.

She enrolled in the program on developing urban areas.

FOREIGN TERMS

See chapter 8 for a list of capitalized terms in familiar foreign languages.

GEOGRAPHY

Places and Regions

Capitalize the specific geographical and topographical names of most places, regions, and other areas or parts of countries, continents, and the world. Lowercase most adjectives pertaining to the place or region (the *Orient/oriental culture*). Capitalize *southern, northern,* and so on when they are part of the name (*Northern Hemisphere*) or have gained prominence through usage (*Southern California*). Lowercase them when they refer to a general location (*northern France*). To determine when words such as *north* are part of an official name, consult a modern atlas.

the Arctic, an arctic winter

South Pole, polar climate

Tropic of Cancer, the equator, the tropics

the Occident, occidental customs

Eastern Hemisphere, Western Hemisphere

South America, Central America, North America

the continent (U.S.), the Continent (Europe), continental United States, continental Europe

Middle East, Far East, Near East

Western Europe, Eastern Europe (post-World War II division)

Central Europe (World War I division)

Southeast Asia, southern Asia

Northern Ireland, northern Canada

West Africa, East Africa, central Africa

Middle West; Lincoln, Nebraska; Nebraska State; state of Nebraska

Pacific Northwest; Seattle, Washington; Washington State; state of Washington

the Roman Empire, the empire

Capitalize *north, south, east,* and *west* when they are part of a proper name or when they designate a specific region. Lowercase the words when they refer to directions. Capitalize *Northern(er)* and *Southern(er)* in Civil War contexts. Lowercase *northern(er), southern(er), eastern(er),* and *western(er)* in general references to a locality or its inhabitants.

the West (U.S.; world), the East (U.S.; world)

Western (world) culture, Eastern (world) culture

west of the Mississippi, east of the Rockies

Deep South, down South

Far West, far western

easterly wind, southern climate

north of Ohio, the North (U.S. region), driving north, beliefs of Northerners in the Civil War, northern United States

Popular Terms

Capitalize terms that have been coined to describe a particular place or area and have become popular through extensive use.

the Loop (Chicago)

the Twin Cities (Minneapolis, St. Paul)

Badlands (South Dakota)

Bay Area (San Francisco)

the Channel (English)

Old South (U.S.)

the Mississippi Delta

Eastern Shore (Chesapeake Bay)

Left Bank (Paris)

New World, Old World

the Piedmont (eastern U.S.)

South Seas

Sun Belt (U.S.)

the Village (New York City)

West Side (New York City)

the States (U.S.)

Benelux countries (Europe)

City of Brotherly Love (Philadelphia)

French Quarter (New Orleans)

Windy City (Chicago)

Empire State (New York State)

Topographical Terms

Capitalize words such as *river* or *mountain* when they are part of a proper name or when they precede two or more proper names. Lowercase general descriptive references to *rivers, mountains,* and the like, and lowercase the word when it follows two or more proper names. Lowercase a word such as *river* when it is directly preceded by *the*. Do not duplicate the meaning of a foreign word that is part of a proper name. *Rio,* for example, means "river" (*Rio Grande,* not *Rio* Grande *River*). Consult a modern atlas for the proper wording, spelling, and capitalization of topographical names.

Gulf of Mexico, the Gulf

Arkansas River, the river

the river Elbe, the river Thames

Mississippi and Colorado rivers

Belknap Mountains, the mountains

Mounts Washington and Wrangell

Rocky and Appalachian mountains

Atlantic Ocean, the Atlantic, the ocean

Colorado River valley, San Joaquin Valley, the valley

Iberian Peninsula, the peninsula

Pacific coast (topography), Pacific Coast (region)

Lake Erie, the lake

Lakes Michigan and Erie, the lakes

Sierra Nevada (not *Sierra* Nevada *Mountains*)

GOVERNMENT AND POLITICS

Countries, States, and Other Territories

Capitalize the official name of a specific political or governmental territory, for example, *Ohio State*. Lowercase the word that defines the type of division or territory (*state*) in general references or when it stands alone. Capitalize *the* only when it is part of the official name.

Persian Empire, the empire

France, the French republic, République Française, the republic, the country of France

the Netherlands, the Kingdom of the Netherlands, the kingdom, the capital of The Hague

Australia, the Commonwealth of Australia, the commonwealth

United States, United States of America, the States, the country of America

British colonies, the colonies

Massachusetts Bay Colony, the colony at Massachusetts Bay

Missouri, Missouri State, the state of Missouri, the state

South Central states, the states

Arizona Territory, the territory of Arizona, the territory

Wade County, the county of Wade, the county

Morris Township, the township of Morris, the township

New York City, the city of New York, the city

Washington, D.C., the District of Columbia, the district

Public Buildings and Other Structures

Capitalize the official names of public buildings, parks, monuments, landmarks, streets, and other structures. Lowercase the term for structure (e.g., *bridge*) in general references or when used alone. (Do not italicize the names of foreign structures.)

the Capitol (U.S.), Capitol Hill

Yellowstone National Park, the park

Washington Monument, the monument

Jefferson Bridge, the bridge

Oval Office, the president's office

National Gallery of Art, the gallery

the faces of Mount Rushmore

the Mall (Washington, D.C.; London)

the Pyramids, the Egyptian pyramids

Columbus Avenue, the avenue, Columbus and Whittaker avenues

Times Square (New York City)

Champs-Elysées (Paris)

San Diego Zoo, the zoo

Formal Documents and Programs

Capitalize the official titles of formal political and governmental documents and programs. Lowercase general references to the type of document or program.

Treaty of Versailles, the Versailles treaty, the treaty

U.S. Constitution, the Constitution of the United States, the Constitution

New Jersey Constitution, the constitution of New Jersey, the constitution

Fourteenth Amendment of the U.S. Constitution, the amendment

due process clause [*or* Due Process Clause] of the U.S. Constitution

Monroe Doctrine, the doctrine

Public Law 169, the law

Tonkin Resolution, the resolution

Reorganization Bill of 1974, the Reorganization bill, the bill

Civil Rights Act of 1964, the act, the civil rights law, the civil rights bill

the 1991 Energy Conservation Program, the program

the Social Security [*or* social security] programs Medicare and Medicaid

Governmental and Political Bodies

Capitalize the official names of organizations, political and governmental bodies, and any of their official divisions. Lowercase general references to the type of body. The official names of state governing bodies (*general assembly, senate,* and so on) are given in almanacs and other books of facts.

U.S. Congress, the Congress, congressional

U.S. government, the federal government, the Bush administration

U.N. Security Council, the Security Council, the council

the Central Intelligence Agency, the CIA, the agency

U.S. House of Representatives, the House

House of Commons, the Commons, the lower house

British Parliament, the Parliament, a parliament, parliamentary

General Assembly of North Carolina, the North Carolina legislature, the North Carolina assembly, including the senate and house

Nevada Legislature, the legislature, including the senate and assembly

the Federal Reserve Board, the board

the Federal Aviation Agency, the agency

the Bureau of the Census, the Census Bureau, the bureau

the Department of Energy, the Energy Department, the department

the Hillside City Council, the city council, the council

the Word Processing Division of the Military Contracts Board, the division

Professional Titles and Titles of Nobility

Capitalize titles such as *president* and *governor* when they precede a name or appear in formal lists such as an address list. But do not capitalize titles such as *director* and *secretary* preceding a name (except in the case of a high official such as *Secretary of State*); rather, use a personal title (*Mr.*) or scholastic title (*Dr.*). Lowercase titles that follow a name in general text or that are used alone. But capitalize honorific forms of address such as *His Royal Highness* even when used alone.

President George Bush; the president; George Bush, president of the United States; the presidency

Secretary of Defense Dick Cheney; the secretary; Dick Cheney, secretary of defense

Governor Rose Mofford; the governor; Rose Mofford, the governor of Arizona

Representative Norma Briskill, Fifth District; the representative; the congresswoman

Mayor John Roman, the mayor

Alderman Paul Dougherty; Paul Dougherty, Newton Board of Aldermen; the alderman/alderperson; Mr. Paul Dougherty, treasurer, Newton Board of Aldermen

Ms. Janice Tompkins, associate member, Humane Society of the United States; Janice Tompkins, an associate member

HISTORY

Historical and Cultural Periods

Capitalize the proper names and traditionally recognized official names of historical and cultural periods such as the *Middle Ages*. Lowercase general references to most periods, for example, the American *colonial* period. Also, lowercase recent cultural periods such as the *space age*.

Augustan Age

Dark Ages

Guilded Age

antiquity, ancient Greece

Middle Ages, High Middle Ages, early Middle Ages, late Middle Ages

Stone Age, Iron Age, Bronze Age

age of steam, atomic age, nuclear age, space age

Neolithic times, Paleolithic times

Renaissance, High Renaissance

the Enlightenment

Age of Reason

Restoration

Progressive Era

Reformation, Counter-Reformation

Old Regime, the ancien régime, *l'ancien régime*

Victorian era

Christian Era

romantic period

colonial period

baroque period

fin de siècle

Important Events and Occasions

Capitalize the traditionally recognized formal names of events and occasions. Lowercase generic terms such as *revolution* (except references to the American Revolution) when standing alone or following a proper name.

Boston Tea Party

Congress of Vienna

Yalta Conference

Reign of Terror

Great Depression, the depression

Reconstruction (U.S.)

Prohibition

American Revolution, the Revolution, the revolutionary war

Industrial Revolution (*or* industrial revolution)

New Deal

War on Poverty

World Series, the Series

California gold rush, the gold rush

Dreyfus affair

cold war (*or* Cold War)

Numerical Designations

Capitalize a numerical reference when it is part of a proper name. Lowercase all other numerical designations of periods or events.

Roaring Twenties

Third Reich

nineteenth century

Five-Year Plan (Soviet)

the third battle at Concord

the IAB First Annual Conference and Technical Exhibition, the IAB's first conference and exhibition

Second World War, World War II, the war

Movements, Schools, and Styles

Capitalize the proper nouns and adjectives in the names of movements, schools, and styles as well as terms derived from proper nouns, such as *Epicurean*. Lowercase most general references or descriptions, such as *neoclassic*.

Gothic

Doric

Epicurean

Socratic

baroque

Romanesque

Aristotelian

rococo

Neoplatonism

Pre-Raphaelite

New Criticism

classical, neoclassical, classicist

surrealism, surrealist

cubism, cubist

symbolism, symbolist

idealism, idealist

impressionism, impressionist

realism, realist

transcendentalism, transcendentalist

Scholasticism, Scholastics

Stoicism, Stoic

op art, pop art

theater of the absurd

Palmatte school of design

Winslow school of thought

civil rights movement

anti-American movement

Languages and Nationalities

Capitalize the names of historically recognized races, peoples, tribes, and other groups and their official languages. Lowercase general descriptive references such as *black*.

Caucasian

Afro-American

Hispanic

Chicano, Chicana

Latino, Latina

Mongol, mongoloid

Negro, negroid

Oriental (person), oriental culture

Pygmy (Central African), pygmy (a dwarf)

American Indian, native American

Apache

Papago

aborigine

Bushman (southern African), bushman (Australia)

English, English language

Russian, Russian language

black, white, yellow, red

HOLIDAYS, TIME, AND SEASONS

Special Days

Capitalize the names of days of the week and of months, religious days and seasons, and special secular days or occasions. Lowercase general descriptive references to an occasion, such as *election day*.

Monday, Tuesday, Wednesday, Thursday, Friday, Saturday, Sunday

January, February, March, April, May, June, July, August, September, October, November, December

Christmas, Christmas Eve, Yuletide

Easter Day

Good Friday, Ash Wednesday

Hanukkah

Passover

Rosh Hashanah

Yom Kippur

Ramadan

Halloween, All Hallows' Eve

Twelfth Night

Holy Week

Lent

Thanksgiving Day

Fourth of July, the Fourth, Independence Day

April Fools' Day, All Fools' Day

New Year, New Year's Eve, New Year's Day

Martin Luther King Day

Arbor Day

Labor Day

Veterans Day

V-E Day

D day

Mother's Day, Father's Day

Energy Conservation Week

election day

registration day

inauguration day

Time

Capitalize proper nouns in the designations of time zones, and capitalize or use small capitals for the abbreviations *A.D.* and *B.C.*. Lowercase or use small capitals for the initials *a.m.* and *p.m.*

eastern standard time (est)

central daylight time (cdt)

Pacific standard time (Pst)

Greenwich mean time (Gmt)

daylight saving time (dst)

a.m, p.m. (*or* A.M., P.M.)

A.D., B.C. (*or* A.D., B.C.)

two o'clock (*or* 2 o'clock)

4 a.m. (*or* 4 A.M.)

10:30 p.m. (*or* 10:30 P.M.)

The Four Seasons

Capitalize the name of a season when it is personified. Lowercase other references to any of the four seasons and to the solstice and equinox.

spring, summer, autumn (fall), winter

summer solstice, winter solstice, spring equinox, fall equinox

Then came Winter's chilling breath.

He returned from college during the winter recess.

THE JUDICIARY

Judicial Bodies

Capitalize the official names of particular judicial bodies. Lowercase most shortened references (except to the U.S. Supreme Court and except when "the Court" refers to the judge) and general, descriptive references to a type of body, such as a *traffic court*.

Supreme Court of the United States, U.S. Supreme Court, the Supreme Court, the Court

U.S. Court of Customs and Patent Appeals, the customs court, the court

The Tax Court of the United States, the tax court, the court

U.S. Court of Appeals for the District of Columbia, the court of appeals, the court

New York Court of Appeals, the Court of Appeals (capitalized to avoid confusion with the U.S. appeals court), the court

New Hampshire Supreme Court, the state supreme court, the court

Municipal Court of Hollyville, Hollyville municipal court, the municipal court, the court

Circuit Court of Wade County, circuit court, county court

Court of Queen's Bench, the court

the family court

the juvenile court

the traffic court

It is the opinion of the Court [i.e., the judge] that the evidence is inadmissible.

The Court's [i.e., the judge's] ruling shall stand.

Titles of Officials

Capitalize titles when they precede a name, in formal listings such as an address list, and in direct address. Capitalize honorific titles such as *Your Honor*. Lowercase titles other than honorific titles or titles used in direct address when they follow a name or when they are used alone.

Judge Sharon Thomas is presiding.

The Honorable Sharon Thomas, associate justice, is presiding.

The judge, Sharon Thomas, is presiding in both cases.

The Honorable Abraham U. Kendall
Chief Justice
Supreme Court of Arizona
Phoenix, AZ 85009

We believe the signature is a forgery, Judge, but the lab report is not clear on this.

According to the record, His Honor requested that the jury disregard that statement.

The judge will decide the merits of the case.

Legal Cases

Capitalize all important words in the names of legal cases. Lowercase the abbreviation *v.* or *vs.* (versus) and lowercase the words *case, decision,* and *trial* in general discussion.

In re York

Hart et al. v. *Pringle, Inc.*

Heberson v. *North Dakota*

Heberson v. *North Dakota*

the *Heberson* case, the *Heberson* decision, the *Heberson* trial, Heberson's case, Heberson's trial

MILITARY SERVICE

Branches and Organizations

Capitalize the official names of military branches and organizations. Lowercase words such as *army* and *air force* when they are used alone or are used collectively.

United States Army, the army

United States Air Force, the air force

United States Navy, the navy

United States Marine Corps, the Marine Corps, the marines

United States Coast Guard, the Coast Guard

United States Signal Corps, the Signal Corps

National Guard, the guard

armed forces

Union army (Civil War), Confederate army

Army of the Potomac, the army

Red Army, the Russian army

Royal Air Force, British air force

French foreign legion

Second Battalion, the battalion

Third Fleet, the fleet

Fifth Army, the army

Pacific Fleet (World War II)

Twenty-first Infantry Division, the division

the armies of the Western alliance

Allied forces, the Allies (World Wars I and II)

Central Powers (World War I)

Joint Chiefs of Staff

Military Rank

Capitalize a title when it precedes a name, in formal listings such as an address list, and when used in direct address. Lowercase titles when used alone (but capitalize *General of the Army* and *Fleet Admiral* in all cases to avoid confusion with other ranks of general or admiral).

General Nelson Wyman, the general

Fleet Admiral Harry Wexler, the Fleet Admiral

Major Anne Steinberg, the major

Sergeant John Porter, the sergeant

Lieutenant Colonel Harriet Domage
United States Navy
Fort Greenbriar
Portland, OR 97227

Tell me, Colonel, is it true that the government may close the base?

Wars and Battles

Capitalize the formal titles of wars, battles, conflicts, revolutions, and military campaigns. Lowercase words such as *war, seige,* or *battle* when used alone.

World War I, the Great War, First World War, the war

World War II, Second World War, the war

American Revolution, the Revolution, the revolutionary war, the War of Independence, the war

French Revolution, the Revolution

American and French revolutions

French and Indian War, the war

Battle of the Bulge, the battle

Spanish-American War, the war

Vietnam War, the war

Whiskey Rebellion, the rebellion

intercoastal water campaign

the seige of Lewisville

Civil War (U.S.), the war

Norman Conquest, conquest of England, the conquest

Battle of Bunker Hill, the battle

War of the Roses, the war

Korean conflict

the Israeli occupation

the invasion of Kuwait

Awards and Honors

Capitalize the official names of special military medals and other awards or honors. Lowercase general references to an award or honor.

Medal of Honor, the medal

Purple Heart

Distinguished Service Cross

Distinguished Flying Cross

Navy Cross

croix de guerre

He received the marines' highest award.

He displayed the medal proudly.

PROPER NOUNS

Organizations

Capitalize the official names of companies, institutions, and other organizations. Lowercase words such as *company* when used alone, and lowercase the word *party* when used with the name of political affiliation (*Republican party*).

U.S. Chamber of Commerce, the Chamber of Commerce

Princeton University, the university

Communist party, Communist bloc, Communist, communism

Democratic party, the party, democracy

the Left, leftist, left wing, left-winger

American Express Company, the company

Trans World Airlines, TWA, the airline

North Atlantic Treaty Organization, NATO, the organization

United Nations, the U.N. organization

Cincinnati East Junior High, the junior high

Amtrak, the railroad

American Psychological Association, the association

First Lutheran Church, the church

Paradise Condominiums, Inc., the condominiums

U.S. Department of Labor, Labor Department, the department

the Phoenix Cardinals, the Cardinals, the team

the executive branch, the legislative branch

Personal and Fictitious Names, Nicknames, and Initials

Capitalize a person's first name, initials, and surname, but follow the individual's preferred spelling of prefixes such as *de* or *la*. If the prefix is the first word in a sentence, however, capitalize it regardless of the individual's preferred style. Also capitalize all important words in a nickname, and capitalize fictitious names and personifications. Lowercase articles and prepositions in nicknames and epithets.

Mary T. K. Rawlins

E. I. du Pont de Nemours

William Van Vliet

Kevin de Kooning

Morris "the Cat" Greenley

Thomas P. "Tip" O'Neill

Calamity Jane

the Virginian

Attila the Hun

Uncle Sam

John Doe

Jack Frost

Then Nature sank into her misty solitude.

Professional and Personal Titles with Names. Capitalize professional or scholastic (*Dr.*) and personal (*Ms.*) titles used before a name, in formal listings such as an address list, and in direct address. Lowercase titles such as *professor* after a name and when used alone, and lowercase business or descriptive titles such as *programmer* both before and after a name and when used alone.

Dr. Madeline McDonald; Madeline McDonald, M.D.; the doctor

Mr. Roy Jones; Professor Roy Jones; Roy Jones, the professor of marketing; the professor

Dr. Rena Forrestor
Associate Professor of Geology
Honolulu College of Geology
Honolulu, HI 96816

I was wondering, Professor, if we could have an extension on our assignment.

computer operator David Tomlin

President Corine Beale; Corine Beale, the president of Beale Industries; the president

administrative assistant Jerry Foxworth

Secretary of State James Baker; James Baker, the secretary of state; the secretary

Vehicles, Crafts, and Vessels

Capitalize the official names of land, sea, and air vehicles. Lowercase general references to a *ship, car,* or the like.

SS *America*, the *America*, the ship

HMS *Seacliff*, the *Seacliff*, the ship

Spirit of Saint Louis, the airplane

Boeing 727, the airplane

Concorde, the airplane

Century Limited, the Century, the train

ICBM, the missile

Sputnik I, Sputnik, the satellite

Discovery, the space shuttle

Ulysses, the solar probe

Honda Civic, the car

Ford F150 XLT, the truck

Winnebago, the recreation vehicle, the RV

Greyhound, the bus

Products, Services, and Trademarks

Capitalize brand names and registered trademarks. Lowercase generic names and general references to a type of product or service, such as *television.* Also lowercase a trademark name that through extensive use has acquired the status of a common noun.

Kleenex, tissue

Realtor, real estate agent

Coca-Cola, Coke, soft drink

Band-Aid

Teflon

Levi's, overalls

Frigidaire, refrigerator

Tide, soap, detergent

Bufferin, aspirin

Computer Terms

Capitalize the official brand names of hardware and software. Terms or initials designating languages, commands, operations, and the like are usually written in all capital letters. Lowercase general references to a program or procedure.

Zenith Data Systems

80286 Personal Computer, the Z-286, the computer

Microsoft Word Version 5.0, word processing software

BASIC, FORTRAN (*or* Fortran), Pascal, the language

DSKSETUP, CONFIGUR, MKDIR, the command

WESTLAW (*or* Westlaw), the database

debug

format

hard copy

on line

time-sharing

Numerical Designations

Capitalize the important words in an official name containing a numerical designation. Lowercase general references to a page number, item, and the like.

Ward 3, the ward

Fourteenth Precinct, the precinct

Flight 201, the flight

Executive Order 217096, the executive order

Fifth Avenue, the avenue

Room 419

Unit 16

chapter 2 (*or* Chapter 2)

book III (*or* Book III)

figure 6.6 (*or* Figure 6.6)

volume 2 (*or* Volume 2)

page 397

line 13

verse 5

note 28

paragraph 7

size 8

question 9

Words Based on Proper Nouns

Lowercase words that are derived from proper names and created to convey a particular meaning, as in *Louis Pasteur/pasteurize.*

bohemian

arabic numerals

roman numerals

scotch whiskey

dutch oven

india ink

china (dishes)

morocco (leather)

sienna (color)

venetian blinds

arctic boats

anglicize

manila envelopes

RELIGION

Groups and Organizations

Capitalize the names of religions, churches, denominations, sects, orders, councils, and any other formally recognized religious group or organization. Lowercase general references to a structure (*church*) or organization (*council*).

Zen Buddhism, a Buddhist, the temple

Buddhism, Buddhist monastery, the monastery

Judaism, Jewish synagogue, the synagogue

Islam, Islamic beliefs, a Muslim

Theosophism, Theosophy, a Theosophist

Gentiles, gentile practices

Protestant church, the church, Protestantism

Roman Catholic church, the church, Roman Catholicism

Anglican church, the church, Anglicanism

Reformed Church in America, Reformed church, the church

First Baptist Church, the Baptist church, the church

Saint Luke's Episcopal Church, the Episcopal church, the church

Sisters of Mercy, the order, the sisters

First Vatican Council, Vatican I, the council

Titles

Capitalize religious titles that precede a name, in formal listings such as an address list, and when used in direct address. Lowercase titles after a name and when used alone. (Traditionally, the word *the* preceded the title of *reverend, right reverend,* and so on. Some sources state that this is no longer a requirement in modern usage. But observe the practice of the group you are addressing.)

Pope John Paul II, His Holiness, the pope, the papacy

the Ecumenical patriarch of Constantinople, His Holiness, the patriarch

the Most Reverend Michael Winslow Porter, bishop of Metropolis, Bishop Porter, the Catholic bishop of Metropolis, the bishop (Roman Catholic)

the Right Reverend Donald C. Evanston, bishop of Metropolis, Bishop Evanston, the Anglican bishop of Metropolis, the bishop (Anglican)

the Reverend (*or* the Reverend Dr.) Virginia M. Wharton, minister of the First Reformed Church; Ms. (*or* Dr.) Wharton; Rev. Virginia M. Wharton; the Reverend Ms. (*or* Dr.) Wharton; the minister

Rabbi Benjamin Goldberg, Rabbi Goldberg, Mr. (*or* Dr.) Goldberg, the rabbi

Father Harold T. Royal, Father Royal, the father

Deities and Divine Persons

Capitalize the names of deities (*God*) and divine persons (*Saint Peter*) and references to a supreme being. Lowercase pronouns referring to a deity as well as words such as *godlike* that are derived from the name of a deity.

God, the Lord, the Almighty, the Father, the Omnipotent, the Supreme Being

Allah, Jehovah, Yahweh, El

Buddha

the Prophet Muhammad

The Lord, in his infinite wisdom, has spoken, and he shall be heard by all who believe.

John the Baptist

Saint Paul

the Virgin Mary, the Blessed Virgin, Mother of God

the Apostles, the Divine Apostle

Literature

Capitalize the titles of sacred works and their parts or divisions. Lowercase general terms such as *book* when used alone and most terms that are based on or derived from a religious work such as *biblical*. (The titles of sacred works are not italicized or enclosed in quotation marks.)

Bible, Holy Bible, Holy Writ, biblical

Talmud, talmudic

Dead Sea Scrolls, the scrolls

Book of the Dead, the book

Koran, Koranic, the book, the sacred work

Authorized Version, King James Version

Revised Standard Version

Gospels, the gospel truth

New Testament, Old Testament

Pentateuch

the pastoral Epistles

Psalms, a psalm

Acts, the Acts of the Apostles

Revelation, the Apocalypse

Sermon on the Mount

Ten Commandments

the Lord's Prayer

Ave Maria

the Beatitudes

Apostles' Creed

Rites and Services

Capitalize *Mass* when it refers to the eucharistic rite. Lowercase general references to rites and services, for example, *baptism*; and lowercase *high mass* and *low mass* in reference to a specific, individual service. Also lowercase the names of items used in rites and services, such as the *rosary*.

Mass, the eucharistic sacrament

He was late for today's high mass.

There will be masses every day this week.

the Sacrament in Holy Communion

the Body and Blood of Christ in Holy Communion

bar mitzvah, bas mitzvah

baptism

confirmation

vesper service

holy water

sanctuary

chalice and paten

Important Events

Capitalize the formal names of traditionally recognized special events, predictions, and beliefs. Lowercase informal, general references, such as *the death of Christ*, and words derived from the formal name of an event, such as *creationism*.

Creation, creationism

the Crucifixion, the crucifying of Christ

the Resurrection

the Second Coming of Christ

Original Sin

Redemption, redemptive

the Inquisition, the tribunal

the Flood, the Deluge

the Diaspora, the settlement of Jews

the Exodus, the departure

the Fall

the Crusades

SCIENCE

Astronomy and Meteorology

Capitalize the official names of planets and other celestial bodies, but capitalize *earth, sun,* and *moon* only when discussed in connection with other celestial bodies. Lowercase the names of meteorological phenomena.

Venus

Mars

Saturn

Sirius

Pleiades

Ursa Major

Big Dipper

North Star

Alpha Centauri

Milky Way

the Galaxy, a galaxy

Halley's comet

Solar System

aurora borealis, northern lights

We studied the planets Uranus and Pluto.

The satellite bounced beacons between the Earth and the Moon while scientists studied the latest photographs of Mars.

The earth is like a living organism.

The sun is a bright star.

The light of the moon is casting deep shadows.

Chemistry and Physics

Capitalize chemical symbols and proper nouns in theorems, laws, and the like. Lowercase the names of the chemical elements and words such as *law* and *principle.* (Capitalize *law, principle,* and so on only in popular or fictitious names such as "Murphy's Law.")

aluminum, Al

iron, Fe

zinc, Zn

the Pythagorean theorem

Einstein's theory of relativity

Boyle's law

the Peter Principle

Murphy's Law

Medicine

Capitalize proper nouns in the names of diseases and related terms, and capitalize the brand names of drugs. Also capitalize genus names and lowercase species' names of infectious organisms. Lowercase the generic names of drugs and general terms such as *disease* and *syndrome*.

leukemia

cancer

Hodgkin's disease

chronic fatigue syndrome

Phthirus (lice), *P. pubis*

Tunga (sand flea), *T. penetrans*

diazepam, Valium

estrogen, Clinestrone

insulin, Humulin L

Biology

Capitalize genus names and names of larger divisions (phylum, class, order, and family). Lowercase species and subspecies names. Capitalize only the proper nouns and adjectives in most common names. Italicize genus, species, subspecies, and variety names, and use roman type for the names of phylum, class, order, and family. (Note that authorities in different disciplines may observe different rules concerning capitalization of Latin terms.)

Conopholis americana, C. americana, squawroot

Eschscholtzia californica, E. californica, California poppy

Pinus palustris, P. palustris, longleaf pine

Opuntia fulgida, O. fulgida, jumping cholla

Phoca vitulina, P. vitulina, harbor seal

Cervus elaphus, C. elaphus, elk

Hylocicha mustelina, H. mustelina, wood thrush

Accipiter cooperii, A. cooperii, Cooper's hawk

Velvet ants are in the family Mutillidae.

Rabbits are in the order Lagomorpha.

Scallops are in the family Pectinidae.

Scorpion flies are in the order Mecoptera.

Geology

Capitalize the names of periods, eras, and other time designations and words such as *lower* or *middle* when they refer to a particular date or time within a period. Lowercase words such as *period* in most cases, as well as *early, late,* and other adjectives when used descriptively. Also lowercase structural terms such as *basin* unless they are preceded by a proper noun.

Pliocene epoch

Quaternary period

Mesozoic era

Lower Silurian period

Upper Cambrian period

Late Mississippian period

middle Paleocene (general description)

Early Triassic period

interglacial age

red beds (rocks)

syncline (structural)

Nashville Basin, the basin

Piedmont Lowland, the lowland

TITLES AND HEADINGS

Written Material

Capitalize the important words in titles of books, booklets, periodicals, poems, plays, dissertations, reports, and other written material, and capitalize the names of any awards for such works. Also capitalize the titles of articles, chapters, short stories, series, and the like. Capitalize general titles such as *foreword* and *glossary* only in cross-references. Lowercase general references to a chapter, an article, and so on, as well as casual references to common titles such as the bibliography. Also lowercase parts of poems and plays such as *act* and *canto*.

Prentice Hall Style Manual (book)

Oxford English Dictionary, OED, the dictionary

Time (magazine)

Ode to Spring (long poem), stanza 3

"Springfest" (short poem)

Phantom of the Opera (play), act 2, scene 1

"The Economic Structure of the Welsh Highlands" (unpublished dissertation)

Marketing Strategy for the X-1400 Copiers (formal report)

Nobel Prize, Pulitzer Prize, the award

"The New Women Entrepreneurs" (magazine article)

"Capitalization" (chapter)

"The Lost Loves of Sheila" (short story)

Fielding Studies in Hypersensitivity, No. 1 (series)

Classic Gold edition

See part II. (cross-reference)

Refer to the Introduction, page 14. (cross-reference)

It is a follow-up on the discussion in chapter 6.

The author explains his procedure in the preface.

Film and Broadcast Material

Capitalize important words in the titles of motion pictures, television programs, and radio programs. Lowercase general references to a movie, program, or show.

When Harry Met Sally (motion picture), the movie

Dick Tracy (motion picture), the film

"Quantum Leap" (television program), the program

"Sunrise Semester" (television program), the show

"Children's Hour" (radio program), the broadcast

Musical Compositions

Capitalize the important words in the titles of long musical works, such as operas and symphonies, and short works, such as songs. Lowercase most abbreviations such as *op.* (opus) and *no.* (number), and lowercase general references to an opera, song, and the like.

King David, the oratorio

Sonata in C Minor, op. 3

Minute Waltz, the waltz

Symphony no. [*or* No.] 8 in B Minor ("Unfinished"), the symphony

The Barber of Seville, the opera

Madame Butterfly, the opera

William Tell Overture

Handel's *Messiah*

String Quartet no. 3

Prelude ("Song of the Hoodlum"), the movement

"Star-Spangled Banner," the song

"Amazing Grace," the hymn

Artwork

Capitalize important words in the titles of paintings, sculptures, and other works of art. Lowercase general references to a drawing, statue, and the like.

Van Gogh's *Irises,* the painting

Turner's *Seascape,* the painting

the Mona Lisa (a traditional work of art)

Boccioni's *Unique Forms of Continuity in Space,* the sculpture

Praxiteles's *Hermes with the Infant Dionysus,* the sculpture

Woman Possessed, a drawing

The Field Workers, an etching

Signs and Slogans

Capitalize important words in signs, notices, slogans, and mottoes. Lowercase general references to a motto, slogan, and the like.

No Through Traffic, the sign

Live Free or Die, the motto

He Lived Every Moment of Every Day, the inscription

California or Bust, the slogan

Closed by Order of the Sheriff, the notice

Chapter 4

SPELLING

The rules of spelling described in this chapter can be used as a guide to determine how to spell names, titles, abbreviations, numbers, foreign words, compounds, possessives, and various common nouns. The usefulness of the rules, however, is limited by the numerous exceptions that must be observed. With most compound nouns, for example, *s* or *es* is added to the end of the word to make it plural: *standby/standbys*. But another word that also ends in *by* is an exception to that rule: *passerby/passersby* (not *passerbys*).

Often there is no additional rule or guide to tell you when to depart from a primary rule. It is a matter of memorizing the individual exceptions to a rule or consulting a dictionary when in doubt. One of the best dictionaries for this purpose is *Webster's Third New International Dictionary* or the abridged version, *Webster's New Collegiate Dictionary*.

The guidelines given here are based on American spelling (*labor*) rather than British spelling (*labour*). Other variations may occur, however, since different disciplines have different preferred spellings for certain terms. *Webster's*, for instance, shows *esthete* to be a variation of *aesthete,* and it lists *nickle* as an alternative for *nickel*. In the absence of instructions, you should usually select the spelling indicated in the dictionary as preferred. (Dictionaries state the preferred spelling first.) Regardless of the variation you choose, though, consistency is essential so that readers are not distracted and confused by switching back and forth from one spelling to another.

PLURALS

Names

Add *s* or *es* to form the plural of most first and last names. Add *es* when the last name ends in *ch, s, sh, x,* or *z,* unless doing so makes the pronunciation awkward. With all proper names, do not change the original spelling before adding *s* or *es*.

Sampson/the Sampsons

Burns/the Burnses

Hodges/the Hodges (*not* Hodgeses: *awkward*)

Schwartz/the Schwartzes

Haddox/the Haddoxes

Rush/the Rushes

Larch/the Larches

the Cecil Krauses Sr. (*or* the Cecil Kraus Srs.)

Mary/the two Marys

Douglas/the two Douglases

North and South Carolina/the two Carolinas

Kansas City, Kansas and Missouri/the two Kansas Citys (*not* Cities)

Mondays and Thursdays

Exception: Rocky Mountains/Rockies (*not* Rockys)

Personal Titles

Personal titles are usually made plural only in formal usage. The familiar plurals are *Mmes.* (*Mrs.*), *Messrs.* (*Mr.*), *Misses* (*Miss*), and *Mss.* [or *Mses.*] (*Ms.*).

Mrs. Hill and Mrs. Barrows/Mmes. Hill and Barrows

Mr. Blackstone and Mr. Gross/Messrs. Blackstone and Gross

Miss Jolla and Miss Purdy/Misses Jolla and Purdy

Ms. Soloman and Ms. Horsfeld/Mss. Soloman and Horsfeld

Abbreviations

Add *s* to most abbreviations to form the plural, but double the initial of abbreviations for page, note, and line. Omit the *s* with metric units and many standard weights and measures.

mgr./mgrs.

Dr./Drs.

no./nos.

dos and don'ts

p./pp.

n./nn.

l./ll.

mm/mm (metric)

cl/cl (metric)

oz./oz.

ft./ft.

Numbers and Letters

Add an *s* to most numbers and letters to form the plural. Include an apostrophe only when necessary for clarity.

twos and threes

two s's

p's and q's

the Rs and Vs

YMCAs

A.A.'s

Foreign Words

The style for foreign plurals varies depending on whether you retain the foreign plural or use the English variation. Since meaning could be altered by changing foreign terms, consult a dictionary when in doubt. In the following examples the common English plural is given first. Notice that in many cases the foreign plural is preferred.

focus/focuses (*preferred*)/foci

syllabus/syllabuses/syllabi (*preferred*)

formula/formulas (*preferred*)/formulae

millennium/millenniums/millennia (*preferred*)

symposium/symposiums/symposia (*preferred*)

tempo/tempos (*preferred*)/tempi

phenomenon/phenomenons/phenomena (*preferred*)

appendix/appendixes (*preferred*)/appendices

tableau/tableaus/tableaux (*preferred*)

Compounds

Usually, add *s* or *es* to the end of a compound term or change the spelling of the compound to make it plural. In some cases, however, the *s* is added to the first part of the compound. In other cases the *s* may be added to either element. No clear rule exists to help make a determination.

standby/standbys

passerby/passersby

hanger-on/hangers-on

bucketful/bucketsful *or* bucketfuls

judge advocate/judge advocates

printout/printouts

spokesman/spokesmen

saleswoman/saleswomen

put-down/put-downs

aide de camp/aides de camp

attorney at law/attorneys at law

jack of all trades/jacks of all trades

foreword/forewords

heir apparent/heirs apparent

bookshelf/bookshelves

Common Nouns

The rules for forming the plural of common nouns differ depending on the way the noun ends. Some require an added *s* and others require *es*. With some words it may be necessary to change the form of the word before adding *s* or *es*. In a few cases the spelling of the singular and plural is the same. No clear rules exist for exceptions to any of the following rules.

Ch, S, Sh, Ss, X, or Z. Usually, add *es* to a noun ending with any of these letters. But if a final *s* is silent, keep the same form for both singular and plural.

church/churches

yes/yeses

bias/biases

corps/corps

dish/dishes

glass/glasses

box/boxes

quartz/quartzes

F, Fe, or Ff. Either add *s* to a noun ending with any of these letters or change the final *f* to *v* and add *es*. In a few cases more than one plural form is acceptable. No rule exists to determine when the form of the word should be changed.

proof/proofs

shelf/shelves

scarf/scarfs/scarves (*preferred*)

dwarf/dwarfs(*preferred*)/dwarves

safe/safes

life/lives

cliff/cliffs

O. Two rules apply to nouns ending in *o*. The first rule states that when the word ends with a vowel followed by *o*, add *s*.

studio/studios
stereo/stereos
ratio/ratios
duo/duos

The second rule states that when the word ends with a consonant followed by *o*, add *es* in most cases, *s* in a few cases, and either *s* or *es* in a few cases. For musical terms, regardless, add only *s*. No clear rule exists for making this determination.

potato/potatoes
veto/vetoes
photo/photos
memo/memos
cargo/cargoes (*preferred*)/cargos
zero/zeros (*preferred*)/zeroes
soprano/sopranos
cello/cellos

Y. Two rules apply to nouns ending in *y*, but no clear rule exists for determining exceptions to either rule. The first rule states that when the word ends with a vowel followed by *y*, add *s*.

attorney/attorneys
boy/boys
Exception: soliloquy/soliloquies

The second rule states that when the word ends with a consonant followed by *y*, change the *y* to *i* and add *es*.

copy/copies
holly/hollies
category/categories

Irregular Nouns. To form the plural of some words, change the spelling rather than add *s* or *es*.

ox/oxen
woman/women
child/children
foot/feet
mouse/mice

brother/brothers (*preferred*)/brethren

goose/geese

Other Nouns. To form the plural in cases other than those described previously, simply add *s*.

house/houses

chance/chances

harp/harps

plate/plates

college/colleges

dog/dogs

POSSESSIVES

Several rules apply to forming the possessive of nouns. For a singular noun that does not end with an *s* sound, add an apostrophe and *s*.

Harper Corp.'s policy

neighbor's car

Colorado's scenery

one hour's time

government's program

UCC's release

Wall Street Journal's report

Bengaux's restaurant

sisters-in-law's gift

When a singular noun ends with an *s* sound and forming the possessive causes a new syllable to be pronounced, add an apostrophe and *s*. But if it is awkward to pronounce the new syllable, add an apostrophe alone.

witness's testimony

Harris's boss

for conscience' sake

Add an apostrophe alone to most plural nouns. For a few irregular nouns, change the form of the singular to plural and add an apostrophe and *s*.

states' rights

doctors' hours

two years' growth

the Harrises' daughter

children's school

men's suits

Add an apostrophe alone to the words *Jesus* and *Moses*.

Jesus' teachings

Moses' prophecy

Add an apostrophe alone to names whose ending is pronounced *eez*.

Euripides' writings

M. N. Furtees' company

Zerkes' theorem

When something possessed belongs to two or more people or things, make only the last unit possessive. But when a difference is implied, make each unit possessive.

Jeanne and Harry's trip (*same trip*)

the Burnses' and Williamses' trips (*different trips*)

COMPOUNDS

Closed Compounds

Most compounds—a combination of two or more words—are written closed (solid) to form a single word. The following guidelines apply in the treatment of compounds.

Close most words that have been combined to form a specialized term. (But some are written hyphenated [*life-style*] or open [*trade name*].)

footnote

checkbook

greenhouse

bookkeeper

headache

checklist

courtyard

lightweight

bookstore

paperwork

schoolteacher

Close most compounds with prefixes or suffixes except when a prefix precedes a proper noun (*pro-Constitution*), when it doubles the letter *i* (*anti-insurance*), or when it causes three *l*'s to be combined (*gull-like*).

preempt

antireligious

postgraduate

supranatural

interoffice

microeconomics

grandfather

threefold

industrywide

trustworthy

Close compounds with *one, body, thing,* and the like, unless a different meaning is intended.

Someone should volunteer to go.

Anyone is eligible to enter.

Any one of the committee members is qualified.

The paper must be somewhere in the house.

Everything is in order.

Close most compounds with *back, down, out, over, up, off, away, about,* and *by.* (But many are hyphenated [*call-up, rip-off*].)

backup

breakdown

fallout

leftover

setup

payoff

layaway

turnabout

runaround

standby

Close many of the compound verbs. Others such as *dry-clean* are hyphenated, however.

proofread

whitewash

downgrade

blackball

backstop

highlight

mastermind

pinpoint

shortchange

sidetrack

Hyphenated Compounds

Many compounds are written with a hyphen. The following guidelines apply.

Hyphenate certain compounds that are combined to form a specialized term. (But many are written closed [*lifeline*] or open [*life raft*].)

cross-reference

half-truth

close-up

life-style

eye-opener

light-year

Hyphenate prefixes when they precede a proper noun or when they cause the vowel *i* or *a* to be doubled. Hyphenate suffixes that create three *l*'s in succession. Most prefixes and suffixes are written closed (*nonessential, oversupply, uppermost, nationwide*), but a few are hyphenated for clarity (*re-form,* meaning "to form again") or to distinguish a prefix from a base word (*self-confident, selfhood*). Some such as *great-grandmother* and *sister-in-law* are always hyphenated.

non-American

pre-World War II

self-education

anti-intellectual

semi-independent

ultra-amplifier

re-lease ("lease again")

re-create ("create again")

great-uncle

mother-in-law

Hyphenate certain compounds with *down, out, over, up, off, between, through,* or *together*. (But many of these compounds are written closed [*setup, takeoff*].)

put-down

fade-out

once-over

start-up

spin-off

go-between

follow-through

get-together

Hyphenate certain compound nouns, coined terms, and compounds used as a noun that don't have a noun as one of the elements. (But a few of these terms are written closed [*brainstorming, whodunit*] and several open [*rule of thumb*].)

know-how

go-getter

good-for-nothing

nitty-gritty

right-of-way

jack-of-all-trades

Hyphenate nouns of equal weight, the titles *vice-chancellor* and *vice-consul,* and words with *-elect* or *ex-*. (But do not hyphenate other words with *vice-* such as *vice president*.)

clerk-typist

secretary-treasurer

vice-consul

vice president-elect

ex-senator

Hyphenate some compounds containing a single initial letter. Others such as *T square* are written open.

H-bomb

T-shirt

U-shaped

x-axis

c-curve

Hyphenate some compound verbs. Others such as *proofread* are written closed.

double-space
field-test
spot-check
air-condition
soft-pedal

Hyphenate most compound adjectives before a noun. Include a hyphen in numbers *twenty-one* to *ninety-nine*. Well-known compounds such as *social security* or *public relations* need not be hyphenated.

well-known entertainer
Spanish-American treaty
four-, five-, and six-year programs
company-owned plant
48-inch opening
twentieth-century customs
thirty-one-day billing cycle

Open Compounds

Some compounds are written open, as two or more words. The following guidelines apply.

Write certain compounds combined to form a specialized term open. (But many are written closed [*crossroad*] or hyphenated [*trade-off*].)

time sheet
book review
sick pay
work load
master plan
eye shadow

Write various compound nouns and coined terms open. (But most are hyphenated [*higher-ups, well-to-do*].)

wear and tear
power of attorney
problem solving
decision making

Write some compounds with single letters open. (But most are hyphenated [*A-frame*].)

X ray

T square

V neck

Write most titles open. (But those with *ex-* [*ex-governor*] or *elect-* [*mayor-elect*] are hyphenated as are two titles with *vice-* [*vice-chancellor* and *vice-consul*]. Also, two nouns designating one person are hyphenated [*actor-director*].)

chief of staff

attorney general

rear admiral

staff sergeant

general manager

vice president

vice admiral

When a compound verb is used as a noun or a gerund, write it open.

to field-test/the field test

to rubber-stamp/the rubber stamp

to air-condition/air conditioning is . . .

to speed-read/speed reading is . . .

Write most compound adjectives that follow a noun or are used as a noun open (most that precede a noun are hyphenated).

well-known man/The man is well known.

twentieth-century politics/Politics in the twentieth century is confusing.

three-by-five-inch cards/The cards are three by five inches.

two-week seminar/The seminar lasts two weeks.

up-to-date facts/The facts are up to date.

Leave open compounds with an adverb ending in *ly* and compounds with two adverbs.

hastily written report

very well liked commentator

carefully planned campaign

technically oriented instructions

Write temporary compounds with the word *master* open, but close permanent terms such as *masterpiece.*

master artist

master builder

master teacher

Write *quasi*-noun compounds open (but hyphenate adjectives, such as quasi-legal company).

quasi corporation

quasi agreement

quasi author

Write compounds expressing a relationship open.

mother country

father figure

foster child

parent company

fellow employee

Leave open color compounds both before and after a noun when one color modifies the other.

emerald green

yellowish orange

bluish green

grayish white

Leave open adjective compounds consisting of proper nouns unless the two elements are of equal weight (*Russian-American cooperation*).

Civil War

Latin American

Central African

East Asian

Old English

Common Compounds

The following list includes many compounds commonly used in written material. The abbreviations in parentheses following each compound designate the different parts of speech as which the compound may be used: *adj* (adjective), *adv* (adverb), *n* (noun), *pron* (pronoun), and *v* (verb).

aforementioned (*adj*)

after-hours(*adj*)

afterthought (*n*)

air conditioner (*n*)

all-important (*adj*)

all right (*adj, adv*)

also-ran (*n*)

anti-intellectual(*adj, n*)

antiwar (*adj*)

anybody (*pron*)

anyone (*pron*)

attorney general (*n*)

audiovisual (*adj*)

audiovisuals (*n*)

backup (*n*)

ballpoint (*adj, n*)

bankbook (*n*)

beforehand (*adj, adv*)

billboard (*n, v*)

birthrate (*n*)

blue-collar (*adj*)

blue jeans, bluejeans (*n*)

blueprint (*n*)

blue ribbon (*n*)

blue-ribbon (*adj*)

boardinghouse (*n*)

bondholder (*n*)

bookcase (*n*)

bookkeeping (*n*)

bookstore (*n*)

bottom-line (*adj*)

box office (*n*)

box-office (*adj*)

brainstorm (*n, v*)

breadwinner (*n*)

break-in (*n*)

breakthrough (*n*)

breakup (*n*)

briefcase (*n*)

broadcast (*n*)

buildup (*n*)

built-in (*adj, n*)

burnout (*n*)

businessperson (*n*)

bylaw (*n*)

bypass (*n, v*)

by-product (*n*)

cardboard (*adj, n*)

car pool (*n*)

carpool (*v*)

carryall (*n*)

carryover (*n*)

caseload (*n*)

casework (*n*)

catchall (*adj, n*)

catchword (*n*)

catlike (*adj*)

checkbook (*n*)

check-in (*adj*)

checklist (*n*)

check mark (*n,v*)

checkout (*adj, n*)

checkup (*n*)

city-state (*n*)

classmate (*n*)

classroom (*n*)

clean-cut (*adj*)

cleanup (*n*)

clear-cut (*adj*)

clearinghouse (*n*)

clipboard (*n*)

closeout (*n*)

coauthor (*n*)

coed (*n*)

cold-blooded (*adj*)

cold shoulder (*n*)

cold-shoulder (*v*)

comeback (*n*)

common sense (*n*)

commonsense (*adj*)

consciousness-raising (*n*)

co-op (*n*)

co-opt (*v*)

copyedit (*v*)

copywriter (*n*)

cost-effective (*adj*)

countdown (*n*)

court-martial (*n*)

courtroom (*n*)

crackdown (*n*)

crack-up (*n*)

crossover (*n*)

cross-reference (*n, v*)

crossroad (*n*)

cross section (*n*)

cross-section (*adj, v*)

day-care (*adj*)

daytime (*adj, n*)

deadline (*n*)

deathbed (*n*)

death rate (*n*)

devil-may-care (*adj*)

diehard (*n*)

die-hard (*adj*)

double-check (*v*)

double-cross (*v*)

double entry (*n*)

double-space (*v*)

downplay (*v*)

downtime (*n*)

downtown (*n*)

dry-clean (*v*)

dry cleaner (*n*)

everywhere (*adv*)

ex officio (*adj, adv*)

ex-president (*n*)

extracurricular (*adj, n*)

fireproof (*adj, v*)

first aid (*n*)

foolproof (*adj*)

foothold (*n*)

free lance (*n*)

free-lance (*adj, v*)

free trade (*n*)

free will (*n*)

freewill (*adj*)

ghostwriter (*n*)

good-bye, good-by (*n*)

goodwill (*n*)

grandmother (*n*)

groundwork (*n*)

half-hour (*n*)

halftime (*n*)

halfway (*adj, adv*)

handmade (*adj*)

headline (*n*)

holdover (*n*)

holdup (*n*)

hometown (*n*)

horsepower (*n*)

interrelate (*v*)

jet lag (*n*)

keypunch (*n, v*)

keystroke (*n, v*)

laborsaving (*adj*)

landholder (*n*)

landowner (*n*)

lawmaker (*n*)

layoff (*n*)

layout (*n*)

letterhead (*n*)

lifeline (*n*)

life-style (*n*)

lightweight (*adj, n*)

lineup (*n*)

loose-leaf (*adj*)

lowdown (*n*)

low-down (*adj*)

markdown (*n*)

marketplace (*n*)

moreover (*adv*)

nation-state (*n*)

nationwide (*adj*)

nearby (*adj, adv*)

nevertheless (*adv*)

newfound (*adj*)

newscast (*n*)

newsstand (*n*)

nightlife (*n*)

nonessential (*adj*)

nonetheless (*adv*)

nonprofit (*adj*)

noontime (*n*)

notebook (*n*)

offhand (*adj, adv*)

officeholder (*n*)

offset (*adj, adv, n, v*)

once-over (*n*)

one-half (*n*)

on-line (*adj, adv*)

overall (*adj, adv, n*)

paperwork (*n*)

passerby (*n*)

percent (*adj, adv, n*)

postwar (*adj*)

preeminent (*adj*)

president-elect (*n*)

prodemocratic (*adj*)

proofread (*v*)

pseudointellectual (*n*)

push button, pushbutton (*n*)

pushbutton, push-button (*adj*)

put-down (*n*)

readout (*n*)

rewrite (*n, v*)

rundown (*n*)

run-down (*adj*)

salesperson (*n*)

say-so (*n*)

schoolteacher (*n*)

self-concern (*n*)

semiconscious (*adj*)

send-off (*n*)

setback (*n*)

setup (*n*)

shortcut (*n*)

showdown (*n*)

standby (*n*)

stand-in (*n*)

statewide (*adj, adv*)

stopgap (*n*)

subdivision (*n*)

takeoff (*n*)

takeover (*n*)

textbook (*n*)

tie-in (*n*)

tie-up (*n*)

timesaving (*adj*)

timetable (*n*)

trade-in (*n*)

trade-off (*n*)

transcontinental (*adj*)

turnover (*adj, n*)

twofold (*adj, adv*)

underrate (*v*)

underway (*adj*)

viewpoint (*n*)

waterpower (*n*)

workday (*n*)

work force (*n*)

work load (*n*)

PREFIXES

Most prefixes, such as *pre-, pro-, non-,* and *anti-,* are written closed (*prearranged, proauthority, nongovernmental, antirevolutionary*) unless they precede a proper noun (*pre–Civil War*) or create a double letter that would be hard to read without a hyphen (*anti-institution*).

The following list contains many prefixes that can be added to original word forms.

after-/aftertaste

ambi-/ambidextrous

ante-/antebellum

anti-/antireligion

aqua-/aquaplane

audio-/audiovisual

auto-/autobiography

bi-/bicycle

bio-/biophysical

by-/byroad

cata-/cataclinal

centi-/centimeter

co-/coexist

contra-/contraband

counter-/countermeasure

de-/decompose

deci-/deciliter

deka-/dekagram

dis-/disapprove

duo-/duotone

epi-/epicenter

equi-/equidistant

ex-/ex-husband

extra-/extrajudicial

for-/forspent

fore-/foresight

hecto-/hectometer

hemi-/hemisphere

hemo-/hemoglobin

hyper-/hyperactive

in-/indiscreet

infra-/infrastructure

inter-/international

intra-/intrastate

intro-/introjection

ir-/irreversible

kilo-/kiloton

lacto-/lactoprotein

macro-/macroprogram

mal-/maladjusted

meta-/metaethical

micro-/microscope

mid-/midcentury

milli-/milligram

mini-/minibus

mis-/mislead

mono-/monosyllable

multi-/multifaceted

neo-/neoclassic

non-/nonlegal

off-/offbeat

out-/outboard

over-/overhead

pan-/panchromatic

para-/parapsychology

peri-/periscope

photo-/photosensitive

post-/postwar

pre-/preexamine

pro-/proecology

pseudo-/pseudopsychologist

re-/rejoin

semi-/semicircle

sub-/subterrain

super-/supersede

supra-/supranatural

trans-/transnational

twi-/twilight

ultra-/ultraconservative

un-/unnoticed

under-/underground

up-/upstairs

SUFFIXES

Although numerous rules apply to the addition of suffixes and other word endings, the number of exceptions to the rules are equally numerous, and thus the rules are of limited value. Most of the confusion arises in determining whether to double a final consonant before adding a suffix or other word ending: *ship/shipped, bus/buses, begin/beginning, offer/offering, joy/joyfully, mass/massive, sale, salable or saleable,* and so on.

The following list illustrates the accepted form for many common suffixes and other word endings.

-able/regrettable

-age/breakage

-al/arrival

-ance/continuance

-ancy/redundancy

-ant/dependant

-ary/contrary

-ation/cancellation

-by/passerby

-cade/motorcade

-cation/notification
-cede/concede
-ceed/exceed
-chrome/monochrome
-cide/insecticide
-dom/kingdom
-ed/dropped
-ee/payee
-en/earthen
-ence/dependence
-ency/insistency
-ent/prevalent
-er/speaker
-ery/stationery
-es/buses
-est/closest
-ful/fearful
-fy/amplify
-gamy/polygamy
-gram/telegram
-graph/monograph
-hood/statehood
-ial/managerial
-ian/beautician
-ible/digestible
-ier/easier
-ing/beginning
-ise/advertise
-ish/outlandish
-ism/ageism
-ite/Brooklynite

-ition/proposition
-ity/alkalinity
-ive/passive
-ize/apologize
-kin/catkin
-less/homeless
-let/piglet
-like/childlike
-lithic/neolithic
-logical/biological
-ly/ordinarily
-mania/lettermania
-ment/accompaniment
-meter/pedometer
-most/utmost
-ness/darkness
-oid/humanoid
-or/surveyor
-ous/courageous
-proof/foolproof
-sect/bisect
-ship/governorship
-some/handsome
-sphere/hemisphere
-ster/gangster
-tude/altitude
-ule/capsule
-ward/forward
-wide/nationwide
-work/piecework
-worthy/trustworthy

COMMONLY MISSPELLED WORDS

This list contains five hundred words that are particularly troublesome to many people and are frequently misspelled.

absence	affect
accede	affidavit
accept	aggravate
acceptance	agreeable
accessible	allotment
accessory	allotted
accidentally	allowable
accommodate	allowance
accompanying	all right
accordance	almost
accrued	already
accumulate	altogether
accuracy	amendment
achievement	among
acknowledgment	analysis
acquaintance	analyze
acquiesce	announce
acquire	announcement
across	annoyance
adapt	annual
address	anticipate
adequate	anxious
adjustment	apologize
admirable	apparel
advantageous	apparent
advertisement	appearance
advertising	appliance
advice	applicable
advisable	applicant
advise	appointment
advisory	

appraisal

appreciable

appropriate

approximate

archaeology

architect

argument

arrangement

article

ascertain

assessment

assignment

assistance

associate

assured

attendance

attention

attorneys

authorize

available

baccalaureate

bankruptcy

bargain

basis

beginning

believe

beneficial

beneficiary

benefited

bookkeeper

brilliant

brochure

budget

bulletin

bureau

business

businessperson

busy

calendar

campaign

canceled (*cancelled*)

cancellation

cannot

capital

capitol (*building*)

career

casualty

catalog(*ue*)

choice

choose (*present tense*)

chose (*past tense*)

circumstances

client

clientele

collateral

column

coming

commission

commitment

committee

comparable

comparison

compelled

competent

competitor

complement (*that which completes*)

compliment (*an expression of respect*)

compromise

concede

conceivable

concern

concession

concurred

conference

confident

confidential

congratulate

conscience

conscientious

conscious

consensus

consequence

consignment

consistent

continuous

controlling

controversy

convenience

convenient

cordially

corporation

correspondence (*communication*)

correspondent (*one who communicates*)

council

counsel

courteous

courtesy

coverage

creditor

criticism

criticize

current

customer

debtor

deceive

decide

decision

deductible

defendant

defense

deferred

deficit

definite

definitely

delegate

dependent

depositor

describe

description

desirable

deteriorate

develop

development

device (*noun*)

devise (*verb*)

difference

director

disappear

disappoint

discrepancy

dissatisfied

eagerly

economical

edition

effect

efficiency

efficient

eligible

eliminate

embarrass

emergency

emphasis

emphasize

employee

enclose
endeavor
endorsement
enterprise
enthusiasm
envelope
environment
equipment
equipped
especially
essential
etiquette
exaggerate
exceed
excellence
excellent
except
excessive
exercise
existence
expedite
expenditure
expense
experience
explanation
extensions
extraordinary
extremely
facilities
familiarize
fascinate
favorable
favorite
February
finally
financial

forcible
foreign
forfeit
formerly
forty
forward
fourth
freight
friend
fulfillment
furthermore
gauge
genuine
government
governor
grateful
grievance
guarantee
handled
harass
hardware
hazardous
height
hesitant
hoping
identical
illegible
immediately
imperative
impossible
inasmuch as
incidentally
inconvenience
incurred
indebtedness

independent

indispensable

individual

inducement

influential

initial

inquiry

installment

intelligence

intention

intercede

interfere

interrupted

inventory

investor

irrelevant

itemized

itinerary

it's (*it is*)

its (*adjective*)

jeopardize

judgment

justifiable

knowledge

laboratory

legible

legitimate

leisure

length

letterhead

liaison

library

license

likable

livelihood

loose (*not secure*)

lose (*suffer loss*)

magazine

maintenance

management

manufacturer

manuscript

maximum

medical

memorandum

menus

merchandise

mileage

minimum

miscellaneous

mischievous

modernize

mortgage

necessary

negligible

negotiate

neighborhood

nevertheless

ninety

ninth

noticeable

oblige

occasion

occupant

occurred

occurrence

occurring

offense

offering

official

omission

omitted

opportunity

ordinary

organization

organize

original

overdue

paid

pamphlet

parallel

partial

participant

particularly

patronage

percent

permanent

permissible

permitted

personal (*private*)

personnel (*employees*)

persuade

phase

physician

planning

pleasant

pleasure

possession

practical

practically

practice

precede

precision

preferable

preference

preferred

prejudice

preliminary

premium

previous

price list

principal (*person [noun]; chief [adjective]*)

principle (*rule or doctrine*)

privilege

probably

proceed

professor

prominent

prosecute

psychology

purchase

pursue

quantity

questionnaire

quiet

quite

realize

really

reasonable

receipt

receive

recipe

recognize

recognized

recommend

recurrence

reference

referred

referring

regrettable

reimburse

remember

remittance

renewal

repetition

representative

requirement

respectfully

response

responsibility

responsible

restaurant

ridiculous

route

salable, saleable

salary

satisfactorily

schedule

secretary

securities

seized

separate

serviceable

shipment

shipping

siege

significant

similar

simultaneous

sincerity

someone

somewhat

specialize

stationary (*immobile*)

stationery (*paper*)

statistics

strictly

submitted

subscriber

substantial

succeed

successful

sufficient

superintendent

supersede

supervisor

surprise

survey

tariff

temporary

their

there

thorough

throughout

too

tragedy

transferred

typing

ultimately

unanimous

undoubtedly

unfortunately

unnecessary

until

urgent

usable

usually

vacuum

valuable

various

vehicle

vendor

vengeance

vicinity

visible

volume

voluntary

volunteer

warehouse

weather

whether

wholesale

withhold

worthwhile

writing

yield

Chapter 5

WORD DIVISION

Whether your material is justified (with an even right margin) or prepared ragged right (with an uneven right margin), you will usually find it necessary to divide some words at the end of a line.

INCORRECT DIVISION: A READING HANDICAP

When words are divided incorrectly, it impairs both reading speed and reading comprehension. Review the following examples of incorrect division; notice how you must pause to determine what each word really is.

```
av-
    ailable
pu-
    blished
bene-
    ath
wor-
    ld
cha-
    racter
co-
    nsideration
```

For reading ease and understanding, words should be divided between syllables, although there are exceptions to this general guideline, as illustrated below.

Both spelling dictionaries and regular dictionaries provide the syllable divisions of words. Some dictionaries give both pronunciation and word division, which is useful in distinguishing between words such as *rec-re-ate* ("to give new life or freshness") and *re-cre-ate* ("to create again") or *pre-sent* ("to give or introduce") and *pres-ent* ("a gift").

SYLLABLES AND LETTERS

Words That Should Not Be Divided

Do not divide words that are pronounced as a single syllable.

helped (*not* help-ed)

gained (*not* gain-ed)

planned (*not* plan-ned)

through (*not* th-rough)

straight (*not* st-raight)

hour (*not* ho-ur)

Do not divide words of fewer than five letters.

into (*not* in-to)

only (*not* on-ly)

oven (*not* ov-en)

user (*not* us-er)

Do not separate a single letter from the beginning or end of a word.

enough (*not* e-nough)

around (*not* a-round)

ideal (*not* i-deal)

tro-phy (*not* troph-y)

lucky (*not* luck-y)

Do not divide vowels that are pronounced together.

per-c*ei*ved

ap-p*oi*nted

pa-t*ie*nce

por-t*io*n

an-n*ou*nce

Where to Divide Words

When a word has a single-letter syllable within it, make the division after that letter unless pronunciation requires a different division.

simi-lar (*not* sim-ilar)

busi-ness (*not* bus-iness)

acti-vate (*not* act-ivate)

nega-tive (*not* neg-ative)

congratu-late (*not* congrat-ulate)

But do not divide the suffixes *-able* or *-ible*.

reduc-ible (*not* reduci-ble)

consider-able (*not* considera-ble)

pos-sible (*not* possi-ble)

read-able (*not* reada-ble)

When two vowels within a word are pronounced separately, divide the word between them.

compli-ance

influ-ential

courte-ous

experi-ence

situ-ation

recre-ation

continu-ous

When two consonants occur between two vowels, divide between the consonants unless pronunciation requires a different division.

im-por-tant

struc-ture

ad-van-tage

cir-cum-fer-ence

in-ter-ro-gate

moun-tain

Divide a word only if at least two letters and the hyphen will be on the top line and three characters, including any punctuation mark, will be on the lower line.

Top:		**Bottom:**	
re-			new
	go-		ing
	ad-		mit
	dit-		to:

PREFIXES AND SUFFIXES

Whenever possible, make the division after a prefix or before a suffix rather than within the root word. Do not divide a prefix or suffix itself.

    pre-eminent (*not* preemi-nent)

    trust-worthy (*not* trustwor-thy)

    co-operate (*not* cooper-ate)

    manage-ment (*not* man-agement)

    re-arrange (*not* rear-range)

    success-ful (*not* suc-cessful)

Usually, divide gerunds and present participles before -*ing*. But if the final consonant is doubled, divide between the consonants.

    giv-ing

    learn-ing

    spin-ning

    chang-ing

    run-ning

    control-ling

    occur-ring

If the original word already has a double consonant, divide it after the double letters.

    mill-ing

    spell-ing

    fill-ing

    thrill-ing

    spill-ing

When a word has an *le* syllable pronounced as "ul," divide the word before the syllable.

    han-dling

    siz-zling

    bris-tling

COMPOUNDS

Preferably, divide a hyphenated compound only at the hyphen and divide a solid compound between the key parts.

    master-piece (*not* mas-terpiece)

    grand-mother (*not* grandmo-ther)

    clearing-house (*not* clear-inghouse)

    school-teacher (*not* schooltea-cher)

eye-witness (*not* eyewit-ness)

president-elect (*not* presi-dent-elect)

ex-senator (*not* ex-sena-tor)

all-important (*not* all-im-portant)

ABBREVIATIONS

Do not divide abbreviations, initialisms, acronyms, or contractions unless there already is a hyphen in a two-part abbreviation.

admin. (*not* ad-min.)

eta (*not* e-ta)

NATO (*not* NA-TO)

doesn't (*not* does-n't)

o'clock (*not* o'-clock)

AFL-CIO (*not* AFL-CI-O)

NAMES

Try to avoid dividing names, but if necessary, divide only before the last name.

Preferred: John A. / Jones

                 R. M. / Harrison

Avoid: John / A. Jones

                 R. / M. Har-rison

If a title is used, divide between the title and the name.

Mayor / Helen Cole (*not* Mayor Helen / Cole)

Vice President / M. M. Jacobs (*not* Vice President M. M. / Jacobs)

NUMBERS

Try to avoid dividing numbers, but if necessary, divide only at a comma and at least two digits.

6,457,-000 (*not* 6,-457,000)

350,-000 (*not* 35-0,000)

2,750,-632.43 (*not* 2,750,632.-43)

Avoid dividing short units, such as page and number or month and day.

page 16 (*not* page / 16)

section 5 (*not* section / 5)

March 1992 (*not* March / 1992)

35 mm (*not* 35 / mm)

If necessary, divide dates between day and year.

January 6, / 1992 (*not* January / 6, 1992)

Divide places between city and state or state and zip code or between words within the city or state.

Charleston, / South Carolina 29406

Des Moines, Iowa / 50322

San / Antonio, Texas 78213

Divide addresses between the street name and the words *street, avenue, boulevard,* and so on, or between words within the street name.

1625 East / Avenue (*not* 1625 / East Avenue)

124 Grand / Mesa Boulevard (*not* 124 / Grand Mesa Boulevard)

Divide numbered or lettered items before a number or letter.

(1) faith, / (2) hope, and (3) charity [*not* (1) faith, (2) / hope, and (3) charity]

Chapter 6

ABBREVIATIONS

Abbreviations abound in technical and specialized writing, and their use is increasing. Simultaneously, in formal and general writing the use of abbreviations is decreasing. Most authorities, in fact, recommend that all words and terms be spelled out in formal material, except for those that are almost always abbreviated, such as *Mr., Dr., a.m., B.C.,* or *Ph.D.*

ABBREVIATION STYLE

Words, terms, and phrases are abbreviated in different ways. Some abbreviations omit the last part of the word (*admin./administration*). Others omit letters within the word (*acct./accountant*). In American-style punctuation, a period is always used in the first case and often in the second case. (British style omits the period after an abbreviation that is formed by omitting letters within the word.)

Sometimes a phrase or term is abbreviated by combining the first letter of all its words or all its important words, which is known as *initialism* (*asap/as soon as possible*). A combination of letters that can be pronounced as a word in itself (*ARM/adjustable rate mortgage*) is referred to as an acronym. All of these short forms of words, terms, and phrases are informally called abbreviations.

Abbreviation Trends

Two trends are evident in abbreviation style: less capitalization and less punctuation, for example, *cm* (centimeter), *fob* (free on board), *rms* (root mean square). Through use, some abbreviations have been accepted as words in themselves and are never punctuated (*memo, ad*). Contractions should never have a period (*nat'l, don't*). Many technical terms, such as metric measures, also omit the period (*km, ml*). Organizational abbreviations, too, are written without periods (*YMCA, IBM*).

But most general abbreviations are punctuated (*col., dept.*), and any abbreviation that could be confused with a word that is spelled the same should be punctuated to distinguish it from that word (abbreviation *in.*/word *in;* abbreviation *cot.*/word *cot*).

Academic degrees, time designations, titles, initials in a name, and the like are always punctuated (*Sc.D., p.m.,* A.D., *Mrs.*).

Examples of Abbreviation Style

The following lists provide examples of the variety of abbreviations and appropriate capitalization and punctuation style in these categories: general abbreviations (*hosp./hospital*), technical abbreviations (*nF/nanofarad*), organizations (*ACUG/Association of Computing User Groups*), academic degrees (*B.S.J./bachelor of science in journalism*), and postal abbreviations (*MD, Md./Maryland*).

GENERAL ABBREVIATIONS

Confine the use of most abbreviated words, such as *st.* for *street*, to note taking and rough drafts. In letters, reports, and other communications or publications, most terms should be spelled out. The only exceptions are titles, degrees, and references to time, as described above. Notes and bibliographies as well as tabular and graphics material, however, commonly use abbreviations. Business forms and records use abbreviations as codes and references for retrieval purposes or simply to conserve space.

Abbreviations of nouns are usually capitalized in the case of a proper noun (*St. Peter/Saint Peter*) and lowercased in the case of a common noun (*sec'y/secretary*). Spell out titles, however, when they are used with a last name only (*General Miller*), and spell out *reverend* if preceded by *the* (*the Reverend James T. McHenry*). A period follows the short form of names (*Jas.*), titles (*Dr.*), degrees (*M.D.*), and the like but is omitted when all capital letters are used for organizational names (*CORE/Congress of Racial Equality*), the initials of famous persons (*FDR/Franklin Delano Roosevelt*), or acronyms (*RAM/random-access memory*).

Some words can be abbreviated in more than one way; for example, *verb* can appear as *v.* or *vb.* Since organizations and individuals may differ in their preferred style of capitalization, punctuation, and even spelling, follow the requirements of your employer in business and professional situations.

The following list contains examples of general abbreviation style. For further examples consult a book of abbreviations such as *The New American Dictionary of Abbreviations* (New American Library, 1990) or a large library reference work such as *Acronyms, Initialisms & Abbreviations Dictionary* (Gale Research Company, current year).

aa	always afloat; author's alteration(s)
a&a	additions and amendments
aap	advise if able to proceed; affirmative action program

a&b	assault and battery
abbr.	abbreviate(d); abbreviation
a/c	account; account current; air conditioning
accred.	accredited
acct.	account(ant)(ing)
a/c pay.	accounts payable
a/c rec.	accounts receivable
acron.	acronym
act. wt.	actual weight
acv	actual cash value
a&d	accounting and disbursing; ascending and descending
ad fin.	to the end (Latin: *ad finem*)
ad inf.	to infinity (Latin: *ad infinitum*)
adj.	adjacent; adjective; adjust; adjutant
ad loc.	to or at this place (Latin: *ad locum*)
admin.	administration; administrative; administrator
ad naus.	dull to the point of nausea (Latin: *ad nauseam*)
adsc	average daily service charge
Adt	Atlantic daylight time
adv. pmt.	advance payment
aec	additional extended coverage; at earliest convenience
afc	average fixed cost
afsd.	aforesaid
ag.	agricultural; agriculture
agb	any good brand
agi	adjusted gross income; annual general inspection
agric.	agricultural; agriculture
agt.	agent
agy.	agency
a&i	abstracting and indexing; accident and indemnity
aia	advise if available

AIDS	acquired immune deficiency syndrome
aka	also known as
ald	a later date; acceptable limit for dispersion
alg.	algebra; algebraic
alloc.	allocate; allocation
alpha.	alphabetical
a.m.	before noon (Latin: *ante meridiem*)
Am.	America(n)
a&m	agricultural and mechanical; ancient and modern; architectural and mechanical
amb.	ambassador; amber; ambient; ambulance
am. cur.	friend of the court (Latin: *amicus curiae*)
Amer.	America(n)
amr	automatic message routing
an.	above named; annual
anat.	anatomy
annot.	annotate(d); annotation
anon.	nameless (Greek: *anonymous*)
a/o	account of
aod	as of date
aper.	aperture
apos.	apostrophe
appl.	applicable; application; applied
appr.	approval; approve(d)
appt.	appointment
apr	annual percentage rate
apt.	apartment
arith.	arithmetic
a/s	after sight; alongside
Asl	American sign language
ast	absolute space time
Ast	Atlantic standard time
At	Atlantic time
A/t	American terms
ata	actual time of arrival; air to air
ATM	automated teller machine

atten.	attention
atv	all-terrain vehicle
aux.	auxiliary
av	acid value; assessed valuation; audiovisual
av.	avenue; average
a/w	actual weight; all-water; all-weather
awol	absent without leave; absent without official leave
AWOL	absent without leave; absent without official leave
b.	born; brother
bal.	balance; balcony
b&b	bed and board; bed and breakfast
b/c	bales of cotton; bills for collection; birth control; broadcast
B.C.	before Christ
bf	backfeed; boldface
b/f	black female; brought forward
bib.	biblical; bibliography
bio.	biographical; biography; biological; biology
biog.	biographer; biographical; biography
bkpt.	bankrupt
blvd.	boulevard
bo	back order; blackout; body odor; branch office
b/o	back order; brought over; budget outlay
bop	balance of payments; best operating procedure
b/r	bills receivable
Bros.	Brothers
bs	backspace
b/st	bill of sight
bu.	bureau
bull.	bulletin
bus.	business
b.w.	please turn over (German: *bitte wenden*)
b/w	black and white; bread and water
c	about; calorie; candle; carat; cent; century; chapter; child

C	Centigrade
cad.	cadet; cash against documents; computer-aided design; contract-award date
CAD	computer-aided design
cad/cam	computer-aided design/computer-aided manufacturing
CAD/CAM	computer-aided design/computer-aided manufacturing
cap.	capacity; capital; capital letter; capitol; capsule; client assessment package; computer-aided production
caps.	capital letters
CB	citizen's band (radio)
cbx	computerized branch exchange; computerized business exchange
CBX	computerized branch exchange; computerized business exchange
cc	carbon copy; chief complaint; color code; command and control
c/d	carried down; cash against documents; certificate of deposit
CD	certificate of deposit
cdst	central daylight saving time
cdt	central daylight time
ceo	chief executive officer
cert.	certificate; certify
cf.	compare (Latin: *confer*)
c/f	carried forward
cfi	cost, freight, and insurance
c&lc	capital and lowercase letters
c/o	care of; carried over; cash order; complaint/complaints of
c.o.d.	cash on delivery
C.O.D.	cash on delivery
cola	cost-of-living adjustment; cost-of-living allowance
COLA	cost-of-living adjustment; cost-of-living allowance
coop.	cooperation

co-op	cooperative
copr.	copyright
corres.	correspond(ence)(ent)(ing)
CPI	consumer price index
cr.	credit; creek; crown
cr. bal.	credit balance
crt	cathode ray tube
CRT	cathode ray tube
c&sc	caps and small caps
c/t	certificate of title
cwo	cash with order
d	daughter; day; degree; died
d/a	deposit account
db.	debit
dba	doing business as/at
d&c	dilation and curettage
dd	days after date; deferred delivery; delayed delivery; double draft; dry dock; due date
deb.	debenture; debit
def.	defeat(ed); defect(ion)(or); defend(ant); defense; defer(red); definite; definition; deflect(ing)(ion); defrost(er)(ing); defunct
deg.	degenerate; degree
del.	delegate; delegation; delete; deletion; deliberate; deliberation; delineate(d); delineation; deliver(y)
dem.	demand; democracy; democrat(ic); demolish; demolition; demonstrate; demonstration; demote; demotion
democ.	democracy
demod.	demodulator
diam.	diameter
dig.	digest(ion)(ive)
disc.	discount
diss.	dissent(er); dissertation
dkt.	docket
dls.	dollars

dn	debit note
d/n	debit note
dos	date of sale
dp	data processing; deal pending; departure point; dew point; displaced person; distribution point
dr.	debit; doctor; dram; drill; drive
dst	daylight saving time
dtp	desktop publishing
DTP	desktop publishing
d/v	declared value
D.V.	God willing (Latin: *Deo volente*)
dwi	driving while intoxicated
ea.	each
eaon	except as otherwise noted
econ.	economic(s); economist; economy
edit.	editing; edition; editor; editorial
ed. note	editorial note; editor's note
eds.	editors
edt	eastern daylight time
ee	errors excepted; eye and ear
EE	Early English
eeo	equal employment opportunity
eer	energy efficiency ratio
efa	essential fatty acids
e.g.	for example (Latin: *exempli gratia*)
enc.	enclose(d); enclosure; encumbrance
encl.	enclose(d); enclosure
ency.	encyclopedia
eo	by authority of his or her office (Latin: *ex officio*)
eod	every other day
eoe	equal opportunity employer
e&oe	errors and omissions excepted
eoph	except as otherwise herein provided
equip.	equipment
Esl	English as a second language

est	eastern standard time; electroshock therapy
est.	estate; estimate(d); estimation
et	eastern time; educational therapy; elapsed time; electric/electronic typewriter; extraterrestrial
eta	estimated time of arrival
et al.	and elsewhere (Latin: *et alibi*); and others (Latin: *et alia*)
etc.	and so forth; and so on (Latin: *et cetera*)
et seq.	and following (Latin: *et sequens*)
f	family; farthing; father; female
f.	folio; following page
F	Fahrenheit
f/b	feedback; female black; front to back
fifo	first in, first out
filo	first in, last out
fka	formerly known as
fl.	flourished (Latin: *floruit*)
fol.	folio; follow(ing)
ft	free of tax; free trade; full term
fv.	back of the page (Latin: *folio verso*)
FY	fiscal year
fyi	for your information
FYI	for your information
Gk.	Greek
gnp	gross national product
GNP	gross national product
govt.	government
gov't	government
hab. corp.	may you have the body (Latin: *habeas corpus*)
hc	hard copy; hydrocarbon
hdqrs.	headquarters
hi fi	high fidelity
hosp.	hospital
i&a	indexing and abstracting
id.	the same (Latin: *idem*)
i.e.	that is (Latin: *id est*)

i/o	in and/or over; input/output; instead of
i&o	input and output
IOU	I owe you
IQ	import quota; intelligence quotient
i.q.e.d.	that which was to be proved (Latin: *id quod erat demonstrandum*)
ISBN	International Standard Book Number
ital.	italics
j.	journal
JFK	John Fitzgerald Kennedy
kia	killed in action
KIA	killed in action
k-o	knockout
KO	knockout
l.	line
lang.	language
lc	lowercase
lifo	last in, first out
lp	long play
LP	long play
m	male; married; masculine
M	noon (Latin: *meridies*)
mad.	mind-altering drug; mutual(ly) assured destruction
MAD	mutual(ly) assured destruction
math	mathematics
math.	mathematician
mbo	management by objectives
MBO	management by objectives
Mesd.	Ladies (French: *Mesdames*)
Messrs.	Gentlemen (French: *Messieurs*)
mfg.	manufacturing
mfr.	manufacture(d)(r)
mgr.	manager
Mgr.	Monseigneur (French: *Monsignor*); Monsignore (Italian: *Monsignor*)
mia	missing in action
MIA	missing in action
Mlle.	Miss (French: *Mademoiselle*)

Mlles.	Misses (French: *Mesdemoiselles*)
m.m.	with the necessary changes (Latin: *mutatis mutandis*)
Mme.	Missus (French: *Madame*)
Mmes.	Ladies (French: *Mesdames*)
MP	member of Parliament; military police; mounted police
ms.	manuscript
mss.	manuscripts
mst	mean solar time; mountain standard time
mt	mountain time
n	note; number
n.	note; number
natl.	national
nat'l	national
n.b.	note well (Latin: *nota bene*)
n/c	no charge; numerical control
nf	no funds
n/f	no funds
nol. pros.	do not want to prosecute (Latin: *nolle prosequi*)
non obs.	notwithstanding (Latin: *non obstante*)
non seq.	it does not follow (Latin: *non sequitur*)
nop	not otherwise provided for
nos	not otherwise specified
np	no place; no publisher; notary public; note payable
n.p.	no place; no publisher
ns	new series; not specified
NS	new style
N.S.	new style
ntp	no title page
ob.	died (Latin: *obiit*)
obit.	obituary
op. cit.	in the work cited (Latin: *opere citato*)
os	old series; operating system; out of stock
o.s.	old series
OS	old style

O.S.	old style
pbx	private branch exchange
PBX	private branch exchange
p&i	principal and interest
pp.	pages
ppd.	prepaid
pro tem.	for the time being (Latin: *pro tempore*)
P.S.	written after (Latin: *post scriptum*)
Pst	Pacific standard time
Pt	Pacific time
pto	please turn over
q.e.d.	that which was to be proved or demonstrated (Latin: *quod erat demonstrandum*)
q.v.	which see (Latin: *quod vide*)
r.	recto; reigned
rom.	roman (type style)
rop	run of paper; run of press
Rsvp	please reply (French: *réspondez s'il vous plaît*)
R.s.v.p.	please reply (French: *réspondez s'il vous plaît*)
sae	self-addressed envelope
SALT	Strategic Arms Limitation Talks
sase	self-addressed stamped envelope
sc	separate; small capitals; statistical control
sect.	section; sector
s&l	savings and loan
sm. caps	small capitals
smsa	standard metropolitan statistical area
SMSA	standard metropolitan statistical area
st.	saint; stanza; state; street
st.	let it stand (Latin: *stet*)
t	temperature
T	temperature
temp.	temper(ature)(ed)(ing); temporary
TLC	tender loving care
tm	trademark

u.	university
ufo	unidentified flying object
UFO	unidentified flying object
u&lc	upper and lowercase
univ.	universal; university
v.	verb; verse; verso; versus
vb.	verb(al)
viz.	namely (Latin: *videlicet*)
vol.	volume; volunteer
vs.	versus
wats	wide-area telephone service
WATS	Wide Area Telecommunications Service
wf	wrong font
w/o	without
wp	will proceed; word processing; working paper; working party
yr.	year
z	zero; zone

TECHNICAL ABBREVIATIONS

Technical abbreviations are widely used in most areas of science and technology and are being used increasingly in certain general business material such as records, forms, and reports. But terms such as *aperture (aper.)* and *energy consumption rate (ecr)* should always be spelled out in correspondence, formal documents, and nontechnical publications. Many scientific organizations, however, regularly use technical abbreviations in most of their written material.

Technical abbreviations such as metric measures (*mm/millimeter*), chemical elements (*cl/chlorine*), and other abbreviations and initialisms (*emt/electromotive force*) are frequently set without periods. But a period should follow any abbreviation that might be confused with an actual word that is spelled the same (*elf./extralow frequency*). Also, a period should follow any abbreviation that is formed by omitting letters from the word (*cal./calorie*). Although many technical abbreviations are written with small letters, some, such as computer commands and other computer terminology (*ADDR/address*), are written in all capitals. In chemical elements the first letter of the abbreviation is usually capitalized (*Ag/silver*).

The following list has a variety of technical abbreviations in a generally accepted style of capitalization and punctuation. Since style may vary from one discipline to another, however, follow the requirements of your profession.

a	ampere; arc; atto-
Å	angstrom
abm	automated batch mixing
ABM	automated batch mixing
ac	alternating current; automatic analog computer; axiocervical
ACC	accumulator
a/d	analog to digital
ADDR	address
ADR	adder
ADV	advance
agz	actual ground zero
ah	ampere-hour
a-h	ampere-hour
Ah	ampere-hour; hyperopic astigmatism
ALGOL	Algebraically Oriented Language; Algorithmic Language
alphanumeric	alphabetical and numerical
alt.	alternator; altimeter
amp.	ampere; amplification; amplifier; amplitude
amr	automatic message routing
AMR	automatic message routing
aoi	angle of incidence
arcos	arc cosine
are.	air reactor experiment
ARE	air reactor experiment
ASCII	American Standard Code for Information Interchange
ast	absolute space time
at.	ampere-ton; ampere-turn
At	ampere-ton; ampere-turn
at. no.	atomic number
at. vol.	atomic volume
at. wt.	atomic weight
av.	average; avoirdupois

avdp.	avoirdupois
ax.	axes; axial; axiom; axis
az.	azimuth
BAM	basic access method
bar.	barometer; barometric; base address register; buffer address register
BAR	buffer address register
BASIC	Beginner's All-Purpose Symbolic Instruction Code
bev	billion electron volts
BeV	billion electron volts
bfr.	buffer
bhp	boiler horsepower; brake horsepower
bi.	binary
BI	binary
bn	binary number
BN	binary number
bof	beginning of file
BOF	beginning of file
bot	beginning of tape
BOT	beginning of tape
bps	bits per second; bytes per second
bs	backspace; binary subtraction
BS	backspace
btu	basic transmission unit; British thermal unit
Btu	British thermal unit
BTU	British thermal unit
bu.	bushel
c	calorie (large); carbohydrates; centi-; coefficient; computer; cycle; speed of light
C	calculated weight; candle; Celsius; Centigrade
cad.	cartridge-activated device; computer-aided design
CAD	computer-aided design
cad/cam	computer-aided design/computer-aided manufacturing
CAD/CAM	computer-aided design/computer-aided manufacturing

cal	computer-aided learning; conversational algebraic language
cal.	calorie (small)
cam.	central-address memory; computer-addressed memory; computer-aided manufacturing
CAM	computer-aided manufacturing
CAN	cancel
Cd	coefficient of drag
cg	center of gravity; centigram
c-h	candle-hour
char.	character
CHAR	character
cl	centiliter
clu	central logic unit
cm^2	square centimeter
CMND	command
COBOL	Common Business-Oriented Language
coef.	coefficient
cos.	cosine
cot.	cotangent
cp/m	control program/microcomputers
cpr	cardiopulmonary resuscitation
CPU	central processing unit
crt	cathode-ray tube
CRT	cathode-ray tube
CTRL	control
cub.	control unit busy
cv	coefficient of variation
cwt	centum weight; counterweight; hundredweight
cx	central exchange; control transmitter
CX	central exchange
cyb.	cybernetics
d	day; deci-
da	deka-; density altitude; drift angle
dag	dekagram
dal	dekaliter

dam.	dekameter; direct-access method
DAM	direct-access method
dav	data above voice
db	decibel; diode block
dB	decibel
dbu	decibel unit
dBu	decibel unit
dc	direct current
dde	direct data entry
del.	delete
DEL	delete
dg	decigram
diam.	diameter
dl	data link; deciliter
d/l	data link
do.	diamine oxidase; dissolved oxygen
dos	disk operating system
DOS	disk operating system
dov	data over voice
dp	data processing; dew point; diametral pitch; diffusion pressure
dr.	dram
dwt	deadweight ton; pennyweight
dyn.	dyne
ecr	energy consumption rate
edp	electronic data processing
EDP	electronic data processing
eer	energy-efficiency ratio
efi	electronic fuel injection
ekg	electrocardiogram
EKG	electrocardiogram
emf	electromotive force
Emos	Earth's mean orbital speed
eo	end of operation
EO	end of operation
eob	end of block

EOB	end of block
eof	end of file
EOF	end of file
eoj	end of job
EOJ	end of job
eolb	end-of-line block
EOLB	end-of-line block
eom	end of message
EOM	end of message
eor	end of record; end of run
EOR	end of record; end of run
eot	end of tape; end of transmission
EOT	end of tape; end of transmission
esc	escape
ESC	escape
est	electroshock therapy
etb	end-of-transmission block
ETB	end-of-transmission block
etx	end of text
ETX	end of text
f	farad; fathom; feedback; feet
F	Fahrenheit; farad; fathom; feedback
f/b	feedback; front to back
fc	foot-candle
ff	form feed
FF	form feed
fL	foot-lambert
fl. dr.	fluid dram
fl. oz.	fluid ounce
fl. pt.	fluid pint
FORTRAN	Formula Translation
ft.	foot; feet
ft.^{2}	square feet; square foot
ft.-lb.	foot-pound
G	gauss; giga-
gal.	gallon

Gb	gilbert
gc	geographical coordinates; gigacycle; gyrocompass
gev	gigaelectronvolt
GeV	gigaelectronvolt
g gr.	great gross
GHz	gigahertz
gi	gill
gr.	grain; gross
Gv	gigavolt
GV	gigavolt
gw	gigawatt; ground wave
Gw	gigawatt
h	hectare; hecto-; height; hour
H	henry
ha	hectare; hour angle; hour aspect; humic acid
hepa	high-efficiency particulate air
hz	hertz
Hz	hertz
ic	input circuit; integrated circuit
i gal.	imperial gallon
imp. gal.	imperial gallon
in.	inch
i/o	input/output
i/p	input
i&r	information and retrieval
J	joule
k	about one thousand (computer-storage capacity); carat (karat); Kelvin; kilo-; knot
K	about one thousand (computer-storage capacity)
kb	keyboard; kilobit; kilobyte
kc	kilocycle
kg	kilogram
kG	kilogauss
khz	kilohertz
kHz	kilohertz
kΩ	kilohm

kt	karat (carat); kiloton
kv	kilovolt
kV	kilovolt
kva	kilovoltampere
kVa	kilovoltampere
kw	kilowatt
kW	kilowatt
l	line; liter; locus
L	lambert
LAN	local area network
lb.	pound
lbs.	pounds
lcd	liquid crystal display; lowest common denominator
LCD	liquid crystal display
lm	lumen
lms	least mean square; lumen second; lunar mass spectrometer
log.	logarithm
lsc	least significant character
m	mega-; meter; milli-
m^2	square meter
ma	milliampere
mA	milliampere
mc	magnetic center; master control; megacycle; metric carat; millicycle
mcg	microgram
mf	medium frequency; millifarad
mF	millifarad
mg	megagram; milligram
mG	milligauss
mh	magnetic heading; millihenry
mH	millihenry
mhz	megahertz; millihertz
mHz	megahertz; millihertz
mi.	mile
mK	millikelvin

mL	millilambert
mm	megameter; millimeter; millimicron
modem	modulator-demodulator
mΩ	megaohm
mr	milliroentgen
mR	milliroentgen
ms	mean square; metric system; millisecond
msg	monosodium glutamate
MSG	monosodium glutamate
mv	mean variation; megavolt; millivolt
mV	megavolt; millivolt
mw	megawatt; milliwatt; molecular weight
mW	megawatt; milliwatt
μ	micro-
μg	microgram
μm	micrometer
n	nano-
N	newton
nF	nanofarod
ocr	optical-character reader; optical-character recognition
OCR	optional-character recognition; optical-character reader
os	oil solvent; operating system
OS	operating system
oz.	ounce
p	pico-; probability
Pa	pascal
pot.	point of tangency; potentiometer
pW	picowatt
ql	quintal
qt.	quart
ram.	random-access memory
RAM	random-access memory
rem	recognition memory
REM	recognition memory
rms	root mean square

rom	read-only memory
ROM	read-only memory
s/c	short circuit
sq. rt.	square root
t	tonne (metric); troy
T	tera-
tan.	tangent
uhf	ultrahigh frequency
UHF	ultrahigh frequency
USASCII	USA Standard Code for Information Interchange
uv	ultraviolet
u-v	ultraviolet
v	volt
V	volt
w	watt
W	watt
xmt	transmit
yd.	yard
z	zero
zn.	zenith

ORGANIZATIONS

Organization names are commonly abbreviated by combining the first letters of all important words (*AA/Alcoholics Anonymous*). In contemporary usage no periods follow the letters and no space is added between them. Although the names of organizations should be spelled out in formal writing and in official documents, some organizations permit the use of initials, provided that the organization name is spelled out on first use with the initials appearing in parentheses immediately after the name: *American Broadcasting Company (ABC)*. The following examples illustrate the contemporary style for organization names.

AA	Addicts Anonymous; Alcoholics Anonymous
AAA	American Academy of Advertising; American Anthropological Association; American Automobile Association
ABC	American Broadcasting Company; Audit Bureau of Circulation
ACTA	American Community Theatre Association

ACUG	Association of Computing User Groups
AFB	American Farm Bureau; American Foundation for the Blind
AHA	American Heart Association; American Historical Association; Animal Hospital Association; American Humane Association
AIA	Aerospace Industries Association; American Institute of Accountants; American Institute of Aeronautics; American Institute of Architects
AMA	Aircraft Manufacturers Association; American Machinery Association; American Management Association; American Maritime Association; American Marketing Association; American Medical Association; American Motel Association; American Municipal Association; Automobile Manufacturers Association
ASE	American Stock Exchange
ATLA	American Trial Lawyers Association
BBB	Better Business Bureau
BIAA	Bureau of Inter-American Affairs
CAA	Civil Aeronautics Administration; Civil Aeronautics Authority; Collectors of American Art; Community Action Agencies; Custom Agents Association
CBO	Congressional Budget Office
CHR	Commission on Human Rights
CMEA	Council for Mutual Economic Assistance
DOD	Department of Defense
FDA	Food and Drug Administration
GAO	General Accounting Office; General Auditing Office; Government Accounting Office
IMF	International Monetary Fund
IRS	Internal Revenue Service; International Rorschach Society
ISO	International Standards Organization
LWV	League of Women Voters
NCAPC	National Center for Air Pollution Control

NGS	National Geodetic Survey; National Geographic Society
OAS	Organization of American States
OECD	Organization for Economic Growth and Development
OEO	Office of Economic Opportunity
PC	Peace Corps
PETA	People for the Ethical Treatment of Animals
SAG	Screen Actors Guild
SEC	Securities and Exchange Commission
SGO	Surgeon General's Office
SPCA	Society for the Prevention of Cruelty to Animals
TVA	Tennessee Valley Authority
UN	United Nations
WHO	World Health Organization

ACADEMIC DEGREES

Scholarly degrees written after a name are always abbreviated (*Madaline Driscoll, Litt.D.*). The title *professor* should be spelled out before and after a name, whereas *Dr.* should be abbreviated before a name and spelled out in general text (*The doctor arrived in time*). In all cases the abbreviated degree should be punctuated, as illustrated in the following examples.

A.A.	associate in accounting; associate in arts
A.B.	bachelor of arts
A.M.	master of arts
A.Sc.	associate in science
B.A.	bachelor of arts (Latin: *Baccalaureus Artium*)
B.Ar.	bachelor of architecture
B.C.L.	bachelor of civil law
B.F.A.	bachelor of fine arts
B.L.S.	bachelor of library science; bachelor of library service
B.M.	bachelor of medicine; bachelor of music
B.S.	bachelor of science
B.S.J.	bachelor of science in journalism

Ch.D.	doctor of chemistry
D.Ag.	doctor of agriculture
D.D.	doctor of divinity
D.D.S.	doctor of dental science
D.Med.	doctor of medicine
D.P.	doctor of pharmacy; doctor of podiatry
D.Pharm.	doctor of pharmacy
Dr.Jr.	doctor of law (Latin: *Doctor Juris*)
D.S.	doctor of science
D.Sc.	doctor of science
D.T.	doctor of theology
D.Th.	doctor of theology
D.V.M.	doctor of veterinary medicine
Ed.M.	master of education
Eng.D.	doctor of engineering
J.D.	doctor of jurisprudence; doctor of law(s) (Latin: *Juris* or *Jurum Doctor*)
L.B.	bachelor of letters (Latin: *Baccalaureus Litterarum*)
LL.B.	bachelor of laws (Latin: *Legum Baccalaureus*)
LL.D.	doctor of laws (Latin: *Legum Doctor*)
LL.M.	master of laws (Latin: *Legum Magister*)
M.B.A.	master of business administration
M.E.E.	master of electrical engineering
M.I.E.	master of industrial engineering
M.Ph.	master of philosophy
M.S.B.A.	master of science in business administration
M.Sc.	master of science
M.Th.	master of theology
Mus.D.	doctor of music
Phar.D.	doctor of pharmacy
Ph.D.	doctor of philosophy (Latin: *Philosophiae Doctor*)
Pod.D.	doctor of podiatry
Sc.D.	doctor of science
Sci.D.	doctor of science
Sc.M.	master of science (Latin: *Scientiae Magister*)

S.M.	master of science (Latin: *Scientiae Magister*)
Th.D.	doctor of theology (Latin: *Theologiae Doctor*)
V.M.D.	doctor of veterinary medicine (Latin: *Veterinariae Medicinae Doctor*)

STATE AND COUNTRY ABBREVIATIONS

Although the names of states and countries should be spelled out in general text discussion, they are commonly abbreviated in postal addresses and in notes and bibliographies (see examples in chapter 9). Words such as *avenue* and directions such as *west* should also be spelled out in general text material and in traditional correspondence. But they are commonly abbreviated in condensed or fast-messaging postal addresses and in notes and bibliographies. A period should follow abbreviations such as *St.* (*Street*) when used in addresses.

Avenue/Ave.

Boulevard/Blvd.

Building/Bldg.

Court/Ct.

Drive/Dr.

Parkway/Pkwy.

Place/Pl.

Square/Sq.

Street/St.

Terrace/Terr.

When using the condensed format, place a period after a directional abbreviation that precedes the name of a street. But omit the period when the direction follows the street name.

130 W. Holliston

130 Washington Street, NW

State Abbreviations

Mail that is prepared for sorting by optical-character readers must contain the two-letter state abbreviations designated by the U.S. Postal Service.

State	Traditional	Postal
Alabama	Ala.	AL
Alaska	Alaska	AK
American Samoa	Amer. Samoa	AS

Arizona	Ariz.	AZ
Arkansas	Ark.	AR
California	Calif.	CA
Canal Zone	C.Z.	CZ
Colorado	Colo.	CO
Connecticut	Conn	CT
Delaware	Del.	DE
District of Columbia	D.C	DC
Florida	Fla.	FL
Georgia	Ga.	GA
Guam	Guam	GU
Hawaii	Hawaii	HI
Idaho	Idaho	ID
Illinois	Ill.	IL
Indiana	Ind.	IN
Iowa	Iowa	IA
Kansas	Kans	KS
Kentucky	Ky.	KY
Louisiana	La.	LA
Maine	Maine	ME
Maryland	Md.	MD
Massachusetts	Mass.	MA
Michigan	Mich.	MI
Minnesota	Minn.	MN
Mississippi	Miss.	MS
Missouri	Mo.	MO
Montana	Mont.	MT
Nebraska	Nebr.	NE
Nevada	Nev.	NV
New Hampshire	N.H.	NH
New Jersey	N.J.	NJ
New Mexico	N. Mex.	NM
New York	N.Y.	NY
North Carolina	N.C.	NC
North Dakota	N. Dak.	ND
Ohio	Ohio	OH

Oklahoma	Okla.	OK
Oregon	Oreg.	OR
Pennsylvania	Pa.	PA
Puerto Rico	P.R.	PR
Rhode Island	R.I.	RI
South Carolina	S.C.	SC
South Dakota	S. Dak.	SD
Tennessee	Tenn.	TN
Texas	Tex.	TX
Utah	Utah	UT
Vermont	Vt.	VT
Virginia	Va.	VA
Virgin Islands	V.I.	VI
Washington	Wash.	WA
West Virginia	W. Va.	WV
Wisconsin	Wis.	WI
Wyoming	Wyo.	WY

Country Abbreviations

The following are traditional abbreviations used for major countries of the world.

Afghanistan	Afghan.
Albania	Alb.
Algeria	Alg.
Andorra	And.
Angola	Ang.
Antigua	Ant.
Argentina	Argen.
Australia	Aust., Austl.
Austria	Aus.
Bahamas, The	Bah.
Bahrain	Bah.
Bangladesh	Bangla.
Barbuda	Barbuda, Bar.
Barbados	Barb.
Belgium	Belg.
Belize	Bel.

Benin	Benin, Ben.
Bhutan	Bhu.
Bolivia	Bol.
Botswana	Botswana, Bots.
Brazil	Braz.
Bulgaria	Bulg.
Burkina Faso	Burk. Fas.
Burma	Bur.
Burundi	Burun.
Cameroon	Cam.
Canada	Can.
Cape Verde	C.V., CV
Central African Empire	C.A.E., CAE, C. Afr. Emp.
Chad	Chad
Chile	Chile
China	Chin.
Colombia	Col., Colom.
Commonwealth of Independent States	C.I.S., CIS
Comoros	Comoros, Com.
Congo	Congo, Cong.
Costa Rica	C.R., CR
Cuba	Cuba
Cyprus	Cyp.
Czechoslovakia	Czech.
Denmark	Den.
Djibouti	Djib.
Dominica	Dom.
Dominican Republic	D.R., DR, Dom. Rep.
Ecuador	Ecua.
Egypt	Egyp.
El Salvador	E. Sal.
Equatorial Guinea	E.G., EG, Eq. Guin.
Estonia	Est.
Ethiopia	Eth.
Fiji	Fiji

Finland	Fin.
France	Fr.
Gabon	Gab.
Gambia	Gam.
Germany	Ger.
Ghana	Ghana
Greece	Greece
Grenada	Gren.
Guatemala	Guat.
Guinea	Guinea
Guinea-Bissau	Guinea-Bissau
Guyana	Guy.
Haiti	Haiti
Honduras	Hond.
Hungary	Hung.
Iceland	Ice.
India	Ind.
Indonesia	Indon.
Iran	Ir.
Iraq	Iraq
Ireland	Ir.
Israel	Isr.
Italy	It.
Ivory Coast	I.C., IC, Iv. Cst.
Jamaica	Jam.
Japan	Jap.
Jordan	Jord.
Kampuchea (Cambodia)	Kamp. (Cambod.)
Kenya	Ken.
Kiribati	Kir.
Kuwait	Kuw.
Laos	Laos
Latvia	Lat.
Lebanon	Leb.
Lesotho	Leso.
Liberia	Lib., Liberia

Libya	Lib.
Liechtenstein	Liech.
Lithuania	Lith.
Luxembourg	Lux.
Madagascar	Madag.
Malawi	Malawi, Mal.
Malaysia	Mal.
Maldives	Mald.
Mali	Mali
Malta	Mal.
Mauritania	Maurit.
Mauritius	Maur.
Mexico	Mex.
Monaco	Mon.
Mongolia	Mong.
Morocco	Mor.
Mozambique	Mozam.
Nauru	Nau.
Nepal	Nep.
Netherlands, The	Neth.
New Zealand	N.Z., NZ
Nicaragua	Nica.
Niger	Nig.
Nigeria	Nig.
North Korea	N. Kor.
Norway	Nor.
Oman	Om.
Pakistan	Pak.
Panama	Pan.
Papua New Guinea	Pap. N.G., Pap. NG
Paraguay	Para.
Peru	Peru
Philippines	Phil.
Poland	Pol.
Portugal	Port.
Qatar	Qatar, Qa.

Romania	Rom.
Rwanda	Rwanda
Saint Lucia	S.L., SL, St. Lu.
Saint Vincent and the Grenadines	St. V.&G., St. V&G
San Marino	S.M., SM
São Tomé and Príncipe	São Tomé and Príncipe
Saudi Arabia	S.A., SA
Senegal	Seneg.
Seychelles	Seychelles, Sey.
Sierra Leone	S.L., SL
Singapore	Sing.
Solomon Islands	S.I., SI
Somalia	Som.
South Africa	S.A., SA, S. Afr.
South Korea	S. Kor.
Spain	Sp.
Sri Lanka (Ceylon)	S.L., SL, Sri Lan. (Cey.)
Sudan	Sud.
Suriname	Suri.
Swaziland	Swaz.
Sweden	Swed.
Switzerland	Switz.
Syria	Syr.
Tanzania	Tanz.
Thailand	Thai., Thail.
Tobago	Tob.
Togo	To.
Tonga	Ton.
Trinidad	Trin.
Tunisia	Tun.
Turkey	Turk.
Tuvalu	Tuv.
Uganda	Ugan.
Union of Soviet Socialist Republics	U.S.S.R., USSR
United Arab Emirates	U.A.E., UAE

United Kingdom	U.K., UK
United States	U.S., US
Uruguay	Uru.
Vanuatu	Vanu.
Vatican City	V.C., VC
Venezuela	Venez.
Vietnam	Viet.
Western Samoa	W.S., WS
Yemen (South Yemen)	S. Yem.
Yemen (Arab Republic)	Yem.
Yugoslavia	Yug.
Zaire	Zai.
Zambia	Zam.
Zimbabwe	Zimb.

For rules concerning the abbreviations of numbers see "Inclusive Numbers" in chapter 7.

Chapter 7

NUMBERS AND SYMBOLS

One of the main decisions to be made concerning the use of numbers and symbols is when to spell them out and when to use a figure, sign, or symbol. Rules differ among the various disciplines, with figures and symbols more common in scientific usage and words more common in general literature. (If the first thing in a sentence is a figure, sign, or symbol, it should be spelled out, regardless of the style chosen.)

It is always important to use a selected style consistently. Readers are annoyed and distracted when a writer uses *$10* in one sentence and writes *ten dollars* in the next sentence.

For rules concerning the division of numbers at the end of a line, see "Numbers" in chapter 5.

NUMBERS

General Rules

A popular style in general usage is to spell out numbers *one* through *ninety-nine* and large round numbers such as *one hundred* or *two thousand*. If a paragraph has one or more uneven numbers greater than *one hundred*, however, such as *113*, figures should be used for everything within the category involved.

> Each of the four meeting rooms held 200 people, and 113 men and 87 women attended the lecture in Room 709.

> Each of the four meeting rooms held two hundred people, and nearly one hundred men and one hundred women attended the lecture in Room 709.

In scientific material writers often spell out numbers *one* through *nine* (or *ten*), using figures for all other numbers. If a figure larger than *nine* (or *ten*) is used in a paragraph, all numbers should be written as figures for items within the category involved.

> He ordered 4 additional textbooks and 11 study guides, although as yet only seven people had registered for the course.

He ordered four additional textbooks and nine study guides, although as yet only 12 people had registered for the course.

The same rules apply to rankings (ordinal numbers).

She was in 3d place, whereas he was in 124th place.

She was in third place, whereas he was in ninth place.

Note that *d* rather than *nd* or *rd* is preferred with second (*142d*) and third (*153d*).

Round numbers in the millions may be written with the word *million* (*12 million*) rather than using zeros if no other uneven number in the millions appears in the paragraph.

The votes exceeded 4 million this year compared with 3 million last year.

The Republicans received 2,174,912 votes; the Democrats, 2,000,000 votes; and the Independents, 183,000 votes.

Approximations

Spell out any approximate or inexact general references.

More than a million people voted.

You can see thousands of lights in the city at night.

I have a dozen reasons why we should continue.

Plurals

Add *s* to a figure (without an apostrophe) to form the plural.

The world political order changed drastically in the 1990s.

His score was in the high 80s.

For spelled-out numbers, refer to chapter 4 for rules concerning the addition of *s* or *es* to form the plural of nouns.

Her boss was in his sixties.

They listed the options in fours and sixes.

Inclusive Numbers

Numbers of one hundred and above that use a hyphen (or en dash in typeset copy) instead of the words *to, from,* or *between* may be abbreviated in certain cases. Numbers that end in a double zero, however, should not be abbreviated, nor should years that pertain to different centuries or similar numerical spans. Also, numbers in titles are usually not abbreviated.

chapters 5-11, 20-21, 39-40

pp. 100-107, 108-9, 237-341, 340-86, 1191-95, 1200-1201, 1259-1300 the years A.D. 419-21, 421-419 B.C., 1800-1850, 1860-1902, 1940-47, 1990-91

"A Study of the Rise and Fall of Governor Porter, 1931-1933" (article title)

Fractions and Ratios

Specific decimals, percentages, and ratios are usually written as figures; the word *percent* is commonly spelled out in general text but is expressed as a symbol in scientific material. A general or imprecise reference to a ratio is often spelled out.

The percentages were 0.15 and 1.20.

The odds are 10 to 1.

His chances of winning are one in a million.

It is a 6:2 ratio.

A zero precedes a decimal fraction such as *0.21* only if the quantity might exceed 1.00. Otherwise, the zero should be omitted (*R = .13*).

Common fractions are usually spelled out unless they are lengthy or awkward.

The measure requires a two-thirds vote to pass.

The size of the paper is 8½ by 11 inches.

Technical Measures

Figures are commonly used for all weights and measures in scientific copy, but the numbers *one* through *ninety-nine* and large round numbers are usually spelled out in general references in nontechnical material. When a paragraph of text in general literature is heavily laden with statistics, however, figures are usually preferred. It is important to be consistent in all cases (not *5 millimeters and sixteen centimeters*).

Technical: 12 feet

4 kilometers

6 fathoms

55 miles an hour

Nontechnical: twelve feet

four kilometers

six fathoms

fifty-five miles an hour

If the weight or measure is expressed by an abbreviation or symbol, a figure should always be used. See "Symbols," below.

35 mm (*not* thirty-five mm)

9′12″ (*not* nine′twelve″)

8 lbs. (*not* eight lbs.)

65 km (*not* sixty-five km)

Special Designations

Figures are always used for specific years and days of the month. Roman numerals are often used for numbered vehicles such as Starship IV, names of sovereigns, and the like. Pages, chapters, room numbers, highway numbers, and so on, are also written as figures. A number referred to as a number may be expressed with a figure too. But references to money, military units, wards, and precincts are treated the same as other numbers, as described under "General Rules," on page 135.

General references to centuries, dynasties, congresses, and the like are usually spelled out. Numbers designating clock time are generally spelled out when used with *o'clock* and written as figures when used with *a.m.* or *p.m.* In typeset material *a.m.* and *p.m.* are sometimes set as small capitals. In typewriter and computer preparation they are written as lowercase letters. The abbreviations A.D. and B.C. are typed as capital letters but usually typeset as small capitals.

the year 1991	$0.25 and $216.07
the 1990s (*or* the nineties)	First Lutheran Church
January 7, 1989	Sixth Army
Sputnik I	297th Fighter Wing
Queen Elizabeth II	Third World
John Soleto III	First Congressional District
page 141	Seventh Avenue
chapter 16	Ninety-eighth Street
Room 1000	2101 Sixth Street
the number *4*	the twentieth century
U.S. Route 80	101st Congress
Patriots Post No. 1307	Third Reich
a thousand dollars	four o'clock (*or* 4 o'clock)
$101.39	12:00 a.m. and 1:30 p.m.
twenty-five cents	A.D. 900 and 200 B.C.

Roman Numerals

The following table lists the roman numeral equivalent of arabic numbers. Repeating a letter repeats its value (*XX = 20*). A letter placed after one of greater value adds to it (*LX = 60*). A letter placed before one of greater value subtracts from it (*XL = 40*). A line over a numeral (overbar) multiplies the value by 1,000 ($\overline{X}$ = *10,000*).

I	1	XL	40
II	2	L	50
III	3	LX	60
IV	4	LXX	70
V	5	LXXX	80
VI	6	XC	90
VII	7	C	100
VIII	8	CC	200
IX	9	CCC	300
X	10	CD	400
XI	11	D	500
XII	12	DC	600
XIII	13	DCC	700
XIV	14	DCCC	800
XV	15	CM	900
XVI	16	M	1,000
XVII	17	MM	2,000
XVIII	18	MMM	3,000
XIX	19	$\overline{\text{MV}}$	4,000
XX	20	$\overline{\text{V}}$	5,000
XXX	30		

SYMBOLS

Signs and symbols are commonly used in technical material but are usually spelled out, when possible, in nontechnical material. Two important rules are (1) to be consistent in using either symbols or words and (2) to use figures when symbols are used and to use spelled-out numbers (according to the style described under "Numbers" on page 135) when the symbols are written as words. (*Exception:* Figures are usually used with both % and *percent.*)

35° F (*or* thirty-five degrees Fahrenheit)

6 < 7 (*or* six is less than seven)

35¢, $0.35 (*or* thirty-five cents)

Refer to the preceding section, "Numbers," for further guidelines.

The following list contains familiar symbols commonly used in scientific and other technical material.

Accents

- ˊ acute
- ˘ breve
- ˒ cedilla
- ˆ circumflex
- ¨ dieresis
- ˋ grave
- − macron
- ~ tilde
- ˇ haček

Chemical

- ‰ salinity
- ℳ minim
- ⇅ exchange
- ↑ gas

Electrical

ℜ reluctance

↔ reaction goes both right and left

↕ reaction goes both up and down

↕ reversible

→ direction of flow; yields

→ direct current

⇋ electrical current

⇋ reversible reaction

⇌ reversible reaction

⇋ alternating current

⇌ alternating current

⇌ reversible reaction beginning at left

⇋ reversible reaction beginning at right

Ω ohm; omega

MΩ megohm; omega

μΩ microohm; mu omega

ω angular frequency, solid angle; omega

Φ magnetic flux; phi

Ψ dielectric flux; electrostatic flux; psi

γ conductivity; gamma

ρ resistivity; rho

Λ equivalent conductivity

HP horsepower

Geological Systems

J   Jurassic
Ŧ   Triassic
P   Permian
IP Pennsylvania
M   Mississippian
D   Devonian
S   Silurian
O   Ordovician
Є   Cambrian
pЄ Precambrian
C   Carboniferous
Q   Quaternary
T   Tertiary
K   Cretaceous

Note: These symbols are the standard ones used by the Geological Survey on geological maps. The capital letter indicates the system and the one or more lower-cased letters designate the formation and member where used.

Mathematical

— vinculum (above letters)
÷ geometrical proportion
—: difference, excess
‖ parallel
‖s parallels
≠ not parallels
| | absolute value
· multiplied by
: is to; ratio
÷ divided by
∴ therefore; hence
∵ because
:: proportion; as
≪ is dominated by
> greater than
⊏ greater than
≥ greater than or equal to
≧ greater than or equal to
≷ greater than or less than
≯ is not greater than
< less than
⊐ less than
≶ less than or greater than
≮ is not less than
⋖ smaller than
≤ less than or equal to
≦ less than or equal to
≧ or ≥ greater than or equal to
≲ equal to or less than
≦ equal to or less than
≦ is not greater than equal to or less than
≳ equal to or greater than
≧ is not less than equal to or greater than

⊥ equilateral
⊥ perpendicular to
⊢ assertion sign
≐ approaches
≑ approaches a limit
⋁ equal angles
≠ not equal to
≡ identical with
≢ not identical with
⁄X⁄ score
≈ or ≒ nearly equal to
= equal to
~ difference
≃ perspective to
≅ congruent to approximately equal
≏ difference between
≎ geometrically equivalent to
(included in
) excluded from
⊂ is contained in
∪ logical sum or union
∩ logical product or intersection
√ radical
√ root
√ square root
∛ cube root
∜ fourth root
√ fifth root
√ sixth root
π pi
ε base (2.718) of natural system of logarithms; epsilon

ε is a member of; dielectric constant; mean error; epsilon
+ plus
+ bold plus
− minus
− bold minus
/ shill(ing); slash; virgule
± plus or minus
∓ minus or plus
× multiplied by
= bold equal
number
₱ per
% percent
∫ integral
| single bond
\ single bond
/ single bond
‖ double bond
⧵ double bond
∥ double bond
⟨⟩ benzene ring
∂ or δ differential; variation
∂ Italian differential
→ approaches limit of
~ cycle sine
→ horizontal integral
∮ contour integral
∝ variation; varies as
Π product
Σ summation of; sum; sigma
! or ⌊ factorial product

Miscellaneous

§   section
†   dagger
‡   double dagger
%c account of
%   care of
/XX/ score
¶   paragraph
þ   Anglo-Saxon
¢   center line
♂   conjunction
⊥   perpendicular to
″   or " ditto
∝   variation
℞   recipe
]   move right
[move left
○ or ⊙ or ① annual
⊙ ⊙ or ② biennial
∈   element of
Ɔ   scruple
ƒ   function
!   exclamation mark
⊞   plus in square
♃   perennial
φ   diameter
c̄   mean value of c
∪   mathmodifier
⊂   mathmodifier
⊡   dot in square
△   dot in triangle
⊠   station mark
@   at
℔   pound
℥   dram
ƒ ℥ fluid dram
℥   ounce
ƒ ℥ fluid ounce
O   pint

Planets

☿ Mercury

♀ Venus

⊕ Earth

♂ Mars

♃ Jupiter

♄ Saturn

♅ Uranus

♆ Neptune

♇ Pluto

☊ dragon's head, ascending node

☋ dragon's tail, descending node

☌ conjunction

☍ opposition

☉ or ☺ Sun

☉ Sun's lower limb

☉ Sun's upper limb

◐ solar corona

⊕ solar halo

🌑 Moon

● new Moon

☽ first quarter

◑ first quarter

🌓 third quarter

◐ last quarter

☾ last quarter

◑ last quarter

○ full Moon

☺ full Moon

⊖ eclipse of Moon

⏑ lunar halo

⏒ lunar corona

⚳ Ceres

⚷ Juno

Weather

T   thunder

R   thunderstorm; sheet
        lightning

⋖   sheet lightning

↓   precipitate

◍   rain

←   floating ice crystals

↔   ice needles

▲   hail

⊗   sleet

∞   glazed frost

⊔   hoarfrost

∨   frostwork

✳   snow or sextile

⊠   snow on ground

⇃   drifting snow (low)

≡   fog

∞   haze

⌒   Aurora

Zodiac

♈   Aries; Ram

♉   Taurus; Bull

♊   Gemini; Twins

♋   Cancer; Crab

♌   Leo; Lion

♍   Virgo; Virgin

♎   Libra; Balance

♏   Scorpio; Scorpion

♐   Sagittarius; Archer

♑   Capricornus; Goat

♒   Aquarius; Water bear-
        er

♓   Pisces; Fishes

Chapter 8

FOREIGN TERMS

Writers, editors, and compositors who deal with foreign expressions incorporated into English texts must be concerned with proper capitalization, punctuation, word division, and the use of diacritical marks and italics. These points of style are all discussed in this chapter; however, since the rules pertaining to these concerns differ from one language to another, an instructional text or stylebook pertaining to the language in question should be consulted for futher information. (For examples of foreign alphabets and rules on characters, syllabication, and so on, see "Familiar Foreign Languages," on page 150.)

CAPITALIZATION

Generally, in languages using the Latin alphabet writers capitalize the first word of a title or sentence and all proper nouns. Some languages capitalize other words as well. In the German language, for example, writers also capitalize common nouns. Moreover, authorities using the same language sometimes apply different rules. Because of the differences in rules of capitalization in different languages, it is necessary to follow a guide to the specific language under consideration.

A list of capital and lowercase letters for seven familiar languages is provided at the end of this chapter.

PUNCTUATION

Like the rules of capitalization, the rules of punctuation differ among the various languages, and an instructional text or stylebook should be consulted for a complete guide to the punctuation of the language in question. When foreign material is used in an English work, however, writers generally punctuate the material according to the rules of English punctuation (see chapter 2).

WORD DIVISION

The division of words at the end of a line also differs from one language to another. For a summary of rules pertaining to syllabication in the French, German, modern Greek, Italian, Latin, Russian, and Spanish languages, see "Familiar Foreign Languages" below.

USE OF ITALICS AND DIACRITICAL MARKS

The rule followed by most writers concerning the use of italics and diacritical marks for foreign terms is to italicize and accent unfamiliar words and expressions and to use roman type and omit the diacritical for familiar words and expressions. Large passages or complete texts of foreign material should be set in roman type in any case; only individual words or brief expressions (generally less than a sentence) introduced into English material are italicized. Proper names, such as of companies and individuals, should not be italicized in English works.

The diacritical marks illustrated in Chapter 7 under "Symbols" are those most often used in foreign works.

Although most foreign words use diacritical marks as an essential part of their spelling (*chargé, doña, entrepôt, père*), the following anglicized terms may be set in roman type without diacritical marks.

abaca	cause celebre
aide memoire	chateau
a la carte	cliche
a la king	cloisonne
a la mode	comedienne
angstrom	comme ci comme ca
aperitif	communique
applique	confrere
apropos	consomme
auto(s)-da-fe	cortege
blase	coulee
boutonniere	coup de grace
brassiere	coupe d'etat
cabana	coupe
cafe	creme
cafeteria	crepe
caique	crepe de chine
canape	

critique

critiquing

debacle

debris

debut

debutante

decollete

dejeuner

denouement

depot

dos-a-dos

eclair

eclat

ecru

elan

elite

entree

etude

facade

faience

fete

fiance (masc., fem.)

frappe

garcon

glace

grille

gruyere

habitue

ingenue

jardiniere

litterateur

material

matinee

melange

melee

menage

mesalliance

metier

moire

naive

naivete

nee

opera bouffe

opera comique

papier mache

piece de resistance

pleiade

porte cochere

porte lumiere

portiere

pousse cafe

premiere

protege (masc., fem.)

puree

rale

recherche

regime

risque (masc., fem.)

role

rotisserie

roue

saute

seance

smorgasbord

soiree

souffle

suede

table d'hote

tete-a-tete

tragedienne

vicuna

vis-a-vis

FAMILIAR FOREIGN LANGUAGES

The following alphabets of seven familiar foreign languages are provided to help writers, editors, and compositors recognize and use foreign characters, accents, syllabication, and other features that vary from one language to another.

French

Alphabet and pronunciation

A	a	} between *a* in pat and *o* in pot
A	à	
A	â	*a* in hah
B	b	*b*
C	c	*c* in city before *e, i, y* (= *s*); *c* in car, elsewhere (= *k*)
Ç	ç	*c* in city (= *s*)
D	d	*d*
E	e	*e* in met when followed by two consonants, or by a single final consonant, digraph, or consonantal unit; silent when final and in *-ent,* third person plural verb ending; *e* in moment, before a single consonant, digraph, or consonantal unit, followed by a vowel
È	è	*e* in met
Ê	ê	*e* in met or there
Ë	ë	dieresis indicates that preceding vowel has its usual value and does not form a diphthong with *e*
É	é	*a* in late
F	f	*f*
G	g	*s* in pleasure (= *zh*) before *e, i, y; g* in game elsewhere
H	h	silent
I	i	*ee* in meet
Î	î	*ee* in meet
Ï	ï	*y* in yet, between vowels; *ee* in meet elsewhere
J	j	*s* in pleasure (= *zh*)
K	k	*k*
L	l	*l;* silent in a few cases—*gentil, outil, fils;* frequently letters *il* in final position, and after vowel, and *ill* before vowel pronounced like *y* in yet—*travail, fille*
M	m	*m*
N	n	*n; -ent,* third person plural verb ending, is silent
O	o	*o* in no when final; *o* in for elsewhere
Ô	ô	*o* in no
P	p	*p*
Q	q	*q* in quick (= *k*)
R	r	sound made by scraping of air between back of tongue and roof of mouth; silent when final in ending *-er*
S	s	*z* between vowels; usually silent when final; *s* elsewhere
T	t	*t* with few exceptions; usually silent when final
U	u	} like German *ü* (*ee* with lips rounded as for *oo*) in Esaü; usually silent after *g* and *q* before *e,*
Û	û	*i, y*
Ü	ü	
V	v	*v*
W	w	*w* or *v*
X	x	*gz* at beginning of word (Xavier, xylophone) and sometimes between vowels (exister); otherwise *ks*

Y   y   *ee*
Z   z   *z;* usually silent when final

Special Characters

French uses the Latin alphabet with the addition of the following special characters: *à, â, ç, é, è, ê, ë, ï, ô, ù, û, ü.*

Vowels and Consonants

The vowel letters are *a, e, i, o, u, y;* the other letters are consonants. Vowel sounds are represented by one of the vowel letters or by a combination of two or three of them. Consonant sounds are represented by one or two consonant letters.

Combinations of Two Vowel Letters (Diphthongs)

ai, ay, ei, ey as *e* in met or there
au, eau as *o* in no
eu, œ, œu as *u* in fur [1]
oi, oy as *wa* in watt

ou, oû, aoû as *oo* in moon
oui like English we
ui somewhat like English we

Combinations of Two Consonant Letters (Digraphs)

ch as *sh* in shoe; occasionally as *k*
gn as *ny* in canyon
gu as *g* in give before *e, i, y;* occasionally as *gw*
ll as *y* in yet (in -*ille*)

ph as in English
qu as *k;* occasionally as *kw*
rh as *r*
th as *t*

Sequences of Vowel(s) and n or m (Nasals)

In French, there are four nasal sounds. These are produced by allowing air to pass through the nose and the mouth at the same time, but without any actual sound of *m, n,* or *ng* after them. These sounds are represented by the syllables:

1. *am, an, em, en,* the vowel sound of each being like *a* in far;
2. *aim, ain, eim, ein, im, in, oin, ym, yn,* the vowel sound of each being *a* in sang;
3. *om, on,* with the vowel like *o* in song;
4. *eun, um, un,* with the vowel like *u* in sung.

Nasals occur at the end of a word or in the middle of a word before another consonant except *m* or *n: faim,* bi*en,* lo*in,* m*a*nger, m*e*mbre; otherwise, the above combinations are not nasalized: *ananas* (pronounced *ànànà*), *nommer* (pronounced *nomé*). There are a few exceptions.

Consonantal Units

In French, certain consonants followed by *l* or *r* or preceded by *s* are pronounced in the same syllable with the following vowel. These consonant groups are:

bl, br	*fl, fr*	*sc, sp, sph, squ, st*
chl, chr, cl, cr	*gl, gr*	*thr, tr*
dr	*phl, phr, pl, pr*	*vl, vr*

Rules for Syllabification

In French, words are divided into syllables according to the following rules:

(1) *A consonant between two vowels commences a new syllable:*
ca-pi-tal, ca-pi-ta-li-sa-ble, ca-pi-ta-li-ser, ca-pi-ta-lis-me, ca-pi-ta-lis-te, mo-no-mé-tal-lis-te, li-bé-ra-toi-re, dé-sap-pro-vi-si-on-ne-ment, a-rith-mé-ti-que-ment, an-tis-ta-tu-tai-re-ment, pri-vi-lè-ge, su-bor-don-né, su-res-ta-ries, é-ti-que-ta-ge, e-xa-mi-na-teur, e-xer-ci-ce, e-xis-ten-ce, e-xo-né-rer, i-ne-xac-te-ment, in-de-xa-ti-on, i-nu-ti-le, u-ne, u-na-ni-me-ment, vi-gueur, vi-gou-reux, vi-gou-reu-se, paie-ment, pa-ral-lé-lé-pi-pé-di-que. ·

---

[1] Note that *œ* is printed as a single piece of type when it has this pronunciation, and also in some words of Latin origin, where it is pronounced as French *e.* When *o* and *e* are printed separately, they represent separate sounds in different syllables.

(2) *Two adjoining consonants (except rule 4 digraphs) between two vowels separate into two syllables:*

ac-com-mo-der, ac-quit-te-ment, at-ter-ris-sa-ge, bail-le-res-se, chan-geant, chan-gean-te, con-cur-ren-ti-el-le, cor-res-pon-dan-ce, des-cen-dre, ex-cep-ti-on-nel-le-ment, ex-pé-di-ti-on-nai-re, in-na-vi-ga-ble, in-te-ro-cé-a-ni-que, in-ter-val-le, ir-res-pon-sa-bi-li-té, os-cil-ler, ras-seoir, re-con-nais-san-ce, res-ti-tu-er, sub-di-vi-ser, sur-taux, veil-le.

(3) *A vowel can only begin a syllable, other than an initial syllable, when preceded by another vowel:*

a-é-ro-pla-ne, a-gré-er, an-ci-en, ar-ri-è-re, bé-né-fi-ci-ai-re, ca-mi-on, ca-out-chouc, co-as-so-ci-é, co-ef-fi-ci-ent, co-ïn-ci-der, dé-pou-il-le-ment, ex-tra-or-di-nai-re, feu-il-le, in-né-go-ci-a-ble, li-er, mi-eux, na-ti-on, ou-est, ré-é-va-lu-er, ré-u-ni-on, ro-yau-me, vic-tu-ail-les, vi-e-il-lir, vi-eux, voi-li-er, vo-ya-ge.

(4) *The following digraph consonants are inseparable:*

bl: câ-blo-gram-me, chan-gea-ble, o-bli-té-rer, pu-bli-que. *Exception:* sub-lu-nai-re.

br: dé-brou-il-ler, li-bre, su-bré-car-gue. *Exception:* sub-ro-ger *and derivatives.*

ch: dis-pa-cheur, é-chan-til-lon, é-chauf-fer, gui-chet, re-cher-che.

cl: ac-cla-mer, ac-cli-ma-ter, é-clai-ra-ge, é-clu-se, ex-clu-sif.

cr: des-crip-ti-ve, é-cri-tu-re, ma-nus-crit, pres-cri-re, sous-cri-re.

dh: ré-dhi-bi-toi-re.

dr: a-dres-ser, cor-res-pon-dre, en-tre-pren-dre, or-dre.

fl: af-flux, ef-fleu-rer, in-fla-ti-on, in-flu-ent.

fr: af-fran-chir, en-cof-frer, in-dé-chif-fra-ble, ré-af-frè-te-ment, re-frap-pa-ge.

gl: ag-glo-mé-rer, a-veu-gle, é-tran-gle-ment, né-gli-gen-ce, rè-gle-ment.

gn: com-pa-gnie, é-par-gnant, ren-sei-gne-ment, si-gnal, vi-gnet-te.

gr: ag-gra-va-ti-on, dé-gros-sir, dé-ni-grer, in-té-gral, re-gret.

ph: chi-ro-gra-phai-re, dac-ty-lo-gra-phi-er, té-lé-pho-ne, u-ni-gra-phi-que.

pl: ac-com-plis-se-ment, ap-pli-ca-ti-on, com-plè-te-ment, ex-ploit.

pr: an-ti-pro-tec-ti-on-nis-te, ap-pren-dre, ex-pri-mer, pro-pri-é-té.

rh: ar-rhe-ment, ar-rhes, bi-blo-rhapt, e-nar-rher, trans-rhé-na-ne.

th: au-then-ti-que, dés-hy-po-thé-quer, hy-po-thé-cai-re, mé-tho-de.

tr: ad-mi-nis-tra-tif, cen-tre, co-di-rec-tri-ce, con-tre-si-gner, con-tres-ta-ries, il-lus-trée.

vr: a-vril, li-vrai-son, li-vre, ma-nœu-vrer, ou-vri-er.

(5) (*a*) ns, bs, *and* rs *are separable if followed by a vowel:*

con-sa-crer, con-seil-la-ble, con-si-dé-rer, in-sé-rer, in-sol-va-ble, in-suf-fi-sant, tran-sac-ti-on, tran-sat-lan-ti-que, tran-si-ter; ab-sor-ber, ob-ser-ver; per-su-a-der.

(*b*) ns, bs, *and* rs *are inseparable if followed by a consonant:*

cons-pi-rer, cons-ta-ter, cons-ti-tu-er, ins-pec-ter, ins-tal-ler, trans-cen-dant, trans-fè-re-ment, trans-port; no-nobs-tant, obs-ta-cles, subs-tan-ce; in-ters-ti-ce, pers-pec-ti-ve.

(*c*) ns *and* bs *are inseparable if followed by a consonant coupled with* r:

cons-trui-re, ins-cri-re, trans-cri-re, trans-gres-ser; abs-trac-ti-on, obs-truc-ti-on.

(*d*) ns *and* bs *are separable before* ci:

con-sci-en-ci-eux, in-sci-em-ment; ab-scis-se.

(6) (*a*) mp *and* nc *followed by* t *are inseparable:*

a-comp-te, comp-ta-ble, es-comp-ter, pré-emp-ti-on; fonc-ti-on, sanc-ti-on.

(*b*) *In all other combinations* mp *and* nc *are separable:*

em-plo-yer, em-prun-ter, im-por-tant; a-van-cer, fran-çais, fran-che, fran-co.

(7) *In writing or in print no syllable is separable which does not include a vowel;* thus, trigraph consonants are inseparable initially; scru-tin, but separable medially: ins-cru-ta-ble.

8. Foreign words and components of foreign words (not naturalized) follow the conventions of the language of origin: *alpen-stock, reichs-amt, cre-scendo, sky-scraper, Wash-ington.* Under this rule are also included scientific and technical words, which editors prefer to treat etymologically: *dia-gnostique, hémi-sphère, hémo-ptysies.*

Some of the small syllables, especially initial vowel uniliterals and final biliterals beginning with a vowel, are not usually separated from the body of the word in writing or print, but they are of importance in the pronunciation; thus, émission is pronounced *é-mi-si-on,* but the written or printed word is ordinarily only divided émis-

(*end of line*) sion, not é- (*end of line*) mission, nor émissi- (*end of line*) on, though d'é- (*end of line*) mission, l'é- (*end of line*) mission, are better than d' (*end of line*) émission, l' (*end of line*) émission.

Divisions of words at the ends of lines should, of course, be avoided as far as possible, and not be carried to extremes.

Illustrative Word Divisions

[The numbers in parentheses refer to the syllabification rules]

ab-so-lu-ment	(2, 1, 1)	i-nex-pu-gna-ble	(1, 2, 4, 4)
abs-trac-ti-on	(4, 2, 3)	ins-pi-ra-tion	(5, 1, 1, 3)
ad-mi-nis-tra-ti-on	(2, 1, 4, 1, 3)	ins-tan-ta-née	(5, 2, 1)
a-mé-ri-cai-nes	(1, 1, 1, 1)	ins-truc-ti-on	(5, 2, 3)
an-ti-scor-bu-ti-que	(2, 2, 2, 1, 1)	in-tro-duc-ti-on	(4, 1, 2, 3)
at-mos-phé-ri-que	(2, 4, 1, 1)	Ja-ma-ï-que	(1, 3, 1)
au-to-gno-sie	(1, 4, 1)	Kam-tchat-ka	(8, 2)
bi-blio-thè-que	(4, 4, 1)	ki-lo-mé-tri-que	(1, 1, 4, 1)
bi-en-heu-reux	(3, 2, 1)	ma-la-droi-te-ment	(1, 4, 1, 1)
ca-out-chou-ter	(3, 4, 1)	ma-nus-crits	(1, 4)
cir-cons-tan-ces	(2, 5, 2)	mi-cro-sco-pi-que	(4, 2, 1, 1)
com-pri-ma-ble	(4, 1, 1)	non-ac-ti-vi-té	(1, 2, 1, 1)
cons-cien-cieu-se-ment	(5, 2, 1, 1)	no-nobs-tant	(1, 5)
cons-ti-tu-ti-on-nel	(5, 1, 1, 3, 2)	ob-jec-ti-vi-té	(2, 2, 1, 1)
des-cen-dant	(2, 2)	obli-ga-ti-on	(1, 1, 3)
des-crip-ti-on	(4, 2)	obs-cu-ri-té	(5, 1, 1)
dia-gnos-ti-quer	(4, 2, 1)	per-cep-ti-ble	(2, 2, 4)
dis-ci-pli-ner	(2, 4, 1)	pé-remp-ti-on	(1, 6, 3)
en-tr'ac-cor-der	(4, 2, 2)	pré-oc-cu-pa-ti-on	(3, 2, 1, 1, 3)
e-xé-cu-ti-ves	(1, 1, 1, 1)	pro-blè-mes	(4, 1)
ex-haus-se-ment	(2, 2, 1)	pro-pre-ment	(4,1)
e-xo-cel-lu-lai-res	(1, 1, 2, 1, 1)	pros-crip-ti-on	(7, 2, 3)
ex-tra-or-di-nai-res	(4, 3, 2, 1, 1)	pros-pé-ri-té	(2, 1, 1)
gym-no-sper-mes	(2, 2, 2)	sub-cons-ci-en-ce	(2, 7, 3, 2)
hé-té-ro-do-xie	(1, 1, 1, 1)	su-bor-don-ner	(1, 2, 2)
hy-dro-sco-pie	(2, 2, 1)	sub-ro-ger	(4)
ig-ni-ti-on	(2, 1, 3)	subs-tan-ti-el	(7, 2, 3)

Stress and Diacritics

In French, words do not have any syllabic stress, each syllable being uttered with almost equal force with a slight stress falling on the last.

The diacritics used in French are the acute, the circumflex, the grave, the dieresis (trema), and the cedilla.

The circumflex occurs on the vowels. It may indicate that an *s* followed the vowel in Old French, as in *île* from *isle*, island, and *pâté* from *paste*, paste; it may distinguish homonyms like *dû* (due) and *du* (of the); *â, ê, ô* may represent vowels longer than those spelled *a, e, o*, as in *âne, bête, môle*.

The acute accent occurs only on the *e; é* represents a close *e* sound, more like the *a* in late than the *e* in met. It will be found on an *e* followed by a single consonant or digraph or consonantal unit, followed by a vowel as in *érable, église, étrenne*. It will not be on an *e* followed by two consonants (i.e., two consonants which do not form a digraph or consonantal unit), as in *esclaves, elbeuf*. The letter *é* is common at the end of words (*été, passé*), and frequently initially, and medially as well, under the conditions already stated.

The grave accent occurs on *a, e,* and *u*. One of its functions is to distinguish homonyms: *a* (has) and *à* (to); *des* (of the) and *dès* (since); *ou* (or) and *où* (where). Far more frequent is the occurrence of *è*, indicating an open *e* sound, more like the *e* in met than the *a* in late. It occurs in one-syllable words in which mute *e* is the last letter, and a single consonant or digraph, or consonantal unit, is the next-to-last letter, as in *ère, lèvre, sèche;* in word-final syllables like *-ère, -ière, -ègre, -èbre, -èvre, -èdre, -ères, -ières, -ègres,* etc.; occasionally, in a word ending in *es,* to indicate that the *e* is not silent, as in *progrès, succès*.

The dieresis occurs on the second of two consecutive vowel letters to indicate that the sequence does not have its usual value.

ai as *e* in met (*plaisir*)
ei as *e* in met (*reine*)
oi as *wa* in watt (*toi*)
œ as *u* in fur (*œil*)
gue as *g* in go plus mute *e* in vague
gui as *g* in go plus *ee* as in meet (*guide*); sometimes
    g as in go plus *we* as in we (*aiguille*)
aï as *a* in watt plus *ee* as in meet (*naïf*)

eï as *e* in met plus *ee* as in meet
oï as *o* in for plus *ee* as in meet (*colloïde*)
oë as *o* in for plus *a* as in late (*canoë*); as *o* in for
    plus *e* as in met (*noël*)
guë as *g* in go plus *u* as in German *ü* plus mute *e*
    (*aiguë*)
guï as *g* in go plus *u* as in German *ü* plus *ee* as in
    meet (*contiguïté*)

The cedilla occurs under the letter *c* before *a*, *o*, or *u*, to indicate that *c* is pronounced like *s; reçu*, received.

Capitalization

1. Capitalize the first word of sentences, phrases, verses, speeches, citations: *Un homme dit: "Je passerai la mer . . . ."*

2. After interrogation, exclamation, and suspension points when they end the sentence.

3. In proper names in general: *Jeanne, la France, la Seine*.

a. The names designating God, the three holy persons, Jesus Christ: *Le Créateur, la Providence, le Messie, le Tout-Puissant*.

b. The names of mythological divinities and abstractions personified by poetry or mythology, as well as the names of stars, constellations, and planets: *Jupiter, les Furies, Sirius, le Cygne*.

c. The proper names of people, families, and dynasties: *Les Français, les Bourbons;* but *l'Etat allemand, le drapeau français*.

4. The names of holidays: *La Toussaint, à Noël:* but not the names of days or months.

5. The names that have become proper names: *L'Orateur romain* (Cicero), *la Vierge* (Virgin Mary).

6. The proper names of scholarly, political, and religious organizations, or orders of chivalry: *L'Eglise, l'Institut de France, la Chambre de représentants, l'Université catholique de Paris, l'Ordre de la Couronne*.

7. Ordinarily the cardinal points when they are used absolutely, as in: *Les peuples de l'Orient;* otherwise the lowercase is used.

8. The proper names of streets, monuments, buildings, ships, etc.: *La rue des Tuileries, le Parthénon, le Titanic*.

9. The titles of books, poems, pictures, works of art, etc.

10. Titles, such as: *Sa Majesté, Son Excellence,* when addressing the person himself.

a. Nous, Vous, etc., in encyclicals, pastoral letters, etc.

b. Historical events: *La Renaissance, la Révolution*.

11. The adjective is capitalized when it is intimately connected with the proper name: *Etats-Unis, la Comédie-Française, Charles le Téméraire*.

a. When it precedes the name: *Le Saint-Office, la Sainte-Alliance*.

b. When it accompanies a geographic term: *La mer Méditerranée*.

Punctuation and Hyphenation

The period indicates the end of the sentence. It is used sometimes to give greater emphasis to a subordinate clause.

The interrogation point is used in general as in English; an indirect interrogation is never followed by an interrogation point. When an interrogative phrase is followed by an insertion, the interrogation point is placed immediately after that phrase, the sentence continuing in lower case.

The exclamation point is placed directly after the exclamation; the interjection *ô* is never used by itself, as in *O regret!*, and the exclamation point is placed after the complete exclamation.

The comma marks a brief pause. In spelled out figures the decimal part is separated from the main part by a comma (instead of a period, as in English). It must be used after the place in the date: *Paris, le 4 juin . . . .*

The comma follows salutations, such as: *Ma chère Marie, ...*

It is used before *et, ou,* or *ni* when coordinating more than two elements, such as: *Un bon financier, dit . . . , ne pleure ni ses amis, ni sa femme, ni ses enfants.*

The semicolon marks a medium long pause.

The colon is used as in English.

The suspension points are used as in English.

The quotation marks in French are written: « ». However, *Le Grand Larousse,* in the preface to its 1960–64 edition, uses the English version: '' ''.

The punctuation is usually placed at the end of the quote, if the citation is a complete phrase, as in: *Je répondis: «J'attends le départ.»* Otherwise '' precede the punctuation, as in: *Quel homme, que ce «Père la Victoire»!*

The apostrophe is used to mark the omission of *a, e, i,* as in: *l'arme, d'abord, s'il vous plaît.*

The hyphen is used much more widely than in English, and care should be exercised not to mistake the marginal hyphen in copy used orthographically as one of syllabification. The various orthographic uses of the hyphen are as follows:

1. Between verbs and the pronouns in questions: *Parlez-vous?* Do you speak?
2. Between verbs and object pronouns: *Parlez-moi,* speak to me.
3. Between verbs and the participles *en, y, ce, on: Portez-leur-en,* bring them some.
4. Between the personal pronoun and the adjective *même, moi-même,* myself.
5. On each side of the euphonic *t: A-t-il?* Has he? *Parlera-t-elle?* Will she speak?
6. Before *ci* and *là: celui-ci;* and in certain expressions after *ci* and *là,* as in *ces choses là-dessus.*
7. After *entre* in all reciprocal verbs: *s'entre-tuer,* to kill one another.
8. Between *demi* and its noun: *une demi-heure,* half an hour.
9. In compound nouns and adjectives, especially with prepositional particles, as in *arc-en-ciel,* rainbow; *nouveau-né,* newborn.
10. In spelled numbers.
11. Between first names: *Louis-Charles-Alfred de Musset.*
12. Between the word *Saint* and the following name, when used to designate a locality, a feast-day, a street, an era, etc., but not when it concerns the Saint himself: *la rue Saint-Jacques, La Saint-Nicolas.*
13. In geographic names: *Saint-Valéry-en-Caux,* etc.
14. In certain invariable phrases: *Pêle-mêle, avant-hier,* etc.

Abbreviations

a.	accepté, accepted	Mlle	Mademoiselle, Miss
a.c.	année courante, current year	Mgr	monseigneur, my lord
art.	article, article	N.-D.	Notre Dame, Our Lady
av.	avec, with	N.D.L.R.	note de la rédaction, editor's note.
B.B.	billet de bank, bank note	p.ex.	par exemple, for example
c (c^es)	centime(s), centime(s)	p.f.s.a.	pour faire ses adieux, to say good-by
c.à-d.	c'est-à-dire, that is (i.e.)		
ch.	chapitre, chapter	R.F.	République française, French Republic
ch. de f.	chemin de fer, railway		
Cie, Cie	compagnie, company	R.S.V.P., or r.s.v.p.	répondez, s'il vous plaît, please answer
C.V.	cheval vapeur, H.P.		
C., c., c^te	compte, account	S.A.R.	Son Altesse Royale, His Royal Highness
f., fr.(s)	franc, franc(s)		
h.	heure, hour	S.E.	Son Excellence, His Excellency
J.-C.	Jésus-Christ, Jesus Christ	S.E.O.	sauf erreur ou omission, error or omission excepted
M., MM.	Monsieur, Messieurs, Mr., Messrs.		
Mme	Madame, Mrs.	S.M.	Sa Majesté, His Majesty

NOTE.—It will be noted that the period is not used where the last letter in the abbreviation is the last letter of the complete word.

S.A., Soc. an^e	Société anonyme, similar to limited liability company	t.s.v.p.	tournez, s'il vous plaît, please turn
S.S.	Sa Sainteté, His Holiness	voy., v.	voyez, voir, see
s.v.p.	s'il vous plaît, please	Vve	veuve, widow
t., T.	tome, book	1er	premier (*m.*), first
tît.	tître, title	1ère	première (*f.*), first
		IIe, 2^e	deuxième, second

Abbreviations of Metric Terms

Mm	mégamètre	mm^3	millimètre cube	g	gramme
hkm	hectokilomètre	ha	hectare	dg	décigramme
mam	myriamètre	a	are	cg	centigramme
km	kilomètre	ca	centiare	mg	milligramme
hm	hectomètre	dast	décastère	kl	kilolitre
dam	décamètre	st	stère	hl	hectolitre
m	mètre	dst	décistère	dal	décalitre
dm	décimètre	t	tonne	l	litre
cm	centimètre	q	quintal	dl	décilitre
m^2	mètre carré	kg	kilogramme	cl	centilitre
mm	millimètre	hg	hectogramme	ml	millilitre
mm^2	millimètre carré	dag	décagramme		

Cardinal Numbers

un, *m.* une, *f.*	one	soixante-dix	seventy
deux	two	soixante et onze	seventy-one
trois	three	soixante-douze	seventy-two
quatre	four	soixante-treize	seventy-three
cinq	five	soixante-quatorze	seventy-four
six	six	soixante-quinze	seventy-five
sept	seven	soixante-seize	seventy-six
huit	eight	soixante-dix-sept	seventy-seven
neuf	nine	soixante-dix-huit	seventy-eight
dix	ten	soixante-dix-neuf	seventy-nine
onze	eleven	quatre-vingts	eighty
douze	twelve	quatre-vingt-un	eighty-one
treize	thirteen	quatre-vingt-deux	eighty-two
quatorze	fourteen	quatre-vingt-trois	eighty-three
quinze	fifteen	quatre-vingt-quatre	eighty-four
seize	sixteen	quatre-vingt-cinq	eighty-five
dix-sept	seventeen	quatre-vingt-six, etc.	eighty-six, etc.
dix-huit	eighteen	quatre-vingt-dix	ninety
dix-neuf	nineteen	quatre-vingt-onze, etc.	ninety-one, etc.
vingt	twenty	quatre-vingt-dix-sept	ninety-seven
vingt et un	twenty-one	quatre-vingt-dix-huit	ninety-eight
vingt-deux, etc.	twenty-two, etc.	quatre-vingt-dix-neuf	ninety-nine
trente	thirty	cent	hundred
trente et un	thirty-one	cent un, etc.	one hundred and one, etc.
trente-deux, etc.	thirty-two, etc.	deux cents, etc.	two hundred, etc.
quarante	forty	mille (mil)	thousand
cinquante	fifty	million	million
soixante	sixty	milliard	billion

Ordinal Numbers

premier, *m.* ⎫ premère, *f.* ⎭	first	septième	seventh
		huitième	eighth
second, *m.;* seconde, *f.* ⎫ deuxième ⎭	second	neuvième	ninth
		dixième	tenth
troisième	third	onzième, etc.	eleventh, etc.
quatrième	fourth	vingt et unième	twenty-first
cinquième	fifth	vingt-deuxième, etc.	twenty-second, etc.
sixième	sixth	centième	hundredth

Months

janvier (janv.)	January	juillet (juil.)	July
février (fév.)	February	août	August
mars	March	septembre (sept.)	September
avril (av.)	April	octobre (oct.)	October
mai	May	novembre (nov.)	November
juin	June	décembre (déc.)	December

Days

dimanche	Sunday	jeudi	Thursday
lundi	Monday	vendredi	Friday
mardi	Tuesday	samedi	Saturday
mercredi	Wednesday		

Seasons

printemps	spring	automne	autumn
été	summer	hiver	winter

Time

seconde	second	semaine	week
minute	minute	mois	month
demi-heure	half an hour	année	year
heure	hour	saison	season
jour	day		

Sets of figures, separated in English by commas, in French are separated either by spaces, as in: 1 005; 1 000 000, or by periods as in: 1.005; 1.000.000. Percentages printed in English in lowercase are in French frequently printed in uppercase: 2 1/2 0/0.

Authors and their works are cited in the text as follows: first name (mostly by initial), last name in caps; followed by a comma, then the name of the work in italics, followed by a comma, then volume in Roman numerals, followed by a comma, then the page: p. 211, for example. If the source is a newspaper or a periodical, the name of the author appears, as above, followed by *dans* (in) *le Temps* (a newspaper), or the name of the periodical, followed by a comma and the date, as in: *7 août 1962,* followed by a comman, then p. . . . . The source appears in parentheses, and, followed if cited at the end of a sentence, by a period. Sometimes *t.* (volume) precedes the volume, and *ch.* (chapter), the chapter referred to.

German

Alphabet and Pronunciation [1]

A	a	short: *a* like *u* in cup; long: *a* in father
Ä	ä	short: *e* in bet; long: *e* in there or *a* in bad
B	b	*b;* at end of word or syllable, bulb or as *p* in lip
C	c	before *e, i, ä* and usually *y*, as *ts* in bits; before other vowels, as *c* in can ($=k$)
D	d	*d;* at end of word or syllable, as *t* in hit
E	e	short: *e* in bet; long: somewhat like *a* in gate; in unstressed syllables, like *e* in aspen
F	f	*f*
G	g	*g;* at end of word after *e, ei,* and *i,* many Germans pronounce *g* like German *ch* (see under consonant sequences)
H	h	*h;* at end of word or syllable or before consonant, merely shows that preceding vowel is long; between vowels *h* has the effect of a dieresis
I	i	short: *i* in bit; long: *ee* in meet
J	j	*y* in yes
K	k	*k*
L	l	*l* in let
M	m	*m*
N	n	*n*
O	o	short: between *o* in not and *u* in nut; long: *o* in tone
Ö	ö	short: as in French neuf; (as in fur) long (tongue in long *e* position, lips in long *o* position): *u* in hurt or *eu* in fur
P	p	*p;* after initial *s,* as *p* in spin

[1] All German vowels are pronounced short or long. German spelling does not consistently indicate vowel quantity, but two dependable conversion rules may be mentioned. A double vowel and a vowel followed by a single consonant are pronounced long; a single vowel followed by a double consonant is pronounced short. Consonant quantity is fairly stable; a double consonant does not indicate a lengthened sound.

Q   q   *k; qu* pronounced as *kv*

R   r   *r* in three or parade; at end of word or syllable, usually as in alter

S   s   before vowel, as *z* in zoo or *s* in rose; at end of word, as *s* in miss; before *p* or *t* at
            beginning of word, as *sh* in ship

T   t   *t;* after initial *s,* as *t* in stop

U   u   short: *oo* in cook; long: *oo* in boot

Ü   ü   short: tongue in short *u* position, lips in short *i* position; long (tongue in long *u* posi-
            tion, lips in long *i* position): *u* in French du

V   v   *v* or *f* at beginning of words, *f* at beginning and end of words, elsewhere usually *v*

W   w   *v*

X   x   *x* (= *ks*)

Y   y   short and long: as German *i* or German *ü;* occasionally (before vowel) as *y* in yet

Z   z   *ts* in bits

Special Characters

German used to be set, traditionally, in the Fraktur alphabet (German text). It was abolished for official publications in 1941 and is virtually no longer used. For information on Fraktur, see earlier editions of the U.S. Government Printing Office Style Manual. The Latin alphabet, which is now generally used, has, however, retained the following special characters, called umlauts: Ä ä, Ö ö, and Ü ü.

The Fraktur alphabet employed four ligatures: ch (*ch*), ck (*ck*), ß (ß, *ss*), and tz (*tz*). However, German style when using a Latin alphabet has retained the following usages: In syllabification, tz may be divided, ch and ß may never be divided, and ck, if division is called for, must be changed to k-k. This is because the character c may never end a word or a syllable and, hence, may not terminate a line.

When German is set in Latin characters, the only ligature employed is ß; the other ligatures are represented by their respective individual characters. When ß is not available, it may be replaced by *ss.*

Vowels and Consonants

The vowels are *a, e, i, o, u,* and *y* (including the umlauts *ä, ö,* and *ü*). The other letters of the alphabet are consonants.

Vowel Sequences (Diphthongs)

The diphthongs and their sounds are:

aa as German long *a*
ai as *ai* in aisle
au as *ou* in our
äu as *oi* in noise
ee as German long *e*
ei as *ai* in aisle

eu as *oi* in noise
ie as German long *i*
oo as German long *o*
oe as German long *o* in some proper names (as distinguished from *oe* for the umlaut *ö*)
oi as German long *o* in some proper names

To the *ie* there are a few exceptions, as in a few words *ie* is not a diphthong but the two letters are sounded separately, as *ee-uh.* These exceptions occur usually at the end of words of foreign origin, the *ie* being equivalent to the Latin *ia: Linie, Materie,* etc.

To the above diphthongs should be added also *ae, oe,* and *ue,* which are sometimes used in place of *ä, ö,* and *ü,* respectively, and are sounded as *ä, ö, ü.*

Consonant Sequences (Digraphs)

The digraphs and their sounds are:

ph as English *ph=f*   *th* as *t*
sch as *sh* in shall

The sound for *ch* may be approximated by making a strong *h* sound. In words some, *ch* is pronounced like *k.* The digraph *sch* must be distinguished from the mere coincidental juxtaposition of those letters, pronounced like *s* and *ch* separately: *biß-chen,* little bit; *Fäß-chen,* little barrel; *Häus-chen* little house.

Consonantal Units

The combinations *qu* (pronounced *kv*), *st,* and *ß* are treated as consonantal units. Some editors treat *pf* as a consonantal unit, especially after another consonant; but this is not favored by Duden, Rechtschreibung der deutschen Sprache, which divides *kämp-fen, Karp-fen, rup-fen* as indicated. The rule is that *pf* is separated when followed by a vowel.

When ß is replaced by *ss, ss* is never divided.

Rules for Syllabification

1. Diphthongs, digraphs, and consonantal units may not be divided with the exception of *ng.*

2. Division is made on a vowel or on a diphthong before a single consonant, a digraph, or a consonantal unit: *le-ben, lie-ben, wa-chen, wa-schen, Mei-ster, gro-ßen, Re-qui-sit.*

3. In a group of two or more consonants, division is made before the last consonant, digraph, or consonantal unit: *Mut-ter, Was-ser, stimm-ten, kämp-fen, wün-schen, Fen-ster, Pfing-sten.*

4. Division may be made between two vowels not constituting a diphthong or between a diphthong and a vowel: *Oze-an, Trau-ung.*

5. Certain adverbial prefixes are kept intact. These are: *ab, an, auf, aus, be, bei, durch, ein, emp, ent, er, fort, ge, her, hin, hinter, in, miß, mit, nach, nieder, ob, um, un, unter, ver, vor, weg, wider, wieder, zer, zu, zurück,* and *zusammen: ab-ändern, An-erbe, auf-arbeiten,* etc.

6. Certain suffixes are kept intact. These are: *artig, chen, haft, heit, schaft,* and *tum: eigen-artig, Hühn-chen, Knapp-heit, Wachs-tum.*

7. Compound words are divided according to their component parts (and each part according to rules 1 to 6): *alt-italienisch, Tür-angel.* The compounding *r* and *s,* if used, are kept with the preceding component: *dar-auf, wor-auf, Redens-art, Orts-angabe.*

8. Foreign words and components of foreign words follow the conventions of the language of origin: *Repu-blik, Hy-drant, Wash-ington, Shake-speare.* Under this rule are also included scientific and technical words, which editors prefer to treat etymologically: *Dia-gnose, Mikro-skop.*

9. When division is made on or before a syllable from which a letter was elided, the letter is restored to render the syllable integral: *glitschst* is divided *glit-schest, Luftschiffahrt* is divided *Luftschiff-fahrt;* and when the double consonant *ck* is divided, the *c* is changed to *k,* thus *Hacke* and *Zucker* are divided *Hak-ke* and *Zuk-ker.* It is important to bear in mind that words divided under this rule, if subsequently reset and run over, must have their original spelling restored.

10. No division should be made that results in a single letter being separated or a syllable of two letters occupying the second line. Wrong: *O-zean, koch-te.*

11. When, in a compound word, the first word ends with *s* and the second begins with *t,* the *st* rule does not apply: *Reichs-tag* not *Reich-stag.*

12. No division is permitted that affects the meaning adversely: *Spar-gelder* not *Spargel-der; Ur-instinkt* not *Urin-stinkt.*

Illustrative Word Divisions

[The numbers in parentheses refer to the syllabification rules]

Ab-gren-zung	(5, 2)	Nach-ord-nung	(5, 3)
ame-ri-ka-ni-sche	(2, 2, 2, 2)	ne-ben-an	(2, 7)
Amts-an-tritt	(7, 5)	nie-der-bre-chen	(2, 5, 2)
an-ord-nen	(5, 3)	nied-rig-ste	(3, 3)
Auf-pflan-zung	(5, 3)	Ober-stabs-arzt	(7, 7)
Aus-zah-lung	(5, 3)	Ob-lie-gen-heit	(5, 2, 3)
bei-tra-gen	(5, 2)	ord-nungs-mä-ßig	(3, 7, 2)
Be-ob-ach-tung	(5, 5, 3)	Orts-an-ga-be	(7, 5, 2)
Be-quem-lich-keit	(2, 3, 3)	öster-rei-chi-sche	(7, 2, 2)
bläs-chen-för-mige	(3, 7, 3, 2, 1)	ost-in-di-sche	(7, 3, 2)
dar-ein-schla-gen	(7, 5, 2)	pas-sie-ren	(3, 2)
deut-sche	(2)	pflicht-schul-dig	(7, 3)
Deutsch-land	(7)	Plan-wirt-schaft	(7, 6)
Dienst-al-ter	(7, 3)	Platz-an-wei-sung	(7, 5, 2)
durch-ar-bei-ten	(5, 3, 2)	plat-zen-de	(3, 3)
ein-spre-chen	(5, 2)	Rat-haus-saal	(7, 7)
emp-fäng-lich	(5, 3)	Rich-ter-amt	(3, 3)
eng-li-sche	(3, 2)	recht-fer-ti-gen	(7, 3, 2)
ent-spre-chen	(5, 2)	Rechts-ge-schich-te	(7, 2, 3)
er-schreck-lich	(5, 3)	re-pu-bli-ka-nisch	(2, 8, 2, 2)
eu-ro-pä-i-sche	(2, 2, 4, 2)	Sach-ver-zeich-nis	(7, 5, 3)
Far-ben-auf-trag	(3, 7, 5)	schwei-ze-ri-sche	(2, 2, 2)
Fin-ster-nis	(3, 3)	Selbst-ach-tung	(7, 3)
fort-ar-bei-ten	(5, 3, 2)	Selb-stän-dig-keit	(7, 3, 3)
fünf-und-zwan-zig	(7, 7, 3)	sy-ste-ma-ti-sche	(2, 2, 2, 2)
ge-brau-chen	(5, 2)	über-ein-kom-men	(5, 5, 3)
her-aus-zie-hen	(5, 5, 2)	um-än-dern	(5, 3)
hin-ar-bei-ten	(5, 3, 2)	un-ab-hän-gig	(5, 5, 3)
hin-ter-brin-gen	(3, 5, 3, 11)	Un-ter-ab-tei-lung	(3, 5, 5, 2)
In-an-spruch-nahme	(5, 5, 7, 3)	ver-ei-nig-te	(5, 2, 3)
in-ein-an-der	(5, 5, 3)	Vor-an-schlag	(5, 5)
In-ter-esse	(3, 8, 3, 10)	weg-schlei-chen	(5, 2)
Jah-res-tag	(3, 7)	Werk-ar-beit	(7, 3)
Ka-me-ra-den	(2, 2, 2)	wi-der-spre-chen	(2, 5, 2)
Leb-haf-tig-keit	(3, 3, 3)	Wie-der-ab-druck	(2, 5, 5)
Maß-sy-stem	(7, 2)	Wirt-schaf-ter	(6, 3)
me-di-zi-ni-sche	(2, 2, 2, 2)	zer-split-tern	(5, 3)
Miß-er-folg	(5, 3)	zu-dre-hen	(5, 2)
mit-hel-fen	(5, 3)	zu-rück-er-o-bern	(2, 5, 5, 2)
mitt-le-rer	(3, 2)	zu-sam-men-flie-ßen	(2, 3, 5, 2)

Diacritics and Stress

Other than the umlauts, no diacritical marks are used in German. The chief stress falls on the root syllable in simple words (*SINGen*, to sing), and on the leading component, usually the first, in compound words (*FESTland,* mainland). Words of foreign origin have their own characteristic stress.

Capitalization

With the exception of the following, capitalization conventions are the same as in English:

1. All nouns and words used as nouns are capitalized: [1] *das Geben,* the giving; *die Armen,* the poor.

---

[1] In the interest of simplicity, works in philology and bibliography often allow all common nouns to go lowercase.

2. Proper adjectives are lowercased: *die deutsche Sprache,* the German language.

3. Adjectives derived from personal names are capitalized: *die Lutherische Übersetzung,* Luther's translation; but when used descriptively, lowercased: *die lutherische Kirche,* the Lutheran Church; *ciceronische Beredsamkeit,* Ciceronic eloquence.

4. The pronouns *Sie,* you, *Ihr,* your, and *Ihnen,* to you, are capitalized, but not *ich,* I. The pronouns *Du,* you, *Dein,* your, and their various forms are capitalized in correspondence.

In solid matter, where the umlaut on capital letters is likely to cause trouble in alinement, it will be omitted and a lowercase *e* added after the capital, as *Ae (Aerger), Oe (Oel), Ue (Uebel).*

Punctuation and Hyphenation

Punctuation is practically as in English. The comma, however, is used to set off subordinate clauses of all kinds; e.g., *ich glaube, daß er kommen wird,* I believe that he will come.

In series of words made up of two parts, where one part is common to both words, the hyphen is used as follows: *Feld- und Gartenfrüchte* (field- and garden produce), the word *früchte* being common to both *Feld* and *Garten;* but *Haftpflicht-Versicherungsgesellschaft und -Versicherte* (liability-insurance company and -insured), because *Haftpflicht* is common to both *Versicherungsgesellschaft* and *Versicherte.*

Abbreviations

a.	an, am, an der, on (the), at (the)	d.M.	dieses Monats, of the . . . instant
a.a.O.	am angeführten Ort, in the place cited (loc. cit.)	do.	ditto, the same
Abb.	Abbildung, illustration, figure	Dr.	Doktor, doctor
Abk.	Abkürzung, abbreviation	Dtzd.	Dutzend, dozen
Abt.	Abteilung, section	einschl.	einschließlich, including, inclusive
a.d.	an der, on the	entspr.	entsprechend, corresponding
a.D.	außer Dienst, retired	e.V.	eingetragener Verein, incorporated society or association
Adr.	Adresse, address	ev.	evangelisch, Protestant
A.G.	Aktiengesellschaft, corporation	evtl.	eventuell, perhaps, possibly
allg.	allgemein, general(ly)	Fa.	Firma, firm
Anm.	Anmerkung, note	ff.	folgende (Seiten), following (pages)
Art.	Artikel, article	F.f.	Fortsetzung folgt, to be continued
Aufl.	Auflage, edition	Forts.	Fortsetzung, continuation
b.	bei, beim, near, with, c/o	Frl.	Fräulein, Miss
Bd.	Band, volume	geb.	geboren, born; gebunden, bound; geborene, née
bes.	besonders, especially		
betr.	betreffs, betreffend, concerning	Gebr.	Gebrüder, Brothers
bez.	bezüglich, respecting	gef.	gefälligst, kindly
Bez.	Bezirk, district	gegr.	gegründet, founded
bezw., bzw.	beziehungsweise, respectively	ges., gesch.	gesetzlich geschützt, registered trademark
Blg.	Beilage, enclosure	G.m.b.H.	Gesellschaft mit beschränkter Haftung, Ltd., or Inc.
b.w.	bitte wenden, please turn page		
ca.	circa, zirka, about	hrsg.	herausgegeben, edited or published
d.Ä.	der Ältere, Sr.	i.	in, im, in, in the
ders.	derselbe, the same	Ing.	Ingenieur, engineer
dgl.	dergleichen, the like, of that kind	inkl.	inklusive, inclusive, included
d.h.	das heißt, that is, i.e.	insb.	insbesondere, in particular
d.i.	das ist, that is, i.e.	Kap.	Kapitel, chapter
d.J.	der Jüngere, junior; dieses Jahres, of this year	kath.	kathalisch, Catholic
		Kl.	Klasse, class
DM	Deutsche Mark, mark (after World War II)	lfd.	laufend, current
		Lfg.	Lieferung, fascicle

M.	Mark, mark (coin)		T.	Teil, part
m.E.	meines Erachtens, in my opinion		teilw.	teilweise, partly
Nachf.	Nachfolger, successor(s)		u.	und, and
nachm.	nachmittags, p.m., afternoon		u.a.	und andere, and others; unter anderem, among other things; unter andern, among others (inter alia)
näml.	nämlich, namely, i.e.			
NB	(nota bene) beachte, note, remark (P.S.)			
n.Chr.	nach Christus, A.D.		u.a.m.	und andere mehr, and many others
n.F.	neue Folge, new series		U.A. w.g.	Um Antwort wird gebeten, an answer is requested
No., Nr.	Numero, number			
no., ntto.	Netto, net		usw.	und so weiter, and so forth, etc.
od.	oder, or		v.	(vide) siehe, see (cf.); von, of, from, by
ö., österr.	österreichisch, Austrian			
p.A.	per Adresse, care of (c/o)		v.Chr.	vor Christus, B.C.
Pf.	Pfennig, penny		Verf.	Verfasser, author
Pfd.	Pfund, pound (lb.)		Verl.	Verleger, publisher
PS	Pferdestärke, horsepower		vgl.	vergleiche, compare
resp.	respektiv, respectively		v.H.	vom Hundert, percent (%)
rglm.	regelmäjßg, regular		v.J.	vorigen Jahres, of last year
S.	Seite, page		v.M.	vorigen Monats, of last month
s.	siehe, see (cf.)		vorm.	vormittags, morning, a.m.
sel.	selig, late		Vors.	Vorsitzender, chairman
Skt., St.	Sankt, Saint		w.o.	wie oben, as above
s.o.	siehe oben, see above		Wwe.	Witwe, widow
sog.	sogenannt, so called		z.	zu, zum, zur, to, to the, at
Sp.	Spalte, column		z.B.	zum Beispiel, for example
St.	Stück, individual piece		z.H.	zu Händen, attention of
staatl.	staatlich, State or Federal		Ztschr.	Zeitschrift, periodical
Str.	Strasse, street		z.T.	zum Teil, in part
s.u.	siehe unten, see below		zus.	zusammen, together
			z.Z.	zur Zeit, at the time, acting (e.g., secretary)

Cardinal Numbers

eins	one		neunzehn	nineteen
zwei	two		zwanzig	twenty
drei	three		einundzwanzig	twenty-one
vier	four		zweiundzwanzig	twenty-two
fünf	five		dreiundzwanzig, etc.	twenty-three, etc.
sechs	six		dreißig	thirty
sieben	seven		vierzig	forty
acht	eight		fünfzig	fifty
neun	nine		sechzig	sixty
zehn	ten		siebzig	seventy
elf	eleven		achtzig	eighty
zwölf	twelve		neunzig	ninety
dreizehn	thirteen		hundert	hundred
vierzehn	fourteen		hundertundeins	one hundred and one
fünfzehn	fifteen		hundertundzwei, etc.	one hundred and two, etc.
sechzehn	sixteen			
siebzehn	seventeen		zweihundert, etc.	two hundred, etc.
achtzehn	eighteen		tausend	thousand

Ordinal numbers

erste	first	dreizehnte, etc.	thirteenth, etc.
zweite	second	zwanzigste	twentieth
dritte	third	einundzwanzigste	twenty-first
vierte	fourth	zweiundzwanzigste,	twenty-second,
fünfte	fifth	etc.	etc.
sechste	sixth	dreißigste	thirtieth, etc.
siebente	seventh	vierzigste, etc.	fortieth
achte	eighth	hundertste	hundredth
neunte	ninth	hundertunderste, etc.	one hundred and first,
zehnte	tenth		etc.
elfte	eleventh	zweihundertste	two hundredth
zwölfte	twelfth	tausendste	thousandth

After ordinal numbers a period is placed where in English the form would be 1st, 2d, etc., as *1. Heft; 2. Band.*

Months

Januar (Jan.)	January	Juli (Jul.)	July
Februar (Feb.)	February	August (Aug.)	August
März	March	September (Sept.)	September
April (Apr.)	April	Oktober (Okt.)	October
Mai	May	November (Nov.)	November
Juni (Jun.)	June	Dezember (Dez.)	December

Days

Sonntag	Sunday	Donnerstag	Thursday
Montag	Monday	Freitag	Friday
Dienstag	Tuesday	Sonnabend, Samstag	Saturday
Mittwoch	Wednesday		

Seasons

Frühling	spring	Herbst	autumn
Sommer	summer	Winter	winter

Time

Stunde	hour	Monat	month
Tag	day	Jahr	year
Woche	week		

Greek

Alphabet and Pronunciation

A	α	*Aa*	alpha	*a* in father; see αι, αυ, under Diphthongs
B	6	*Bb*	beta	*v*
Γ	γ	*Tr*	gamma	*y* in yes before αι, ε, ει, η, ι, οι, υ, υι; *ng* in singer before γ, κ, ξ, χ; somewhat like *g* in go everywhere else; see γγ, γκ, under Digraphs
Δ	δ	*Dd*	delta	*th* in this, except in νδρ, pronounced *ndr*
E	ε	*Ee*	epsilon	*e* in met; see ει, ευ, under Diphthongs
Z	ζ	*Zz*	zeta	*z*
H	η	*Hn*	eta	*ee* in eel; *y* in yet, when after a consonant and before a vowel; see ηυ, under Diphthongs
Θ	θ	*θθ*	theta	*th* in thin
I	ι	*I.ι*	iota	*ee* in eel; *y* in yet when initial or after a consonant, before a vowel; see αι, ει, οι, υι, under Diphthongs
K	κ	*Ku*	kappa	*k;* see γκ, under Digraphs
Λ	λ	*Λλ*	lambda	*l*
M	μ	*Mμ*	mu	*m;* see μπ, under Digraphs
N	ν	*Nv*	nu	*n;* see ντ, under Digraphs
Ξ	ξ	*Ξξ*	xi	*x* (= ks)
O	o	*Oo*	omicron	*o* in for; see οι, ου, under Diphthongs
Π	π	*Πω*	pi	*p;* see μπ, under Digraphs
P	ρ	*Pρ*	rho	*r,* somewhat like the Scotch trilled *r*
Σ	σ ς[1]	*Lσs*	sigma	*z* before β, γ, δ, λ, μ, ν, ρ; *s* everywhere else
T	τ	*Tt(τ)*	tau	*t;* see ντ, τζ, τσ, under Digraphs
Y	υ	*Vv*	upsilon	*ee* in eel; *y* in yet, after a consonant and before a vowel; see αυ, ευ, ηυ, ου, υι, under Diphthongs
Φ	φ	*Φφ*	phi	*f*
X	χ	*Xx*	chi	like a strong *h* (like German *ch*)
Ψ	ψ	*Ψy*	psi	*ps*
Ω	ω	*Ωω*	omega	*o* in or

---

[1] The character σ is used in initial and medial positions in a word; the character ς, in the final position.

In connected speech, many phonetic changes occur: word-final *n* often drops or becomes *m,* and the first sound of the next word may change, for example, from *p* to *b; ts* at the beginning of a word becomes *dz* after a word ending in *n;* many other such differences in pronunciation, between an isolated word and a word in connected speech, are observable. These phenomena, however, are not reflected in the spelling.

Modern Greek uses the same alphabet as Classical Greek, but many of the letters stand for different sounds now because of the linguistic changes that have taken place since classical times. The names of the letters are given here in the usual English version of their Classical Greek form. These names are usually pronounced in English as follows: alpha (*al* as in Alfred), bayta, gamma, delta, épsilon (*o* as in don), zayta, ayta, thayta, eye-ó-ta, kappa, lamda, mew, new, zie (*ie* as in die or sigh), óm-i-kron (*o*'s as in don), pie, roe, sigma, tou (*ou* as in house), yóu-psi-lon (or úp-silon), fie, kie, sie, o-máy-ga. In Modern Greek, the letter names are pronounced ahlfa, veeta, gahma, thelta (*th* as in then), eh-psee-láwn, zeeta, eeta, theeta (*th* as in thin), yoeta, kahpa, lahmvtha (*th* as in then), mee, nee, ksee, oh-mee-kráwn, pee, ro, seeg-ma, tahv, ae-psee-láwn, fee, hee, p-see, o-mée-ga.

It is suggested that for transliterating Modern Greek names, etc., the usual transliteration of the letters be used, regardless of pronunciation: *a, b, g, d, e, z, ē, th, i, k, l, m, n, x, o, p, r, s, t, u, ph, ch, ps, ō*. For β, *v* may be used if desired.

There are two quite different styles of Modern Greek: one is an extremely formal academic style, known as katharevousa; the other, called Demotic Greek, is used by everybody in daily speech, and in modern novels, stories, poetry, and some newspapers. There are considerable differences between the two styles in grammatical structure and vocabulary, but their pronunciation and spelling are largely the same.

Special Characters

Some of the letters of the alphabet have variant forms: for alpha, α and ɑ; for beta, б and β; for theta, ϑ and θ; for kappa, κ and ϰ; for pi, π and ϖ; for phi, φ and ϕ; for psi, ψ and y. These are used interchangeably.

Some Greek letters are exactly or nearly like the corresponding Latin letters: A α, B β, E ϵ, Z, I ι, K κ, M, N, O o, ς, T τ, υ. The other letters are characteristically Greek: Γ γ, Δ δ, ζ, H η, Θ θ, Λ λ, μ, ν, Ξ ξ, Π π, P ρ, Σ σ, Y, Φ ϕ, X χ, Ω ω.

Vowels

The vowels are α, ϵ, η, ι, o, ν, and ω, including the three vowels with a subscript (ᾳ, ῃ, and ῳ), which are pronounced the same as their respective vowels without the subscript. The remaining letters are consonants.

Combinations of Two Vowel Letters (Diphthongs)

αι   as *e* in met

αυ   as *a* in watt, plus *f* before voiceless consonants (θ, κ, ζ, π, σ, τ, ϕ, χ, ψ); as *a* in watt, plus *v* before vowels and voiced consonants (β, γ, δ, ζ, λ, μ, ν, ρ)

ϵι   as *ee* in eel; *y* in yet, when after a consonant and before a vowel

ϵυ   as *e* in met, plus *f,* before voiceless consonants; as *e* in met, plus *v* before vowels and voiced consonants

ηυ   as *ee* in eel, plus *f,* before voiceless consonants; as *ee* in eel, plus *v,* before vowels and voiced consonants

οι   as *ee* in eel; *y* in yet, when after a consonant and before a vowel

ου   as *ou* in group, same as *oo* in food

υι   as *ee* in eel

Note that ϵι, οι, and υι are pronounced the same as the simple vowels η, ι, υ, all like *ee* in eel.

Combinations of Two Consonant Letters (Digraphs)

γκ as *g* in go initially; *ng* in finger, rarely *nk* in sink, elsewhere

γγ as *g* in go initially; *ng* in finger, rarely *nk* in sink, elsewhere

μπ as *b* in bet initially; *mb* in ember, rarely *mp* in empty, elsewhere

ντ as *d* in did initially; *nd* in end, rarely *nt* in enter, elsewhere

τζ as *dz* in adz; *j* in judge in some foreign words

τσ as *ts* in hats; *ch* in chug in some foreign words

Consonantal Units

For purposes of syllabification, any combination of consonants that may begin a Greek word is a unit. Hence, the following are consonantal units:

βδ, βλ, βρ	πλ, πν, πρ, πτ
γλ, γν, γρ	σβ, σθ, σκ, σμ, σπ, στ, στρ, σφ, σχ
δμ, δν, δρ	τλ, τμ, τρ
θλ, θν, θρ	φθ, φλ, φν, φρ
κλ, κμ, κν, κρ	χθ, χλ, χν, χρ
μν	

Also, any group of three consonants, the first two and the last two of which are units, as listed above, are likewise regarded as consonantal units. Thus, χθρ is a unit, because χθ and θρ are units.

Rules for Syllabification

1. Diphthongs, digraphs when they represent a single sound, and consonantal units may not be divided.
2. Division is made on a vowel or on a diphthong before a single consonant, digraph, or consonantal unit: πα-τέ-ρας, παι-διά, βί-βλος.
3. In a group of two or more consonants, the division is made before the last consonant, digraph, or consonantal unit: γλῶσ-σα, πορθ-μός, Ἀγ-γλία, ἄν-θραξ.
4. Division may be made between vowels not constituting a diphthong or between a diphthong and another vowel: εὐ-ειδής, θέ-ατρον, λα-ϊκός, οὔ-ϊα.
5. Certain adverbial prefixes are kept intact. These are: ἀν, δια, δισ, δυσ, εἰσ, ἐκ, ἐν, ἐξ, μισ, προς, συν, ὑπερ, and ὡσ: ἀν-αρχία, ἐξ-άδελφος, ὥσ-τε.
6. Compound words are divided according to their component parts (and each part according to rules 1 to 5): φιλ-άνθρωπος, τρισ-άθλιος.
7. Foreign words in Greek orthography are regarded as naturalized words and divided according to rules 1 to 5: Ἀγ-γλία, Βά-σιγ-κτων, Ἐδου-άρ-δος; but foreign compound words are divided according to their component parts: Τσεχο-σλοβακία.

Illustrative Word Divisions

[The numbers in parentheses refer to the syllabification rules]

ἀγνω-στι-κὸς	(2, 2)	Ἠνω-μέ-ναι	(2, 2)
αἱ-μορ-ρο-ϊ-δες	(2, 3, 4, 2)	θε-ο-κρα-τι-κὸς	(4, 6, 2, 2)
αἰ-σθαν-τι-κὸς	(2, 3, 2)	ἰδι-ο-συγ-κρα-σία	(4, 6, 3, 2)
Ἀμε-ρι-κα-νὸς	(2, 2, 2)	κα-τά-θλι-ψις	(2, 2, 2)
ἀν-ω-δύ-νως	(5, 2, 2)	κα-ταρ-τι-σμὸς	(2, 3, 2)
ἀπο-στρα-τεύ-ο-μαι	(2, 2, 4, 2)	Κων-σταν-τῖ-νος	(3, 3, 2)
βα-σί-λει-ον	(2, 2, 4)	λε-ξι-κο-γρά-φος	(2, 2, 6, 2)
γλαύ-κω-μα	(2, 2)	μα-γνη-τι-σμὸς	(2, 2, 2)
δι-ά-γνω-σις	(4, 5, 2)	μαι-ευ-τι-κή	(4, 2, 2)
δισ-ε-κα-τομ-μύ-ρι-ον	(5, 2, 2, 3, 2, 4)	με-γα-λει-ὸ-της	(2, 2, 4, 2)
δύσ-καμ-πτος	(5, 3)	με-λαγ-χο-λία	(2, 3, 2)
εἰσ-έρ-χο-μαι	(5, 3, 2)	με-τα-βάλ-λον-ται	(2, 2, 3, 3)
ἐκ-λαμ-πρό-της	(5, 3, 2)	μισ-αν-θρω-πία	(5, 3, 2)
Ἑλ-λά-δος	(3, 2)	μπαρ-μπέ-ρης	(3, 2)
Ἐξ-ο-χό-τη-τα	(5, 2, 2, 2)	ναυ-αρ-χεῖ-ον	(6, 3, 4)
Ἐξ-ω-τε-ρι-κὸς	(5, 2, 2, 2)	νε-ο-ελ-λη-νι-κὸς	(4, 6, 3, 2, 2)
εὐ-ερ-γέ-της	(6, 3, 2)	Οὐά-σιγ-κτων	(2, 3)
Εὐ-ρω-πα-ϊ-κὸς	(2, 2, 4, 2)	πο-λι-τεῖ-αι	(2, 2, 4)
Ζω-άρ-κεια	(4, 3)	πλη-ρε-ξού-σι-οι	(2, 2, 2, 4)
Ἠλεκ-τρο-σκό-πι-ον	(2, 2, 2, 4)	προσ-έγ-γι-σις	(5, 3, 2)

συμ-βαλ-λό-με-νοι	(3, 3, 2, 2)	τρισ-ά-γι-ος	(6, 2, 4)
συν-οι-κέ-σι-ον	(5, 2, 2, 4)	τρισ-χί-λι-οι	(6, 2, 4)
συν-ο-μο-λο-γῶ	(5, 2, 2, 2)	ὑπερ-ά-γα-θος	(5, 2, 2)
συ-στη-μα-τι-κός	(2, 2, 2, 2)	ὑπερ-άν-θρω-πος	(5, 3, 2)
σχο-λαρ-χεῖ-ον	(2, 3, 4)	ὑπέρ-λαμ-προς	(5, 3)
σω-μα-τεμ-πο-ρία	(2, 2, 3, 2)	φιλ-ά-δελ-φος	(6, 2, 3)
σω-φρο-νι-στή-ρι-ον	(2, 2, 2, 2, 4)	χα-λύ-βδι-νος	(2, 2, 2)
τε-λει-ο-ποί-η-σις	(2, 4, 2, 4, 2)	ψευ-δο-μάρ-τυς	(2, 2, 3)
τη-λέ-γραμ-μα	(2, 2, 3)	ὠρύ-ο-μαι	(4, 2)
τμη-μα-τάρ-χης	(2, 2, 3)	ὠφε-λι-μό-της	(2, 2, 2)

Accents and Diacritics

The three accent marks used in Greek now all represent the same thing—loud stress, although in Classical Greek they are supposed to have represented different pitch accents:

1. The acute (´), which may occur on the vowel, or on the second vowel of a diphthong, in any one of the last three syllables of a word.

2. The circumflex (˜, ^), which may occur on the vowel, or on the second vowel of a diphthong, in either of the last two syllables of a word. The circumflex never appears over ε or ο.

3. The grave (`), which may occur only on the vowel, or on the second vowel of a diphthong, in the last syllable of a word; such a word must be followed directly by another word, not a period or comma.

Greek orthography also employs two "breathing" marks:

1. The rough breathing, or spiritus asper ('), which occurs on an initial vowel, or on the second vowel of an initial diphthong. It has no phonetic value, although in Classical Greek it represented an *h* sound before the vowel or diphthong; in transliteration, it may be represented by *h*.

2. The smooth breathing, or spiritus lenis ('), which occurs on an initial vowel, or second vowel of an initial diphthong. It has no phonetic value, and in Classical Greek represented a lack of *h* sound before the vowel.

In text, these breathings and the grave and acute accent marks are placed above and to the left of capital vowel letters, rather than directly above.

Some words, called enclitics, may appear with no written accent at all; the word preceding an enclitic, however (unless it too is an enclitic), will always have at least one accent mark and may have two; e.g., τυιαῦτά ἐστι.

Another diacritical mark is the dieresis (trema) (¨), which occurs on the second of two vowels to indicate that they do not form a diphthong, which otherwise they would form: καϋμένος (pronounced *kaeeménos* instead of *kavménos*).

These diacritical marks may form combinations, as follows:

῍ lenis acute	῝ asper grave	῎ dieresis acute
῎ lenis grave	῏ circumflex lenis	῏ dieresis grave
῞ asper acute	῟ circumflex asper	

An iota is often placed beneath the vowel α, η, or ω, mainly to indicate a declensional or conjugational inflection: ῇ, the nominative plural of ἡ; τιμᾷ, third person singular of τιμῶ. This iota is called iota subscript.

Capitalization

Capitalization is practically the same as in English. The pronoun of address is usually capitalized. (This does not apply to Classical Greek.) Capital letters do not take diacritical marks. If a lowercase accented vowel is capitalized, the accent mark is dropped. (In Classical Greek this is quite true but this statement should perhaps be modified to the effect that it applies to whole words spelled out in capitals, not to those beginning with capitals; the example illustrates the case well.) An initial capital vowel, however, carries the accent mark before it. The iota subscript may be placed either beneath the vowel or changed into a regular iota and placed right after the vowel. Thus the words ἅγιος, ᾅδης, and ἀπό, if capitalized, are set ῞ΑΓΙΟΣ, ῞ΑΔΗΣ, and ᾿ΑΠΟ. ῞Αϲης may also be set ῞Αιδης. In Classical Greek iota subscript cannot stand under capital; if the letter under which it stands is capitalized then iota subscript becomes iota adscript; e.g., ΤΗΙ ΩΙΔΗΙ—τῇ ᾠδῇ or Ὠιδῇ.

Punctuation

The comma, the period, and the exclamation point are the same as in English and are used similarly. The semicolon and the colon are represented by a point above the line. The question mark resembles the English semicolon. The scheme for quotation marks is the same as in the western languages.

Abbreviations

A. E.	Αὐτοῦ Ἐξοχότης, His Excellency		ν. ἡμ.	νέον ἡμερολόγιον, New Calendar
A. M.	Αὐτοῦ Μεγαλειότης, His Majesty		Ο´	Ἑβδομήκοντα, Septuagint
B. Δ.	Βασιλικὸν Διάταγμα, Royal Decree		Π. Δ.	παλαιὰ Διαθήκη, Old Testament; Προεδρικὸν Διάταγμα, Presidential Order
βλ.	βλέπε, see			
δηλ.	δηλαδή, that is, namely, to wit		πλ.	πληθυντικός, plural
δρ.	δραχμή, drachma		π. μ.	πρὸ μεσημβρίας, a.m.
δράμ.	δράμιον, dram		πρβλ.	παράβαλε, compare, cf.
Δ. Φ.	Διδάκτωρ Φιλοσοφίας, Ph.D.		π. Χ.	πρὸ Χριστοῦ, B.C.
Δ. Ν.	Διδάκτωρ Νομικῆς, LL.D.		π. χ.	παραδείγματος χάριν, for example, e.g.
ἔ. ἀ.	ἔνθα ἀνωτέρω, loc. cit.			
ἰδ.	ἰδέ, see		σεβ.	σεβαστός, Hon.
I. X.	Ἰησοῦς Χριστός, Jesus Christ		σελ.	σελίς, page
Καθ.	Καθηγητής, Prof.		στήλ.	στήλη, column
Κος	Κύριος, Mr.		σύγκρ.	σύγκρινε, compare, cf.
Κα	Κυρία, Mrs.		τ. ἔ.	τοῦτ’ ἔστιν, that is, i.e.
κτλ.	καὶ τὰ λοιπά, etc.		τόμ.	τόμος, volume
κ. τ. ὅ.	καὶ τά ὅμοια, and the like		Τ. Σ.	τόπος σφραγίδος, L.S., locosigilli
κφλ.	κεφάλαιον, chapter		τρ. ἔτ.	τρέχοντος ἔτους, current year
λπτ.	λεπτά, lepta		φ.	φύλλον, folio
μέρ.	μέρος, part		χιλ.	χιλιόμετρον, kilometer
μ. μ.	μετὰ μεσημβρίαν, p.m.			
μ. Χ.	μετὰ Χριστόν, A.D.			
N. Δ.	Νέα Διαθήκη, New Testament; Νομοθετικὸν Διάταγμα, Legislative Ordinance			

Cardinal Numbers

εἷς (ἕνας), μία, ἕν(α)	one		δεκατέσσαρες (m. and f.), δεκατέσσαρα (n.)	fourteen
δύο	two			
τρεῖς, τρία	three		δεκαπέντε, etc.	fifteen, etc.
τέσσαρες, -α	four		εἴκοσι	twenty
πέντε	five		εἴκοσι ἕνα (m. and n.), εἴκοσι μία (f.)	twenty-one
ἕξ(ι)	six			
ἑπτά (ἑφτά)	seven			
ὀκτὼ	eight		εἴκοσι δύο, etc.	twenty-two, etc.
ἐννέα	nine		τριά(κο)ντα	thirty
δέκα	ten		σαράντα	forty
ἕνδεκα	eleven		πενῆντα	fifty
δώδεκα	twelve		ἑξῆντα	sixty
δεκατρεῖς (m. and f.), δεκατρία (n.)	thirteen		ἑβδομῆντα	seventy
			ὀγδῶντα	eighty

ἐνενῆντα	ninety	τριακόσια	three hundred
ἑκατόν	one hundred	τετ ρακόσια, etc.	four hundred, etc.
ἑκατὸν ἕνας, etc.	one hundred and one, etc.	χίλια	thousand
		δύο χιλιάδες, etc.	two thousand, etc.
διακόσια	two hundred	ἕν ἑκατομμύριον	one million

NOTE: Modern Greek uses the Arabic figures for ordinary number work. Where Western languages use Roman numerals, the Modern Greek uses the same scheme of letters as used in Classical Greek.

Ordinal Numbers

πρῶτος	first	εἰκοστὸς	twentieth
δεύτερος	second	εἰκοστὸς πρῶτος, etc.	twenty-first, etc.
τρίτος	third		
τέταρτος	fourth	τριακοστὸς	thirtieth
πέμπτος	fifth	τεσσαρακοστὸς	fortieth
ἕκτος	sixth	πεντηκοστὸς	fiftieth
ἕβδομος	seventh	ἑξηκοστὸς	sixtieth
ὄγδοος	eighth	ἑβδομηκοστὸς	seventieth
ἔννατος	ninth	ὀγδοηκοστὸς	eightieth
δέκατος	tenth	ἐνενηκοστὸς, etc.	ninetieth, etc.
ἑνδέκατος	eleventh	ἑκατοστὸς	hundredth
δωδέκατος	twelfth	χιλιοστὸς	thousandth
δέκατος τ ρίτος, etc.	thirteenth, etc.	ἑκατομμυριοστὸς	millionth

Months

Ἰανουάριος	January	Ἰούλιος	July
Φεβρουάριος	February	Αὔγουστος	August
Μάρτιος	March	Σεπτέμβριος	September
Ἀπρίλιος	April	Ὀκτώβριος	October
Μάϊος	May	Νοέμβριος	November
Ἰούνιος	June	Δεκέμβριος	December

Days

Κυριακή	Sunday	Πέμπτη	Thursday
Δευτέρα	Monday	Παρασκευὴ	Friday
Τρίτη	Tuesday	Σάββατο(ν)	Saturday
Τετάρτη	Wednesday		

Seasons

ἄνοιξις	spring	φθινόπωρον	autumn
καλοκαῖρι	summer	χειμών (χειμῶνας)	winter

Time

ὥρα	hour	μήνας	month
ἡμέρα	day	ἔτος	year
ἑβδομὰς	week		

Italian

Alphabet and Pronunciation

A	a	*a* in far
B	b	*b;* all consonant letters may be doubled, and then pronounced long, as *n* (*k*) *n* in penknife, etc.
C	c	*c* in scan (= *k*) before *a, o, u,* and consonants; before *e* or *i*, similar to *ch* in chant; *cia, cie, cio,* and *ciu* pronounced as *cha* in chart, *che* in check or *cha* in chafe, *cho* in chortle, and *chu* in Manchu, respectively; *ccia,* etc., sound like *tch,* etc.; *scia, scie, scio,* and *sciu* pronounced as *sha* in sharp, *she* in shepherd, *sho* in show, and *sho* in shoe, respectively
D	d	*d*
E	e	*a* in grate; *e* in bell
F	f	*f*
G	g	*g* in gay before *a, o, u,* and consonants; before *e* or *i* like *j; gia, gie, gio,* and *giu* pronounced as *ja* in jar, *je* in jet, between *ja* in jaw and *jo* in joke, and *ju* in jury, respectively; *ggia,* etc., sound like *d* plus *ja,* etc.
H	h	silent, but makes a preceding *c* or *g* hard
I	i	*e* in me; *i* preceded by *c, sc,* or *g* and followed by *a, o,* or *u* is silent unless stressed; before or after more highly stressed vowel, *i* is similar to *y* in yes and in boy, respectively
J	j	*y* in yes; now obsolete and replaced by *i*
K	k	*k;* only in foreign words
L	l	*l* in million
M	m	*m*
N	n	*n*
O	o	*o* in note; *aw* in saw
P	p	*p* in spin
Q	q	always with following *u; qu* pronounced as in quick
R	r	*r* in three
S	s	*s;* usually *z* between two vowels; *scia, scie, scio,* and *sciu* are pronounced *sha, she, sho,* and *shu,* respectively
T	t	*t* in step
U	u	*oo* in coo; before or after more highly stressed vowel, *u* is similar to *w* in wet and how, respectively
V	v	*v*
W	w	} only in foreign words
X	x	
Y	y	*i;* only in foreign words
Z	z	*ts* in quarts or *ds* in adz

Special Characters

Italian uses the Latin alphabet. It has no special characters; accents are employed only to a limited extent.

Vowels and Consonants

The vowels are *a, e, i, o, u,* and *y;* the other letters of the alphabet are consonants.

Diphthongs

The combination of an *i* or *u* with another, more highly stressed, vowel may be regarded as diphthongal.

Digraphs

The digraphs and their sounds are:

ch as *c* in cat only before *e, i*

gh as *g* in go only before *e, i*

gl as *ll* in million [1]

gn as in cognac (= *ny* in canyon)

qu as in squalor

sc as *sh* in shall (before *e* or *i*)

Consonantal Units

For the purpose of syllabification, a mute consonant followed by a liquid consonant is a consonantal unit. Hence, the following are consonantal units:

bl, br	*dr,*	*gl, gr*	*tl, tr*
chr, cl, cr	*fl, fr*	*pl, pr*	*vl, vr*

Also the combination of the letter *s* with any other following consonant, digraph, or consonantal unit is a unit for purposes of syllabification.

Rules for Syllabification

1. Digraphs and consonantal units may not be divided.

2. Division is made on a vowel before a single consonant, digraph, or consonantal unit: *ami-co, ba-gno, ca-pra, giu-sto, ma-schera, ro-stro.*

3. In a group of two or more consonants, division is made before the last consonant, digraph, or consonantal unit: *sab-bia, ac-qua, ist-mo, an-che, com-pro.*

4. Division may be made between vowels only if they are strong, that is, *a, e, o*. Hence, only the following vowel groups may be divided: *aa, ae, ao; ea, ee, eo; oa, oe, oo: be-ato, co-atto, po-eta*, etc.

5. Prefixes are kept intact only if this conforms to rules 2 to 4: *con-stare* (rule 3), *pro-emio* (rule 4), *pro-getto* (rule 2), *sub-marino* (rule 3); but *co-nestabile* (rule 2), *proi-bire* (rule 2), *su-bordinare* (rule 2). [2]

6. Compound words are divided according to their component parts (and each part according to rules 1 to 5): *gentil-uomo, cento-uno.*

If a compound is formed with an apostrophe, division may not be made on the apostrophe; thus *dell'albero, un'arte, dovrebb'essere* may be divided only *del-l'al-be-ro, un'ar-te, do-vreb-b'es-se-re*, respectively. A compound may be divided also by making use of the full article or word: *dello albero, dovrebbe essere.*

7. Foreign words and components of foreign words (not naturalized) follow the conventions of the language of origin: *Wash-ington, Haps-burg, Hamp-shire, reichs-bank, Wag-ner.*

Illustrative Word Divisions

[The numbers in parentheses refer to the syllabification rules]

ab-bo-na-men-to	(3, 2, 2, 3)	de-mo-cra-ti-co	(2, 2, 2, 2)
ac-quie-sce-re	(3, 2, 2)	dia-gno-sti-co	(2, 2, 2)
ae-re-o-li-to	(2, 4, 2, 2)	di-scor-so	(2, 3)
af-fli-to	(3, 2)	di-sgra-zia	(2, 2)
ame-ri-ca-no	(2, 2, 2)	di-sor-di-ne	(2, 3, 2, 2)
bi-gliet-taio	(2, 3)	di-spo-si-zio-ne	(2, 2, 2, 2)
bis-a-vo-lo	(6, 2, 2)	di-stin-ti-vo	(2, 3, 2)
bi-so-gni-no	(2, 2, 2)	emi-sfe-ro	(2, 2)
Bre-ta-gna	(2, 2)	Epi-sco-pa-to	(2, 2, 2)
Buck-ing-ham	(7, 7)	esa-e-dro	(4, 2)
co-o-pe-ra-zio-ne	(4, 2, 2, 2, 2)	espa-tria-zio-ne	(2, 2, 2)
co-stret-to	(2, 3)	espe-rien-za	(2, 3)
cre-sce-re	(2, 2)	estra-di-zio-ne	(2, 2, 2)

---

[1] In a few words *gl* is not a digraph and is pronounced as *gl* in angle; for example: *Ganglio, glicerina, geroglifico, glifo, gloria, negligere*, etc.

[2] Usage varies as to this rule; some orthographers still prefer dividing on the prefix. The rule given in the text above follows the recommendation of Leone Donati, *Corso Pràtico di Lingua Italiana*, 207, 1934, Orell Füssli Editori, Zurigo e Lipsia. It is followed by most dictionaries as well as general works extant.

exe-qua-tur	(2, 2)	ist-mi-co	(3, 2)
fan-ta-sma-go-ria	(3, 2, 2, 2)	isto-lo-gi-co	(2, 2, 2)
fa-sci-smo	(2, 2)	istru-men-to	(2, 3)
fi-lan-tro-pi-smo	(2, 3, 2, 2)	ita-lia-no	(2, 2)
fo-sfo-re-scen-za	(2, 2, 2, 3)	Kam-tsciat-ka	(7, 3)
fo-to-e-lio-gra-fia	(2, 6, 2, 2, 2)	l'al-tr'ie-ri	(3, 2)
Fre-de-ris-bur-go	(2, 2, 7, 3)	ma-gne-ti-co	(2, 2, 2)
gen-til-uo-mo	(3, 6, 2)	ma-gni-fi-cen-te	(2, 2, 2, 3)
ge-o-gno-sti-co	(4, 2, 2, 2)	me-sme-ri-smo	(2, 2, 2)
in-du-stria-le	(3, 2, 2)	me-te-o-ri-te	(2, 4, 2, 2)
ine-scu-sa-bi-le	(2, 2, 2, 2)	mil-li-gram-mo	(3, 2, 3)
ine-spli-ca-bi-le	(2, 2, 2, 2)	mi-san-tro-po	(2, 3, 2)
in-fi-schio	(3, 2)	mi-scre-den-te	(2, 2, 3)
inin-tel-li-gen-te	(3, 3, 2, 3)	neu-tra-liz-za-re	(2, 2, 3, 2)
inor-ga-ni-co	(3, 2, 2)	tra-sfor-ma-zio-ne	(2, 3, 2, 2)
in-scrit-to-re	(3, 3, 2)	tra-spor-ta-re	(2, 3, 2)
in-te-res-se	(3, 2, 3)	ve-sci-chet-ta	(2, 2, 3)
iscri-zio-ne	(2, 2)	zo-o-sper-ma	(4, 2, 3)

Stress and Diacritics

No simple rules can be formulated for word stress in Italian. The majority of words receive their stress on the penultimate (next to the last) syllable: *aMIco, comPLEto;* fewer words are stressed on the antepenultimate (third from the last) syllable: *FABrico, gramMAtica;* only a limited number are stressed on the ultimate (last) syllable, but in this case the vowel carries the grave accent: *citTÀ fabbriCO.*

☆ Accent marks are used only to a limited degree—chiefly to indicate a final stressed syllable. Generally a grave (`) is used when the final vowel is open and an acute (´) is used when that vowel is closed. Word types illustrating these usages are:

(*a*) Nouns ending in *ta* or *tu* having the singular and plural alike: *libertà, virtú* (from the Latin *libertade, virtude,* etc.).

(*b*) Verbs in the third person singular past absolute and first and third persons singular future: *comprò* (he bought), *comprerò* (I shall buy), *comprerà* (he will buy); similarly in the second and third conjugations: *vendé, venderò, venderà; finí, finirò, finirà.*

(*c*) Homonyms. The most common of these homonyms are:

ché, because	*che*, that	*né*, neither, nor	*ne*, of it, of them
colà, there	*cola*, strainer	*piè*, foot	*pie*, pious
costà, there	*costa*, shore	*però*, therefore	*pero*, pear tree
dà, gives	*da*, by, from, to	*sè*, himself	*se*, if
dí, day	*di*, of	*sí*, yes	*si*, himself, one
è, is	*e*, and	*tè*, tea	*te*, thee
là, there	*la*, the, her	*testè*, just now	*teste*, heads
lí, there	*li*, the, them		

(*d*) Monosyllables terminating in two vowels, to indicate that the preceding vowel is shortened: *ciò, già, giú, piú, può, quà.*

(*e*) Terminations *ia* and *io* in which the *i* is to be stressed: *magìa, desìo.*

The acute is used by some editors to distinguish words differently stressed, where otherwise a misunderstanding might arise: *malvágia* (wicked), *malvagía* (malmsey, a wine). This use is rare.

The circumflex is used to indicate contraction: *cacciâr* (for *cacciarono*), *ginnasî* (for *ginnasii*). This use is rare.

The dieresis (trema) is used in poetry over the *i* to indicate that it is to be sounded separately from a following vowel: *armonïoso* (pronounced *armoni-oso,* instead of *armonio-so*). This use is rare.

Capitalization

Capitalization in Italian is similar to that in English, with a few exceptions:

(*a*) Proper adjectives are lowercased: *la lingua italiana*, the Italian language, but *gl'Italiani*, the Italians (proper noun).

(*b*) The names of days and months are lowercased.

(*c*) Titles followed by name are lowercased: *il signor Donati*, Mr. Donati; *il principe Umberto*, Prince Umberto.

(*d*) The pronoun *io, I*, is lowercased, but the pronouns of formal address, *Ella, Lei, Loro*, all meaning *you*, are sometimes capitalized. These pronouns, however, in modern Italian usage, and *Lei* in particular, are *not* capitalized in a written text except for that of a letter, and a formal one at that. *Ella* is often capitalized in poetry.

(*e*) In poetry, the first word of each line is usually lowercased.

Punctuation

Punctuation is similar to that of English. The comma is used to point off all clauses, restrictive as well as descriptive. Commas are not used, however, with the conjunction *e* in a series of several words. The apostrophe is used to indicate vowel elision only: *un'opera d'arte* (for *una opera di arte*), *sopra 'l letto* (for *sopra il letto*). The space after the apostrophe is no longer required.

Quotation Marks

Used less often than in English.

In the text of a dialog they are often substituted by a new paragraph for each speech, sometimes preceded by a long dash.

Titles of books, poems, and articles are usually entered in quotation marks in a text. Titles of books are sometimes entered in italic, and periodicals, more often than books, are also entered in italic in a text.

[No authority specifically stating this found. However, the use of quotation marks as stated above can be seen in Hall's text. In any Italian text or newspaper the above use of italic can also be observed.]

Abbreviations

a/c.	a conto, account	fasc.	fascicolo, number, part
a.c.	anno corrente, current year	f(err).	ferrovia, railroad
a.D.	anno Domini, in the year of our Lord	f.co	franco, post free
a.m., ant.	antimeridiano, a. m.	F.lli	Fratelli, brothers
a.p.	anno passato, last year	Giun.	Giuniore, junior
c.m.	corrente mese, instant	I. Cl.	prima classe, first class
C.ª	Compagnia, company	Ill.mo	Illustrissimo, most illustrious
d.C.	dopo Cristo, after Christ	lit., £	lire
Dep.prov.	Deputato provinciale, member of the provincial parliament	LL. MM.	Loro Maestà, Their Majesties
		N.ⁱ	Numeri, numbers
disp.	dispensa, number, part	N.º	Numero, number
ecc.	eccetera, etc.	On.	Onorevole, Honorable
Ed.	Edizione, edition; Editore, editor	p.m.,	pomeridiane, p.m.
es.	esempio, example	pom.	

Cardinal Numbers

uno	one	tredici	thirteen
due	two	quattordici	fourteen
tre	three	quindici	fifteen
quattro	four	sedici	sixteen
cinque	five	diciassette ⎫	
sei	six	diciasette ⎭	seventeen
sette	seven	diciotto	eighteen
otto	eight	diciannove ⎫	
nove	nine	dicianove ⎭	nineteen
dieci	ten	venti	twenty
undici	eleven	ventuno	twenty-one
dodici	twelve	ventidue	twenty-two

ventitrè, etc.	twenty-three, etc.	novanta	ninety
ventotto, etc.	twenty-eight, etc.	novantuno, etc.	ninety-one, etc.
trenta	thirty	cento	hundred
quaranta	forty	cent(o) uno, etc.	one hundred and one, etc.
cinquanta	fifty		
sessanta	sixty	duecento, etc.	two hundred, etc.
settanta	seventy	mille, mila	thousand
ottanta	eighty	duemila, etc.	two thousand, etc.

Ordinal Numbers

primo, -a	first	ventesimo	twentieth
secondo	second	ventunesimo	twenty-first,
terzo	third	ventesimo primo, etc.	etc.
quarto	fourth	trentesimo	thirtieth
quinto	fifth	quarantesimo	fortieth
sesto	sixth	cinquantesimo	fiftieth
settimo	seventh	sessantesimo, etc.	sixtieth, etc.
ottavo	eighth	centesimo	hundredth
nono	ninth	centesimo primo, etc.	one hundred and first, etc.
decimo	tenth		
decimo primo } undicesimo	eleventh	duecentesimo	two hundredth
		trecentesimo, etc.	three hundredth, etc.
dodicesimo	twelfth	millesimo	thousandth
tredicesimo	thirteenth		
quattordicesimo } decimo quarto, etc.	fourteenth, etc.		

Months

gennaio (genn.)	January	luglio	July
febbraio (febb.)	February	agosto	August
marzo	March	settembre (sett.)	September
aprile	April	ottobre (ott.)	October
maggio (magg.)	May	novembre (nov.)	November
giugno	June	dicembre (dic.)	December

Days

domenica	Sunday	giovedì	Thursday
lunedì	Monday	venerdì	Friday
martedì	Tuesday	sabato	Saturday
mercoledì	Wednesday		

Seasons

| primavera | spring | autunno | autumn |
| estate | summer | inverno | winter |

Time

ora	hour	mese	month
giorno	day	anno	year
settimana	week		

Latin

Alphabet and Pronunciation

A	a	long: *ah;* short: *o* in hot	O	o	long: *o* in note; short: *o* in fort
B	b	*b*	P	p	*p*
C	c	*k*	Q	q	*k*
D	d	*d*	R	r	*r*
E	e	long: *e* in there; short: *e* in met	S	s	*s*
F	f	*f*	T	t	*t*
G	g	*g* in go	U	u	long; *oo* in food; short: *oo* in good; like *w* after *q*, and usually after other consonants before another vowel
H	h	*h*			
I	i	long: *ee;* short: *i* in sit			
J	j	*y* in yet			
K	k	*k*	V	v	*w*
L	l	*l*	X	x	*ks*
M	m	*m*	Y	y	*ee; i* as for *i*
N	n	*n*	Z	z	*z*

Consonants

Formerly *u* and *v* were written with *v*, and *i* and *j* with *i*. Modern texts customarily distinguish both pairs. Thus: *uva, visu, janua, Jove.*

K, z, and *y* are rather rare, occurring mostly in loanwords. *Q* is used only in the combination *qu*, pronounced *kw*.

The digraphs *ch, ph,* and *th* are pronounced as *k, f,* and *t,* respectively.

Vowels

Each of the five vowels is either long or short in each occurrence, and an accurate pronunciation will reflect this difference. Elementary texts usually mark the long vowels with a macron; thus: *ā, ē, ī, ō, ū.*

Diphthongs

Two short vowels may occur together in the same syllable, in which case the second of the two is a semivowel; i.e., *u* as the second element of a diphthong is pronounced like *w*, and *i* or *e* in this position is pronounced like *y*. The commonest diphthongs are *ae* and *au*, pronounced to rhyme with high and how. Less common are *ei* (as in vein), *eu, oe* (as *oi* in oil), and *ui.*

Consonantal Units [1]

The following combinations are referred to as consonant clusters in the rules given below for syllabification: *bl, br, cl, cr, dr, fl, fr, gl, gr, pl, pr, tl, tr, scr, str, spl, spr.*

The digraphs *ch, ph,* and *th* are treated just like *c, f,* and *t* in consonant clusters.

Rules for Syllabification

1. Diphthongs, digraphs, and consonant clusters may not be divided.
2. Division is made on a vowel or on a diphthong before a single consonant, a digraph, or a consonant cluster: *ca-sus, si-pho, pa-tres, cae-lum.*
3. In a group of two or more consonants, division is made before the last consonant, digraph, or consonant cluster: *vit-ta, mag-nus, punc-tus, bac-chor, am-plus.*
4. Division may be made between vowels not constituting a diphthong: *pu-er, di-es, fili-us, Tro-ius.*

---

[1] Some Latin lexicographers still use the classic method of determining consonantal units; namely, any group of consonants which can begin a word constitutes a consonantal unit and may begin a syllable. This method is still in use in Greek syllabification; but in present-day Latin orthography it has been largely replaced by the Romance-language method.

5. Certain adverbial prefixes are kept intact. These are: *ab, ante, circum, cis, con, de, ex, extra, in, inter, intro, ob, per, prae, praeter, per, post, pro(d), propter, re(d), sub, super, supra,* and *trans: ab-eo, con-scrip-tum, inter-esse.*

6. Compound words are divided according to their component parts (and each part according to rules 1 to 5): *quot-annis, et-enim, sic-ut.*

7. The letter *x* is retained with the preceding syllable: *dix-it.*

NOTE.—The above rules do not apply to anglicized Latin scientific names used in English works. Their syllabification follows the English practice.

Illustrative Word Divisions

[The numbers in parentheses refer to the syllabification rules]

ab-a-li-e-no	(5, 2, 4, 2)	prod-es-se	(5, 3)
ab-scin-do	(5, 3)	proe-li-um	(2,4)
ac-cli-na-tus	(3, 2, 2)	pro-stra-tum	(5, 2)
ad-ae-qua-tus	(5, 2, 2)	pro-sub-ac-tum	(5, 5, 3)
ad-emp-tus	(5, 3)	pu-bli-ca-tus	(2, 2, 2)
am-plex-us	(3, 7)	quam-ob-rem	(6, 6)
cir-cum-ac-tus	(3, 5, 3)	quem-ad-mo-dum	(6, 6, 2)
Cis-al-pi-nus	(5, 3, 2)	re-cru-des-co	(5, 2, 3)
con-sue-tus	(5, 2)	red-ac-tus	(5, 3)
de-spon-sum	(5, 3)	re-duc-tus	(5, 3)
et-e-nim	(6, 2)	re-frac-tum	(5, 3)
ex-em-plum	(7, 3)	re-spec-tus	(5, 3)
in-a-nis	(5, 2)	res-pu-bli-ca	(6, 2, 2)
in-ep-ti	(5, 3)	ses-cen-ti	(6, 3)
in-ter-ea	(3, 5)	sua-de-re	(2, 2)
ne-sci-tus	(6, 2)	sub-ac-tio	(5, 3)
ob-la-tus	(5, 2)	su-pra-scan-do	(2, 5, 3)
per-ac-tus	(5, 3)	trans-ab-i-tum	(5, 5, 2)
per-e-git	(5, 2)	trans-ad-ac-tum	(5, 5, 3)
pe-ri-cli-ta-tio	(2, 2, 2, 2)	tran-su-tum	(3, 2)
post-ea-quam	(5, 6)	tri-um-pho	(4, 3)
post-hu-mus	(5, 2)	tu-mul-tu-o-sus	(2, 3, 4, 2)
post-sce-ni-um	(5, 2, 4)	una-ni-mus	(2, 2)
pos-tu-la-tus	(3, 2, 2)	usus-fruc-tus	(6, 3)
prae-scrip-tus	(5, 3)	va-li-dus	(2, 2)
prae-ter-i-tum	(2, 5, 2)	Xe-no-phon	(2,2)

Stress

Words of two syllables are always stressed on the first syllable: *ROma, LIber.*

In words of more than two syllables, the stress is on the next to the last syllable if that syllable ends in a consonant, a long vowel, or a diphthong. Otherwise the stress is on the third from the last syllable. Thus: ho-NO-ris, CON-su-lis.

Capitalization and Punctuation

American editors usually follow the English conventions in capitalization and punctuation.

Abbreviations

a., annus, year; ante, before

A.A.C., anno ante Christum, in the year before Christ

A.A.S., Academiae Americanae Socius, Fellow of the American Academy [Academy of Arts and Sciences]

A.B., artium baccalaureus, bachelor of arts

ab init., ab initio, from the beginning

abs. re., absente reo, the defendant being absent

A.C., ante Christum, before Christ

A.D., anno Domini, in the year of our Lord

a.d., ante diem, before the day

ad fin., ad finem, at the end, to one end

ad h.l., ad hunc locum, to this place, on this passage

ad inf., ad infinitum, to infinity

ad init., ad initium, at the beginning

ad int., ad interim, in the meantime

ad lib., ad libitum, at pleasure

ad loc., ad locum, at the place

ad val., ad valorem, according to value

A.I., anno inventionis, in the year of the discovery

al., alia, alii, other things, other persons

A.M., anno mundi, in the year of the world; Annus mirabilis, the wonderful year [1666]; a.m., ante meridiem, before noon

an., anno, in the year; ante, before

ann., annales, annals; anni, years

A.R.S.S., Antiquariorum Regiae Societatis Socius, Fellow of the Royal Society of Antiquaries

A.U.C., anno urbis conditae, ab urbe conolita, in [the year from] the building of the City [Rome], 753 B.C.

B.A., baccalaureus artium, bachelor of arts

B.Sc., baccalaureus scientiae, bachelor of science

C., centum, a hundred; condemno, I condemn, find guilty

c., circa, about

cent., centum, a hundred

cf., confer, compare

C.M., chirurgiae magister, master of surgery

coch., cochlear, a spoon, spoonful

coch. amp., cochlear amplum, a tablespoonful

coch. mag., cochlear magnum, a large spoonful

coch. med., cochlear medium, a dessert spoonful

coch. parv., cochlear parvum, a teaspoonful

con., contra, against; conjunx, wife

C.P.S., custos privati sigilli, keeper of the privy seal

C.S., custos sigilli, keeper of the seal

cwt., c. for centum, wt. for weight, hundredweight

D., Deus, God; Dominus, Lord; d., decretum, a decree; denarius, a penny; da, give

D.D., divinitatis doctor, doctor of divinity

D.G., Dei gratia, by the grace of God; Deo gratias, thanks to God

D.N., Dominus noster, our Lord

D.Sc., doctor scientiae, doctor of science

d.s.p., decessit sine prole, died without issue

D.V., Deo volente, God willing

dwt., d. for denarius, wt. for weight pennyweight

e.g., exempli gratia, for example

et al., et alibi, and elsewhere; et alii, or aliae, and others

etc., et cetera, and others, and so forth

et seq., et sequentes, and those that follow

et ux., et uxor, and wife

F., filius, son

f., fiat, let it be made; forte, strong

fac., factum similis, facsimile, an exact copy

fasc., fasciculus, a bundle

fl., flores, flowers; floruit, flourished; fluidus, fluid

f.r., folio recto, right-hand page

F.R.S., Fraternitatis Regiae Socius, Fellow of the Royal Society

f.v., folio verso, on the back of the leaf

guttat., guttatim, by drops

H., hora, hour

h.a., hoc anno, in this year; hujus anni, this year's

hab. corp., habeas corpus, have the body—a writ

h.e., hic est, this is; hoc est, that is

h.m., hoc mense, in this month; huius mensis, this month's

h.q., hoc quaere, look for this

H.R.I.P., hic requiescat in pace, here rests in peace

H.S., hic sepultus, here is buried; hic situs, here lies; h.s., hoc sensu, in this sense

H.S.S., Historiae Societatis Socius, Fellow of the Historical Society

h.t., hoc tempore, at this time; hoc titulo, in or under this title

I, Idus, the Ides; i., id, that; immortalis, immortal

ib. or ibid., ibidem, in the same place

id., idem, the same

i.e., id est, that is

imp., imprimatur, sanction, let it be printed

I.N.D., in nomine Dei, in the name of God

in f., in fine, at the end

inf., infra, below

init., initio, in the beginning

in lim., in limine, on the threshold, at the outset

in loc., in loco, in its place

in loc. cit., in loco citato, in the place cited

in pr., in principio, in the beginning

in trans., in transitu, on the way

i.q., idem quod, the same as

i.q.e.d., id quod erat demonstrandum, what was to be proved

J., judex, judge

J.C.D., juris civilis doctor, doctor of civil law

J.D., jurum doctor, doctor of laws

J.U.D., juris utriusque doctor, doctor of both civil and canon law

L., liber, a book; locus, a place

£, libra, pound; placed before figures, thus £10; if l., to be placed after, as 40 l.

L.A.M., liberalium artium magister, master of the liberal arts

L.B., baccalaureus literarum, bachelor of letters

lb., libra, pound (singular and plural)

L.H.D., literarum humaniorum doctor, doctor of the more humane letters

Litt. D., literarum doctor, doctor of letters

LL.B., legum baccalaureus, bachelor of laws

LL.D., legum doctor, doctor of laws

LL.M., legum magister, master of laws

loc. cit., loco citato, in the place cited

loq., loquitur, he, or she, speaks

L.S., locus sigilli, the place of the seal

l.s.c., loco supra citato, in the place above cited

£ s. d., librae, solidi, denarii, pounds, shillings, pence

M., magister, master; manipulus, handful; medicinae, of medicine; m., meridies, noon

M.A., magister artium, master of arts

M.B., medicinae baccalaureus, bachelor of medicine

M. Ch., magister chirurgiae, master of surgery

M.D., medicinae doctor, doctor of medicine

m.m., mutatis mutandis, with the necessary changes

m.n., mutato nomine, the name being changed

MS., manuscriptum, manuscript; MSS., manuscripta, manuscripts

Mus. B., musicae baccalaureus, bachelor of music

Mus. D., musicae doctor, doctor of music

Mus. M., musicae magister, master of music

N., Nepos, grandson; nomen, name; nomina, names; noster, our; n., natus, born; nocte, at night

N.B., nota bene, mark well

ni. pri., nisi prius, unless before

nob., nobis, for (or on) our part

nol. pros., nolle prosequi, will not prosecute

non cul., non culpabilis, not guilty

n.l., non licet, it is not permitted; non liquet, it is not clear; non longe, not far

non obs., non obstante, notwithstanding

non pros., non prosequitur, he does not prosecute

non seq., non sequitur, it does not follow logically

O., octarius, a pint

ob., obiit, he, or she, died; obiter, incidentally

ob. s.p., obiit sine prole, died without issue

o.c., opere citato, in the work cited

op., opus, work; opera, works

op. cit., opere citato, in the work cited

P., papa, pope; pater, father; pontifex, bishop; populus, people; p., partim, in part; per, by, for; pius, holy; pondere, by weight; post, after; primus, first; pro, for

p.a., or per ann., per annum, yearly; pro anno, for the year

p. ae., partes aequales, equal parts

pass., passim, everywhere

percent., per centum, by the hundred

pil., pilula, pill

Ph. B., philosophiae baccalaureus, bachelor of philosophy

P.M., post mortem, after death

p.m., post meridiem, afternoon

pro tem., pro tempore, for the time being

prox., proximo, in or of the next [month]

P.S., postscriptum, postscript; P.SS., postscripta, postscripts

q.d., quasi dicat, as if one should say; quasi dictum, as if said; quasi dixisset, as if he had said

q.e., quod est, which is

Q.E.D., quod erat demonstrandum, which was to be demonstrated

Q.E.F., quod erat faciendum, which was to be done

Q.E.I., quod erat inveniendum, which was to be found out

q.l., quantum libet, as much as you please

q. pl., quantum placet, as much as seems good

q.s., quantum sufficit, sufficient quantity

q.v., quantum vis, as much as you will; quem, quam, quod vide, which see; qq. v., quos, quas, or quae vide, which see (plural)

R., regina, queen; recto, right-hand page; respublica, commonwealth

℞, recipe, take

R.I.P., requiescat, or requiescant, in pace, may he, she, or they, rest in peace

R.P.D., rerum politicarum doctor, doctor of political science

rr., rarissime, very rarely

R.S.S., Regiae Societatis Sodalis, Fellow of the Royal Society

S., sepultus, buried; situs, lies; societas, society; socius or sodalis, fellow; s., semi, half; solidus, shilling

s.a., sine anno, without date; secundum artem, according to art

S.A.S., Societatis Antiquariorum Socius, Fellow of the Society of Antiquaries

sc., scilicet, namely; sculpsit, he, or she, carved or engraved it

Sc.B., scientiae baccalaureus, bachelor of science

Sc.D., scientiae doctor, doctor of science

S.D., salutem dicit, sends greetings

s.d., sine die, indefinitely

sec., secundum, according to

sec. leg., secundum legem, according to law

sec. nat., secundum naturam, according to nature, or naturally

sec. reg., secundum regulam, according to rule

seq., sequens, sequentes, sequentia, the following

S.H.S., Societatis Historiae Socius, Fellow of the Historical Society

s.h.v., sub hac voce or sub hoc verbo, under this word

s.l.a.n., sine loco, anno, vel nomine, without place, date, or name

s.l.p., sine legitima prole, without lawful issue

s.m.p., sine mascula prole, without male issue

s.n., sine nomine, without name

s.p., sine prole, without issue

S.P.A.S., Societatis Philosophiae Americanae Socius, Fellow of the American Philosophical Society

s.p.s., sine prole superstite, without surviving issue

S.R.S., Societatis Regiae Socius or Sodalis, Fellow of the Royal Society

ss, scilicet, namely (in law)

S.S.C., Societas Sanctae Crucis, Society of the Holy Cross

stat., statim, immediately

S.T.B., sacrae theologiae baccalaureus, bachelor of sacred theology

S.T.D., sacrae theologiae doctor, doctor of sacred theology

S.T.P., sacrae theologiae professor, professor of sacred theology

sub., subaudi, understand, supply

sup., supra, above

t. or temp., tempore, in the time of

tal. qual., talis qualis, just as they come; average quality

U.J.D., utriusque juris doctor, doctor of both civil and canon law

ult., ultimo, last month (may be abbreviated in writing but should be spelled out in printing)

ung., unguentum, ointment

u.s., ubi supra, in the place above mentioned

ut dict., ut dictum, as directed

ut sup., ut supra, as above

ux., uxor, wife

v., versus, against; vide, see; voce, voice, word

v. — a., vixit — annos, lived [so many] years

verb. sap., verbum [satis] sapienti, a word to the wise suffices

v.g., verbi gratia, for example

viz., videlicet, namely

v.s., vide supra, see above

Cardinal Numbers

unus, una, unum	one	duodetriginta	twenty-eight
duo, duae, duo	two	undetriginta	twenty-nine
tres, tria	three	triginta	thirty
quattuor	four	quadraginta	forty
quinque	five	quinquaginta	fifty
sex	six	sexaginta	sixty
septem	seven	septuaginta	seventy
octo	eight	octoginta	eighty
novem	nine	nonaginta	ninety
decem	ten	centum	hundred
undecim	eleven	centum et unus, etc.	hundred and one, etc.
duodecim	twelve		
tredecim	thirteen	ducenti, -ae, -a	two hundred
quattuordecim	fourteen	trecenti	three hundred
quindecim	fifteen	quadringenti	four hundred
sedecim	sixteen	quingenti	five hundred
septendecim	seventeen	sescenti	six hundred
duodeviginti	eighteen	septingenti	seven hundred
undeviginti	nineteen	octingenti	eight hundred
viginti	twenty	nongenti	nine hundred
viginti unus, etc.	twenty-one, etc.	mille	thousand

Ordinal Numbers

primus	first	undecimus	eleventh
secundus	second	duodecimus	twelfth
tertius	third	tertius decimus, etc.	thirteenth, etc.
quartus	fourth	duodevicesimus	eighteenth
quintus	fifth	undevicesimus	nineteenth
sextus	sixth	vicesimus, vigesimus	twentieth
septimus	seventh	vicesimus primus, etc.	twenty-first, etc.
octavus	eighth	centesimus	hundredth
nonus	ninth	millesimus	thousandth
decimus	tenth		

Months

Januarius	January	Julius	July
Februarius	February	Augustus	August
Martius	March	September	September
Aprilis	April	October	October
Maius	May	November	November
Junius	June	December	December

Days

dies solis dies dominica	Sunday	dies Mercurii	Wednesday
		dies Iovis	Thursday
dies lunae	Monday	dies Veneris	Friday
dies Martis	Tuesday	dies Saturni	Saturday

Seasons

ver	spring	autumnus	autumn
aestas	summer	hiems	winter

time

hora	hour	mensis	month
dies	day	annus	year
hebdomas	week	saeculum	century

Russian

Alphabet, Transliteration, [1] and Pronunciation

А	а	a	*a* in far [2]
Б	б	b	*b*
В	в	v	*v*
Г	г	g	*g* in go [3]
Д	д	d	*d*
Е	е	ye, e [4]	*ye* in yell, *e* in fell [5]
Ё	ё	yë, ë [6]	*yo* in yore, *o* in order [7]
Ж	ж	zh	*z* in azure
З	з	z	*z* in zeal
И	и	i	*i* in machine [8]
Й	й	y	*y* in boy
К	к	k	*k*
Л	л	l	*l*
М	м	m	*m*
Н	н	n	*n*
О	о	o	*o* in order [9]
П	п	p	*p*
Р	р	r	*r*
С	с	s	*s* in so
Т	т	t	*t*
У	у	u	*u* like the *oo* in Moon.
Ф	ф	f	*f*
Х	х	kh	*h* in how, but stronger, or *ch* in Scottish loch
Ц	ц	ts	*ts* in hats
Ч	ч	ch	*ch* in church
Ш	ш	sh	*sh* in shoe
Щ	щ	shch	*sh* plus *ch*, somewhat like *sti* in question
Ъ	ъ	'' [10]	([11])
Ы	ы	y	*y* in rhythm
Ь	ь	' [12]	([13])
Э	э	e	*e* in elder

---

[1] U.S. Board on Geographic Names transliteration, 1944.

[2] When stressed; when unstressed, like *a* in sofa.

[3] Also pronounced as *v* in the genitive ending -uj; often used for original *h* in non-Russian words, but is pronounced as *g* by Russians.

[4] *Ye* initially after vowels, and after ъ, ь.

[5] Pronounced as *i* in habit, or the same sound with preceding *y*, when unstressed.

[6] *Yë* as for *ye*. The sign *ë* is not considered a separate letter of the alphabet, and the ¨ is often omitted. Transliterate as *ë, yë* when printed in Russian as *ë:* otherwise use *e, ye*.

[7] Only stressed.

[8] Like *i* in habit when unstressed; like *yie* in yield after a vowel and after ь.

[9] Like *o* in abbot when unstressed.

[10] The symbol '' (double apostrophe), not a repetition of the line above.

[11] No sound; used only after certain prefixes before the vowel letters ь, ё, я, э. Formerly used also at the end of all words now ending in a consonant letter.

[12] ' (apostrophe).

[13] Palatalizes a preceding consonant, giving a sound resembling the consonant plus *y*, somewhat as in English meet you, did you.

| Ю | ю | yu | *u* in union |
| Я | я | ya | *ya* in yard |

Special Characters

Russian uses the Cyrillic alphabet. Many of the characters are the same as in Latin, with the following special ones: Б б, Г г, Д д, Ж ж, Й й, Л л, П п, Ф ф, Ц ц, Ш ш, Щ щ, Ъ ъ, Ы ы, Э э, Ю ю, and Я я. Note the following somewhat similar characters: З Э, Л П, У Ч, Ш Щ, з э, л п, ш щ. The Ы is a separate character and not a combination of Ь and I.

Transliteration

This is a mechanical process of substituting the transliteration letter or combination of letters for each Russian letter: Москва = *Moskva,* Киев = *Kiyev,* Русский = *Russkiy,* etc.

Vowels and Consonants

The vowel letters are а, е ё, и, о, у, ы, э, ю, and я, represented, respectively, by *a, e* or *ye, ё* or *yё, i, o, u, y, e, yu, ya.* The letters й, ъ, and ь are not called either vowels or consonants. All other letters are consonants.

Diphthongs

The sequences of a vowel followed by й are often called diphthongs. Their sounds are:

ай (*ay*) *ai* in aisle

ей (*ey, yey*) *ey* in they, or as *yea* (= yes)

ий (*iy*) like prolonged English *ee*

ой (*oy*) *oy*

уй (*uy*) *uoy* in buoy as pronounced by some ($\overline{oo}$ plus *y*)

ый (*yy*) *y* in rhythm plus *y* in yield

эй (*ey*) *ey* in they

юй (*yuy*) *you* plus *y* in yield

яй (*yay*) *ya* in yard plus *y* in yield

Digraphs

The transliterations *ye, zh, kh, ts, ch, sh, shch, yu, ya* represent single Russian letters and should not be divided in syllabification.

Consonantal Units

The following combinations of consonants should be treated, for syllabification purposes, as indivisible units:

бл, бр (*bl, br*)

вл, вр (*vl, vr*)

гл, гр (*gl, gr*)

дв, др (*dv, dr*)

жд (*zhd*)

кл, кр (*kl, kr*)

мл (*ml*)

пл, пр (*pl, pr*)

ск, скв, скр, ст, ств, стр (*sk, skv, skr, st, stv, str*)

тв, тр (*tv, tr*)

фл, фр (*fl, fr*)

These simplified rules have been followed for the past 2 years by the Library of Congress Card Division. (Based on practice in Bol'shaīā sovetskaīā enīsiklopedīā, v. 36.)

General:

1. A single letter is not separated from the rest of the word.

2. A soft or hard sign is not separated from the preceding consonant.

3. Division is made at the end of the prefix (a fill-vowel is considered part of the prefix): со-глас-но   воз-дух   по-треб-ле-ние   объ-ем   пре-до-ста-вить.

4. In compound words, letters are not separated from the component parts of the word, and a fill-vowel goes with the preceding syllable:

сов-хоз   зем-ле-вла-де-лец

Two vowels together:

1. Division is made between the vowels: сто-ит (*but:* рос-сий-ский).

One consonant between two vowels:

1. The consonant goes with the following vowel:

ма-не-ры   по-вы-ше-ни-ем   ста-тья-ми.

Two consonants between two vowels:

1. Division is made between the consonants. (*Exception:* ст goes with the following vowel): топ-ли-во управ-ле-ние ре-ак-тив-ный биб-ли-о-те-ка Поль-ша (*but:* пу-скает   ча-сти).

Three or more consonants between two vowels:

1. If a consonant is doubled, division is made between the the two:

искус-ство   диф-фрак-ция.

2. ст is never separated.

3. Division is not made before the first nor after the last consonant. (*Exception:* When ст begins the consonant group, it may be separated from the preceding vowel): мест-ность *or* ме-стность

4. Otherwise, division is optional: элек-три-че-ство *or* элект-ри-че-ство. Ан-глия *or* Анг-лия цент-раль-ный *or* цен-траль-ный

Exception: The following are consistently divided as shown: марк-сизм Мо-сква

Rules for Syllabification [1]

1. Diphthongs, digraphs, and consonantal units may not be divided.

2. Division is made on a vowel or on a diphthong before a single consonant, a digraph, or a consonantal unit: ба-гаж (*ba-gazh*), Бай-кал (*Bay-kal*), му-ха (*mu-kha*), рё-бра (*rë-bra*), каче-ство (*kache-stvo*), свой-ство (*svoy-stvo*).

3. In a group of two or more consonants, division is made before the last consonant, digraph, or consonantal unit: мас-ло (*mas-lo*), мас-са (*mas-sa*), мар-шал (*mar-shal*), точ-ка (*toch-ka*), долж-ность (*dolzh-nost'*), сред-ство (*sred-stvo*).

4. Division may be made between vowels not constituting a diphthong or between a diphthong and another vowel: оке-ан (*oke-an*), ма-як (*ma-yak*).

5. Certain adverbial prefixes are kept intact, except before ы. These are: без (бес), во, воз (вос), вы, до, за, из (ис), на, над, не, ни, низ (нис), о, об, обо, от, ото, пере, по, под, пред(и), пред(о), при, про, раз (рас), с(о), and у. In transliteration these prefixes are respectively *bez* (*bes*), *vo*, *voz* (*vos*), *vy*, *do*, *za*, *iz* (*is*), *na, nad, ne, ni, niz* (*nis*), *o, ob, obo, ot, oto, pere, po, pod, pred*(*i*), *pred*(*o*), pri, pro, raz (*ras*), *s*(*o*), and *u*: без-вкусный (*bez-vkusnyy*), бес-связь (*bes-svyaz'*), во-круг (*vo-krug*), but раэ-ыскать (*ra-zyskat'*), etc.

6. Compound words are divided according to their component parts (and each part according to rules 1 to 5): радио-связь (*radio-svyaz'*), фото-снимка (*foto-snimka*).

7. It is to be noted that the й (*ĭ*) always terminates a syllable: бой-кий (*boy-kiy*), рай-он (*ray-on*); the ъ ('') terminates a syllable except in words beginning with въ (*v''*), взъ (*vz''*), and съ (*s''*): отъ-ехать (*ot''-yekhat'*) but съём-ка (*s''yëm-ka*), съест-ной (*s''yest-noy*); the ь (') terminates a syllable except before the soft vowels е (*e*), и (*i*), ю (*yu*), and я (*ya*): маль-чик (*mal'-chik*), but соло-вьев (*solo-v'yev*), брн-льянт (*bri-l'yant*), се-мья (*se-m'ya*).

8. Foreign words and components of foreign words (not naturalized) follow the conventions of the language of origin: Шек-спир (*Shek-spir*), мас-штаб (*mas-shtab*), Лоа-ра (*Loa-ra*) [not Ло-ара (*Lo-ara*) (from the French *Loire*)], се-ньор (*se-n'or*).

Illustrative Word Divisions

[The numbers in parentheses refer to the syllabification rules]

аме-ри-кан-ский *ame-ri-kan-skiy*	(2, 2, 3)	воз-зре-ние *voz-zre-niye*	(5, 2)
ан-глий-ская *an-gliy-skaya*	(3, 2)	вос-хва-ле-ние *vos-khva-le-niye*	(5, 2, 2)
беа-ал-ко-голь-ный *bez-al-ko-gol'-nyy*	(5, 3, 2, 7)	вы-здо-ро-веть *vy-zdo-ro-vet'*	(5, 2, 2)
бес-сроч-ный *bes-sroch-nyy*	(5, 3)	вы-со-ко-нрав-ство *vy-so-ko-nrav-stvo*	(2, 2, 6, 3)
ва-ку-ум *va-ku-um*	(2, 4)	го-су-дар-ствен-ный *go-su-dar-stven-nyy*	(2, 2, 3, 3)
во-гну-тость *vo-gnu-tost'*	(5, 2)	до-школь-ное *do-shkol'-noe*	(5, 7)
во-до-вме-сти-ли-ще *vo-do-vme-sti-li-shche*	(2, 6, 2, 2, 2)	зав-траш-ний *zav-trash-niy*	(3, 3)

---

[1] Since the orthographic reform of 1918, the rules for syllabification have been considerably liberalized. It is generally permitted now to divide according to convenience, provided that phonetics and etymology are not severely overridden. These rules, designed as a guide for workers who might not be thoroughly familiar with the Russian language, are of necessity somewhat restrictive, but they insure invariably correct word division in conformity with generally approved usage.

As a great deal of Russian matter, especially bibliography, is printed in transliterated form, these rules have been formulated so as to apply with equal accuracy whether matter is in Russian characters or in transliteration.

изъ-яс-не-ние *iz''-yas-ne-niye*	(7, 3, 2)	по-глуб-же *po-glub-zhe*	(5, 3)
ис-сле-до-ва-тель-ский *is-sle-do-va-tel'-skiy*	(5, 2, 2, 2, 7)	по-гля-ды-вать *po-glya-dy-vat'*	(5, 2, 2)
Крон-штадт-ский *Kron-shtadt-skiy*	(8, 3)	по-да-вать-ся *po-da-vat'-sya*	(5, 2, 7)
на-всег-да *na-vseg-da*	(5, 3)	под-жи-да-ние *pod-zhi-da-niye*	(5, 2, 2)
на-двн-га-ю-щий-ся *na-dvi-ga-yu-shchiy-sya*	(5, 2, 4, 2, 7)	пред-ва-ри-тель-ный *pred-va-ri-tel'-nyy*	(5, 2, 2, 7)
над-вя-зать *nad-vya-zat'*	(5, 2)	пре-ди-сло-вие *pre-di-slo-viye*	(2, 5, 2)
не-сго-ра-е-мый *ne-sgo-ra-e-myy*	(5, 2, 4, 2)	пре-до-хра-нять *pre-do-khra-nyat'*	(2, 5, 2)
неф-те-хра-ни-ли-ше *nef-te-khra-ni-li-shche*	(3, 6, 2, 2, 2)	при-вхо-дя-щий *pri-vkho-dya-shchiy*	(5, 2, 2)
ни-сколь-ко *ni-skol'-ko*	(5, 7)	про-све-ще-ние *pro-sve-shche-niye*	(5, 2, 2)
об-ло-же-ние *ob-lo-zhe-niye*	(5, 2, 2)	про-те-стант-ство *pro-te-stant-stvo*	(2, 2, 3)
обо-зна-че-ние *obo-zna-che-niye*	(5, 2, 2)	про-хва-тить *pro-khva-tit'*	(5, 2)
объ-яс-ни-тель-ный *ob''-yas-ni-tel'-nyy*	(7, 3, 2, 7)	раз-вью-чи-вать *raz-v'yu-chi-vat'*	(5, 2, 2)
од-но-звуч-ный *od-no-zvuch-nyy*	(3, 6, 3)	раз-мно-жать *raz-mno-zhat'*	(5, 2)
от-зву-чать *ot-zvu-chat'*	(5, 2)	рас-ска-зы-вать *ras-ska-zy-vat'*	(5, 2, 2)
ото-зва-ние *oto-zva-niye*	(5, 2)	соб-ствен-ный *sob-stven-nyy*	(3, 3)
отъ-ез-жа-ю-щий *ot''-yez-zha-yu-shchiy*	(7, 3, 4, 2)	со-дей-ство-вать *so-dey-stvo-vat'*	(5, 7, 2)
Па-ра-гвай *Pa-ra-gvay*	(2, 8)	со-е-ди-нён-ные *so-ye-di-nën-nyye*	(5, 2, 2, 3)
пе-ре-гнать *pe-re-gnat'*	(2, 5)	сол-неч-ный *sol-nech-nyy*	(3, 3)
пер-спек-ти-ва *per-spek-ti-va*	(8, 3, 2)	солн-це-сто-я-ние *soln-tse-sto-ya-niye*	(3, 6, 4, 2)
пи-о-нер-ский *pi-o-ner-skiy*	(4, 2, 3)	удоб-ней-ше *udob-ney-she*	(3, 7)

Stress and Diacritics

No simple set of rules for syllabic stress can be formulated. The only dependable guide is a native, or a dictionary in the case of basic forms and a grammar for their inflectional shiftings.

The only diacritics are the dieresis and the breve. These do not indicate stress but modification of sound. Note alphabet.

Capitalization

Capitalization is practically as in English, except that proper adjectives, names of the months (except when abbreviated), and days of the week are lowercased.

Punctuation

Punctuation is very similar to that of English, but the comma is used for restrictive as well as nonrestrictive clauses. The dash is used between a subject and a complement when there is no verb *is* or *are*, and sometimes before a clause where the equivalent of the conjunction *that* has been omitted. Dialog is usually shown by dashes rather than quotation marks. Cited material is enclosed in quotation marks, which are usually in the French form—« », though sometimes in the German form—,, '', and rarely as in English.

Abbreviations

амер.	американский, American
АН	Академия наук, Academy of Sciences
б.г.	без года, no date
б.м.	без места, no place
ВКП (б)	Всесоюзная Коммунистическая Партия (большевиков) All-Union Communist Party (Bolshevik)
г.	год, year; город, city; господин, Mr.
г-жа	госпожа, Mrs.
гл	глава, chapter
гр.	гражданин, citizen; гражданка, citizen (female)
до н. э.	до нашей эры, B.C.
ж. д.	железная дорога, railroad
и т. д.	и так далее etc.
км.	километр, kilometer
КПСС	Коммунистическая партия Советского, Союза, Communist Party of the Soviet Union
м.	метр, meter
мм.	миллиметр, millimeter

н. ст.	новый стиль, new style
н. э.	нашей эры, A.D.
обл.	область, oblast
отд.	отделение, section
по Р. Х.	по Рождестве Христове, anno Domini
см.	сентиметр, centimeter; смотри, see, cf.
СССР	Соцз Советских Социалистических Республик, Union of Soviet Socialist Republics
с. ст.	старый стиль, old style
США	Соединенные Штаты Америки, United States of America
ст.	статья, article; столбец, column
стр.	страница, page
т.	том, volume; товарищ, comrade
т.е.	то есть, that is
ЦК	Центральный Комитет, Central Committee
ч.	часть, part

Cardinal Numbers

один, одна, одно *m., f., n.*	one	семнадцать	seventeen
два, две *m. & n., f.*	two	восемнадцать	eighteen
три	three	девятнадцать	nineteen
четыре	four	двадцать	twenty
пять	five	двадцать один, etc.	twenty-one, etc.
шесть	six	тридцать	thirty
семь	seven	сорок	forty
восемь	eight	пятьдесят, etc.	fifty, etc.
девять	nine	девяносто	ninety
десять	ten	сто	hundred
одиннадцать	eleven	сто один, etc.	one hundred and one, etc.
двенадцать	twelve	двести	two hundred
тринадцать	thirteen	триста, etc.	three hundred, etc.
четырнадцать	fourteen	пятьсот, etc.	five hundred, etc.
пятнадцать	fifteen	тысяча	thousand
шестнадцать	sixteen		

Ordinal Numbers [2]

первый	first	одиннадцатый	eleventh
второй	second	двенадцатый	twelfth
третий	third	тринадцатый	thirteenth
четвёртый	fourth	четырнадцатый	fourteenth
пятый	fifth	пятнадцатый	fifteenth
шестой	sixth	шестнадцатый	sixteenth
седьмой	seventh	семнадцатый	seventeenth
восьмой	eighth	восемнадцатый	eighteenth
девятый	ninth	девятнадцатый	nineteenth
десятый	tenth	двадцатый	twentieth

---

[2] The ordinal numbers here given are of the masculine gender. To convert them to feminine or neuter, it is only necessary to effect the proper gender changes: For the feminine, change ый to ая, ий to ья, ой to ая. For the neuter, change ый to ое, ий to ье, and ой to ое.

двадцать первый	twenty-first	трехсотый	three hundredth
сотый	hundredth	четырехсотый	four hundredth
сто первый, etc.	one hundred and first, etc.	пятьсотый, etc.	five hundredth, etc.
двухсотый	two hundredth	тысячный	thousandth

Months

январь (Янв.)	January	июль	July
февраль (Февр.)	February	август (Авг.)	August
март	March	сентябрь (Сент.)	September
апрель (Апр.)	April	октябрь (Окт.)	October
май	May	ноябрь	November
июнь	June	декабрь (Дек.)	December

Days

воскресенье	Sunday	четверг	Thursday
понедельник	Monday	пятница	Friday
вторник	Tuesday	суббота	Saturday
среда	Wednesday		

Seasons

| весна | spring | осень | autumn |
| лето | summer | зима | winter |

Time

час	hour	месяц	month
день	day	год	year
неделя	week		

Note on Old Spelling

On October 10, 1918, the Council of People's Commissars decreed the introduction of a spelling reform that had been proposed many years before but never adopted. The spelling used from that time in all official publications, except those of the Academy of Sciences (Akademiya Nauk), was this new spelling. The academy adopted the new spelling in 1924. All Russian publications, except for a few printed outside the Soviet Union, have used the new spelling since the institution of the reform.

The old spelling, found in books printed before the dates mentioned, differed in the following ways:

1. There were used the additional *i* (in the alphabet, after и and before к, as й was not considered a separate letter), ѣ (after ь), ѳ (after я), and ѵ (after ѳ).

2. *I* was used only before another vowel letter and in the word мірѣ, world. It is now replaced by и (мірѣ became мир).

3. ѣ occurred in certain words and in some grammatical endings. It represented the same sound as *e* and is now replaced by *e* everywhere. In a few cases ѣ was pronounced like *ё*, and where *e* is now printed with dieresis (¨), the replacement of ѣ is, of course, *ё*.

4. Ѳ was used in words of Greek origin, for Greek θ (th). It was pronounced *f*, and is now replaced by *f*.

5. Ѵ was used in a few ecclesiastical words, for Greek ν (*u, y*). It was pronounced like и, and is replaced by that letter.

6. Ъ was used at the end of all words after a consonant not followed by ь. In this position ъ has simply been omitted since the reform. For some years after 1918, some publishers omitted ъ altogether, using an apostrophe for it after prefixes, but the use of the apostrophe is now discouraged, and ъ is used.

7. The prefixes из, воз, вз, раз, без, чрез, через were written with final з everywhere, whereas now they are written ис, вос, etc., before к, п, с, т, х, ц, ч, ш, ф, щ.

8. Some adjective endings in the genitive singular were written -аго, -яго; these were replaced by -ого, -его.

9. The plural nominative of adjectives agreeing with feminine and neuter nouns was written -ыя, -ія; these endings were replaced by -ые, -ие, which had formerly been used only for adjectives agreeing with masculine nouns.

10. The pronoun "they" in referring to the feminine gender was written онѣ; this was replaced by они, previously used only for masculine reference.

11. Similarly, однѣ, однѣх, однѣми were replaced by одни, одних, одними.

12. The genitive pronoun "her" was written ея; this was replaced by её, formerly used only as accusative.

13. Ё was printed only in schoolbooks.

Spanish

Alphabet and Pronunciation

A	a	*a* in watt; *ai* as in aisle
B	b	*b,* at beginning of words and after *m;* more like *v* everywhere else
C	c	*c* in car, before *a, o, u,* and consonants; before *e, i* pronounced as *s* in so, in Spanish America; as *th* in thin, in Spain
Ch	ch	*ch* in chart
D	d	*d*
E	e	*e* in met; *ei* as in vein
F	f	*f*
G	g	*g* in go, before *a, o, u,* and consonants; like strong *h* before *e* and *i; gu* like *gw* before *a, o; gü* like gw before *e, i*
H	h	not pronounced
I	i	*i* in machine; *y* in yet, before and after vowels
J	j	*h,* but with more friction (same as *g* before *e, i*)
K	k	*k;* only in foreign words
L	l	*l* in lily
LL	ll	*y* in yet, in most of Spanish America; *lli* in million, in Spain, Colombia, and Ecuador
M	m	*m*
N	n	*n; nv* like *mb* in lumber
Ñ	ñ	*ny* in canyon
O	o	*o* in obey; *oi* as in oil
P	p	*p*
Q	q	always followed by silent *u, qu* being pronounced *k*
R	r	*r,* like tongue-tap *r* in British pronunciation of very
Rr	rr	*r* trilled, as in Scotch English or Italian
S	s	*s* in so, before most consonants and between vowels; *z* in zeal, before voiced consonants (*b, d, g, l, m, n, r, y*)
T	t	*t*
U	u	*u* in rule (=*oo* as in coo); *w* in wet, before vowels; silent in *gue, gui, qu*
V	v	*b* at beginning of words; more like *v* everywhere else
W	w	*w, v;* only in foreign words
X	x	*x* in ax (=*ks*), between vowels; *s* before consonants
Y	y	*y* in yet, initially and between vowels; *ay* as *ai* in aisle; *ey* as in they; *oy* as in boy
Z	z	*s* in so, in Spanish America; *th* in thin, in Spain

Special Characters

Spanish uses the Latin alphabet with the addition of the characters Ñ ñ. Note that *ch, ll,* and *rr* are regarded as separate units; i.e., words beginning with *ch* will be entered in the dictionary after words beginning with *cz,* not between the groups of words beginning with *ce* and *ci.* The acute accent appears very frequently over one of the vowel letters in a word. The dieresis appears occasionally over *u* following *g;* its occurrence elsewhere is so rare as to be negligible.

Vowels and Consonants

The vowels are *a, e, i, o, u,* and sometimes *y.* The other letters are consonants. The letter *y* is a consonant at the beginning of a word (before a vowel) and between two vowels.

Combinations of Vowel Letters (Diphthongs and Triphthongs)

The vowel *i* or *u* preceding *a, e, i, o, u,* or following *a, e, o,* is pronounced as a single syllable with the preceding or following vowel; if the diphthong occurs in a syllable which needs an accent mark (see Stress and Diacritics), the acute accent is placed over the vowel other than *i* or *u.* The diphthongs are:

ai	ei	oi		ái	éi	ói	
au	eu	ou		áu	éu	óu	
ia	ie	io	iu	iá	ié	ió	iú
ua	ue	uo	ui	uá	ué	uó	uí

At the end of a word and in one-syllable words, *ay, ey, oy* replace the diphthongs ending in *i.*

Sequences of vowel letters which are not diphthongs, and which may be divided, are those in which *í* or *ú* precedes or follows another vowel: *aí, eí, oí, aú, eú, oú, ía, íe, ío, íu, úa, úe, úo, úi.*

Spanish also has triphthongs. A triphthong is a combination of three vowels, the middle one of which is stressed, the others unstressed; the combination is pronounced as a single syllable. The triphthongs are:

iai	iei	ioi	iui	uai	uei	uoi	
iau	ieu	iou		uau	ueu	uou	uiu

If the *i* or *u* at the beginning or the end of a sequence of three vowel letters has an acute accent, it is not part of a triphthong, and division may be made accordingly; e.g., *í-ai, ua-ú, ú-oi.*

Combinations of Consonant Letters (Digraphs)

The digraphs are *ch, ll,* and *rr.*

Consonantal Units

In Spanish certain consonants followed by *l* or *r* are pronounced in the same syllable with the following vowel. These consonant groups are: *bl, br; cl, cr; dr; fl, fr; gl, gr; pl, pr; tr.*

Rules for Syllabification

1. Diphthongs, triphthongs, digraphs, and consonantal units may not be divided.

2. Division is made on a vowel or on a diphthong before a single consonant, a digraph, or a consonantal unit: *ca-sa, bue-no, re-yes, mu-cho, po-llo, co-rrer, ha-blar, li-bro.*

3. In a group of two or more consonants, division is made before the last consonant, digraph, or consonantal unit: *ac-ta, ac-ción, ist-mo, mar-cha, cen-tro.*

4. Division may be made between vowels not constituting a diphthong or triphthong or between a diphthong and another vowel: *ca-er, le-er, ba-úl, flú-ido, temí-ais.*

5. Certain adverbial prefixes are kept intact. These are: *anti, bis, circum, cis, des, inter, mal, pan, sub, super, trans,* and *tras: anti-artístico, bis-anuo* (never *bi-sanuo*), *circum-ambiente* (never *circu-mambiente*), *des-unión* (never *de-sunión*). Other prefixes are also divisible from the stem, provided the division conforms to rules 2 to 4: *contra-parte* (rule 2), *ab-negación* (rule 3), *ex-traer* (rule 3), *co-existir* (rule 4). Otherwise division on prefixes should be avoided, except in cases of exigency, such as very narrow measure: *ab-usar* (better *abu-sar*), *re-unir* (better *reu-nir*), *ex-ánime* (better *exá-nime*), *in-afectado* (better *ina-fectado*), *co-incidencia* (better *coin-cidencia*). In no case may division on a prefix be made, however, before an *s* followed by another consonant: *cons-titución* (never *con-stitución*), *pers-pectivo* (never *per-spectivo*), *subs-tancia* (never *sub-stancia*). [1]

6. Compound words are divided according to their component parts (and each part according to rules 1 to 5): *estado-unidense* (rather than *estadou-nidense*), *bien-estar* (There are not many compound words in Spanish the correct division of which does not coincide with rules 1 to 5.)

7. Foreign words and components of foreign words (not naturalized) follow the conventions of the language of origin: *Wásh-ington, Groen-landia* (never *Gro-enlandia*), *Gegen-stand, Frei-schütz, Ingol-stadt, Ste-phenson.*

---

[1] This rule of the *s* is rigidly adhered to, because no Spanish word and hence no syllable can begin with a group of consonants the first of which is *s.*

Scientific and technical words derived from Latin and Greek are treated as naturalized Spanish words and are divided according to rules 1 to 6: *diag-nóstico, hemis-ferio, anas-tomosis.*

Illustrative Word Divisions
[The numbers in parentheses refer to the syllabification rules]

Amé-ri-ca	(2, 2)	in-clu-yen-do	(3, 2, 3)
anas-to-mo-sis	(3, 2, 2)	in-ter-a-me-ri-ca-no	(3, 5, 2, 2, 2, 2)
an-te-o-jos	(3, 6, 2)	in-te-re-ses	(3, 2, 2)
an-ti-es-pas-mó-di-co	(3, 5, 3, 3, 2, 2)	in-te-rro-ga-ción	(3, 2, 2, 2)
an-ti-psó-ri-co	(3, 5, 2, 2)	íst-mi-co	(3, 2)
apro-xi-ma-ción	(2, 2, 2)	lla-me-an-te	(2, 4, 3)
au-to-ex-ci-tan-te	(2, 4, 3, 2, 3)	lu-ga-ri-llo	(2, 2, 2)
au-xi-liar	(2, 2)	ma-la-men-te	(2, 2, 3)
ba-le-á-ri-co	(2, 4, 2, 2)	mal-in-ten-cio-na-do	(5, 3, 3, 2, 2)
bis-a-nuo	(5, 2)	ma-yo-ría	(2, 2)
bri-llan-te	(2, 3)	me-tró-po-li	(2, 2, 2)
cas-te-lla-no	(3, 2, 2)	me-xi-ca-no	(2, 2, 2)
chan-chu-lle-ro	(3, 2, 2)	mid-ship-man	(7, 3)
cir-cum-am-bien-te	(3, 5, 3, 3)	mi-llo-na-rio	(2, 2, 2)
cir-cuns-tan-cia	(3, 3, 3)	mi-nis-tro	(2, 3)
cis-al-pi-no	(5, 3, 2)	mo-nos-per-mas	(2, 3, 3)
co-ne-xión	(2, 2)	ne-o-im-pre-sio-nis-mo	(4, 7, 3, 2, 2, 3)
con-se-cuen-cia	(3, 2, 3)	ne-o-yor-qui-no	(4, 2, 3, 2)
cons-ti-tu-cio-nal	(3, 2, 2, 2)	nos-o-tros	(6, 2)
cons-truc-ción	(3, 3)	obs-truir-se	(3, 3)
co-rres-pon-den-cia	(2, 3, 3, 3)	pa-í-ses	(4, 2)
cre-í-an	(4, 4)	pan-a-me-ri-ca-nis-mo	(5, 2, 2, 2, 2, 3)
cre-yen-do	(2, 3)	pa-ra-gua-yo	(2, 2, 2)
cual-quie-ra	(6, 2)	pe-re-gri-no	(2, 2, 2)
des-a-rro-llar-se	(5, 2, 2, 3)	pe-rió-di-co	(2, 2, 2)
des-em-ba-rrar	(5, 3, 2)	pe-rí-o-do	(2, 4, 2)
de-se-o-so	(2, 4, 2)	pe-ris-có-pi-co	(2, 3, 2, 2)
des-u-nir	(5, 2)	post-is-lá-mi-co	(7, 3, 2, 2)
diag-nós-ti-co	(3, 3, 2)	pro-rro-gar	(2, 2)
elip-soi-dal	(3, 2)	pú-bli-co	(2, 2)
en-te-rrar	(3, 2)	re-pú-bli-ca	(2, 2, 2)
es-o-tro	(6, 2)	san-güe-sa	(3, 2)
es-pa-ño-les	(3, 2, 2)	si-guien-tes	(2, 3)
es-ta-do-uni-den-se	(3, 2, 6, 2, 3)	sub-al-ter-nar	(5, 3, 3)
exac-ta-men-te	(3, 2, 3)	su-per-e-mi-nen-te	(2, 5, 2, 2, 3)
exa-mi-nar	(2, 2)	trans-al-pi-no	(5, 3, 2)
exe-quá-tur	(2, 2)	tras-an-te-a-yer	(5, 3, 6, 2)
ex-hi-bi-ción	(3, 2, 2)	vos-o-tros	(6, 2)
fre-cuen-te-men-te	(2, 3, 2, 3)	Wal-len-stein	(7, 7)
ge-o-grá-fi-co	(4, 2, 2, 2)	Wásh-ing-ton	(7, 3)
he-mis-fé-ri-co	(2, 3, 2, 2)	Welt-an-schau-ung	(7, 7, 4)
ina-pli-ca-ble	(2, 2, 2)		

Stress and Diacritics

The tilde, the dieresis, and the acute accent are the diacritical marks used in Spanish. The tilde is used only over the *n,* and *ñ* is a special character representing a separate phoneme, the palatal *n.* The dieresis mark (¨)

called *diéresis* or *crema* in Spanish, is to be found in a limited number of words, such as *vergüenza*, and *argüir*, to indicate that the vowel *u* must be pronounced.

The acute accent is used over a vowel to indicate that it is stressed; it is also used to distinguish homonyms. If there is no accent mark, a word ending in a consonant (including *y*, except *n* and *s*) is stressed on the last syllable; a word ending in a vowel, *n*, or *s* is stressed on the next-to-last syllable. Specifically, the acute accent is used as follows:

1. To indicate that the vowel is stressed.
2. To indicate vowels not forming a diphthong (see Diphthongs).
3. To distinguish words of the same spelling but of different meanings: *aún*, still, yet, *aun*, even; *dé*, give, *de*, of; *él*, he, him, *el*, the (but *el que, el cual*, he who, him who); *há*, ago, *ha*, has; *hé*, behold, *he*, I have; *mí*, me, *mi*, my; *más*, more, *mas*, but; *sé*, I know, be thou, *se*, oneself; *sí*, yes, oneself, *si*, if; *sólo*, only, *solo*, alone, single; *té*, tea, *te*, thee; *tú*, thou, *tu* thy; *vé*, go, *ve*, sees.
4. To distinguish interrogative or exclamatory use from relative or declarative: *adónde*, where? *adonde*, where; *cómo*, how? *como*, as; *cuán*, how! *cuan*, how; *cuándo*, when? *cuando*, when; *cuánto*, how much? *cuanto*, as much; *cúyo*, whose? *cuyo*, whose; *dónde*, where? *donde*, where; *qué*, what? *que*, which; *quién*, who(m)?, *quien*, who(m).
5. To distinguish pronouns from adjectives: *éste*, this one, *este*, this; *ése*, that one, *ese*, that; *aquél*, that one yonder, *aquel*, that.
6. Arbitrarily on monosyllabic aorists: *dí*, I gave; *fuí*, I was; *fué*, he was; *rió*, he laughed; *ví*, I saw; *vió*, he saw.
7. To avoid confusing the word *o* (or) with the zero: *2 ó 3*, but *dos o tres*, two or three.

Capitalization

The English style of capitalization is followed with few exceptions.

Adjectives derived from proper nouns are lowercased, as in *música colombiana* (Colombian music) and *teatro español* (Spanish theater).

Days of the week and months begin with a lowercase letter.

In titles of books, the general practice is to capitalize only the initial word and the proper nouns, as in *El ingenioso hidalgo don Quijote de la Mancha* (The ingenuous gentleman Don Quixote of the Mancha) and *Con los indios cuna de Panamá* (With the Cuna Indians of Panama). In the case of short titles there is a tendency to capitalize adjectives and common nouns, as in *Ortografía Castellana* (Castilian orthography) and *Enciclopedia de la Cocina* (Encyclopedia of cooking).

Punctuation and Hyphenation

Punctuation is practically the same as in English. One conspicuous exception is the use of inverted interrogation and exclamation marks, which are placed at the exact beginning of the question or exclamation: *¿Habla usted español?* (Do you speak Spanish?) *Si quiere visitar el Brasil, ¿por qué no estudia portugués?* (If you want to visit Brazil, why don't you study Portuguese?) *¡Viva el astronauta!* (Long live the astronaut!) *No recibí invitación, ¡y no comprendo por qué!* (I did not receive an invitation, and I cannot understand why!)

Quotation marks are used to reproduce a statement, text, etc., but not a dialog as developed in prose fiction. In the latter case, preference is given in Spanish to em dashes at the beginning of each interlocuter's paragraph. Example:

—*Yo soy Juan de Aguirre, el marino, el hermano de su madre de usted, el que desapareció.*
—*¡Usted es Juan de Aguirre!*
—*Sí.*
—*¿Mi tío?*
—*El mismo.*
—*¡Y por qué no habérmelo dicho antes!*

(Pío Baroja, *Las inquietudes de Shanti Andía*)

The hyphen, as a rule, is used only in syllabification. The apostrophe is not employed in modern Spanish.

Abbreviations

a. de J. C.	antes de Jesucristo	N.S.	Nuestro Señor, Nuestra Señora
a.m.	ante meridiano	núm.	número
C.A.	Centro América	O.	Oeste
Cía.	Compañía	pág., págs.	página, páginas
cm.	centímetro	Pbro.	Presbítero
d. de J. C.	después de Jesucristo	P.D.	Post Data
D.	Don	P.ej.	Por ejemplo
D.F.	Distrito Federal	p.m.	pasado meridiano
Dr., Dra.	Doctor, Doctora	Prov.	Provincia
E.	Este	Q.E.P.D.	Que en paz descanse
EE. UU.	Estados Unidos	R.P.	Reverendo Padre
E.U.A.	Estados Unidos de América	S.	Sur
Excmo., Excma.	Excelentísimo, Excelentísima	S.A.	Sociedad Anónima
Gral.	General	S.A.R.	Su Alteza Real
Hnos.	Hermanos	S.E.	Su Excelencia
Ilmo., Ilma.	Ilustrísimo, Illustrísima	S.E. u O.	Salvo error u omisión
kg.	kilógramo	S.M.	Su Majestad
km.	kilómetro	Sr., Sres.	Señor, Señores
Lic.	Licenciado	Sra., Sras.	Señora, Señoras
m.	metro, metros	S.R.L.	Sociedad de Responsabilidad Limitada
m/n	moneda nacional		
Mons.	Monseñor	Srta.	Señorita
M.S.	Manuscrito	S.S.	Su Santidad
M.S.S.	Manuscritos	S.S.S.	Su seguro servidor, Su segura servidora
N.	Norte		
N.B.	Nota bene	Sta., Sto.	Santa, Santo
N. de la R.	Nota de la Redacción	T.	Tomo
N. del A.	Nota del Autor	Ud., Uds.	Usted, Ustedes
N. del T.	Nota del Traductor	V.º B.º	Visto bueno
no.	número		

Cardinal Numbers

uno, una	one	veinte y dos, veintidós, etc.	twenty-two, etc.
dos	two		
tres	three	treinta	thirty
cuatro	four	cuarenta	forty
cinco	five	cincuenta	fifty
seis	six	sesenta	sixty
siete	seven	setenta	seventy
ocho	eight	ochenta	eighty
nueve	nine	noventa	ninety
diez	ten	ciento, cien	hundred
once	eleven	ciento uno, etc.	one hundred and one, etc.
doce	twelve		
trece	thirteen	doscientos, -as, etc.	two hundred, etc.
catorce	fourteen	quinientos, -as	five hundred
quince	fifteen	seiscientos, -as	six hundred
diez y seis, dieciséis	sixteen	setecientos, -as	seven hundred
diez y siete, diecisiete, etc.	seventeen, etc.	ochocientos, -as	eight hundred
veinte	twenty	novecientos, -as	nine hundred
veinte y uno (veintiuno)	twenty-one	mil	thousand

Round millions preceding units of quantity are followed by the preposition *de: tres millones de pesos, 3,000,000 de pesos.*

Ordinal Numbers

prim(er)o, -a (1°)	first	quincuagésimo	fiftieth
segundo, -a (2°)	second	sexagésimo	sixtieth
tercero, tercer	third	septuagésimo	seventieth
cuarto	fourth	octogésimo	eightieth
quinto	fifth	nonagésimo	ninetieth
sexto	sixth	centésimo	hundredth
sé(p)timo	seventh	centésimo primo, etc.	one hundred and first, etc.
octavo	eighth		
noveno, nono	ninth	ducentésimo	two hundredth
décimo	tenth	tricentésimo	three hundredth
undécimo	eleventh	cuadringentésimo	four hundredth
duodécimo	twelfth	quingentésimo	five hundredth
décimotercio	thirteenth	sexcentésimo	six hundredth
décimocuarto, etc.	fourteenth, etc.	septingentésimo	seven hundredth
vigésimo	twentieth	octingentésimo	eight hundredth
vigésimo primero, etc.	twenty-first, etc.	noningentésimo	nine hundredth
trigésimo	thirtieth	milésimo	thousandth
cuadragésimo	fortieth		

Months

enero	January	julio	July
febrero	February	agosto	August
marzo	March	se(p)tiembre	September
abril	April	octubre	October
mayo	May	noviembre	November
junio	June	diciembre	December

Days

domingo	Sunday	jueves	Thursday
lunes	Monday	viernes	Friday
martes	Tuesday	sábado	Saturday
miércoles	Wednesday		

Seasons

primavera	spring	otoño	autumn
verano	summer	invierno	winter

Time

hora	hour	mes	month
día	day	año	year
semana	week	siglo	century

Chapter 9

REFERENCES

When writers use material from another source, they should identify that source and, in the case of an exact quote, secure permission from the copyright owner or other source to use it. This does not include common material such as a list of the names of planets. But a writer should document the source if he or she discusses the results of a study reported in XYZ Company's newsletter about the impact of formaldehyde on the immune system.

The type of documentation to use depends on whether the text being prepared is a book, an article, a report, or something else. A book, for example, might have an end-of-chapter notes section, whereas an article might use footnotes, which are placed at the bottom of the page where cited.

The type of documentation used and the style of notes or arrangement of source data differ among the various disciplines. The name-date system (see "Reference Lists," on page 199), for instance, is often preferred for scientific works, but the footnote system is more popular in the humanities. This chapter describes notes, reference lists, and bibliographies. Although the systems illustrated here are all commonly used, writers and editors should follow the system and data-presentation style used by their employers or the one widely accepted in their professions.

NOTES

When lettered or numbered documentation is placed at the foot of a page to correspond to letters or numbers in the text, the notes are called *footnotes*. When the notes are collected at the end of a chapter or the end of a book or article, they are called *endnotes*. When all are collected at the end of a book, they should be arranged by chapter, with subheads to designate each chapter.

Although lower case letters (*a, b, c,* and so on) may be used, numbered notes (*1, 2, 3,* and so on) are more common in most professions.

If end-of-book notes are used, the note numbers in the text may start over with the number 1 in each chapter or may run consecutively throughout the entire book. (For note forms, see the following example and also in chapter 21.)

An *unnumbered note*, however, is often placed at the foot of a chapter-opening page or as the first note preceding numbered endnotes. Its purpose is to give special credit to the source of the entire chapter or to someone who made a special contribution to the chapter or to make some other comment that applies to the entire chapter or a specific section of it. The other notes in the chapter, which apply to a particular fact or discussion within the chapter, are numbered consecutively throughout an individual chapter or throughout the entire work in the case of an article or some other material that has no chapters.

Text Numbers

Within the text discussion the number that corresponds to the note number should be placed after the concluding punctuation of the pertinent sentence. Although note numbers in the middle of sentences should be avoided, if they must be used, they are placed after the appropriate word in the sentence or after any internal punctuation except a dash—the note number should always *precede* a dash.

The numbers in the text are set as superscript, or superior (raised), numbers. Writers whose equipment cannot print superscripts should simply type the number on line in the correct place in the text. In material to be published, an editor will use the appropriate proofreading symbol (see "Writing and Editing" in chapter 14) to indicate that the number is to be set and printed raised. In unpublished material, when numbers cannot be printed out as superscripts, some writers place the note number in parentheses or between virgules. Copyeditors, however, often find it easier to mark a note number when it is standing alone.

Manuscript:	This evidence was reported by Beryl Mason.[1]
	This evidence was reported by Beryl Mason.1
	This evidence was reported by Beryl Mason.(1)
	This evidence was reported by Beryl Mason./1/
Typeset Version:	This evidence was reported by Beryl Mason.[1]

When several sources appear within the same sentence, it is not necessary to use a separate number for each. Place a single number at the end of the sentence, and in the corresponding note, list all sources in the order mentioned in the sentence. An extract (blocked quotation) should always have a concluding note number. In a succession of such blocked quotations from different sources, each one will then have its own note number.

Chapter titles, illustration titles, subheads, and other display lines should not have note numbers. If possible, the number should be placed in an appropriate spot in the text. If the note is a general comment pertaining to the entire chapter, article, illustration, subsection, or the like, an unnumbered footnote may be used, as previously described.

Dual System

Occasionally, notes are so long and cumbersome that it is helpful to the reader to separate substantive notes from source notes. In that case all references to sources could be numbered and set as endnotes. Commentary, meanwhile, could be set as footnotes. The footnotes might be lettered (*a, b, c,* and so on) within each chapter or throughout, as in the case of an article or report. Symbols such as asterisks, daggers, and section signs might also be used, although if there are many such notes, the use of symbols can be cumbersome.

Note Style

A common style for notes—whether footnotes or endnotes—is to write the note in indented paragraph style, with the note number positioned on line (even though the corresponding text number is set as a superior figure; see previous discussion). An unnumbered or lettered note follows the same style. The heading for an end-of-chapter notes section could be "Notes" and that for an end-of-book collection could be "Notes" or "Endnotes."

Footnotes should be placed on the page where cited in the text. Because of the typesetting problems in fitting extensive note copy onto a text page, endnotes are preferred when notes are long. If footnotes are used, however, it is desirable to have only one paragraph for each one if possible. Very lengthy note commentary should be condensed when practical or incorporated into the text discussion.

When the note contains both the source of material mentioned in the text and additional commentary, mention the source first. When several sources are given, separate each one with a semicolon. If a quotation is included in the note, (1) put the source for that in parentheses after the closing quotation mark and before the final period of the sentence or (2) treat the source data as a new sentence without parentheses.

Use "ibid." (abbreviation for *ibidem,* meaning "in the same place") for a succeeding note referring to the same data as in the preceding note. Use a short form (author's last name and a shortened version of the title of the work) for references to the same source mentioned in a preceding note other than the one immediately preceding. Use traditional state and country abbreviations as given in chapter 6. The abbreviation *Inc.* may be omitted from the names of publishers. Otherwise, the name should conform to that listed in the work being cited. (Some disciplines abbreviate journal names and use only the first initial of authors. For such variations, consult a style manual for the discipline in question.) *See* and *see also* are often italicized. "Cf." (meaning "compare") is set in roman type in most disciplines except in the legal profession.

The following are examples of note style and are applicable to both footnotes and endnotes. For additional examples of data arrangement for various types of literature, see the models in chapter 21.

> 14. Crystal Oglethorpe, *The New Finance,* vol. 2 (New York: Edgemont Press, 1991), 391-402, 404-5. Oglethorpe has chosen the "new finance" over the traditional system but for reasons that critics claim are subject to dispute.
>
> 15. Ibid., 387.
>
> 16. Wertmeier, *The New Finance Reexamined,* 24.
>
> 17. Unless otherwise stated, all comments by Henry Juneau are quoted from *The Complete Letters of Henry Juneau,* ed. Francis Orwell (Chicago: Oldstead Publications, 1988).

Sample note 17, above, illustrates a way to avoid using numerous successive notes giving nothing more than "ibid." and a page number. After note 17 has been cited, the page numbers enclosed in parentheses appear in the text after further quotations.

> Juneau pointedly objected to Miller's "arrogance under fire" (p. 65).

Credit Lines

When a particular part of a published work such as a chapter, a table, or a photograph draws on and uses material from another source, permission to use the material and to credit the source must be secured. Usually, an author writes to the copyright owner of the material being used and describes what will be quoted or what the author wishes to reprint, what work it will be used in, and so on. When an author is under contract to a particular publisher, that publisher may have a standard form letter the author can use to write for permission to reproduce the material in question.

If permission to use material is granted, the copyright owner will often provide the credit-line wording to be followed. In that case an author should repeat the wording precisely. But if no credit line is provided, an author can use a style such as this (the word *source* often precedes the note in a table or figure).

> Reprinted, by permission, from Alan Torres, *Masterpieces of Cuisine* (Philadelphia: A-Z Books, 1986), 51-53.

Credit lines are usually placed below or along the edge of an illustration. If the note pertains to a chapter or a section, it is usually set as an unnumbered note at the bottom of the chapter- or section-opening page. Table source notes immediately follow the table body, appearing before any general note or table footnotes.

Portions of this chapter were adapted from Woodward Carlyle, "Jewelry High Style," *Cosmetics,* June 1990, 16-21. Used with permission.

Source: Department of Commerce statistics, 1988-89.

Some unpublished, uncopyrighted material is provided by the owner without charge and is given without limitation on its use. In such cases a courtesy line should be used. But an author should carefully determine that the material has no restrictions, and he or she should not merely assume that anything received can be used in any way without further permission.

Photograph by Jami Tillet, courtesy of the Iron Works, Jackson, Mississippi.

Work by the author or someone hired to provide it could also carry a courtesy line.

Map by the author.

Drawing by Nancy Keller.

For more examples of credit lines, see the models in chapter 21.

REFERENCE LISTS

One of the most popular systems of citation in scientific fields is the name-date system, which is used with a corresponding reference list. Because of its practicality, this system's popularity has been increasing in nonscientific areas as well. With this system, a source is signaled within the text not by inserting a superscript number but by enclosing in parentheses the last name of the author, the year of publication of the author's work, and the page number (if any) of the source material. Full data on the source are given in an alphabetical list of works cited.

Text Reference

Like note numbers in the text, name-date references should be placed at the end of a sentence if possible but *before* the concluding mark of punctuation (a note number is placed *after* the final punctuation). In the example below, however, 1924 appears in parentheses immediately after the name *Hindemith,* rather than at the end of the sentence, to insure that readers do not mistakenly assume that it is another reference to Blum, cited in the two previous sentences. Notice that if the text discussion already mentions an author's name, it is not necessary to repeat the name in the parenthetical reference. Succeeding references to the same name and date within a paragraph may consist of the page number alone, provided that no other source has intervened, as illustrated below.

In implementing these procedures, "Karl Hindemith made some crucial mistakes" (Blum 1981, 319-24). His greatest error was one of judgment, not computation, and his later days were spent as an "invocation for deliverance" (p. 317). Hindemith (1924) never openly admitted any failure, however.

Do not place any punctuation between the name and the date, but do place a comma (or a colon) between the date and any page number, table, or the like. Use commas or colons consistently.

(Brown 1975)

(Brown 1975, 161-63)

(Brown 1975: table 2)

Place a semicolon between two or more name-date references. In cases of multiple authors, use *and* (preferred) or & between names. Name-date references in the text are usually listed in the order preferred by the author of a work, and an editor should not rearrange them alphabetically or chronologically without being instructed to do so.

(Brown 1975; Parsons and Parsons 1986; Dunkirk 1990)

Use a colon between a volume number and page number (no space before or after the colon). But if a volume number alone is given, use the abbreviation *vol.* to distinguish it from a page number.

(Brown 1975, 2:169)

(Brown 1975, vol. 2)

For three or fewer names, list all names. But use "et al." (abbreviation for *et alii*, meaning "and others") in roman type when there are four or more authors. If this would cause confusion in cases of similar entries, use all names for one and "et al." for the other. Editors should query authors to be certain that the entries are not referring to the same source.

(Brown, Steiner, and Wallace 1987)

(Brown et al. 1988)

(Brown, Misak, Shields, and Stone 1988)

When two authors have both the same last name and their works carry the same date, use their first names (or initials) to avoid confusion.

(Larry Brown 1975) *or* (L. Brown 1975)

(Jennifer Brown 1975) *or* (J. Brown 1975)

If the same author has two or more works all with the same date, put the works in alphabetical order and add *a, b, c,* and so on to distinguish them.

(Brown 1991a, 1991b)

When a new edition of an older work is cited, include both dates and place the date of the original edition in brackets.

(Hegel [1832] 1980)

Exceptionally long organizational names such as "Shreveport Institute for the Study of Primitive Cultures in South America" may be shortened in the text citation, provided that the first word is retained so that the reader can still easily locate the full citation in the alphabetical reference list.

(Shreveport Institute 1984)

Some sources that do not have publication data, such as a personal interview, may be mentioned in the text without having a corresponding entry in the alphabetical reference list.

The coeducation experience has improved the quality of education at Whittmore Junior College but not necessarily the disposition of the formerly all-male enrollment (Dean Harvey Pruett, letter to the author, April 1991).

Dual System

Although the name-date system is a relatively easy way to handle source citations, it doesn't provide for substantive material. When additional commentary is needed, writers may use both footnotes or endnotes and the name-date reference list. In this case even the notes may refer to the reference list.

9. Rossamer and Rossamer (1988) expounded on this subject from the entrepreneur's perspective.

Reference-List Style

The full entries that correspond to the name-date text references should be arranged in alphabetical order and placed at the end of each chapter or in a single list at the end of the book. A chapter list contains only entries cited within the chapter in question. An end-of-book list has entries for all citations throughout the work.

Usually, the title of the list is "References" or "Works Cited"; sometimes "Bibliography" or another title is used. But the arrangement of data in the name-date system differs from that in a bibliography for a work with a numbered note system. (See "Bibliographies," on page 202.) In the name-date system, the reference list has the date of a work immediately after the author's name. Otherwise, the arrangement of data is generally the same in both types of lists.

Alphabetizing is done by author, or by title when there is no author for a particular work. A single-author entry precedes a multiauthor entry beginning with the same last name. The names of the coauthors need not be inverted.

Forbas, Michael. 1985.

Forbas, Michael, and Mary Reysack. 1990.

A reference list should include all authors' names, but in the text citation "et al." may be used when there are four or more authors.

Reference list: Forbas, Michael, Mary Reysack, John Steiner, and Jeanne Fisk. 1992.

Text citation: (Forbas et al. 1992)

A long dash (3-em dash in typography) precedes repeated single-author and multiauthor names after all works by the authors are placed in chronological order from earliest to latest, regardless of whether the persons were authors or editors. But a dash should not be used when the succeeding work has a coauthor. When two or more books have the same date, they should be placed in alphabetical order, and the letters *a, b,* and so on should be added to the date.

Forbas, Michael. 1985a.

_____. 1985b.

_____. 1990.

_____. 1991.

Forbas, Michael, and Donald West. 1973.

Forbas, Michael, Donald West, and Sharon Pyle. 1965.

_____. 1966.

_____. 1981.

_____, ed. 1992.

The following are examples of reference-list style, usually written with the first line flush left and succeeding lines indented. (For additional examples of data arrangement for various types of literature, see the models in chapter 21.) A cross-reference to a previous entry may be used to avoid repetition of data, as illustrated in the second example below.

Dalmi, Doris M. 1969. "The Expanding Heavens." In *An Introduction to Astronomy.* Edited by Paul Thomas. Cincinnati: Formula Publishing Co., 1-32.

Jerico, Herbert. 1969. "Constellations." In *An Introduction to Astronomy. See* Dalmi 1969.

Jerico, Herbert, and Doris M. Dalmi. 1978. "Astromathematics." *Astronomy Review* 3:410-54.

_____. 1979. *Above and Beyond Planet Earth.* Sacramento: Sunside Publishers.

BIBLIOGRAPHIES

A *bibliography* is a list of works that the author consulted when preparing written material. It consists of an alphabetical list of sources and is usually placed at the end of a book just before the index, although each chapter may have its own bibliography, especially in a multiauthor work.

Whereas a reference list (see "Reference Lists," on page 199) includes only the works cited in the text and cites them by name and date, a bibliography may include other pertinent works. When the list contains only references cited in the text, it is called "Select(ed) Bibliography," "Works Cited," or, in the case of a name-date system, "References."

Bibliography Style

The style of a bibliography is similar to that of a reference list, with a few exceptions. The date in an alphabetical bibliography appears later in the entry; for example, in a book entry it appears after the publisher's name. In a name-date reference list, on the other hand, the date appears after the author's name. (In scholarly publishing some bibliographies are styled similar to a reference list, with the date placed after the name of the author or editor.)

In both a reference list and a bibliography, a 3-em dash is used to designate succeeding works by the same author without repeating the author's name each time. But in a reference list the succeeding works are arranged chronologically, whereas in a bibliography they may be arranged chronologically or alphabetically by title. Also, original books precede edited books by the same author in a bibliography. The letters *a, b, c,* and so on need not be added to the year when the listing is alphabetical by title. (For more examples of bibliography entries, see chapter 21.)

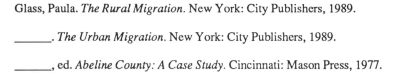

Glass, Paula. *The Rural Migration.* New York: City Publishers, 1989.

_____. *The Urban Migration.* New York: City Publishers, 1989.

_____, ed. *Abeline County: A Case Study.* Cincinnati: Mason Press, 1977.

A bibliography is occasionally presented as an essay, sometimes in addition to a reference list. Often it is then called "Bibliographic Essay" or "Suggested Readings." Such an essay would precede an alphabetical list of sources. Even though it would read like a regular chapter commentary, all sources mentioned should include the same complete data that would be found in an alphabetical bibliography. A bibliography may also be annotated, with brief comments at the end of each entry that point out the usefulness of the work or make some other pertinent observation.

In selecting the best form of bibliography to use, a writer must consider the nature of the work and what other type of documentation (footnotes, endnotes, and so on) will be available for the reader. In all cases the source data in notes and in the text must be consistent with the source data in bibliographic or reference-list entries.

Chapter 10

TABLES

Some information, particularly statistical data, is too detailed to convey in a regular text discussion or is intended to be only supplemental to the text. Such information requires a separate clear and logical arrangement in tabular format. This format enables a reader to scan the material and focus on selected facts or figures, and it enables a cluttered, cumbersome, and tedious text discussion to be avoided.

A complex table may have many elements: table number, table title, subtitle, column heads, stub, source note, general note, and footnotes. (For a description of each element, see "Numbered Tables" on page 209.) Brief unnumbered tables, however, rarely have more than a few of these elements.

UNNUMBERED TABLES

Without Heads

When the data to be presented are brief and uncomplicated, a simple unnumbered table may be presented in the middle of a text paragraph or between paragraphs. If it is obvious what the data in the columns are (years, dollars, and so on), and the presentation is very brief and simple, column headings may be unnecessary. Editors often style such material in the same way they would a multicolumn list, with the columns set apart from the general text and often centered on the page. Although such data are single-spaced in printed material, the information should be double-spaced in manuscript preparation.

Between 1988 and 1990, the price of XYZ Corporation's leading typewriter model (1200/14) first rose and then declined:

1988	$1,498
1989	1,611
1990	1,289

The decline in price in 1990 coincides with the introduction of a popular competitive model by another manufacturer.

Notice in the above example that the dollar sign need not be repeated each time when all of the figures in the column are dollars. This principle also applies to the use of other symbols, such as the percent sign. If all figures in a column are percentages, there is no need to repeat the sign after the first use.

With Heads

In the following example, column heads are used since it is not obvious that the percentages pertain to enrollment. Each major word in a column head should begin with a capital letter.

Region	Enrollment
East	25%
West	24
North	17
South	34

If the head used the word *percent(age)* or the symbol %, the symbol would be omitted entirely in the column below. (*Note:* When the word precedes *of,* use *percentage* rather than *percent.*)

Region	% of Enrollment
East	25
West	24
North	17
South	34

Region	Percentage of Enrollment
East	25
West	24
North	17
South	34

The rules under each column head should be as wide as the widest line of the column below. If the head is wider than the column, the rule should be as wide as the heads.

Sales
$ 1,213.95
11,645.89
8,915.79
$21,775.63

Total Regional Sales
$ 1,213.95
11,645.89
8,915.79
$21,775.63

Dollar signs should be aligned as shown above. (See the examples of statistical lists and columns in chapter 18.)

When two levels of heads are used (stacked heads), a rule used to separate the two levels should be as wide as the row of heads beneath the upper level.

	Labor Force				
Age	1980	1982	1984	1986	1988

Some editors omit the rule after a head when the table is very brief and simple.

Region	*% of Enrollment*
East	25
West	24
North	17
South	34

Region	*Percentage of Enrollment*
East	25
West	24
North	17
South	34

Either way, in manuscript preparation, leave a line space after the head before listing the facts or figures in the column. Leave two line spaces before and after the table.

Leaders

Leaders may be used if they will help a reader locate information in a complex table, although some publishers believe they clutter a table and should be omitted.

County assessments $2,743,911.86

Omitted Material

In published material an em dash (two hyphens in computer or typewriter preparation) or the abbreviation *NA* centered in the column is used to signify omitted material. The dash means that no data exist. The abbreviation *NA* means "not applicable."

1990	1990
21.2%	21.2%
13.5%	13.5%
—	NA
47.9	47.9

Table Title

Even when a table is brief and simple and is placed within the text commentary, an unnumbered table may use a title—with or without corresponding heads, as needed— if it helps the reader to understand the data better. A complex, detailed table set apart from the text discussion, often on a separate page, should always have a title, whether or not the table is numbered.

In manuscript preparation, leave two line spaces between the text discussion and the title and one line space between the title and column heads, if any, or the table body. Capitalize each important word in a table title.

The United States had a population gain of 176,353,309 during the one hundred-year period ending in 1980.

U.S. Population, 1880 and 1980

1880	50,189,209
1980	226,542,518

Source: U.S. Bureau of the Census.

New York led all other states during this period with a population of 5,082,871 in 1880 and 17,558,165 in 1980.

In the above example, a source note (see chapter 9) was added since the data came from an outside source. In manuscript preparation, leave one line space between the table body and the source note and two line spaces between the source note and the regular text discussion that follows.

Instead of a table title, column heads could also have been used in the preceding example.

The United States had a population gain of 176,353,309 during the one hundred-year period ending in 1980.

Year	*U.S. Population*
1880	50,189,209
1980	226,542,518

Source: U.S. Bureau of the Census.

New York led all other states during this period with a population of 5,082,871 in 1880 and 17,558,165 in 1980.

Position of Title and Heads

Because of the simplicity of these brief unnumbered tables that are fit into the text discussion as shown above, publishers generally prefer not to use the horizontal and vertical rules that are common in more complex numbered tables (see "Numbered Tables " on page 209). But whether or not the table is ruled, it should be indented from the regular text or centered on the page. Table titles and column heads may be centered above the column data or set flush left with the data.

Pulitzer Prizes, 1988

Category	*Recipient*	*Work*
Fiction	Toni Morrison	Beloved
Drama	Alfred Uhry	Driving Miss Daisy
General nonfiction	Richard Rhodes	The Making of the Atomic Bomb
Music	William Bolcom	12 New Etudes for Piano

Pulitzer Prizes, 1988

Category	*Recipient*	*Work*
Fiction	Toni Morrison	Beloved
Drama	Alfred Uhry	Driving Miss Daisy
General nonfiction	Richard Rhodes	The Making of the Atomic Bomb
Music	William Bolcom	12 New Etudes for Piano

See chapter 21 for additional examples of unnumbered tables and multicolumn lists.

NUMBERED TABLES

When to Number Tables

When a work has numerous tables, they should be numbered consecutively throughout the work (*1, 2, 3*, and so on) or throughout each chapter (*1.1, 1.2, 1.3, 2.1, 2.2, 2.3*, and so on or *1-1, 1-2, 1-3, 2-1, 2-2, 2-3*, and so on). It is permissible even in material with numerous numbered tables, however, to set the brief factual data as multicolumn lists or unnumbered tables in the midst of the text discussion (see the first example in "Unnumbered Tables" on page 204).

Consistency in Style

The styling of detailed, complex tables raises numerous questions. Should the number, title, and subtitle be centered or flush left? Should column heads be centered above each column or flush left with the first word in each column? Should runover lines be indented? Should footnote numbers or letters be typed on line or raised (superior figures)? Should the symbol % or the word *percent(age)* be used in heads?

Many questions of style are a matter of preference. The essential requirement is that the usage be consistent. If the title and column heads are centered in one table, they should be centered in all tables. If runover lines are indented in one table, they should be indented in all tables. If the symbol % is used in the column heads of one table, symbols, when applicable, should be used in the column heads of all tables.

General Guidelines

Other elements of a table should be styled according to traditional rules. Decimal signs, for instance, should be aligned.

```
 8.77
32.10
17.61
41.82
 6.00
 0.23
```

In the last figure above, a zero precedes the fraction 0.23 since the quantities listed exceed or are capable of exceeding 1.00. With probabilities and other quantities that never equal 1.00, the zero would be omitted.

Each important word in a table title or column head should be capitalized in manuscript preparation, although the publisher may select another style, such as capitals and small capitals, for the printed version.

| Total | Pupils per | Expenditure |
| Enrollment | Teacher | per Pupil |

In the body, however, only the first word of each item in each column should be capitalized.

Educational opportunity
grants

Aid to minority and
developing
institutions

If an item in one column consists of a complete sentence, it should be followed by a period, and all other items in that column should then also be followed by a period.

The use of rules is often a matter of preference. Publishers may avoid vertical rules to simplify typesetting and to reduce costs. But at least three horizontal rules are used in detailed tables; one after the table title, one after the column heads, and one after the table body but before any table notes. (See chapter 21 for examples.) When a complex table requires crossheads within the table body, horizontal rules may be used, but are not required, before and after each crosshead (see chapter 21).

Principal Parts of Tables

The elements described below are illustrated in the examples of textual and statistical tables provided in chapter 21.

Number. Except for very brief, simple tables (see "Unnumbered Tables" on page 204), all tables should have a number to provide an easy means for cross-referencing in the text and to facilitate the location of tables throughout a work. Every table should be mentioned by number in the text whether or not the table content is discussed.

Mariner 2, launched on August 27, 1962, passed within 22,000 miles of Venus on December 14, 1962 (table 21).

Mariner 2, launched on August 27, 1962, passed within 22,000 miles of Venus on December 14, 1962 *(see* table 21).

The text discussion might provide additional information about the subject of the table. But it should not merely summarize or repeat the table information.

Writers should avoid cross-references that open a sentence or paragraph with the table number (*not* "As table 21 reveals, Mariner 2 . . . 1962").

In printed work, tables should be positioned on the page containing the text in which the table is first mentioned or on a succeeding page as soon as possible thereafter. In manuscript preparation, publishers often prefer to have each table prepared on a separate page and positioned at the ends of the appropriate chapters or at the end of the work. When there are numerous tables and other illustrations, authors frequently collect them in a separate "illustrations manuscript" that accompanies the text manuscript.

For the table number use single or dual arabic numbers. In a multichapter work, a dual system may be used, with the first number referring to the chapter and the second referring to the table. The number *6.4* (or *6-4*) refers to the fourth table in chapter 6. The designation *B.5* (or *B-5*) refers to the fifth table in appendix B.

In manuscript preparation, leave two line spaces before the table number and one line space between the number and the title. Both number and title may be centered or positioned flush with the left margin of the table body.

Table 17

Nuclear Weapons Tests, 1945-1987

Title. The table title (sometimes called the table caption) is positioned one line space below the table number. In manuscript copy, it should be double-spaced with all important words capitalized. It may be either centered or set flush with the left margin of the table body. A table subtitle, if any, should be typed on a separate line.

The wording of the title should be concise and serve only to identify the table. Any details or additional descriptive material should be confined to the table body or to a general note following the body.

Table 2–9

Distribution of Total Personal Income
(in Billions of Dollars)

Table 7.14

Consumer Price Indexes for Selected Items
(1982–84 = 100)

If the title must run over to a second line, break it at a logical place for clarity and ease of reading.

Grain Storage Capacity
at Principal U.S. Grain Centers: 1990

Heads. The heads in a table consist of column heads (a row of heads above the body columns) and crossheads (heads within the body of the table that separate different categories of data). Heads should be very brief and may use symbols such as % to conserve space. Capitalize all important words in a head and set each word flush left or centered above the column.

Each column in the table body, except the left column, should have a head. The left column may or may not require a head. If one is used, it is usually singular. The heads for other columns may be singular or plural. Subheads are usually placed in parentheses or on a separate line at the end of the head.

Production (kg)

Melting
Point
°C

If columns are numbered to facilitate cross-referencing in the text, arabic numbers should be set in parentheses on the last line of the heads, or if another subhead such as % appears there, the number may be placed on the first line above the head.

Petroleum (1)   Coal (2)

1   2
Petroleum (%)   Coal (%)

Table heads are typically single-spaced both in manuscript and printed copy, but a manuscript should be prepared with one line space above a column head and another line space after it. Detailed tables usually have a horizontal rule above and below column heads.

Leave at least two character spaces between heads. Although it may be necessary to conserve space in a very wide table, readability and clarity may be sacrificed if heads are placed too close to each other.

Table 6

Most Active Common Stocks
on the New York Stock Exchange, 1989

Stock	Volume (Millions of Shares)

A decked head consists of two or more levels of heads. More than two levels may confuse readers, however, and should be avoided. Usually, the different levels of heads are separated by a rule that spans the applicable columns below.

Table A-10
World Mineral Production, 1985–1986

	1985		1986	
Mineral	Quantity	Value (1,000)	Quantity	Value (1,000)

Crossheads may be inserted in the table body to separate categories of data in the table. These heads should be centered above the columns to which they apply, with one line space above and below each head. Horizontal rules may also be used to define the separation of categories. If used, the rules should span the columns to which the crosshead applies.

Table 16.1

Births in New England and Middle Atlantic States, 1989–1990

State	January–December 1989	January–December 1990
	New England	
Maine	19,422	19,772
New Hampshire	19,763	18,943
Vermont	8,471	9,101
Massachusetts	102,907	134,764
Rhode Island	14,655	15,023
Connecticut	31,811	32,649
Total	197,029	230,252
	Middle Atlantic States	
New York	294,862	301,642
New Jersey	112,905	115,010
Pennsylvania	183,749	197,678
Total	591,516	614,330

Source: U.S. Bureau of the Census.

Stub. The stub is the left column that lists the items about which data are presented or comments made in the other columns. If various levels appear, each sublevel is indented about two spaces from the preceding level.

Education
  Grade school
  High school
  College
    Total

Only the first word of a stub entry is capitalized, although all proper nouns are always capitalized.

Voluntary program
  UN Relief Agency
    Regular program
    Special program

Runover lines should also be indented about two spaces.

Data-processing
  repairs
Electrical and electronic
  technicians

Numbers with items in a stub are unnecessary unless they facilitate cross-referencing in the text discussion.

Type Enrollment	1980	1985	1990	Total
1. Learning disabled	2,163	1,985	2,421	2,032
2. Speech impaired	76	51	39	27
3. Visually handicapped	105	69	101	84
4. All conditions	2,344	2,105	2,561	2,143

Body. The stub and the other columns of the table make up the table body. Although occasionally various kinds of data (dollars, percentages, and so on) will appear in the same column, it is clearer to readers to restrict the data to one kind of information within a particular column, when possible.

Sometimes data are not provided for a particular entry in a column. If a fact or figure is not applicable, write *NA* in the space. If no data exist, put a dash in the space (two hyphens with a typewriter). If there is nothing in the space because the heading does not apply, simply leave the space blank.

Bond Income	1980	1990
Under $5,000	3,091	7,692
$5,000–9,999	6,804	9,171
$10,000–14,999	8,913	10,566
$15,000–24,999	NA	11,841
$25,000–49,999	12,505	—
$50,000 and over	21,162	32,754

Decimal points, dollar signs, percent signs, and the like should all be aligned in a column. When zeros precede a decimal point, only the top and bottom figures require a zero. Place a rule above figures that represent a total or leave a line space before writing the figure.

$0.76
.32
.89
0.67
—––—
$2.64

National Park Service	8,671.02
Corps of Engineers	1,437.95
Bureau of Indian Affairs	3,877.64
Total	13,986.61

Notes. The three principal types of table notes are source notes, general notes, and footnotes. In a table with probability levels, asterisked notes specifying the various levels appear after the last lettered or numbered footnote. Each additional asterisk signifies a higher level of probability.

$*p < .01.$

$**p < .001.$

All notes should be double-spaced in manuscript copy and placed below the table body. Leave one line space between the ruled line at the bottom of the table body and the first note. Write each note indented, paragraph style. Although a publisher may set the word *source* or *note* in capitals and small capitals, an author should type each word with a capital letter, underlined and followed by a colon. (See chapter 9 for source note, footnote, and general note style.)

Note: A period of twenty years was used to compute the average daily precipitation.

The footnote numbers or letters may be written on line or as raised (superscript) elements. The numbers or letters in the table body corresponding to those of the footnotes should always be written raised. To avoid confusion, use letters if they are placed next to figures in a column. Place the letters in sequence horizontally, across the page, not up and down the column.

762^a	857
391	109^b
764^c	244
668	903^d

Do not use a lettered, numbered, or asterisked note with a table title. If a comment must be made concerning the table in general, use a general note.

Note: Figures are for nine months for full-time faculty members.

The order of notes is as follows: source note first, general note(s) second, lettered or numbered footnotes third, and probability notes last.

Source: David Folger, *Quick Reference Guide* (New York: ABC Publishers, 1989), 17.

Note: All river lows are calculated according to average discharge at the mouth.

a. Includes flow of the Colorado River.

b. Includes flow diverted from the Mississippi River.

$p < .01.$

OVERSIZED TABLES

Exceptionally long or wide tables may not fit on the page horizontally or vertically and must then be continued on the succeeding page. When it is practical, an author may prepare the table on large paper and have it reduced to a size that will fit on a single page.

Continuation Lines

Continuation lines are used as needed when a very long or wide table must be continued on another page. A continuation line is needed at the bottom of a right-hand page when it is necessary to turn the page to continue a table on the next left-hand page. A continuation line would also be placed at the top of the left-hand page. When a very wide table is positioned broadside on a left-hand page and continued on a facing right-hand page, the continuation line is generally omitted.

Underline the words of the continuation line in manuscript preparation; they will be set in italic type in printed copy.

Continued on page 000

Continued on page 000

Continued on next page

Continued on next page

The continuation line on the next page should identify the table by number (by title if there is no number), with only the word *continued* underlined (italics in printed copy).

Table 9.14- -Continued

Table 9.14—*Continued*

When to Repeat Heads

When a table is very long as well as wide, it may have to be continued broadside on a second facing (right-hand) page. In that case it is not necessary to repeat the column heads. When it is necessary to turn the page to continue a table on a new left-hand page, it *is* necessary to repeat the heads.

A very wide table may also be typed horizontally with half of the columns on a left-hand page and the other half on a facing right-hand page. In that case, column heads (but not the table title) would have to be provided on the second as well as the first page.

Table 17

Consumer Price Indexes,
1980–1990

1980	1981	1982	1983	1984		1985	1986	1987	1988		1989	1990
		[left page]						*[right page]*				

Ways to Avoid Continuing Tables

Before turning a table broadside on the page or splitting it between two facing pages as shown above, try reducing the space between columns, placing the table number and title on the same line, or single-spacing the body. A large table could also be prepared on oversized paper and reduced to fit a standard text page.

Placement of Notes on Continued Tables

In a continued table, footnotes should appear at the foot of the table page where reference is made. Source notes and general notes, however, are positioned at the foot of the first right-hand page (the second page of a two-page facing spread).

For further examples of tables and the position of elements, see the models in chapter 21.

Chapter 11

FORMS OF ADDRESS

The rules concerning the correct forms of address to use in correspondence are often confusing because of the differences in social and business styles and the different rules that exist for men, women, and dignitaries. In addition, some rules have changed in recent years, for example, the almost exclusive use of *Ms.* for women professionally and the fading use of *the* preceding Catholic titles such as *reverend* (see examples in "Forms of Address: Correspondence" on page 225).

Questions that most often arise concern the proper use of personal, professional, and honorary titles. The following guidelines and the examples in "Forms of Address: Correspondence" apply to inside addresses in correspondence. Traditionally, the inside address of a letter and the envelope address were identical. Now the U.S. Postal Service recommends a different envelope style that can be read by its optical-character readers (see the envelope example in chapter 12).

TITLES

A title should always be used before a name in an address unless the abbreviation *Esq.* follows the name. (*Note:* "Esquire" is used with both men's and women's names.) Then the title is omitted. Also, a scholastic title should not be used in combination with the degree pertaining to that title (*not* Dr. John Jones, M.D.). See "Degrees" on page 220.

Ms. Lynda Sloane

Lynda Sloane, Esq.

Dr. Lynda Sloane

Lynda Sloane, M.D.

Lynda Sloane, Sc.D., LL.D.

Professor Lynda Sloane, Sc.D.

A title may be used in combination with designations such as *Sr.*, with business titles such as *President*, and with initials pertaining to a religious order, such as *S. J.*

Mr. Paul Adams, President

Mr. Paul Adams, Sr.

Father Paul Adams, S.J.

Many writers omit the comma before *Jr.* and *Sr.*; follow the individual's preference.

For more about titles, see the following sections about men, women, companies, and prominent persons.

DEGREES

Generally, avoid using degrees in an inside address. But when initials designating academic degrees are used after a name, place the degree pertaining to the person's profession first, for example, *Diane Royal, LL.D, Ph.D.,* if she is a practicing attorney. Although a scholastic title such as *Dr.* should not be used in combination with initials that indicate the degree, another title may be used in combination with abbreviations of degrees. For example, *The Reverend* could be used with initials representing a law degree.

Dr. James A. Killian *or* James A. Killian, Ph.D.

Dr. Harriet Prentice *or* Harriet Prentice, M.D.

Dr. John Host *or* The Reverend John Host *or* The Reverend John Host, LL.D.

Dr. Malcolm Pruett *or* Malcolm Pruett, Ph.D., *or* Professor Malcolm Pruett *or* Professor Malcolm Pruett, Ph.D.

GENDER AND NAME UNKNOWN

Omit titles such as *Mr.* or *Mrs.* in the inside address (and salutation) when the gender is unknown. Use a job title if a name is unavailable. (Acceptable salutations would be *Dear L. T. Barker, Dear Editor,* and so on.)

F. V. Crenshaw

Leslie Crowley

Director of Research

Member(s), ABC Society

MEN

Use *Mr.* when a man has no other title such as *Dr.* Follow the rules specified in "Titles" and "Degrees" on pages 219 and 220.

Mr. Louis Snow

Professor Louis Snow

Dr. Louis Snow

Louis Snow, D.D.S.

Louis Snow, Esq.

WOMEN

Single Woman

Social. In formal usage, address a single woman by her full name preceded by *Miss.* In informal social usage, use the title *Ms.* unless she prefers *Miss,* and use a scholastic title such as *Dr.* when applicable.

Miss Janet Tate

Dr. Janet Tate

Business. Use the title *Ms.* unless the woman prefers *Miss,* and use a scholastic title such as *Dr.* when applicable. See also "Titles" and "Degrees" on pages 219 and 220 and "Professional Woman" on page 223.

Ms. Janet Tate

Miss Janet Tate

Professor Janet Tate

Dr. Janet Tate

Janet Tate, M.D.

Janet Tate, Esq.

Married or Widowed Woman

Social. In formal usage, address a married or widowed woman by her husband's full name and *Mrs.* In informal social usage, use her husband's full name with *Mrs.* or her first name and her married last name with *Mrs.* or, if she prefers, with *Ms.* Some married women retain their maiden names, and some combine their married and maiden names (with or without a hyphen) both socially and professionally. Use the form she prefers. See "Professional Woman" on page 223 for the use of other titles such as *Dr.*

Mrs. Bennett Stillwell (*formal or informal*)

Mrs. Darlene Stillwell (*informal*)

Ms. Darlene Stillwell (*informal*)

Mrs. Darlene Parker Stillwell (*informal*)

Ms. Darlene Parker-Stillwell (*informal*)

Business. In business, address a married or widowed woman as she prefers, either (1) by her husband's full name with *Mrs.* (less common in business), (2) by her first name and married last name with *Ms.* or *Mrs.*, or (3) by her first name and maiden name with *Ms.* or *Miss.* Use her combined maiden-married name if she prefers that. Use *Ms.*

with her first name and her husband's last name when you are uncertain what she prefers. See "Professional Woman" on page 223 for use of other titles such as *Dr.*

Mrs. Bennett Stillwell (*least common*)

Ms. Darlene Stillwell (*most common*)

Ms. Darlene Parker Stillwell

Mrs. Darlene Stillwell

Mrs. Darlene Parker-Stillwell

Ms. Darlene Parker

Miss Darlene Parker

Divorced Woman

Social. In formal usage, address a divorced woman by her maiden and married names combined with *Mrs.* (but no first name). If she prefers her first name with her maiden name only, use *Miss.* If she prefers her first name and maiden-married name combined, use *Mrs.* In informal social usage, use the name she has taken, maiden or married, with *Ms.* or *Miss.* See "Professional Woman" for use of other titles such as *Dr.*

Mrs. Neely McHenry (*formal*)

Miss Denise Neely (*optional formal*)

Mrs. Denise Neely McHenry (*optional formal*)

Ms. Denise Neely (*informal*)

Miss Denise Neely (*informal*)

Ms. Denise McHenry (*informal*)

Business. In business, use a divorced woman's first name with the last name she has taken, maiden, married, or combined. Use *Ms.* or *Miss* with her maiden name; *Ms., Miss,* or *Mrs.* with her married name; or *Ms., Miss,* or *Mrs.* with a combined last name, as she prefers. Use *Ms.* with her married name if you are uncertain what she prefers. See "Professional Woman" for the use of other titles such as *Dr.*

Ms. Denise Neely

Miss Denise Neely

Ms. Denise McHenry

Miss Denise McHenry

Mrs. Denise McHenry

Ms. Denise Neely McHenry

Miss Denise Neely McHenry

Mrs. Denise Neely-McHenry

Professional Woman

A professional woman usually uses her first name with her married name, maiden name, or a combination. If the woman has an honorary or scholastic title, use it (see "Titles" and "Degrees" on pages 219 and 220). Otherwise, use *Ms., Miss,* or *Mrs.* according to the guidelines given previously for single, married, widowed, or divorced women.

Dr. Mary S. Alder

Mary S. Alder, D.D.S.

Professor Mary S. Alder

Professor Mary S. Alder, LL.D.

Dean Mary S. Alder

The Honorable Mary S. Alder, Governor of Idaho

The Honorable Mary S. Alder, Presiding Justice, Appellate Division

President Mary S. Alder

Ms. Mary S. Alder, Manager, Sales Department

MEN AND WOMEN

The principal questions that arise concerning forms of address for men and women are how to handle titles with husbands and wives together and how to address unmarried men and women together.

Social

Socially, when husbands and wives are addressed and both are titled, use the title for both. If one is titled and not the other, use *Mr.* or *Mrs.* for the untitled person. Use *Mr.* and *Mrs.* when neither is titled. Follow the rules for individuals in addressing unmarried persons together. See "Business" on page 224.

Drs. Jennifer and Carl Ortega

Dr. and Mrs. Carl Ortega

Dr. Jennifer and Mr. Carl Ortega

Dr. Jennifer Ortega and Mr. Carl Ortega

Mr. and Mrs. Carl Ortega

Ambassador Jennifer and Mr. Carl Ortega

Ambassador Jennifer Ortega and Mr. Carl Ortega

Ambassador Carl and Dr. Jennifer Ortega

Ambassador and Mrs. Carl Ortega

Business

Unmarried men and women addressed together should be treated as individuals according to the rules for men, women, and professional persons. In an inside address, stack the names, with the person holding the higher title first. If their positions are equal, list the people alphabetically.

> Ms. Joanne Steel, Sales Manager
> Mr. Darwin Warner, Marketing Manager
> ABC Company
> [Address]

COMPANIES

Use *Messrs.* or *Mesdames* only when companies consist solely of men or of women. Do not use these titles with corporations consisting of impersonal names or with firm names including *Inc.*

> National Business Corporation (*not* Messrs. National Business Corporation)

> Mesdames Arnold, Stoley, and Wilson (*not* Mesdames Arnold, Stoley, and Wilson, Inc.)

> John Maxwell & Sons (*not* Messrs. John Maxwell & Sons)

PROMINENT PERSONS

When only a title is known for a prominent person, address the individual by title preceded by *The*. See "Forms of Address: Correspondence" on page 225 for examples of formal and informal salutations.

> The Acting Mayor of Hartford

> The Lieutenant Governor of Indiana

Someone addressed as "The Honorable" before retirement is still addressed as "The Honorable" after retirement, although the person's formal title, such as *Governor,* would not be used in an address or salutation. Even a former president is called *Mr.* (or *Dr.* if applicable). An exception is the title of *judge*, which is retained after retirement. Retired military officers also retain their title, although the retirement is indicated in the address.

> The Honorable Jeremy Burns (*before retirement*)
> Attorney General of the United States
> [Address]

> The Honorable Jeremy Burns (*after retirement*)
> [Address]

> Colonel Martha Vendura, USA (*before retirement*)
> [Address]

> Colonel Martha Vendura, USA, Retired (*after retirement*)
> [Address]

See also the previous rules and guidelines for titles, degrees, men, women, and men and women together.

FORMS OF ADDRESS: CORRESPONDENCE

Examples of the proper inside address, salutation, and complimentary close are provided below in these categories:

- U.S. government
- State and local government
- The judiciary
- U.S. diplomatic representatives
- Foreign officials and representatives
- United Nations
- The armed forces
- Religion
- Colleges and universities

The examples illustrate the correct form of inside address for the various positions. Beneath each inside address, the correct *formal* salutation and complimentary close are listed first and the correct *informal* salutation and complimentary close are listed last. (For guidelines on the use of personal and professional titles, degrees, and other forms, refer to the preceding sections.)

U.S. GOVERNMENT

If a person has a scholastic title such as *Dr.*, use it instead of *Mr.* or *Ms.*

President

The President
The White House
[Address]

Mr./Madam President:
Respectfully yours,

Dear Mr./Madam President:
Very respectfully yours,/Sincerely yours,

Former President

The Honorable Adam Long
[Local Address]

Sir:
Respectfully yours,

Dear Mr. Long:
Sincerely yours,

Vice President

The Vice President of the United States
The White House
[Address]

The Vice President:
Yours very truly,

Dear Mr./Madam Vice President:
Sincerely yours,

Chief Justice, U.S. Supreme Court

The Chief Justice of the United States
The Supreme Court of the United States
[Address]

Sir/Madam:
Yours very truly,

Dear Mr./Madam Chief Justice:
Sincerely yours,

Associate Justice, U.S. Supreme Court

Madam Justice Short
The Supreme Court of the United States
[Address]

Madam:
Yours very truly,

Dear Madam Justice:/Dear Justice Short:
Sincerely yours,

Retired Justice, U.S. Supreme Court

The Honorable Adam Long
[Local Address]

Sir:
Yours very truly,

Dear Justice Long:
Sincerely yours,

Speaker, House of Representatives

The Honorable Eve Short
Speaker of the House of Representatives
[Address]

Madam:
Yours very truly,

Dear Madam Speaker:/Dear Ms. Short:
Sincerely yours,

Former Speaker, House of Representatives

The Honorable Adam Long
[Local Address]

Sir:
Yours very truly,

Dear Mr. Long:
Sincerely yours,

Cabinet Officer

The Honorable Adam Long
Secretary of State
[Address]

If Written from Abroad

The Honorable Adam Long
Secretary of State of the United States of America
[Address]

Sir:
Yours very truly,

Dear Mr. Secretary:
Sincerely yours,

Former Cabinet Officer

The Honorable Eve Short
[Local Address]

Dear Madam:
Yours very truly,

Dear Ms. Short:
Sincerely yours,

Postmaster General

The Honorable Adam Long
Postmaster General
[Address]

Sir:
Yours very truly,

Dear Mr. Postmaster General:
Sincerely yours,

Attorney General

The Honorable Eve Short
Attorney General of the United States
[Address]

Madam:
Yours very truly,

Dear Madam Attorney General:
Sincerely yours,

Under Secretary, Department

The Honorable Adam Long
Under Secretary of Labor
[Address]

Sir:
Yours very truly,

Dear Mr. Long:/Dear Mr. Under Secretary:
Sincerely yours,

Senator

The Honorable Eve Short
United States Senate
[Address]

Madam:
Yours very truly,

Dear Senator Short:
Sincerely yours,

Former Senator

The Honorable Adam Long
[Local Address]

Dear Sir:
Yours very truly,

Dear Mr. Long:
Sincerely yours,

Senator-elect

The Honorable Eve Short
Senator-elect
United States Senate
[Address]

Dear Madam:
Yours very truly,

Dear Ms. Short:
Sincerely yours,

Committee Chair, U.S. Senate

The Honorable Adam Long
Chairman
House Armed Services Committee
United States Senate
[Address]

Dear Mr. Chairman:
Yours very truly,

Dear Mr. Chairman:/Dear Senator Long:
Sincerely yours,

Subcommittee Chair, U.S. Senate

The Honorable Eve Short
Chairperson
Subcommittee on Foreign Affairs
United States Senate
[Address]

Dear Senator Short:
Yours very truly,

Dear Senator Short:
Sincerely yours,

U.S. Representative, Congress

The Honorable Adam Long
House of Representatives
[Address]

When Away from Washington, D.C.

The Honorable Adam Long
Representative in Congress
[Local Address]

Sir:
Yours very truly,

Dear Mr. Long:
Yours sincerely,

Former U.S. Representative

The Honorable Eve Short
[Local Address]

Dear Madam:/Dear Ms. Short:
Yours very truly,

Dear Ms. Short:
Sincerely yours,

Territorial Delegate

The Honorable Adam Long
Delegate of Puerto Rico
House of Representatives
[Address]

Dear Sir:/Dear Mr. Long:
Yours very truly,

Dear Mr. Long:
Sincerely yours,

Resident Commissioner

The Honorable Eve Short
Resident Commissioner of [Territory]
House of Representatives
[Address]

Dear Madam:/Dear Ms. Short:
Yours very truly,

Dear Ms. Short:
Sincerely yours,

Director/Head, Independent Federal Offices, Agencies, Commissions, Organizations

> The Honorable Adam Long, Director
> Federal Emergency Management Agency
> [Address]
>
> Dear Mr. Director:
> Yours very truly,
>
> Dear Mr. Long:
> Sincerely yours,

Other High Officials

> The Honorable Eve Short
> Comptroller General of the United States
> [Address]
>
> Dear Madam:/Dear Ms. Short:
> Yours very truly,
>
> Dear Ms. Short:
> Sincerely yours,

Secretary to the President

> The Honorable Adam Long
> Secretary to the President
> The White House
> [Address]
>
> Dear Sir:/Dear Mr. Long:
> Yours very truly,
>
> Dear Mr. Long:
> Sincerely yours,

Assistant Secretary to the President

> The Honorable Eve Short
> Assistant Secretary to the President
> The White House
> [Address]
>
> Dear Madam:/Dear Ms. Short:
> Yours very truly,
>
> Dear Ms. Short:
> Sincerely yours,

Press Secretary to the President

Mr. Adam Long
Press Secretary to the President
The White House
[Address]

Dear Sir:/Dear Mr. Long:
Yours very truly,

Dear Mr. Long:
Sincerely yours,

STATE AND LOCAL GOVERNMENT

Governor, State or Territory

The form of address given here is used in most states. *His/Her Excellency, the Governor of Massachusetts,* is the form by law in that state, as well as by courtesy in some other states:

Her Excellency, Eve Short
Governer of Massachusetts

The salutation and complimentary close are the same as that illustrated below.

The Honorable Eve Short
Governor of Louisiana
[Address]

Madam:
Yours very truly,

Dear Governor Short:
Sincerely yours,

Acting Governor, State or Territory

The Honorable Adam Long
Acting Governor of Nevada
[Address]

Sir:
Yours very truly,

Dear Mr. Long:
Sincerely yours,

Lieutenant Governor

The Honorable Eve Short
Lieutenant Governor of New Mexico
[Address]

Madam:
Yours very truly,

Dear Ms. Short:
Sincerely yours,

Secretary of State

The Honorable Adam Long
Secretary of the State of New Hampshire
[Address]

Sir:
Yours very truly,

Dear Mr. Secretary:
Sincerely yours,

Attorney General

The Honorable Eve Short
Attorney General of Tennessee
[Address]

Madam:
Yours very truly,

Dear Madam Attorney General:
Sincerely yours,

President, State Senate

The Honorable Adam Long
President of the Senate of the State of Hawaii
[Address]

Sir:
Yours very truly,

Dear Mr. Long:
Sincerely yours,

Speaker, Assembly/House of Representatives

In California, Nevada, New York, and Wisconsin this legislative body is called the Assembly; in Maryland, Virginia, and West Virginia it is the House of Delegates; in New Jersey it is the House of General Assembly.

The Honorable Eve Short
Speaker of the Assembly of the State of California
[Address]

Madam:
Yours very truly,

Dear Ms. Short:
Sincerely yours,

State Treasurer, Auditor, Comptroller

The Honorable Adam Long
Treasurer of the State of Illinois
[Address]

Dear Sir:
Yours very truly,

Dear Mr. Long:
Sincerely yours,

State Senator

The Honorable Eve Short
The State Senate
[Address]

Dear Madam:
Yours very truly,

Dear Senator Short:
Sincerely yours,

State Representative, Assembly Member, Delegate

The Honorable Adam Long
House of Delegates
[Address]

Dear Sir:
Yours very truly,

Dear Mr. Long:
Sincerely yours,

District Attorney

The Honorable Eve Short
District Attorney, March County
County Courthouse
[Address]

Dear Madam:
Yours very truly,

Dear Ms. Short:
Sincerely yours,

Mayor

The Honorable Adam Long
Mayor of Fort Lauderdale
[Address]

Dear Sir:
Yours very truly,

Dear Mr. Mayor:/Dear Mayor Long:
Sincerely yours,

President, Board of Commissioners

The Honorable Eve Short
President
Board of Commissioners of the
   City of Hillside
[Address]

Dear Madam:
Yours very truly,

Dear Ms. Short:
Sincerely yours,

City Attorney, City Counsel, Corporation Counsel

The Honorable Adam Long
City Attorney
[Address]

Dear Sir:
Yours very truly,

Dear Mr. Long:
Sincerely yours,

Alderperson

Alderperson Eve Short
City Hall
[Address]

Dear Madam:
Yours very truly,

Dear Ms. Short:
Sincerely yours,

THE JUDICIARY

See also the U.S. Supreme Court example under "U.S. Government" on page 226.

Chief Justice, Chief Judge, State Supreme Court

The Honorable Adam Long
Chief Justice of the Supreme Court of Arizona
[Address]

Sir:
Yours very truly,

Dear Mr. Chief Justice:
Sincerely yours,

Associate Justice, Highest Court of a State

The Honorable Eve Short
Associate Justice of the Supreme Court of Ohio
[Address]

Madam:
Yours very truly,

Dear Justice:/Dear Justice Short:
Sincerely yours,

Presiding Justice

The Honorable Adam Long
Presiding Justice, Appellate Division
Supreme Court of California
[Address]

Sir:
Yours very truly,

Dear Justice:/Dear Justice Long:
Sincerely yours,

Judge of a Court

This does not apply to the U.S. Supreme Court.

The Honorable Eve Short
Judge of the United States District Court
    for the Northern District of South Carolina
[Address]

Madam:
Yours very truly,

Dear Judge Short:
Sincerely yours,

Clerk of a Court

Adam Long, Esq.
Clerk of the Superior Court of Iowa
[Address]

Dear Sir:
Yours very truly,

Dear Mr. Long:
Sincerely yours,

U.S. DIPLOMATIC REPRESENTATIVES

American Ambassador

Include the name of the country in which an ambassador or minister is based when the person is temporarily away from that post (*The American Ambassador to Great Britain*). If the person holds military rank, the diplomatic complimentary title *The Honorable* is omitted (*General Adam Long, American Ambassador*). For ambassadors and ministers to Central and South American countries, substitute *The Ambassador of the United States* for *American Ambassador/Minister*.

The Honorable Adam Long
American Ambassador
[Address]

Sir:
Yours very truly,

Dear Mr. Ambassador:/Dear Ambassador Long:
Sincerely yours,

American Minister

The Honorable Eve Short
American Minister to Malawi
[Address]

Madam:
Yours very truly,

Dear Madam Minister:/Dear Minister Short:
Sincerely yours,

American Chargé d'Affaires, Consul General, Consul, Vice-Consul

The phrase ad Interim added to a title means "for the intervening time," "temporarily."

Adam Long, Esq.
American Chargé d'Affaires ad Interim
[Address]

Sir:
Yours very truly,

Dear Mr. Long:
Sincerely yours

High Commissioner

The Honorable Eve Short
United States High Commissioner to Brazil
[Address]

Madam:
Yours very truly,

Dear Ms. Short:
Sincerely yours,

FOREIGN OFFICIALS AND REPRESENTATIVES

Foreign Ambassador in the United States

Use this form of address when the representative is British or a member of the British Commonwealth: *The Right Honorable* or *The Honorable* in addition to *His/Her Excellency* wherever appropriate:

His Excellency
The Right Honorable/The Rt. Hon. David Holmes
Ambassador of Great Britain

Use the following form for other countries:

His Excellency, Kjell Eliassen
Ambassador of Norway
[Address]

Excellency:
Yours very truly,

Dear Mr. Ambassador:
Sincerely yours,

Foreign Minister in the United States

The diplomatic title *His/Her Excellency* or *The Honorable* is omitted if the personal title is royal, such as *His/Her Highness* or *Prince*.

The Honorable Ian Stoichici
Minister of Romania
[Address]

Sir:
Yours very truly,

Dear Mr. Minister:
Sincerely yours,

Foreign Diplomatic Representatives with a Personal Title

Titles of special courtesy in Spanish-speaking countries, such as *Dr., Señor,* or *Dom,* may be used with the diplomatic title *His/Her Excellency* or *The Honorable.* Titles of royalty such as *count* or *baron* should always be included as a matter of respect.

His Excellency, Count Rinaldo Petrignani
Ambassador of Italy
[Address]

Excellency:
Yours very truly,

Dear Mr. Ambassador:
Sincerely yours,

Prime Minister

His Excellency, Nobuo Matsunaga
Prime Minister of Japan
[Address]

Excellency:
Yours very truly,

Dear Mr. Prime Minister:
Sincerely yours,

British Prime Minister

The Right Honorable Jonathan Cole, K.G., M.C., M.P.
Prime Minister
[Address]

Sir:
Yours very truly,

Dear Mr. Prime Minister:/Dear Mr. Cole:
Sincerely yours,

Canadian Prime Minister

The Right Honorable Jean Paul Perreault, C.M.G.
Prime Minister of Canada
[Address]

Sir:
Respectfully yours,

Dear Mr. Prime Minister:/Dear Mr. Perreault:
Sincerely yours,

President of a Republic

His Excellency, Joaquin Balaguer
President of the Dominican Republic
[Address]

Excellency:
Respectfully yours,

Dear Mr. President:
Sincerely yours,

Premier

His Excellency, Michel Rocard
Premier of the French Republic
[Address]

Excellency:
Respectfully yours,

Dear Mr. Premier:
Sincerely yours,

Foreign Chargé d'Affaires
in the United States

Mr. Anders Ljunggren
Chargé d'Affaires of Sweden
[Address]

Sir:
Yours very truly,

Dear Mr. Ljunggren:
Sincerely yours,

Foreign Chargé d'Affaires ad Interim in the United States

Mr. Michael O'Reilly
Chargé d'Affaires ad Interim of Ireland
[Address]

Sir:
Yours very truly,

Dear Mr. O'Reilly:
Sincerely yours,

UNITED NATIONS

The United Nations consists of the General Assembly, the Security Council, the Economic and Social Council, the Trusteeship Council, the International Court of Justice, and the Secretariat.

Secretary General

Although it is proper to use *His/Her Excellency* for persons of high official rank from other countries, an American citizen should never be addressed as *His/Her Excellency*. Rather, persons of high official rank from the United States are addressed as *The Honorable* (*The Honorable Adam Long, Secretary General of the United Nations*).

His Excellency, Adam Long
Secretary General of the United Nations
[Address]

Excellency:
Yours very truly,

Dear Mr. Secretary General:
Sincerely yours,

Under Secretary

The Honorable Eve Short
Under Secretary of the United Nations
The Secretariat
United Nations
[Address]

Madam:
Yours very truly,

Dear Ms. Short:/Dear Madam Under Secretary:
Sincerely yours,

Foreign Representative with Ambassadorial Rank

His Excellency, Julian Santamaria
Representative of Spain to the United Nations
[Address]

Excellency:
Yours very truly,

Dear Mr. Ambassador:
Sincerely yours,

U.S. Representative with Ambassadorial Rank

The Honorable Adam Long
United States Representative to the United Nations
[Address]

Sir:/Dear Mr. Ambassador:
Yours very truly,

Dear Mr. Ambassador:
Sincerely yours,

ARMED FORCES: ARMY, AIR FORCE, MARINE CORPS

Civilian writers usually spell out the rank for all branches of the service, but abbreviations are used in the military service, for example, *CPT* for "captain" and *1LT* for "first lieutenant." In the army, regular service is signified by *USA*, and the reserve is indicated by *USAR*. Official correspondence should include the full rank in both the envelope and inside address (not in the salutation).

Titles in the air force are the same as those in the army. Instead of *USA*, the regular air force uses *USAF*, and *USAFR* indicates the air force reserve. Titles in the Marine Corps are also the same as those in the army, except that the top rank is *commandant of the Marine Corps*. Regular service is indicated by *USMC*, and *USMCR* indicates the reserve.

General of the Army

General of the Army Adam Long, USA
Department of the Army
[Address]

Sir:
Yours very truly,

Dear General Long:
Sincerely yours,

General, Lieutenant General, Major General, Brigadier General

General Eve Short, USA
[Address]

Madam:
Yours very truly,

Dear General Short:
Sincerely yours,

Colonel, Lieutenant Colonel

Colonel Adam Long, USA
[Address]

Dear Colonel Long:
Yours very truly,

Dear Colonel Long:
Sincerely yours,

Major

Major Eve Short, USA
[Address]

Dear Major Short:
Yours very truly,

Dear Major Short:
Sincerely yours,

Captain

Captain Adam Long, USA
[Address]

Dear Captain Long:
Yours very truly,

Dear Captain Long:
Sincerely yours,

First Lieutenant, Second Lieutenant

Lieutenant Eve Short, USA
[Address]

Dear Lieutenant Short:
Yours very truly,

Dear Lieutenant Short:
Sincerely yours,

Chief Warrant Officer, Warrant Officer

Chief Warrant Officer Adam Long, USA
[Address]

Dear Mr. Long:
Yours very truly,

Dear Mr. Long:
Sincerely yours,

Chaplain, U.S. Army

Chaplain Eve Short, Captain, USA
[Address]

Dear Chaplain Short:
Yours very truly,

Dear Chaplain Short:
Sincerely yours,

ARMED FORCES: NAVY, COAST GUARD

Titles in the Coast Guard are the same as those in the navy, except that the top rank is *admiral*. In the Coast Guard, regular service is indicated by *USCG*, whereas *USCGR* indicates the reserve. In the navy, regular service is indicated by *USN,* and *USNR* signifies the reserve.

Fleet Admiral

Admiral Adam Long, USN
Chief of Naval Operations
Department of the Navy
[Address]

Sir:
Yours very truly,

Dear Admiral Long:
Sincerely yours,

Admiral, Vice Admiral, Rear Admiral

Admiral Eve Short, USN
United States Naval Academy
[Address]

Madam:
Yours very truly,

Dear Admiral Short:
Sincerely yours,

Commodore, Captain, Commander, Lieutenant Commander

Commodore Adam Long, USN
[Address]

Dear Commodore Long:
Yours very truly,

Dear Commodore Long:
Sincerely yours,

Junior Officers: Lieutenant, Lieutenant Junior Grade, Ensign

Lieutenant Eve Short, USN
USS Hawaii
[Address]

Dear Ms. Short:
Yours very truly,

Dear Ms. Short:
Sincerely yours,

Chief Warrant Officer, Warrant Officer

Chief Warrant Officer Adam Long, USN
USS Idaho
[Address]

Dear Mr. Long:
Yours very truly,

Dear Mr. Long:
Sincerely yours,

Chaplain

Chaplain Adam Long, Captain, USN
Department of the Navy
[Address]

Dear Chaplain Long:
Yours very truly,

Dear Chaplain Long:
Sincerely yours,

CATHOLIC FAITH

The Pope

His Holiness, The Pope/His Holiness, Pope John Paul
Vatican City
[Address]

Your Holiness/Most Holy Father
Respectfully yours,

[formal only]

Apostolic Pro-Nuncio

His Excellency, Most Reverend Adam Long
Titular Archbishop of Mauriana
The Apostolic Pro-Nuncio
[Address]

Your Excellency:
Respectfully yours,

Dear Archbishop Long:
Sincerely yours,

Cardinal in the United States

His Eminence, Alfred Cardinal Long
Archbishop of Boston
[Address]

Your Eminence:
Respectfully yours,

Dear Cardinal Long:
Sincerely yours,

Bishop and Archbishop in the United States

Most Reverend Adam Long, D.D.
Bishop of Miami
[Address]

Your Excellency:
Respectfully yours,

Dear Bishop Long:
Sincerely yours,

Bishop in England

Right Reverend Adam Long
Bishop of Berkshire
[Local Address]

Right Reverend Sir:
Respectfully yours,

Dear Bishop:
Sincerely yours,

Abbot

Right Reverend Adam Long
Abbot of Ealing Abbey
[Address]

Dear Father Abbot:
Respectfully yours,

Dear Father Long:
Sincerely yours,

Monsignor

Reverend Msgr. Adam Long
[Address]

Reverend Monsignor:
Respectfully yours,

Dear Monsignor Long:
Sincerely yours,

Superior of a Brotherhood and Priest

Consult the *Official Catholic Directory* for the address of the superior of a brotherhood, since the wording depends on whether he is a priest or has a title other than superior.

The Very Reverend Adam Long, M.M.
Director
[Address]

Dear Father Superior:
Respectfully yours,

Dear Father Superior:
Sincerely yours,

Priest

With Scholastic Degree

Reverend Adam Long, Ph.D.
[Address]

Dear Dr. Long:
Yours very truly,

Dear Dr. Long:
Sincerely yours,

Without Scholastic Degree

Reverend Adam Long, S.J.
[Address]

Dear Reverend Father Long:
Yours very truly,

Dear Reverend Father Long:
Sincerely yours,

Brother

Brother Adam Long
[Address]

Dear Brother:
Yours very truly,

Dear Brother Long:
Sincerely yours,

Mother Superior of a Sisterhood, Catholic or Protestant

Many religious congregations no longer use the title *superior*. The head of a congregation is known instead by another title, such as *president*.

Reverend Mother Superior, I. B. V. M.
Convent of St. Jude
[Address]

Dear Reverend Mother:/Dear Mother Superior:
Respectfully yours,

Dear Reverend Mother:/Dear Mother Superior:
Sincerely yours,

Sister Superior

Consult the *Official Catholic Directory* for the address of the superior of a sisterhood. This depends on the order to which she belongs, and the abbreviations for the order are not always used.

Reverend Sister Superior
Convent of St. Jude
[Address]

Dear Sister Superior:
Respectfully yours,

Dear Sister Superior:
Sincerely yours,

Sister

If known, use the form of address preferred by the person. Some women religious prefer to be addressed as "Sister Short" rather than "Sister Eve" in business situations, but others object to the use of the last name.

Sister Eve Short
[Address]

Dear Sister:
Yours very truly,

Dear Sister Short:
Sincerely yours,

JEWISH FAITH

Rabbi

With Scholastic Degree

Rabbi Joseph Steinberg, Ph.D.
[Address]

Sir:
Yours very truly,

Dear Dr. Steinberg:/Dear Rabbi Steinberg:
Sincerely yours,

Without Scholastic Degree

Rabbi Joseph Steinberg
[Address]

Sir:
Yours very truly,

Dear Rabbi Steinberg:
Sincerely yours,

PROTESTANT FAITH

Anglican Archbishop

The Most Reverend Archbishop of
    Canterbury/The Most Reverend
Adam Long
Archbishop of Canterbury
[Address]

Your Grace:
Respectfully yours,

Dear Archbishop Long:
Sincerely yours,

Presiding Bishop of the Protestant Episcopal Church in America

The Right Reverend Adam Long, D.D., LL.D.
Presiding Bishop of the Protestant
    Episcopal Church in America
[Address]

Right Reverend Sir:
Respectfully yours,

Dear Bishop Long:
Sincerely yours,

Anglican Bishop

The Right Reverend
The Lord Bishop of London
[Address]

Right Reverend Sir:
Respectfully yours,

Dear Bishop Long:
Sincerely yours,

Methodist Bishop

The Reverend Adam Long
Methodist Bishop
[Address]

Reverend Sir:
Respectfully yours,

Dear Bishop Long:
Sincerely yours,

Protestant Episcopal Bishop

The Right Reverend Adam Long, D.D., LL.D.
Bishop of Tucson
[Address]

Right Reverend Sir:
Respectfully yours,

Dear Bishop Long:
Sincerely yours,

Archdeacon

The Venerable Adam Long
Archdeacon of Columbus
[Address]

Venerable Sir:
Respectfully yours,

Dear Archdeacon:
Sincerely yours,

Dean

This applies only to the head of a cathedral or of a theological seminary.

The Very Reverend Adam Long, D.D.
Dean of St. Luke's
[Address]

Very Reverend Sir:
Respectfully yours,

Dear Dean Long:
Sincerely yours,

Canon

The Reverend Canon Adam Long, D.D.
Canon of St. Andrew's
[Address]

Reverend Sir:
Respectfully yours,

Dear Canon Long:
Sincerely yours,

Protestant Minister

With Scholastic Degree

The Reverend Adam Long, D.D., Litt.D./The Reverend Dr.
   Adam Long
[Address]

Dear Dr. Long:
Yours very truly,

Dear Dr. Long:
Sincerely yours,

Without Scholastic Degree

The Reverend Adam Long
[Address]

Dear Mr. Long:
Yours very truly,

Dear Mr. Long:
Sincerely yours,

Episcopal Priest, High Church

With Scholastic Degree

The Reverend Adam Long, D.D., Litt.D./The Reverend Dr.
   Adam Long
[Address]

Dear Dr. Long:
Yours very truly,

Dear Dr. Long:
Sincerely yours,

Without Scholastic Degree

The Reverend Adam Long
[Address]

Dear Mr. Long:/Dear Father Long:
Yours very truly,

Dear Mr. Long:/Dear Father Long:
Sincerely yours,

COLLEGE AND UNIVERSITY OFFICIALS

President

With a Doctorate

Dr. Eve Short, LL.D., Ph.D.
President
Northern University
[Address]

Madam:
Yours very truly,

Dear Dr. Short:
Sincerely yours,

Without a Doctorate

Ms. Eve Short
President
Northern University
[Address]

Madam:
Yours very truly,

Dear President Short:
Sincerely yours,

Catholic Priest

The Reverend Adam Long, S.J., D.D., Ph.D.
President
Winston University
[Address]

Sir:
Yours very truly,

Dear Dr. Long:
Sincerely yours,

University Chancellor

Dr. Eve Short
Chancellor
Morrisville University
[Address]

Madam:
Yours very truly,

Dear Dr. Short:
Sincerely yours,

Dean, Assistant Dean, College/Graduate School

With a Doctorate

Dr. Adam Long
Dean, School of Law
University of Ohio
[Address]

Dear Sir:/Dear Dean Long:
Yours very truly,

Dear Dean Long:
Sincerely yours,

Without a Doctorate

Dean Adam Long
School of Law
University of Ohio
[Address]

Dear Sir:/Dear Dean Long:
Yours very truly,

Dear Dean Long:
Sincerely yours,

Professor

With a Doctorate

Dr. Eve Short/Eve Short, Ph.D.
Eastern University
[Address]

Dear Madam:/Dear Dr. Short:/Dear Professor Short:
Yours very truly,

Dear Dr. Short:/Professor Short:
Sincerely yours,

Without a Doctorate

Professor Eve Short
Eastern University
[Address]

Dear Madam:/Dear Professor Short:
Yours very truly,

Dear Professor Short:
Sincerely yours,

Associate/Assistant Professor

With a Doctorate

Dr. Adam Long/Adam Long, Ph.D.
Associate Professor
Southern University
[Address]

Dear Sir:/Dear Dr. Long:/Dear Professor Long:
Yours very truly,

Dear Dr. Long:/Dear Professor Long:
Sincerely yours,

Without a Doctorate

Mr. Adam Long
Associate Professor
Southern University
[Address]

Dear Sir:/Dear Professor Long:
Yours very truly,

Dear Professor Long:
Sincerely yours,

Instructor

With a Doctorate

Dr. Eve Short/Eve Short, Ph.D.
Department of Political Science
University of Michigan
[Address]

Dear Madam:/Dear Dr. Short:
Yours very truly,

Dear Dr. Short:
Sincerely yours,

Without a Doctorate

Ms. Eve Short
Department of Political Science
University of Michigan
[Address]

Dear Madam:
Yours very truly,

Dear Ms. Short:
Sincerely yours,

Chaplain, College or University

With a Doctorate

Chaplain Adam Long, D.D., Ph.D.
Presbyterian College
[Address]

Dear Dr. Long:
Yours very truly,

Dear Dr. Long:
Sincerely yours,

Without a Doctorate

The Reverend Adam Long
Chaplain
Presbyterian College
[Address]

Dear Chaplain Long:
Yours very truly,

Dear Chaplain Long:
Sincerely yours,

Chapter 12

LETTERS

FORMATS

Letter writers have five formats from which to choose (see the models in chapter 15; memo formats are described in chapter 13, and memo models are also provided in chapter 15).

1. *Full block* (modern style—all parts flush left)
2. *Simplified* (modern style—a full-block format that omits the salutation and complimentary close)
3. *Block* (combined modern-traditional style—paragraphs flush left but not the date, reference line, complimentary close, or signature)
4. *Modified block* (traditional style—similar to block format with paragraph indents as well)
5. *Official/personal* (traditional style)—like modified block but with inside address beneath the signature line)

Not all formats are suitable for all writers or all occasions. The simplified style, for example, might be too casual for certain formal messages. The official/personal style is seldom used in the business world. The block and modified-block formats may appear too traditional for an individual or firm trying to convey an ultramodern image, whereas the full-block style may appear too modern for a conservative traditionalist. A letter writer, therefore, must evaluate personal and professional needs and objectives rather than randomly select a format or use one out of habit.

PUNCTUATION

Three punctuation styles are used in letters. The most common is the standard, or mixed, style.

Standard: A colon follows the salutation and a comma follows the complimentary close.

Open: No punctuation is used after any line before and after the body unless the line ends with an abbreviation.

Close: Every line before and after the body ends with either a comma or period.

STATIONERY

The common stationery sizes are as follows:

Standard (business): 8½ by 11 inches

Baronial (note, memo, etc.): 5½ by 8½ inches

Monarch (executive): 7¼ by 10½ inches

Envelope sizes are usually selected to accommodate a sheet of paper folded in thirds. The No. 9 or No. 10 envelope, for example, will hold an 8½-by-11-inch sheet folded twice. Consult an office-supply store for currently available letter and envelope sizes and weights (20-pound and 24-pound weights are common for business correspondence; lighter weights may be used for overseas airmail letters or for file copies).

The quality of stationery is geared to its use. Whereas top-level executives might select a white or off-white paper of 100 percent-cotton content, a department engaged in mass mailings might use an inexpensive bond paper of any color that will attract attention. Samples are available in most printing firms and some office-supply and stationery stores.

PARTS OF A LETTER

A letter may have as many as sixteen principal parts as well as an envelope address that corresponds to the letter's inside address. The appearance is the same whether a letter is prepared by computer or typewriter.

Depending on the software used in computer preparation, the operator may be able to store format instructions for instant recall each time a letter is to be prepared. When similar messages are sent over and over, in fact, complete letters may be stored. Only minor modifications (e.g., different date or inside address) would then need to be keyed in before printout. In volume work, it is time consuming, inefficient, and costly to type every letter from scratch.

Format instructions should be entered for the following parts (listed in the order they appear in a letter), including the envelope. For examples of how the position of these elements differs in the five letter styles, see the models in chapter 15.

Dateline
Reference line
Personal or confidential notation
Inside address
Attention line
Salutation

Subject line

Body

Complimentary close

Signature

Identification line

Enclosure notation

Mail notation

Copy notation

Postscript

Continuation-page heading

Envelope

Chapter 15 provides not only model letter formats but model formats for memos, envelopes, mailing labels, business cards, petitions, and other forms of correspondence such as announcements, notices, and invitations.

Dateline

The date the letter is written is the first element to appear below the letterhead address. The traditional order is month, day, and year; the military order is day, month, and year, with no commas.

Leave two to four blank line spaces above the date and one line space between the date and reference line (if any) or about two to twelve blank line spaces between the date and the inside address. Space can be varied to accommodate letters of different sizes.

In full-block and simplified letters the date is positioned flush left. In the other formats it is positioned (1) two to three character spaces to the right of the page center (aligned with the complimentary close in those letters), (2) flush against the right margin, or (3) somewhere in between.

HIGH GARDENS
100 FIRST AVENUE
DURHAM, NC 27701

June 21, 1991

Your reference XYZ-1002BC

Ms. Polly Ferguson, President
Better Nurseries Association
213 Toledo Avenue
Warwick, RI 02888

**HIGH GARDENS
100 FIRST AVENUE
DURHAM, NC 27701**

June 21, 1991

Your reference XYZ-1002BC

Ms. Polly Ferguson, President
Better Nurseries Association
213 Toledo Avenue
Warwick, RI 02888

**HIGH GARDENS
101 FIRST AVENUE
DURHAM, NC 27701**

June 21, 1991

Your reference XYZ-1002BC

Ms. Polly Ferguson, President
Better Nurseries Association
213 Toledo Avenue
Warwick, RI 02888

Reference Line

Reference lines are used to refer the sender and receiver to a file number, code, or other designation. Some letterhead stationery may have a printed line immediately below the letterhead address, for example, *In reply please refer to*: The sender would then write the designation two spaces after the colon or on the line below. The date in this case would be written two lines below the reference line. Some reference lines have two designations (*Our reference, Your reference*). Place your own reference first and the addressee's on the line below.

If no printed line is given, place the reference line two lines below the date. Align it with the first word of the date (see "Dateline" on page 259), which may be flush left, flush right, or slightly right of the page center, depending on the letter format.

**PENN BROKERS
101 KELLY STREET
LEVITTOWN, PA 19054**

When replying, refer to: X094-1

June 4, 1991

PENN BROKERS
101 KELLY STREET
LEVITTOWN, PA 19054

June 4, 1991

Our reference X094-1
Your reference 89376-00JV

Personal or Confidential Notation

If it is critical that no one but the addressee open a letter, a personal or confidential notation may be written on the envelope and a similar notation written on the letter, flush left in all formats. Place the notation about four lines above the inside address (or two lines below the reference line). It may be typed all capitals or may be underlined.

PERSONAL *or* Personal

CONFIDENTIAL *or* Confidential

Inside Address

The inside address is written single-spaced in uppercase and lowercase letters, unlike an envelope address written in all capitals for Postal Service optical-character reading. It is positioned flush left in all letter formats but appears two lines below the signature line in the official/personal style.

In all other formats, leave two to twelve lines of space between the date and the inside address, depending on the length of the letter and any adjustment needed for the letter to be positioned attractively on the page. Extremely long lines should be divided logically and carried over to the next line. Indent any such runover lines two to three character spaces.

Traditionally, writers included job titles and both street addresses and post office box addresses in the inside address. Authorities now recommend that if the inside address will run over four lines, writers should omit the job title and use only the location desired for delivery—street address or post office box number, but not both. When both street address and post office box are listed, the mail will be delivered to the one that is listed last, just before the city and state.

Follow these guidelines for the inside address (but see "Envelope" on page 274 for other rules concerning envelope addresses).

1. Use the company's official name and spell out or abbreviate *Co., Corp.,* and so on accordingly.

2. Do not precede a street number with an abbreviation or symbol for *number* (not *#251 Dexter Street*).

3. Spell out street address numbers of twelve and below. But use figures for all house numbers except *One*. Use a spaced hyphen to separate house and thoroughfare numbers. Do not add *d, st,* or *th* to a figure.

71 West Twelfth Street

71 West 13 Street

One Sixth Avenue

2 Sixth Avenue

147 - 32 Street

4. Do not abbreviate city names unless the abbreviated version is standard, such as *St. Paul.* (See chapter 6 for state abbreviations.)

5. Use personal titles such as *Mr.* or scholastic titles such as *Dr.* before a name even when a business title such as *director* is used. (For more on forms of address, see chapter 11.) Put a short business title on the same line as the name. A long title should be placed on the next line. (Unless the title is essential for delivery of a letter, omit the title if the address will take more than four lines.) If a person has several titles, use only the highest one.

Ms. Jennifer Crawley, Editor

Mr. Michael Henderson
Vice President, New Product Development

6. Although the attention line appears within the address block on an envelope, place it two lines below the inside address of a letter.

7. Place a departmental name after the company name.

8. Stack names (by importance of title or, if no difference, by alphabetical order) if a letter is addressed to two or more persons.

Mr. Robb Porter, Jr.
Ms. Mildred Steiner
Lewis Builders, Inc.
1907 North Street
Milwaukee, WI 53212

Attention Line

A letter may be addressed to a company and include an attention line directing it to an individual. This insures that the letter will be opened even if the person named in the attention line isn't there. A letter may also be addressed to one person with an attention line directing it to another person. This also insures that the letter will be opened (by the person in the attention line) even if the addressee is absent.

An attention line is used only when it is *not* essential that a specific person read the letter or if it *is* essential that the letter be acted on and not delayed just because an individual might be absent. In the examples below, the letter will be opened by someone even if the individual named is absent.

Leave a blank line space before and after the attention line (two line spaces after it in the simplified format), and position it flush left regardless of the letter format (see chapter 15). An attention line is not used in the official/personal format.

Tamarack Bottling Co.
1600 Laurel Street
Downey, CA 90242

Attention Helen Morris, Purchasing Department

Ladies and Gentlemen:

Mr. Herbert Vos
Tamarack Bottling Co.
1600 Laurel Street
Downey, CA 90242

Attention Helen Morris, Purchasing Department

Dear Mr. Vos:

Salutation

The salutation, or greeting, is placed flush left in all letter styles except the simplified format, where it is omitted. It is placed either two lines below the inside address or two lines below the attention line (if any), except, in the official/personal format where it is placed two to twelve lines below the date. A blank line space should follow the salutation before writing the subject line or the first line of the body.

Chapter 11 provides guidelines on the use of titles and the proper forms of address for men, women, companies, dignitaries, and persons whose name or gender is unknown. Generally, in the salutation the word *Dear* precedes the same name and title that is used in the inside address (when the addressee is a person). In standard punctuation a colon follows the salutation in a business letter.

Dear Dr. Adams: (*not* Dear Dr. Adams, M.D.)

Dear Ms. Adams: (*not* Dear Secretary Adams)

Dear Madam Secretary: (*U.S. Cabinet*)

Dear Mr. Adams:

Dear Professor Adams: (*not* Dear Professor)

Dear A. D. Adams: (*gender unknown*)

Dear Manager: (*name unknown*)

Dear Sir: (*name unknown but gender known*)

Dear Madam: (*name unknown but gender known*)

Ladies and Gentlemen: (*company*)

Ladies: (*firm—women only*)

Mesdames: (*firm—women only*)

Gentlemen: (*firm—men only*)

Dear Mr. Adams and Ms. Watson:

Dear Mr. Adams and Mr. Hart:

Dear Messrs. Adams and Hart:

Dear Ms. Adams and Ms. Hart:

Dear Mss. Adams and Hart:

Dear Dr. Adams and Mr. Adams: (*titled wife*)

Dear Dr. and Mr. Adams: (*titled wife*)

Dear Dr. and Mrs. Adams: (*titled husband*)

Dear Drs. Adams: (*both spouses titled*)

Dear Mr. and Mrs. Adams: (*neither spouse titled*)

Dear Friends: (*collective*)

Dear Members: (*collective*)

Subject Line

A subject line summarizes the topic of the letter so that the reader can see at a glance what will be discussed and the writer doesn't have to describe the subject in the letter body. In most letter styles the subject line is written two lines below the salutation, and the letter body begins two lines below the subject line. In the simplified format there is no salutation, so the subject line is written three lines below the last line of the inside address, or the attention line, if any, and the letter body begins three lines below the subject line.

The word *subject*, sometimes followed by a colon, may precede the subject but is often omitted. Legal writers precede the topic with the words *In re or Re,* sometimes followed by a colon. Important words are capitalized, or the entire line may be written in all capitals.

The subject line is written flush left or indented to correspond to the paragraph style.

Dear Ms. Glass:

ZONING COMMITTEE REPORT

Here is the evaluation you requested on August 9. The report concludes with my recommendations for . . .

Dear Ms. Glass:

SUBJECT: Zoning Committee Report

Here is the evaluation you requested on August 9. The report concludes with my recommendations for . . .

Body

The body (message) of a letter begins after the salutation or subject line (if any). Leave a blank line space before and after the body and between each paragraph, regardless of letter style. Single-space all letters except a very brief letter of one or two sentences, which may (but need not) be double-spaced. Indent paragraphs (five to ten character spaces) in the modified-block and official/personal styles. Begin paragraphs flush left in all other styles.

Sometimes the body of a letter contains material that should be displayed or in some way distinguished from the regular text paragraphs. A list, for example, could be set up in stacked fashion rather than itemized within a sentence. It might be indented five to ten spaces as a block or positioned flush left in certain letter formats (e.g., the full-block or simplified style). A blocked quotation (see chapter 2 and the model in chapter 21) should be indented five to ten spaces at the left margin and may also be indented five to ten spaces on the right.

Any displayed material should have at least one blank line space above and below to separate it from the regular text and should have a blank line space between each item or paragraph. Single-space each item in a list the same as the rest of the letter body.

Please review your records and present a status report by December 27, 1991. In particular, I would be interested in the following:

1. Are FICA, unemployment, and sales tax payments current?

2. What were the date and outcome of the most recent IRS audit?

I'll look forward to your comments, Jake. Thanks very much.

Therefore, I believe our approach is wrong. The Small Business Administration discussed this matter of defining a problem in "Researching Your Market":

You must be able to see beyond the symptoms of a problem to get
at the cause. Seeing the problem as a "sales decline" is not defining
a cause; it's listing a symptom.

I propose that we compile a list of influences that can be measured. Call me by Friday, October 8, if you have any candidates for this task from your department, Tom. Many thanks for your help.

If a letter runs over to a second or third page, carry at least two lines of the body over to the continuation page (see also "Continuation-Page Heading" on page 274). If a paragraph begins at the bottom of the previous page, also leave at least two lines of the paragraph on that page. The margins of the letter may need to be adjusted if this is not otherwise possible.

On standard 8½-by-11-inch business stationery, side and bottom margins should be at least 1 inch but may be increased to adjust a letter on the page. The top margin is usually determined by the position of the printed letterhead address. The amount of space occupied by a letter is also determined by the size of type that is used. Computer printers and typewriters may have an elite (smaller) typeface (12-pitch type) or a pica (larger) typeface (10-pitch type).

Complimentary Close

On all letter formats except the simplified style, the complimentary close is the first element to appear after the body of the letter. In the full-block style it is positioned flush left. In the block, modified-block, and official/personal formats it appears two to four character spaces to the right of the center of the page. One blank line space should always be above the closing and three to four blank line spaces should follow it.

Capitalize only the first word of the complimentary close and place a comma after it in the standard style of punctuation. The following are examples of formal and informal complimentary closings.

Formal:	Respectfully
	Respectfully yours
	Very cordially yours
	Very sincerely yours
	Very truly yours
	Yours truly
	Yours very truly
Informal:	Best regards
	Best wishes
	Cordially
	Cordially yours
	Regards
	Sincerely
	Sincerely yours
	Warmest regards

The two common positions—flush left and slightly right of the page center—are illustrated below.

I hope we will not allow these obstacles to prevent us from reaching our goals.

Sincerely,

Robert M. Allison
Project Manager

I hope we will not allow these obstacles to prevent us from reaching our goals.

Best regards,

Robert M. Allison
Project Manager

Signature

The signature line in a business letter consists of the writer's name and, often on a second line immediately below, his or her job title. If a company name is included, it is written two lines below the complimentary close and three to four blank lines follow before the signer's name is written. (The signature line is written about five lines below the letter body in a simplified letter since there is no complimentary close.)

All lines are aligned at the left. Whether the signature line appears flush left in a letter or slightly right of the page center depends on the letter format. If a job title is very long, it should be divided and carried to the next line. Indent the runover line two to three character spaces.

Company names are written exactly as they appear on the letterhead, and personal names are written exactly as the person signs them (not *Robert Kingston* if the person signs *R. A. Kingston*).

Titles such as *Mr.* and *Ms.* are not used unless the gender would not otherwise be known. In business the titles *Miss* or *Mrs.* are used only if the signer prefers to be addressed as such. If they are not used it is assumed that the woman prefers to be called *Ms.*

A woman also indicates her name preference by using her married name, maiden name, or a combined name. In formal social usage a married or widowed woman places *Mrs.* and her husband's full name all in parentheses but signs with her own first name (see example below); a divorced woman may write *Mrs.* with her maiden name and former married name—no first name—in parentheses but also signs using her first name (see example below).

Secretaries may sign their employer's name with their own initials beneath the signature. If a secretary signs his or her own name the employer's name is still included (Secretary to Mr. Thomson, *not* Secretary to Mr. J. V. Thomson).

Firm: Sincerely,

JOHNSON ACCOUNTING SERVICES

William Snow

William Snow
Treasurer

Gender Unknown: Sincerely,

Marion Foxworth

(Ms.) Marion Foxworth

Titles or Degrees: Sincerely,

William Snow

William Snow
President and Director
   of Marketing Research

Sincerely,

William Snow

William Snow, M.D.

Preferred Personal Title: Sincerely,

Janet Dixon

(Mrs.) Janet Dixon

Sincerely,

Janet Dixon

(Miss) Janet Dixon

Preferred Name: Sincerely,

Janet Dixon

Janet Dixon   (*married name*)

Sincerely,

Janet Browne

Janet Browne   (*maiden name*)

Sincerely,

Janet Browne-Dixon

Janet Browne-Dixon   (*combined name*)

Single Woman: Sincerely,

Jeanne Schultz

Jeanne Schultz

Sincerely,

Jeanne Schultz

(Miss) Jeanne Schultz

Married or Widowed Woman: Sincerely,

Joanne Cole

Joanne Cole   (*married name*)

Sincerely,

Joanne Cole

(Mrs.) Joanne Cole   (*married name*)

Sincerely,

Joanne Rogers-Cole   (*combined name*)

(Mrs.) Joanne Rogers-Cole

Sincerely,

Joanne Cole   (*formal social*)

(Mrs. Jack M. Cole)

Divorced Woman: Sincerely,

Pauline Krieger   (*married name*)

Pauline Krieger

Sincerely,

Pauline Jackson   (*maiden name*)

Pauline Jackson

Sincerely,

Pauline Jackson   (*maiden name*)

(Miss) Pauline Jackson

Sincerely,

Pauline Jackson-Krieger   (*formal social*)

(Mrs. Jackson-Krieger)

Sincerely,

Pauline J. Krieger   (*married name*)

(Mrs.) Pauline J. Krieger

Sincerely,

Pauline Jackson-Krieger   (*combined name*)

Pauline Jackson-Krieger

Secretary: Sincerely,

James Pennyworth

James Pennyworth

Sincerely,

Wanda Lewis

Secretary to Mr. Pennyworth

Identification Line

Initials may be added to a letter to show who dictated or wrote the letter and who prepared it. If three persons are involved, three sets of initials may be used, with the signer first, the person dictating the letter next, and the transcriber last. The writer's initials are unnecessary, however, if the writer's name appears in the signature line. Since this information is of use only to the sender, the initials may be omitted entirely from the addressee's copy and added only to the file copy.

The writer's and dictator's initials are written in all capitals and the transcriber's in small letters. A colon, with no space before or after, separates each set.

Place the initials two lines below the signature line. Use double- or single-spacing around the various concluding notations in a letter, as preferred, and depending on whether the letter is long or short.

ATV:om	ATV:JC:om	om
Enc.		Enc.
Registered	Enc.	Registered
pc: K. Abdulette		pc: K. Abdulette
	Registered	
	pc: K. Abdulette	

Enclosure Notation

Enclosures with a letter are indicated by a notation after the identification lines (if any) or otherwise following the signature line. In an official/personal letter format the notation follows the inside address. Enclosure notations may indicate the number or type of enclosures. The examples below illustrate the variety that is acceptable.

Leave a line space before and after the notation if all other notations are double-spaced. (All notations are frequently single-spaced.) Notations are always positioned flush left regardless of the letter format.

AJ:kcm
Enc.
Certified mail
c: Lee S. Marcus

AJ:kcm

Encs.

Certified mail

c: Lee S. Marcus

AJ:kcm
Enclosures: Check; adjustment form
Certified mail
c: Lee S. Marcus

AJ:kcm

Enclosures
  1. Check
  2. Adjustment form

Certified mail

c: Lee S. Marcus

AJ:kcm
1 enclosure
Certified mail
c: Lee S. Marcus

Mail Notation

A mail notation, written flush left, may be placed beneath the enclosure notation. Often it is omitted from the original and added only to file copies.

mtk
Encs. 3
Certified

mtk
Encs. 3
By United Parcel Service

mtk
Encs. 3
By messenger

Copy Notation

When writers send a copy of their letter to one or more persons other than the addressee, a notation to that effect is added flush left at the end of a letter after the enclosure notation. If copies will be sent to several persons, the names should be stacked and a check mark made after the name of the individual who is to receive a particular copy. Different letters or words indicate the type of copy being sent.

A line space may be placed between the various notations (copy notation, enclosure notation, and so on), or they may all be single-spaced.

Copy: Copy, c, *or* pc

Carbon copy: cc

Reprographic copy: rc

Blind copy: bc

The initials *bc* should appear only on the file copy and on the copy being sent to the person receiving the blind copy. The fact that it is a "blind" copy means that no one else is supposed to know that the person is receiving a copy.

The models in chapter 15 illustrate the placement of the copy-distribution notation on letters. The following examples indicate the order in which various notations should appear.

MDV: ac
Enc. 3
pc: A. T. Willis
    M. M. Seymour
    File Department

rd
Encs.: Contract
        Addendum
By registered mail
bc: Joe Parnelli

Postscript

The final part of a letter is the postscript, written flush left or indented the same as the paragraph style and placed two lines below the last line that was written. It usually consists of a comment unrelated to the body of the letter. Any remark that is pertinent to the body should not be added as a postscript since that would indicate the writer's careless composition.

A single postscript usually begins with the initials *P.S.* A second postscript begins with the initials *P.P.S.* After the last word of each postscript the writer should type his or her initials in all capitals.

> P.S. The mailing-list update is progressing rapidly now that we have additional help. KMR

> P.P.S. Please call me this week to select a date for the next sales meeting. KMR

Continuation-Page Heading

Business stationery may include printed continuation sheets; otherwise, blank paper that matches the letterhead may be used. The word *continued* is not required at the bottom of the preceding page or at the top of the continued page.

The continuation heading should include the addressee's name, the date, and the page number. This information may be stacked flush left or spread across the page. Either way, begin two to three lines down from the top of the page (or after any printed line at the top). Leave at least two line spaces after the heading before resuming the body of the letter. Titles such as *Mr.* or *Ms.* may be omitted, but a scholastic or honorary title such as *Dr.* should be used.

BERNS WATER WORKS, 1112 EAST OMAHA DRIVE, COLUMBUS, GA 31903

Dr. Benjamin Cole
August 5, 1991
page three

BERNS WATER WORKS, 1112 EAST OMAHA DRIVE, COLUMBUS, GA 31903

Dr. Benjamin Cole,   August 5, 1991,   page 3

BERNS WATER WORKS, 1112 EAST OMAHA DRIVE, COLUMBUS, GA 31903

Dr. Benjamin Cole   August 5, 1991   page 3

Envelope

Traditionally, the envelope address matched the inside address of a letter in wording and format. But U.S. Postal Service automation now requires a different format for efficient sorting and distribution of mail.

Envelopes should include a printed or typed return address in the upper left corner, which should include any endorsements.

Sheila Furth
1907 Hendricks Lane
St. Louis, MO 63135-1234

FORWARDING & RETURN POSTAGE GUARANTEED
ADDRESS CORRECTION REQUESTED

Delivery notations should appear in all capitals one to two lines below the postage area. Any personal notation should appear in all capitals to the left of and about two lines above the address block. An attention line, however, should be positioned after the addressee's name within the address block. Nonaddress data such as a routing number (optional) are written in the first line of the address block. If both a street and post office box are listed, the mail will be delivered to the one that appears immediately above the city and state.

The Postal Service recommends that the address block be written in all capital letters without punctuation. Leave at least 1-inch left and right margins and at least a 5/8-inch bottom margin. Place unit numbers such as a suite on the same line after the street. Place a box number before a station number. A window envelope should have a ¼-inch margin around the address block. In a foreign address, the country name is spelled out as the last line of the address block.

Sheila Furth   [POSTAGE]
1907 Hendricks Lane
St. Louis, MO 63135-1234   SPECIAL DELIVERY

FORWARDING & RETURN
POSTAGE GUARANTEED

                        JTR: 7011-9-92   *[Begin 2 inches from*
                        BASIC FOODS INC   *bottom of envelope]*
                        ATTN SA WRIGHT
[1-inch   1309 WEST AVENUE   RM 210   *[1-inch*
margin]   ALEXANDRIA VA 22304-2345   *margin]*

            [5/8-inch bottom margin]

Chapter 13

MEMOS

FORMAT

Numerous memo formats exist and many printed forms are available in office-supply stores. Some are ruled, like a writing tablet, and others are plain. Some are message-reply forms, which are combined with a duplicate reply copy or tear-off portion that the receiver can use to send an answer.

Sizes vary as much as other aspects of the memo format, for example, 4 by 5½ inches, 4½ by 11 inches, 5 by 8 inches, 5½ by 8 inches, 8½ by 7⅝ inches, 8½ by 8½ inches, 8½ by 9⅛ inches, and 8½ by 11⅝ inches.

Although not all of the forms are called "memos," they are all intended for informal, brief, easy-to-prepare messages. Chapter 15 illustrates three common formats: a standard interoffice format, a speed message with a reply tear-off, and a simple note form.

Many companies have memo formats designed especially for their needs in a particular size and with or without a reply tear-off. Usually, the company's return address is printed at the top, similar to the letterhead address on regular business or personal stationery. Bond paper is commonly used for memo forms, often in a lower grade than that used for letter stationery.

PARTS OF A MEMO

Memos have fewer parts than letters. There is no inside address, for example, no complimentary close, and often no attention line or signature line. Instead of the usual letter parts, the memo has fill-in lines such as *Date, To, From,* and *Subject* at the top of the page. Although companies may design a form with additional parts to suit their own needs, the conventional memo has three key parts—guide headings, body, and notations—as well as the corresponding envelope. Often the memo is not signed or is only initialed after the memo body.

The reason for sending a memo instead of a formal letter is to save time in contacting associates and colleagues or in sending impersonal messages such as a purchase order. Therefore, the form is usually designed to be prepared quickly and easily by typewriter or computer.

Interoffice memos are frequently routed in a special envelope with names written on the outside. But memos sent to other locations are sent in the same type of envelope as a regular letter.

Guide Headings

Whether you use a form that already has printed headings or write your own headings, the style will be similar. The top of the memo paper (some people use regular letterhead stationery) usually consists of the sender's return address and, additionally, may have a title below or above the address such as *MEMO, MEMO-LETTER, QUICK MESSAGE,* or *NOTE.* The guide headings are placed a few lines below the last line of the return address or the printed title. Depending on the format chosen, they may all be stacked flush left or half may be flush left and the other half on the right side of the page. The body may or may not have ruled lines.

Most memo headings include fill-in spaces or ruled lines after *To, From, Date,* and *Subject.* The guide word *From* may be unnecessary if the sender's name is printed at the top or if the particular design has a *By* or *Signed* guide word and signature line at the bottom. Otherwise, if the return address at the top of the page has a company name, the memo should include a *From* heading to show the name of the person in the company who is sending it. Sometimes other guide headings are needed, such as *Ref. No.*

PETERSON MACHINE TOOLS
19 EBONY LANE
SAN ANTONIO, TX 78228

TO _____   DATE _____

_____   SUBJECT _____

_____

FROM _____

_____

DAVID LAWSON
1239 SUNNYSIDE AVENUE
POCATELLO, ID 83201

TO   DATE

                                                     SUBJECT

WESTCHESTER MUSIC CO.   Date _____
ONE BROWN AVENUE   Ref. No. _____
ROCKFORD, IL 61103   Reply by _____
                                         Attn. _____
To _____   Subject _____
    _____   _____
    _____   _____

Body

The body, or message portion, of a memo is usually written single-spaced with all paragraphs flush left and a line space between paragraphs—the same as a letter. The first line of the body begins about two to three lines below the last guide heading, often the *Subject* line. If titles such as *MESSAGE* or *REPLY* are printed below the last guide word, the body should begin two to three lines below that. Sometimes the memo form has ruled lines that show where the body copy should begin. With two-part message-reply forms, rules or the titles *MESSAGE* and *REPLY* usually show where both senders and receivers should write their messages and replies.

The style for writing lists, blocked quotations (extracts), and other displayed material is the same as that for letters (see chapter 12). Since memos are intended for quick comprehension as well as rapid preparation, text heads are common. In memos used for short reports or proposals, they are often essential (see the memo proposal format in chapter 21). If the memo body has text headings, leave one or two line spaces before and one line space after such heads. Text heads may be in all capitals or uppercase and lowercase, underlined, or in any style that is clear and readable. If several levels of headings are used, a different style should be used for each level.

MAKING THE PLAN WORK

To make your plan work, use your computer to provide periodic feedback. Look for facts that alert you to trouble spots such as inventory control and production.

Inventory Control

To provide maximum service to customers, you need to control inventory. A rapid turnover will insure that fewer dollars are tied up in raw materials and finished goods.

Setting up controls. In setting up controls, keep in mind that the cost of inventory is not your only cost. . . .

Notations

The concluding notations used in a memo (such as *Enc.*) are the same as those used in a letter. They are also written in the same position—all flush left and with or without a line space between each one, as desired or as space permits.

In a regular letter, the notations follow the signature line. In a memo they begin two lines below the last line of the memo body or two lines below the sender's initials, if the writer chooses to add his or her initials (usually handwritten) immediately below the memo body (this is not required, and many writers do not initial their messages).

Memos do not have a regular complimentary close and signature line, but some have guide words at the bottom of the form under the message and reply sections of combination memos. Since the guide words for this are printed on the last line of the memo form, any notations in the memo are written *above* such signatures, under the body of the memo, as described above. If a routing slip is not attached to the memo, a distribution list may be typed two lines under the last notations or the postscript. For instructions on writing identification lines, enclosure and mail notations, copy notations, and postscripts, see chapter 12.

Therefore, we need to know what business information is available, where to get it, and how to use it.

HT

amr
Enc. 2
Registered
pc: Marge Brindley

P.S. The Chamber of Commerce is holding a seminar on this subject next month. I've ordered brochures for all of you. HT

Distribution

M. Carter
G. Hollingsworth
P. Jesuchi
T. Goldberg
A. Zinden

Envelope

Various styles of interoffice routing envelopes are available. Some resemble regular mailing envelopes, whereas others have ruled lines for writing in recipients' names, departmental names, or other information.

INTEROFFICE MAIL

Name	Department	Name	Department

Memos sent outside by regular mail should be enclosed in a regular mailing envelope and addressed for private delivery or U.S. Postal Service automated reading and sorting. Chapter 15 has illustrations of a traditional envelope format and an optical-character-reading format.

See chapters 12 and 15 for descriptions and illustrations of letter formats and chapter 15 for memo models.

Part II

MODEL
FORMATS

Chapter 14

FORMATTING

In the preparation of written material, *format* refers to the general arrangement of elements on a page—size, shape, position or layout, and overall appearance. Whereas part I provided the rules for writing the various parts of different types of material (punctuation, capitalization, word division, and so on), part II provides illustrations of material to show where the various parts go on a page.

Before elements such as titles, headings, lists, tables, and footnotes can be prepared, a writer has to decide how to prepare them (what appearance they should have and where to position them on a page). In other words, a preparer has to *format* the material.

CHOOSING A FORMAT

One of the purposes of chapters 15 through 21 is to help you select a format for many of the basic items prepared by typewriter or computer—anything from a letter to an appointment schedule to a proposal. The models in these chapters are illustrated in widely acceptable formats, although most of them can be modified to suit individual needs or personal preferences.

In choosing a format, writers have to consider the standard rules of style described in this book as well as company requirements or personal taste. In addition, they have to consider equipment capability. Are they using an electric typewriter or a computer with powerful software? Whereas almost all formatting options may have to be determined by the writer for electric and older electronic typewriters, most options are calculated and performed automatically with word processing and desktop publishing programs. Depending on the program being used, you can choose format details such as margin width, position of page numbers, tab settings, and space between columns; key them into the computer; and thereafter have your copy prepared according to those instructions. A simple keystroke will automatically accomplish tasks such as centering a head without personal calculation and manual repetition.

Ease of preparation strongly influences most writers in choosing a format. The greater the equipment capability and software versatility, the more complex a format can be. Not all equipment or software is easy to learn or use, however, and some persons will be influenced by that fact as well.

Writers who prepare material at work must follow the style requirements of their employers. A writer may prefer a modern full-block letter format (see chapter 15), for example, but perhaps his or her employer is a conservative, traditionally oriented company that wants all letters prepared in the traditional modified-block format. Perhaps a company wants all reports prepared as formal documents with title page, letter of authorization, abstract, and so on. Perhaps an organization insists that all meeting minutes have paragraph heads rather than margin heads. Perhaps all file-drawer labels must be coded in numeric format. But whether choosing a format or whether a particular format has already been specified, a writer must learn how to put the various elements of a document on a page to fit the format.

USING MODERN EQUIPMENT

Although many writers use electric typewriters, most preparation of written material is now done at home, at school, or at work with electronic typewriters or computers. Many electronic typewriters have some of the same features that are available on computers.

For general text preparation by computer, a word processing program such as WordPerfect or Microsoft Word is used. Of the various word processing programs, some are very easy to learn but have limited capabilities. Others are difficult to learn but can do complex tasks with ease.

Whereas a word processing operator working at a terminal connected to a central computer may deal only with a video monitor and a keyboard, a writer working with a stand-alone system will have at hand all components necessary to process text: monitor or screen, keyboard, floppy or hard-disk storage, central processing unit and machine memory, and printer. Some systems also have a modem to tap into databases over telephone lines, or they may have a separate or additional hard disk for increased data-storage capability.

The number of separate components and size of components differ among manufacturers. Some small, battery-operated systems (laptop computers) will fit into a briefcase for operation on an airplane, train, or virtually anywhere. Some personal computers require space equivalent to the top of a desk and, once assembled, are relatively permanent. All of the equipment components in a system are known as the *hardware*. Programs that are run on a computer to enable it to do something such as text preparation are referred to as the *software*.

Formatting by Computer

Every word processing program is different. All programs have certain features, such as centering, in common, but the more powerful programs provide additional features, such as multiple on-screen windows for working on different documents or parts of a document at the same time (the documents or parts can be viewed on the screen simultaneously in different windows).

With most word processing software material can be formatted in at least three ways: by character, by paragraph, and by page. The ease with which the instructions can be given to the computer and then carried out will differ from program to program, but in all cases the capability enables writers to choose from a variety of formats and to control the appearance of text on a page. A program with graphics capability increases a writer's options in preparing charts, graphs, various style and size heads, and other graphics material.

Formatting instructions alone do not insure that a page will have the appearance desired. A writer may specify a bold type for an article title or a superscript letter for a raised footnote number, but if the printer does not have bold or superscript capability, the title will simply be printed out in the printer's regular typeface, and the footnote number will appear on line like any other number. Capabilities, then, must be consistent between hardware and software to make full use of all format options.

Character Formatting. Because word processing programs are not standard, the particular keystrokes required to specify character format changes will differ from program to program. Many programs, though, will enable an operator to specify bold, italic, single or double underlining, small capital letters, different sizes of letters, subscript (lowered) and superscript (raised) letters or numbers, strikethrough letters (a dashed line typed across a word as if to strike it out), and different fonts (different-shaped letters).

A program generally has preset formats for writers who do not want to change anything, for example, all characters 10 pitch and regular face (not bold or italic). But a writer can change any or all aspects of the preset format by pressing the appropriate key so that a list of options will appear on the screen. From this list the writer can then choose what changes to make (often by tab or backspace key or by typing in the preferred option in the designated space).

The manuscript for this book was prepared using Microsoft Word, and the character-format choices that were possible included options such as the following (the options in parentheses are preset in the computer):

Bold:	Yes (No)
Italic:	Yes (No)

Underline:	Yes (No)
Strikethrough:	Yes (No)
Uppercase:	Yes (No)
Small caps:	Yes (No)
Double underline:	Yes (No)
Position:	(Normal) Superscript Subscript
Font name:	[*type in choice*]
Font size:	[*type in choice*]

Paragraph Formatting. A writer might want to change the appearance of certain paragraphs such as blocked quotations (extracts) or lists. Word processing programs that provide for paragraph formatting have options such as hanging indents (for lists), justified paragraphs (flush-right as well as flush-left alignment of words), and double- or single-spacing.

The preset options will probably include single-spacing, left alignment, no extra line spaces before or after a paragraph, and no paragraph indention. To change one or more of these options, a writer would choose a paragraph command to bring the list of options and instructions onto the screen. Changes might then be made by using the tab or backspace key or by typing in the desired change.

The following paragraph-format options are examples of choices that can be made with a program such as Microsoft Word. If a writer wants to indent the left margin one-half inch, for example, he or she should type *0.5"* after the words *Left indent.*

Alignment:	(Left) Centered Right Justified
Left indent:	0"
First line:	0"
Right indent:	0"
Line spacing:	1 li
Space before:	0 li
Space after:	0 li
Keep together:	Yes (No)
Side by side:	Yes (No)

Page Formatting. The preset format options for page layout will seldom be suitable for every document that is prepared. The requirements for documents such as a letter and a balance sheet, for example, are much too different. Writers using a computer, then, must learn how to change format specifications for the various elements of a page, including margins, page size, columns, page numbers, running heads, and line numbers (numbers running down the left margin). The same procedure used in character and paragraph formatting applies to page formatting. The appropriate keystroke will bring on screen the list of options and instructions on which to specify desired changes, often by using the tab or backspace key or by typing in the desired change in the designated position.

Using a program such as Microsoft Word to format the page margins, desired changes can be typed over preset numbers such as the following.

Top:	1"
Bottom:	1"
Left:	1.25"
Right:	1.25"
Page length:	11"
Width:	8.5"
Gutter margin:	0"
Running-head position from top:	0.5"
From bottom:	0.5"

Other aspects of page layout include footnote and column options, and preset features such as the following can be changed as desired.

Footnotes:	(Same page) End
Number of columns:	1
Space between columns:	0.5"
Division break:	(Page) Continuous Column Even Odd

Page numbers can also be controlled by changing preset features such as these.

Format page numbers:	Yes (No)
From top:	0.5"
From left:	7.25"
Numbering:	(Continuous) Start
At:	[insert page number]
Number format:	(1) I i A a

Options for formatting running heads might include the following.

Position:	(Top) Bottom
Odd pages:	(Yes) No
Even pages:	(Yes) No
First page:	Yes (No)

The documentation (instructions) that accompanies each word processing program will explain the specific procedures (keystrokes and other steps) for formatting characters, paragraphs, and pages. Depending on the software, it also may describe steps characters, paragraphs, and pages. Depending on the software, it also may describe steps to take in setting tabs; creating tables; creating fill-in forms; and formatting indexes, outlines, tables of contents, and many other parts of documents. By taking time to learn the keystrokes and other steps involved, a writer can become very adept at creating well-designed pages in every imaginable type of document.

Almost all of the models illustrated in chapters 15 through 21 can be formatted on a typewriter or on a computer using the appropriate word processing software.

PREPARING FOR TYPESETTING AND PRINTING

Many documents that were formerly typed in manuscript form and then sent to a printer for production are now prepared by computer using word processing or desktop publishing software. Companies commonly produce reports, newsletters, booklets, and magazines in house by this method. But some work is still prepared in manuscript form and then sent to an outside firm for typesetting, printing, binding, and sometimes even addressing and mailing.

Material can be protected under copyright law by including the proper copyright notice in the material being produced and then completing and submitting an application, with appropriate fee, to the Register of Copyrights. For instructions and forms, write to the Register of Copyrights, Library of Congress, Washington, D.C. 20559. Specify the type of material (e.g., book) that you wish to copyright.

Some material being prepared for publication requires design and preparation of artwork, writing and editing, manuscript typing or computer preparation, and proofreading. A large firm may have departments or at least various people that handle each aspect of production. A small firm or individual may subcontract some or all of the work to freelancers or companies such as graphics firms and advertising agencies.

Design and Art

The designer and artist may be the same person, or one may do a layout and another prepare mechanicals and finished art. A *layout* is a pencil or ink preliminary drawing of each page, showing margins, areas where blocks or columns of type will go, places for illustrations, captions, heads, and so on—all drawn to approximate or exact size to simulate the arrangement of all elements that will appear in the final product.

A *dummy* is also a page-by-page layout, but instead of blank boxes or lines to suggest text, actual copies of typeset text are cut apart and positioned on each page. Hence a dummy looks even more like the proposed final product than a layout.

A *mechanical* (paste-up) is a finished layout ready to be photographed and then printed. Typeset text, final artwork, and so on are "pasted" onto heavy paper exactly as they will appear in the finished work. Boxes are drawn where a halftone (photograph) will be stripped in later.

Editing

The writer of a document to be published prepares a manuscript that will be edited and typemarked (instructions to typesetter) or may be camera-ready and go directly to the printer for production. A manuscript to be typeset should be prepared by typewriter or computer in double-spaced format, following the style guidelines given in chapters 1 through 13 and the formatting guidelines described in this chapter.

The editor's job is to correct the writer's typographical, style, and other errors; to see that punctuation, capitalization, spelling, and other points of style are handled consistently; and often to typemark the manuscript (someone else may do this)—mark type specifications (size, style, etc.), spacing and indention instructions, leading (space between lines), and other matters of format. The standard symbols used in marking corrections are shown in the two charts in the next section "Proofreading." A sample follows.

In manuscript copy, a writer or editor usually makes short corrections by crossing out errors and writing the correct words above. Long corrections should be written on a separate page marked as A, B, or some other designation. In the margin, at the appropriate place, the editor should write "Insert A here" or "Insert page 000 here." Instructions to the typesetter should be circled in the margin to avoid confusion with corrections or new copy to be typeset.

To run one paragraph in to another, the editor draws a line from the last word in one paragraph to the first word in the next. To separate two words written as one, the editor draws a line between them. To retain material accidentally crossed out, the editor inserts a row of dots beneath it and in the margin circles stet (meaning "let it stand").

The editor should keep an alphabetical list of terms and points of style to insure that consistency is maintained. An author, for example, might hyphenate *non-governmental* on page 1 and write it closed, as *nongovernmental*, on page 54. The editor might forget by page 54 whether the closed or hyphenated style was being used. The following are among the many elements considered by an editor.

accuracy

consistency

completeness

readability

opening and ending

headings

paragraph transition

Sample Page of Edited Manuscript

Telephone Service

Though the office manager usually is responsible for ~~looking into what's~~ administering ~~available in~~ efficient telephone service at ~~a low cost~~ minimum, the secretary must know how to use telephone service and equipment, and sometimes ~~how to~~ select ~~it~~. A communications consultant from your local telephone office ~~is available~~ will ~~when you call to~~ give free advice about services and equipment.

Telephone Convenience Aids

Many telephone ~~Lots of~~ arrangements ~~can be arranged~~ are available for meeting the particular requirements of the professional or business executive. ~~Lots~~ The wide assortment of available equipment and accessories makes possible a tailor-made service to fit the exact requirements at any location in your office.

Business Services

Many services are offered to subscribers:

1. WATS. Wide-area telephone service WATS is designed for companies that make and receive many long-distance calls. Access lines to customers are connected to a nationwide dialing network that may include intrastate and interstate service.

2. Switching systems. Private-branch exchange (PBX) and computerized

Source: The Office Sourcebook, by Mary A. De Vries. © 1989 Reprinted by permission of the publisher, Prentice Hall, a division of Simon & Schuster, Englewood Cliffs, NJ. 07632.

sentence structure

footnotes

illustrations

grammar

spelling

punctuation

capitalization

word choice

conciseness

cliches

clarity

jargon

prefix and suffix style

trite expressions

discriminatory language

Proofreading

Whereas a writer may proofread his or her own manuscript, a proofreader (or an editor) may proofread galleys and page proofs. *Galleys* are copies of the typeset material that have not been divided into final pages. The name derives from metal trays into which lines of type are deposited as they come from a typesetting machine (known as the "hot type" process, as opposed to a "cold type" process such as computer preparation). The proofs made from the trays are called *galley proofs,* and the name is now applied to any proofs or copies of typeset material that will later be divided into pages.

The proofreader reads the galleys for any possible errors and marks the errors in the margins as shown in the chart "How to Correct Proof," using the standard symbols shown in the chart "Proofreading Symbols."

After the typesetter has corrected the galleys, running heads and page numbers are added, and the text is divided into page proofs. The proofreader must then check each page proof to see that all galley corrections were made and mark any that were not, using the standard proofreading marks. Additionally, the proofreader must check that running heads and page numbers are correct, that facing pages are of equal length, that illustrations and footnotes are correct, and that there are no widows (very short lines at the top of a page).

After the typesetter has made any necessary corrections in the page proofs, the final pages of type, prepared on specially treated paper, are ready for photographing. In the offset printing process a plate is made from the negatives and used to print the final

Proofreading Symbols

∧	Make correction indicated in margin.	////	Hair space letters.
Stet	Retain crossed-out word or letter; let it stand.	*wf.*	Wrong font; change to proper font.
Stet (dotted)	Retain words under which dots appear; write "Stet" in margin.	*Qu?*	Is this right?
X	Appears battered; examine.	*lc.*	Set in lower case (small letters).
=	Straighten lines.	*sc.*	Set in small capitals.
✓✓✓	Unevenly spaced; correct spacing.	*Caps*	Set in capitals.
‖	Line up; i.e., make lines even with other matter.	*c&sc.*	Set in caps and small caps.
run in	Make no break in the reading; no paragraph.	*rom.*	Change to roman.
no ¶	No paragraph; sometimes written "run in."	*ital.*	Change to italic.
Out—see copy	Here is an omission; see copy.	≡	Under letter or word means caps.
¶	Make a paragraph here.	=	Under letter or word means small caps.
tr.	Transpose words or letters as indicated.	—	Under letter or word means italic.
ℐ	Take out matter indicated; delete.	∿	Under letter or word means boldface.
ℐ	Take out character indicated and close up.	∧	Insert comma.
℘	Line drawn through a cap means lower case.	;	Insert semicolon.
ℰ	Upside down; reverse.	:	Insert colon.
⌒	Close up; no space.	⊙	Insert period.
#	Insert a space here.	/?/	Insert interrogation mark.
↓	Push down this space.	/!/	Insert exclamation mark.
⌂	Indent line one em.	/	Insert hyphen.
[	Move this to the left.	∨	Insert apostrophe.
]	Move this to the right.	∨ ∨	Insert quotation marks.
⊓	Raise to proper position.	⌴	Insert superior letter or figure.
⊔	Lower to proper position.	∧	Insert inferior letter or figure.
		[/]	Insert brackets.
		(/)	Insert parentheses.
		—/—	One-em dash.
		⹀	Two-em parallel dash.
		⊛	Spell out.

Source: Professional Secretary's Encyclopedic Dictionary, 4th ed. rev. by Mary A. De Vries. © 1989 Reprinted by permission of the publisher, Prentice Hall, Inc., a division of Simon & Schuster, Englewood Cliffs, NJ.

How to Correct Proof

HOW TO CORRECT PROOF

It does not appear that the earliest printers had any method of correcting errors before the form was on the press. The learned learned correctors of the first two centuries of printing were not proofreaders in our sense, they were rather what we should term office editors. Their labors were chiefly to see that the proof corresponded to the copy, but that the printed page was correct in its latinity, that the words were there, and that the sense was right. They cared but little about orthography, bad letters or purely printers' errors, and when the text seemed to them wrong they consulted fresh authorities or altered it on their own responsibility. Good proofs, in the modern sense, were impossible until professional readers were employed, men who had first a printer's education, and then spent many years in the correction of proof. The orthography of English, which for the past century has undergone little change, was very fluctuating until after the publication of Johnson's Dictionary, and capitals, which have been used with considerable regularity for the past 80 years, were previously used on the miss or hit plan. The approach to regularity, so far as we have, may be attributed to the growth of a class of professional proofreaders, and it is to them that we owe the correctness of modern printing. More errors have been found in the Bible than in any other one work. For many generations it was frequently the case that Bibles were brought out stealthily, from fear of governmental interference. They were frequently printed from imperfect texts, and were often modified to meet the views of those who published them. The story is related that a certain woman in Germany, who was the wife of a Printer, and had become disgusted with the continual assertion of the superiority of man over woman which she had heard, hurried into the composing room while her husband was at supper and altered a sentence in the Bible, which he was printing, so that it read Narr instead of Herr, thus making the verse read "And he shall be thy fool" instead of "And he shall be thy lord." The word not was omitted by Barker, the King's printer in England in 1632, in printing the seventh commandment. He was fined £3,000 on this account.

---

document. Before copies are printed, however, printers commonly provide a proof of the negative (sometimes called a "blueprint") so that a final check can be made to insure that every correction was made and that everything is in the right position and on the right page.

Some projects have several steps remaining at this point, such as collating, folding, binding, inserting (in envelopes), addressing, and mailing. The various tasks in production may be supervised and coordinated by one person or by several persons, depending on the type of material and the size of the organization.

Chapter 15

CORRESPONDENCE

Correspondence formats differ according to need—degree of formality desired, image desired (conservative-traditional versus progressive-modern), personal preferences, professional or employer requirements, and other factors pertinent to a particular situation. The models in this chapter include common forms of communication such as letters, memos, announcements, invitations, and notices.

There is no single correct format for each type of communication. Five common acceptable formats, for example, are available for letter messages. A visit to a printer or stationery store will reveal the many styles of invitations that exist, from the strictly formal variety to the very casual, informal style. The models in this chapter and the remaining chapters, therefore, are intended only as selected examples of familiar communication formats widely approved by authorities.

Most forms of communication today are prepared by computer or word processor or by some kind of typewriter. The messages are sent conventionally by the U.S. Postal Service or by a private delivery service, or they are transmitted electronically using the telephone lines or direct machine wiring (local area networks).

A letter prepared on a computer might be placed on a facsimile machine (fax), where it is transmitted electronically to its destination in a matter of seconds. Telex, computerized electronic mail, and similar systems function in the same way. A full-sized letter may be transmitted, or a condensed version similar to a conventional telegram message may be sent. Depending on the subscriber-system requirements, various codes may have to be entered as well to effect transmission. Both full-sized and condensed messages are illustrated in this chapter.

BUCHANAN ADVISORY SERVICE
1460 - 80 Street, NW
Helena, MT 59604
406-772-6363

January 2, 199-

Your reference 03AM#-77

Mr. Jeffrey Veneto, President
The Handcrafter Mart
1432 Raleigh Road
Springfield, IL 62704

Attention Elizabeth Pelham

Dear Mr. Veneto:

CRIME-CONTROL PROCEDURES

Thank you for asking about our program of positive steps to
take to curb crime. I'm enclosing a free booklet that
describes our program of effective management safeguards. It
explains how to make your system fraud-proof and how to control
specific problems such as computer crime.

Most of all, we recommend that you continually impress on
employees and customers alike that you are always aware and
that you always care. This is an essential ingredient in any
effort to prevent and control crime.

We appreciate your interest in our management aids, Mr.
Veneto, and will be happy to answer any questions you have
about our program.

Sincerely,

Ellen R. Thayer
Manager

jt.
Enc. 1

P.S. I met your director of marketing, Benjamin Flemming, at
a conference last week. Please say hello for me. ERT

LETTER: FULL BLOCK

BUCHANAN ADVISORY SERVICE
1460 - 80 Street, NW
Helena, MT 59604
406-772-6363

January 2, 199-

Your reference 03AM#-77

Mr. Jeffrey Veneto, President
The Handcrafter Mart
1432 Raleigh Road
Springfield, IL 62704

Attention Elizabeth Pelham

Dear Mr. Veneto:

CRIME-CONTROL PROCEDURES

Thank you for asking about our program of positive steps to
take to curb crime. I'm enclosing a free booklet that
describes our program of effective management safeguards. It
explains how to make your system fraud-proof and how to control
specific problems such as computer crime.

Most of all, we recommend that you continually impress on
employees and customers alike that you are always aware and
that you always care. This is an essential ingredient in any
effort to prevent and control crime.

We appreciate your interest in our management aids, Mr.
Veneto, and will be happy to answer any questions you have
about our program.

Sincerely,

Ellen R. Thayer
Manager

jt.
Enc. 1

P.S. I met your director of marketing, Benjamin Flemming, at
a conference last week. Please say hello for me. ERT

LETTER: BLOCK

BUCHANAN ADVISORY SERVICE
1460 - 80 Street, NW
Helena, MT 59604
406-772-6363

January 2, 199-

Your reference 03AM#-77

Mr. Jeffrey Veneto, President
The Handcrafter Mart
1432 Raleigh Road
Springfield, IL 62704

Attention Elizabeth Pelham

Dear Mr. Veneto:

CRIME-CONTROL PROCEDURES

Thank you for asking about our program of positive steps to take to curb crime. I'm enclosing a free booklet that describes our program of effective management safeguards. It explains how to make your system fraud-proof and how to control specific problems such as computer crime.

Most of all, we recommend that you continually impress on employees and customers alike that you are always aware and that you always care. This is an essential ingredient in any effort to prevent and control crime.

We appreciate your interest in our management aids, Mr. Veneto, and will be happy to answer any questions you have about our program.

Sincerely,

Ellen R. Thayer
Manager

jt.
Enc. 1

P.S. I met your director of marketing, Benjamin Flemming, at a conference last week. Please say hello for me. ERT

LETTER: MODIFIED BLOCK

BUCHANAN ADVISORY SERVICE
1460 - 80 Street, NW
Helena, MT 59604
406-772-6363

January 2, 199-

Your reference 03AM#-77

Mr. Jeffrey Veneto, President
The Handcrafter Mart
1432 Raleigh Road
Springfield, IL 62704

Attention Elizabeth Pelham

CRIME-CONTROL PROCEDURES

Thank you, Mr. Veneto, for asking about our program of positive
steps to take to curb crime. I'm enclosing a free booklet that
describes our program of effective management safeguards. It
explains how to make your system fraud-proof and how to control
specific problems such as computer crime.

Most of all, we recommend that you continually impress on
employees and customers alike that you are always aware and
that you always care. This is an essential ingredient in any
effort to prevent and control crime.

We appreciate your interest in our management aids, Mr. Veneto,
and will be happy to answer any questions you have about our
program.

Ellen R. Thayer
Manager

jt.
Enc. 1

P.S. I met your director of marketing, Benjamin Flemming, at a
conference last week. Please say hello for me. ERT

LETTER: SIMPLIFIED

BUCHANAN ADVISORY SERVICE
1460 - 80 Street, NW
Helena, MT 59604
406-772-6363

January 2, 199-

Dear Mr. Veneto:

CRIME-CONTROL PROCEDURES

Thank you for asking about our program of positive steps to take to curb crime. I'm enclosing a free booklet that describes our program of effective management safeguards. It explains how to make your system fraud-proof and how to control specific problems such as computer crime.

Most of all, we recommend that you continually impress on employees and customers alike that you are always aware and that you always care. This is an essential ingredient in any effort to prevent and control crime.

We appreciate your interest in our management aids, Mr. Veneto, and will be happy to answer any questions you have about our program.

Sincerely,

Ellen R. Thayer
Manager

Mr. Jeffrey Veneto, President
The Handcrafter Mart
1432 Raleigh Road
Springfield, IL 62704

jt.
Enc. 1

P.S. I met your director of marketing, Benjamin Flemming, at a conference last week. Please say hello for me. ERT

LETTER: OFFICIAL/PERSONAL

MALAPAI INDUSTRIES, 2100 MOSS AVENUE, OAKLAND, CA 94610

Delia Pembroke
August 14, 199-
page two

and I know you have always advocated a patent search to
minimize the risk of infringement when the technology is new.
I heartily concur, Delia, and am happy to authorize such
action. Let me know if I can help in any way.

                                        Best regards,

                                        Donald C. Woodcrest
                                        Director of Research

mk

pc: Barbara K. Hartshorne
    Harold L. Mackenzie
    Arthur M. Solomon

LETTER CONTINUATION PAGE

```
            COMMERCE TOOL COMPANY
                 18 MAGIC LANE
              FORT WORTH, TX 75182
                 817-124-3906
```

TO: Thomas Harvey   **DATE:**   May 17, 199–
        General Manager

FROM: Philip Ritter   **COPIES:** Nancy Slater
        Production Manager   Joseph Holland
                                         Aaron Steiner
                                         Laura Howell
                                         Dena Clodine
                                         Michael Toano

SUBJECT: Change in Inventory-Management System

FOR: ( ) **Action**   ( ) **Decision**   (X) **Information**

I am recommending that we replace our somewhat antiquated inventory-management system with a newer system more suitable for our computerized operations. Our present system impedes rather than facilitates computer processing, and we are unable to use our equipment to its fullest potential. This handicap has created cost inefficiencies ranging from 15 to 35 percent (see enclosed table).

The two approaches under investigation are Materials Requirements Planning (MRP) and Just-in-Time (JIT). I expect to give a detailed report on each system at the next departmental meeting in June.

    <u>Materials Requirements Planning</u> is an information system in which sales are converted into loads on a facility by subunit and time period. Since materials are scheduled more closely, inventories are reduced.

    <u>Just-in-Time</u> is a system that helps to eliminate rather than optimize inventories. Raw materials and work-in-process are focused on that needed for a single day, and this is accomplished by reducing setup and lead time to enable small-lot ordering.

During the next two weeks I will be gathering data on the potential impact of each system on our operations. I would welcome any comments, suggestions, or other information you may have that would be useful in developing a report. Thanks very much for your help.

Enc.: Cost-Inefficiency Table

MEMO: STANDARD INTEROFFICE

H. W. WINKEL, INC.
22 Dixie Drive
Jackson, MS 39209
601-735-5901

DATE   September 19, 199-
REF. NO. 22173-90JFRC

TO   Helen Urbana
     West Junior High
     1010 Chatham Road
     Oklahoma City, OK 73132

SUBJECT Training Aids for
Junior High School Students

MESSAGE

  Helen, we finally have those wizard training aids you asked about
several months ago. I'm sorry it took so long for our order to arrive, but it
was worth the wait. They look wonderful. Let me know if you'd like to have
me set aside a supply for your spring term.

Signed ___*Tim May*___

REPLY

Signed _____ Date _____

MEMO: SPEED MESSAGE-REPLY

M E M O

from Carleton Edgewater

March 10, 199–

Kathryn, I just learned that our order of visors
was omitted from the fall shipment. I'm sure you
followed up immediately, and I was wondering if you
have learned when we may expect delivery. I'd
appreciate a call (X730) as soon as you know.

Thanks very much.

MEMO: NOTE

TO   Jerry Maplewood   DATE   October 6, 199_

STREET   399 North Ogden Ave   TELEPHONE   312-647-9999

CITY-STATE   Chicago, IL   ZIP CODE   60607

Your rush order of sixteen SC books confirmed. Will ship October 11.

Colton Suppliers

SENDER'S NAME & ADDRESS   Beverly Shawnee, Colton Suppliers,

3107 Red Fox Drive, Cincinnati, OH 45245   PHONE   513-784-8622

FAST MESSAGE: CONDENSED COPY

```
BOWIE PLANNERS
961 Richard Drive                          (postage)
Warren, OH 44483

Confidential                               REGISTERED


                Mrs. Evelyn Gladstone, President
                Shotwell Manufacturing Co., Inc.
                Kansas City, MO 64120
```

ENVELOPE: TRADITIONAL

```
    GEMINI, INC.
    911 ASH AVENUE                         (postage)
    RAPID CITY, SD 57701

    RETURN POSTAGE GUARANTEED          SPECIAL DELIVERY

                MNO:65473FC-X
                SPORTSWEAR DISTRIBUTORS INC
                ATTN DF MAXWELL
                551 BAILEY AVENUE   RM 600
                BUFFALO NY 14206-4351
```

ENVELOPE: OCR READABLE

```
┌────────────────────────────────────────────┐
│                                              │
│         WESTCLIFFE INDUSTRIES                │
│         One Washington Square                │
│         Evansville, IN 47715                 │
│                                              │
├────────────────────────────────────────────┤
│                                              │
│                                              │
│    TO   Mr. Irving Chakley                   │
│         Campout Supplies                     │
│         1401 Central Parkway                 │
│         Lake Charles, LA 70605               │
│                                              │
├────────────────────────────────────────────┤
│                                              │
│                                              │
│         FIRST CLASS MAIL                     │
│                                              │
│                                              │
└────────────────────────────────────────────┘
```

MAILING ADDRESS LABEL

```
┌──────────────────────┬─────────────────────────┐
│                      │                         │
│  ( ) First Class     │    CRESSFORD SHOES      │
│                      │    109 Sixth Street     │
│  ( ) Priority Mail   │    Nashua, NH 03060     │
│                      │                         │
│  ( ) Third Class     ├─────────────────────────┤
│                      │                         │
│  (X)  UPS            │ RETURN POSTAGE GUARANTEED│
│                      │                         │
│  ( ) _____        ├─────────────────────────┤
│                      │                         │
│  ( ) _____        │  TO   Ms. Sheila K. McBee│
│                      │       1062 - 57 Street, SE│
│                      │       Everett, WA 98204 │
│                      │                         │
└──────────────────────┴─────────────────────────┘
```

MAILING ADDRESS-DATA LABEL

801-392-8711   801-392-8712

THE GOLDEN EAGLE
Signs, Flags, and Specialty Items

Arlene Langston   983 Skyview Drive
Representative   Ogden, UT 84403

For M *s. Julia Carlson*

Date *april 15* ———— at ——— *2* ——— o'clock

EDGAR O. TORENIA, M.D.
Telephone 702-911-5222

16 Lafayette Street, NW   Roanoke, VA 24017

EDITH GUILFORD
Vice President

Jerome & Guilford Associates
102 Hood Circle
Austin, TX 78745
512-633-7178

BUSINESS CARDS

Marsha Barcarole Finchley
Attorney at Law
announces the opening
of law offices
at Two North Avenue
Aurora, Illinois 60505
Thursday, February 6, 199-

Highland Industries
is pleased to announce that
Lynda C. Kristmoor
has been named general manager
July first

137 Heidi Place
Montgomery, Alabama 36117
205-772-1984

Andrew M. Drendel
Wilma S. Peterson
announce the formation of
Drendel-Peterson, Inc.
a management consulting firm
Nine Derby Street
Boston, Massachusetts 02165
617-832-0107

ANNOUNCEMENTS: FORMAL

Bill Colewell
has opened his new store
Music and More
and wants to welcome his friends to
2121 Granville Street
High Point, North Carolina 27263
919-604-2341

Janice Farnsworth
(formerly Mrs. Kenneth Schott)
has changed her address to
623 Mill Street
Naperville, IL 60540

The Fantasy Mart
will open a new booth
featuring books and toys for tots
on December 16, 199-
at 2000 Bellaire Street
Denver
303-621-7444

Bring this card for a free door prize

ANNOUNCEMENTS: INFORMAL

Mr. and Mrs. Sherman Gallagher
request the pleasure of your company
at dinner
on Saturday, the eleventh of October
at half past seven o'clock
231 Ridgecrest Street
Santa Maria, California 93455

R.s.v.p.

EDISON ADVERTISING

[logo]

The Board of Trustees
cordially invite you to
cocktails
to celebrate the company's tenth year of service
Friday, March 17th
5 to 7 p.m.
1901 Hoover Street
Bridgeport

R.s.v.p. card enclosed

INVITATIONS: FORMAL

[logo]

Mr. and Mrs. Elliott C. Schumway
request the pleasure of your company

at *dinner*

on *Friday, the sixth of June*
at *half after eight o'clock*

Two Parkway Drive
San Antonio

R.s.v.p.
372-9000

INVITATION: FORMAL FILL-IN

J O I N U S!

for *a Christmas party*

on *Wednesday, The 21st, 4 o'clock*

at *The Ranch Del; 941-6 St, Billings*

Reply to *292-7001 (Debbie)*

INVITATION: INFORMAL FILL-IN

Cocktail buffet

Mr. and Mrs. Walter Cody

Saturday, April 9th
6 o'clock
21 Glencoe Place

Regrets only
632-5000

INVITATION: INFORMAL FOLDOVER CARD

Mr. and Mrs. Carl Forsbal
accept with pleasure
the kind invitation of
Mr. and Mrs. Drake Epworth
for dinner
on Saturday, the thirteenth of August
at half past seven o'clock

Mrs. Glen Eastwood
accepts with pleasure
Mr. and Mrs. Mitchell Perkins'
kind invitation for
Tuesday, the second of February
at eight o'clock
but regrets that
Mr. Eastwood
will be unable to attend

Miss Julia Seabrook
regrets that she is unable to accept
the kind invitation of
Mr. and Mrs. Henry Brisbany
for Sunday, the eighth of May

REPLIES TO INVITATIONS: FORMAL

[logo]

Mr. *John Linnola*

Name of Guest *Sally Ann Ridgway*

Accept ✓ Regret ___ Tel. No. *325-8707*

Dinner, January 16th at 6 p.m.
Traveller's Inn
14 Old Canyon Road
Cincinnati, Ohio

REPLY TO INVITATION: R.S.V.P. CARD

Accept with pleasure
Friday at 8:00

Lois and Phil Brubaker

**REPLY TO INVITATION:
INFORMAL FOLDOVER CARD**

FEDERAL SUPPLIES, INC.
490 Flag Drive
Miami, FL 33157
305-622-9107

Just a reminder . . .

If your check has already been sent, please disregard this notice. If you haven't sent us a check, we would appreciate your prompt payment.

Invoice No. 61078   **Date Due** May 5, 199–   **Amount** $164.98

TO   Harold K. Mellwood
6042 Nash Drive
Des Moines, IA 50314

**THANK YOU FOR
YOUR BUSINESS**

NOTICES

TOVAR INVESTMENT AND PLANNING
626 Milburn Street
Beaverton, OR 97005

DISTRIBUTION NOTIFICATION

CYNTHIA AMARILLO
101 DAWSON WAY
BEAVERTON, OR 97005

PARTNER I.D. NO: 34-707163-I
FINANCIAL PLANNER: NORA BROCKMAN
TELEPHONE: 503-424-7659

The following information details your distribution for DECEMBER 199–, which was mailed to your custodian and/or bank.

PARTNERSHIP	AMOUNT INVESTED	CURRENT MONTH	YEAR-TO-DATE DISTRIBUTIONS
BOJ 16, LTD.	$12,500	$117.43	$906.15
TOTAL	$12,500	$117.43	$906.15

PUBLIC NOTICE
of
Rate Hearing
for
Western Utilities Company

On May 17, 199–, Western Utilities Company filed an application with the State Commission for an increase in natural gas rates. The commission will hold a hearing on this matter beginning August 6, 199-, at 10:00 a.m. at the commission's offices, 2121 Tiley Drive, N.E., Albuquerque, New Mexico 87110. Public comments will be taken in Albuquerque on the first day of hearing. Public comments sessions to be held in other cities will be announced at a later date.

The new law provides for an open public hearing at which, under appropriate circumstances, interested parties may intervene. Intervention shall be permitted to any person entitled by law to intervene and having a direct and substantial interest in the matter.

Persons desiring to intervene must file a written motion to intervene with the commission, which motion should be sent to the company or its counsel and to all parties of record, and which, at the minimum, shall contain the following:

1. The name, address, and telephone number of the proposed intervenor and of any party upon whom service of documents is to be made if different from the intervenor.
2. A short statement of the proposed intervenor's interest in the proceeding (a customer of the company, a shareholder of the company, a competitor, and so on).

The granting of motions to intervene shall be governed by M.C.V.R. 32-6-499, except that all motions to intervene must be filed on or before July 14, 199-. The granting of intervention, among other things, entitles a party to present sworn evidence at hearing and to cross-examine other witnesses. However, failure to intervene will not preclude any customer from appearing at the hearing and making a statement on such customer's own behalf.

Western Utilities Company

NOTICES

INITIATIVE MEASURE TO BE SUBMITTED DIRECTLY TO ELECTORS

To the Secretary of State:

We, the undersigned citizens and qualified electors of the state of Pennsylvania, respectfully demand that the following proposed law shall be submitted to the qualified electors of the state of Pennsylvania for their approval or rejection at the next regular general election, and each for himself or herself states:

I have personally signed this petition with my first and last names. I have not signed any other petition for the same measure.
I am a qualified elector of the state of Pennsylvania, county of _____.

WARNING: It is a class 1 misdemeanor for any person knowingly to sign an initiative or referendum petition with a name other than his own except in a circumstance where he signs for a person, in the presence of and at the specific request of such person, who is incapable of signing his own name because of physical infirmity, or knowingly to sign his name more than once for the same measure, or knowingly to sign such petition when he is not a qualified elector.

SIGNATURE	NAME (Printed)	Residence Address	PA POST OFFICE ADDRESS/ZIP CODE	CITY OR TOWN (if any)	DATE
1					
2					
3					
4					
5					
6					
7					
8					
9					
10					

The validity of signature on this sheet must be sworn to by the circulator before a notary public on the form appearing on the reverse side.

PETITION: FORMAL

318

PETITION FOR ESTABLISHING

A PRESERVATION DISTRICT

We, the undersigned, hereby request that our properties described below be considered for a Preservation District.

SIGNATURE	ADDRESS	PARCEL #	DATE

PETITION: INFORMAL

Chapter 16

FILING

Filing systems vary in size, type, and complexity. Large organizations usually have a central filing department, which is commonly equipped for electronically controlled storage and retrieval. Small offices may have various individual filing systems that combine container files and computer files. Organizations with massive amounts of information may also use a reduction process such as microfilming. Containers for conventional storage differ also, for example, large file cabinets, small card files, open-shelf files, rotary files, and desk files.

Computer documents must be named according to the requirements of the software being used. Perhaps the file must be limited to eight characters plus a period plus an optional extension of up to three characters (such as *DOC* for "document"). It may further be limited to the letters A through Z, the numbers 0 through 9, and certain signs or symbols such as $ or %. Hence a letter to a client written on April 7 might be named *4-7LETTR.DOC*.

Whereas you must follow the instructions provided for your software in electronic processing, other filing procedures require independent decisions in the preparation of names and records such as container labels, file "out" cards, and inventory records. The models in this chapter illustrate acceptable spacing capitalization, and punctuation of such items for a variety of systems—alphabetic, numeric, subject, geographic, and a combination of two or more systems.

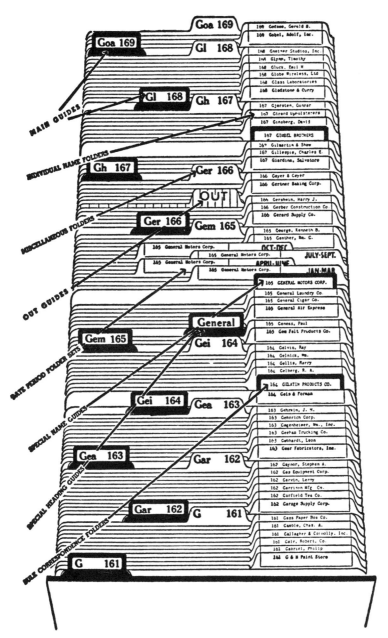

FILE GUIDES AND LABELS

Source: Complete Secretary's Handbook, 6th ed., by Lillian Doris and Besse May Miller, revised by Mary A. De Vries. © 1988, 1983, 1977, 1970, 1960, 1951. Reprinted by permission of the publisher, Prentice Hall, Business & Professional Division, a division of Simon & Schuster, Englewood Cliffs, NJ 07632.

New Services, Inc.

CALIFORNIA

M   24

1690073

FILE GUIDE TABS: PRIMARY

```
┌──────────────────────────────────┐
│                                  │
│        IOWA, Des Moines          │
│        Wm C. Hartwell            │
│        Industrial Park           │
│                                  │
└──────────────────────────────────┘
```

```
┌──────────────────────────────────┐
│                                  │
│        191.07XJV107              │
│        PROSPECTS                 │
│        Midwest Region            │
│                                  │
└──────────────────────────────────┘
```

```
┌──────────────────────────────────┐
│                                  │
│        40   ACCOUNTING           │
│        40.1 Audits               │
│                                  │
└──────────────────────────────────┘
```

LABELS: FILE FOLDER

CONTRACTS

1989 through 1992

XJ1.001

CONTRACTS

1989–1992

LABELS: FILE CABINET

McNEE Window Dressing Co.
SEE Boyle and McNee

CROSS-REFERENCE: FILE LABEL

BYLAWS	206
See Also: Rules and Regulations	

CROSS-REFERENCE: CARDS

CROSS-REFERENCE

Name/Subject: Bylaws   **File No.:** 206

Re: Rules   **Date:** January 6, 199_

SEE

Name/Subject: Rules and Regulations   **File No:** 716

	OUT			
Name/Subject	File No.	Taken by	Date Taken	Document Date
Purdue Project	661	M. Benson	Aug. 5, 199–	Feb. 17, 199–
Tours	21	A. Hart	Oct. 3, 199–	July 1, 199–

OUT GUIDE

REQUEST FOR/RECEIPT OF FILE

Name/Subject   Orientation Program

Address

Requested by   Bill Whittley, Jr.

Department   Personnel

Document Date   Apr. 2, 199–   Date Taken   May 3, 199–

Follow-up Date   July 6, 199–   Date Returned

CHARGE-OUT (REQUISITION) SLIP

BROWNHILL LAUNDRY SERVICE

1403 Wisteria Lane
Princeton, NJ 08540
609-355-9632

Manager: Melanie Brownhill
Delivery: George Brownhill

VERTICAL-CARD-FILE ENTRY

```
Mortgage: $90,000, 2301 Front St. Pullman


Int. due: quarterly
          15th Jan., Apr., Jul., Oct.


Amount: $3,700


Payable to:  Investment Properties Ltd.
             1801 West Street
             Pullman, WA 99164
             (509-772-4300)
```

TICKLER FILE: PAYMENT REMINDER CARD

Chapter 17

LAW

Most legal documents are prepared by specialists in a law office according to the established requirements of the jurisdiction. Some individuals and organizations, however, such as a property manager or a nonprofit organization, may prepare or revise certain material such as a ballot, an amendment to bylaws or other rules and regulations, or an agreement for certain types of services such as maintenance or advertising. The following models are examples of such familiar documents and legal notices.

ARTICLES OF INCORPORATION

OF

SCENIC HILLS HOMEOWNERS' ASSOCIATION

KNOW ALL MEN BY THESE PRESENTS:

That we, the undersigned persons whose residence and post office addresses are set forth below, do hereby adopt these Articles of Incorporation of and for SCENIC HILLS HOMEOWNERS' ASSOCIATION, a nonprofit corporation.

ARTICLE 1

The names and addresses of all the incorporators are

Donna C. Preston   101 Scenic Hills Lane
                                      Phoenix, Arizona 85007

Jack R. Finley   201 Scenic Hills Lane
                                      Phoenix, Arizona 85007

ARTICLE II

The purpose for which this corporation is organized is the transaction of any and all lawful business for which corporations may be incorporated under the laws of the State of Arizona as they may be amended from time to time and specifically but not in limitation thereof the purpose of to acquire and hold title to, manage, maintain, and improve

ARTICLES OF INCORPORATION

-12-

IN WITNESS WHEREOF, we the undersigned, have hereunto placed our signatures this _____ day of _____, 19___.

_____
DONNA C. PRESTON

_____
JACK R. FINLEY

STATE OF ARIZONA   )
) ss.
County of Maricopa   )

On this, the _____ day of _____, 19___, before me, the undersigned Notary Public, personally appeared DONNA C. PRESTON, known to me to be the person whose name is subscribed to the within instrument and acknowledged that she executed the same for the purpose therein contained.

IN WITNESS WHEREOF, I hereunto set my hand and official seal.

_____
Notary Public

My Commission expires:

_____

STATE OF ARIZONA   )
) ss.
County of Maricopa   )

On this, the _____ day of _____, 19___, before me, the undersigned Notary Public, personally appeared JACK R. FINLEY, known to me to be the person whose name is subscribed

ARTICLES OF INCORPORATION

BYLAWS

OF

SCENIC HILLS HOMEOWNERS' ASSOCIATION

ARTICLE I
Recitals, Definitions

1. This corporation has been formed pursuant to the nonprofit corporation laws of the State of Arizona.

2. The specific and primary purposes of this corporation are as set forth in Article V of the Articles of Incorporation.

3. The corporation is herein referred to as "the Association."

4. The term "development" shall mean all of the real property within the boundaries of that certain real estate development in Maricopa County, Arizona, and commonly known as SCENIC HILLS, and any additional property that is annexed thereto pursuant to the provisions of the Restricted Covenants recorded in the office of the Recorder of the County of Maricopa, State of Arizona, in connection with this development.

5. The property that the Association shall initially own and control is that shown on the recorded subdivision plats as common area, as well as all roadways within the subdivision, which are shown on the subdivision plats as easements.

−8−

adopted by the members, only by three-fourths vote of the total votes cast by the membership, provided, however, that Article III, paragraphs 1 and 2, or Article VII shall not be amended or repealed without the affirmative vote of members having at least three-fourths (3/4) of the total votes of the membership approving such amendment or repeal and further provided that no amendment, repeal, or adoption of new Bylaws shall be effective before the sale and conveyance of 75 percent of the lots by the Developer without the consent of the Developer.

10. Any notice or other document permitted or required to be delivered as provided herein may be delivered either personally or by mail. If delivery is made by mail, it shall be deemed to have been delivered twenty-four (24) hours after a copy of same has been deposited in the United States mail, postage prepaid, to the last known address of the addressee.

11. The members shall have the authority to vote, in accordance with Article IV, to direct the Board to transfer or dedicate any or all of the Common Areas or roadways to the City of Phoenix, if the City is willing to accept same for maintenance.

Dated this _____ day of _____, 19___.

_____
Secretary

BYLAWS

NOTICE OF SALE

Request of notice of lien sale be published on the following units(s):

UNIT #21

LOCATION: ROYAL MINI STORAGE, 1672 WINDSOR ROAD

TENANT: JOHN MORSE

STORED GOODS: CONTENTS OF UNIT LIEN SALE WILL BE HELD JULY 7, 9 A.M. TO 12 NOON, ROYAL MINI STORAGE, 1672 WINDSOR ROAD

2TC Pub. June 17, July 1, 199–

NOTICE OF SALE

Request of notice of lien sale be published on the following unit(s):

UNIT #21
LOCATION: ROYAL MINI STORAGE, 1672 WINDSOR ROAD
TENANT: JOHN MORSE
STORED GOODS: CONTENTS OF UNIT LIEN SALE WILL BE HELD JULY 7, 9 A.M. TO 12 NOON, ROYAL MINI STORAGE, 1672 WINDSOR ROAD

2TC Pub. June 17, July 1, 199–

NOTICE: NEWSPAPER

REQUEST FOR BIDS

The Professional Building of Prospect Park, Pennsylvania, is requesting bids from qualified contractors for work that requires trenching for and installing underground utilities consisting of audiovisual conduits, electrical conduits, hot and cold water supply and return pipe lines, fire and domestic water, gas and sewer pipe lines, and for drainage culverts and appurtenances, portland cement concrete paving of streets and parking lot facilities, in conjunction with building program.

Plans and specifications may be obtained from Martin Seers, the Professional Building, 1901 Park Aveneue, Prospect Park, Pennsylvania 19076. Bids will be received until 2 p.m., Monday, September 6, 199–, at the Professional Building.

The Professional Building reserves the right to reject any or all bids and to waive any technicalities.

Martin Seers, Purchasing Agent

5TC Pub. September 2, 3, 4, 5, 6, 199–

P.O. 19088

REQUEST: NEWSPAPER

REQUEST FOR BIDS

The Professional Building of Prospect Park, Pennsylvania, is requesting bids from qualified contractors for work that requires trenching for and installing underground utilities consisting of audiovisual conduits, electrical conduits, hot and cold water supply and return pipe lines, fire and domestic water, gas and sewer pipe lines, and for drainage culverts and appurtenances, portland cement concrete paving of streets and parking lot facilities, in conjunction with building program.

Plans and specifications may be obtained from Martin Seers, the Professional Building, 1901 Park Avenue, Prospect Park, Pennsylvania 19076. Bids will be received until 2 p.m., Monday, September 6, 199–, at the Professional Building.

The Professional Building reserves the right to reject any or all bids and to waive any technicalities.

Martin Seers, Purchasing Agent
5TC Pub. September 2, 3, 4, 5, 6, 199–
P.O. 19088

REQUEST: NEWSPAPER

MAINTENANCE AGREEMENT

This agreement is made this _____ day of _____, 19___, by and between Fredericks Management Company, Inc. (the Company), and Michael J. Sturnam (the Agent). The parties hereto agree as follows:

The Agent shall provide to the Company the following services:

1. _____
2. _____
3. _____

The rate for this service shall be _____.

The agent agrees to keep and submit weekly time record and receipts for any supplies purchased on behalf of the Company and shall receive from the Company monthly compensation for approved time and costs as specified above.

This agreement may be modified by written consent of both parties or may be canceled upon thirty (30) days' notice by either party.

For FREDERICKS MANAGEMENT COMPANY, INC.

President _____ Secretary _____

For MICHAEL J. STURNAM

Agent _____

AGREEMENT: INFORMAL

INDEPENDENT CONTRACTOR SERVICES AGREEMENT

This agreement is made this _____ day of _____, 19___, by and between Fredericks Management Company, Inc. (hereinafter "the Company"), and Michael J. Sturnam (hereinafter "the Contractor"). For and in consideration of the promises exchanged by the parties and for other valuable consideration, the parties enter into this contract in accordance with the terms herein set forth.

1. The Contractor agrees to provide the following services to the Company:

      a. _____

      b. _____

      c. _____

2. In consideration of said services to be provided by the Contractor, the Company agrees to compensate the Contractor in the following amounts and at the following times:

_____

_____.

3. The parties agree that the Contractor shall not be, for any purposes including for tax, workers' compensation, or liability purposes, considered to be an employee or agent of either the Company or of the Company's clients and principals.

CONTRACT: FORMAL

−4−

attorney, then in any court proceedings the prevailing party shall be entitled to its attorney's fees incurred in such proceedings.

11. Any modification or amendment of the contract shall be in writing and shall be executed by all parties.

12. The provisions of the contract shall inure to the benefit of and be binding on the parties thereto, their heirs, executors, administrators, and permitted assignees.

13. Any waiver by any part of a breach of any provision of the contract shall not operate as or be construed as a waiver of any subsequent breach thereof.

14. The parties agree to execute all documents that may be necessary to carry out the intent and purposes of the contract.

15. The terms of the contract and this document constitute the entire agreement between the parties, and the parties represent that there are no collateral agreements or side agreements not otherwise provided for within the terms of the contract.

Agreed and signed this _____ day of _____, 19___.

ATTEST: FREDERICKS MANAGEMENT COMPANY, INC.

_____ By _____
Secretary of the   President
Corporation

ATTEST:

_____ By _____

CONTRACT: FORMAL

ADDENDUM TO LEASE

The Lease made and entered into March 9, 199–, between Jeanette Evans, Lessor, and Henry Brubaker, Lessee, is hereby amended as follows:

> Lessee may make improvements or other alterations in the
> interior of the leased premises at his own expense, provided
> that before commencing any such work, the Lessee shall first
> obtain written consent from the Lessor. Such alteration shall
> become the property of the Lessor and shall remain the
> Lessor's property at the termination of this lease.

Date: _____   _____
                               Lessor

                               _____
                               Lessee

ADDENDUM: DOCUMENT

RESOLVED That Section II of Article IX of the Constitution of The Garden Club is hereby amended to read as follows:

> "SECTION II: Each member of The Garden Club shall pay dues to the Club as follows: The minimum amount to be paid by each member annually shall be twenty-five dollars ($25) for active members, fifteen dollars ($15) for student members, and ten dollars ($10) for senior citizens above the age of sixty-two (62). Bills for dues shall be sent to members at the beginning of the fiscal year. Prorating of dues of members who join during a fiscal year shall be at the discretion of the Club."

FURTHER RESOLVED That the aforesaid amendment shall take effect on January 1, 199–.

AMENDMENT: CONSTITUTION

Chapter 18

STATISTICS AND FINANCE

The preparation of mathematical, statistical, and financial material involves decisions concerning the alignment; indention; spacing; and overall arrangement of figures, signs, and symbols. Some rules are strictly observed; figures, for example, must be aligned at the decimal point in a column. Guidelines in other areas may not be observed as strictly; a carryover, or runover, line, for instance, may be indented two to three character spaces in one office and four to five spaces in another office. (The greater the indention, however, the more likely it is that there will be additional carryover lines.) Regardless of the style chosen, it is important to be consistent. If carryover lines are indented three spaces in one column, they should be indented three spaces in all columns.

The following models illustrate acceptable formats for common financial reports and a variety of statistical lists and columns. The model lists and columns illustrate the alignment of figures, signs, and symbols and the placement of rules around the headings and columns.

GRAPHICS OF AMERICA
22 Lost Lane
Glendora, CA 91740
213-771-8265

DATE: April 21, 199_

TO: Charles J. Brownell
        P.O. Box 7
        Glendora, CA 91740

YOUR PURCHASE ORDER: March 3, 199–

Prepare five b/w pen and ink $342.00
  drawings, 8 × 10   12.00
Set 27 pt. headline $354.00

INVOICE: LETTERHEAD

PETTY CASH VOUCHER

Date ___Dec. 15, 199-___ No. _67_

Charge to _Library_

Paid to _Marcy Evans_ $_9.95_

For _computer dictionary_

_____

Approved by: Payment Received by:

___O.T.S.___   ___Marcy Evans___

<u>Net Gain</u>
$1,973,436.52
236,011.87

Net Gain:
<u>Sales to Date</u>
$1,973,436.52
236,011.87

<u>Net Gain: Sales to Date</u>
$1,973,436.52
236,011.87

Net Gain:
Regional Sales to Date
<u>(Excluding Returns)</u>
$1,973,436.52
236,011.87

Year	Net Gain		
	Total	Western Region	Eastern Region
1991	$1,973,436.52	$ 906,718.26	$1,066,718.26
1992	2,071,356.13	1,020,114.16	1,051,241.97

STATISTICAL LISTS AND COLUMNS:
RULES IN HEADS

```
                         $122.67
                            -
                           0.31
                          14.09
                         $137.07


                          50.10%
                           8.60
                          27.32
                          13.98
                         100.00%
```

```
Cost:                    $1,462.01
Ded.:                    $   123.55
Ratio:                          5:1
No. members:             1,563,070
Net increase:                   25%
```

STATISTICAL LISTS AND COLUMNS:
ALIGNMENT OF DECIMALS, FIGURES, AND SIGNS

CLARKE AND SHILMANN

199– Budget

INCOME

Beginning cash balance	$ 20,000
Sales	301,630
Cash collections	17,901
Total	$339,531

EXPENSES

Labor	$ 80,130
Materials	97,644
Selling expenses	72,500
Overhead	89,257
Total	$339,531
Ending cash balance	$ NONE

BUDGET: INFORMAL

Cash Budget
Year Ended December 31, 199–

	Total	1st Quarter	2nd Quarter	3rd Quarter	4th Quarter
Beginning cash bal.	$ 15,000	$15,000	$ 3,850	$ 13,300	$ 25,750
Cash collections	361,950	69,000	82,800	97,650	112,500
Total	$376,950	$84,000	$86,650	$110,950	$138,250
Cash payments					
Purchases	$ 58,625	$11,750	$13,875	$ 15,375	$ 17,625
Direct labor	98,750	20,000	22,500	26,250	30,000
Mfg. overhead	36,700	7,300	8,300	9,800	11,300
Selling expense	91,600	17,275	21,025	24,775	28,525
Admin. expense	33,300	6,300	7,650	9,000	10,350
Federal income tax	27,525	27,525			
Dividends	20,000				20,000
Interest expense	450				450
Loan repayment	10,000				10,000
Total	$376,950	$90,150	$73,350	$ 85,200	$128,250
Cash deficiency		($6,150)			
Bank loan received	10,000	10,000			
Ending cash balance	$ 10,000	$ 3,850	$13,300	$ 25,750	$ 10,000

BUDGET: FORMAL

RING HARDWARE STORE
Income Statement
Year Ended December 31, 199-

Gross sales		$140,000
Cost of sales:		
Opening inventory	$21,000	
Purchases	30,000	
Total	51,000	
Ending inventory	17,000	
Total cost of sales		34,000
Gross income		106,000
Operating expenses:		
Payroll (employee)	30,000	
Rent	12,000	
Payroll taxes	4,000	
Interest	1,000	
Depreciation	1,400	
Truck expense	11,000	
Telephone	3,000	
Insurance	4,000	
Miscellaneous	1,100	
Total		67,500
Net income (before owner salary)		$ 38,500

INCOME STATEMENT: REPORT FORM

RESOURCES, INC.
Income Statement
Year Ended December 31, 199—

	1992	1991
Income:		
Sales	$786,590	$591,000
Royalties	9,000	3,000
Interest and dividends	4,500	4,000
Total income	$800,090	$598,000
Expenses:		
Cost of goods sold	$540,000	$430,000
Depreciation	43,000	36,000
Selling, gen., & admin.	71,000	69,000
Loss on sale of equipment	4,100	600
Interest expense	6,000	8,000
Federal income tax	42,000	27,000
Total expenses	$706,100	$570,600
Net income	$ 93,990	$ 27,400

INCOME STATEMENT: COMPARATIVE FORM

```
                    THE BRADDOCK COMPANY
                      Income Statement
                Year Ended December 31, 199-


Income:
  Net sales                                        $280,000
  Dividend income                                     1,900
     Total income                                  $281,900


Expenses:
  Cost of goods sold              $171,600
  Selling expenses                   8,200
  Administrative expenses           32,000
  Federal income taxes              16,500
     Total expenses                                 228,300
Net income                                         $ 53,600
```

INCOME STATEMENT: SHORT FORM

```
                     NOVELTIES 'N MORE
                      Income Statement
                Year Ended December 31, 199-


     Income                                        $431,800
     Expenses                                        302,000
     Net income                                    $129,800
```

INCOME STATEMENT: SIMPLIFIED FORM

```
                          ELK-CURRIER CORPORATION
                       Statement of Financial Position
                           December 31, 199-


Current assets:
  Cash                                                           $165,000
  Accounts receivable, net                                         87,000
  Inventories                                                     175,000
     Total current assets                                        $427,000

Less current liabilities:
  Accounts payable                            $181,000
  Income taxes                                  45,000
  Other accrued liabilities                     90,000
     Total current liabilities                                    316,000

Working capital                                                  $111,000

Fixed assets, net:
  Land                                        $ 60,000
  Buildings                                    170,000
  Machinery and equipment                       67,500
                                              $297,500
  Less accumulated deprec.                      30,000            267,500

Other assets                                                      20,000
                                                                 $398,500


Less long-term debt                                              295,300

Net assets                                                      $103,200

Stockholders' equity:
  Common stock, $20 par value, 1,000 shares
    authorized, issued, and outstanding                         $ 20,000
  Retained earnings                                               83,200

     Total stockholders' equity                                 $103,200
```

BALANCE SHEET: REPORT FORM

WARD FORMS COMPANY
Balance Sheet
December 31, 1991, and 1992

ASSETS	1992	1991
Current assets:		
Cash	$ 22,000	$ 31,000
Accounts receivable	48,000	36,000
Inventories	109,000	95,000
Prepaid expenses	17,000	12,000
Total current assets	$196,000	$174,000
Fixed assets:		
Land	30,000	24,000
Buildings	180,000	154,000
Machinery and equipment	95,000	72,000
	305,000	250,000
Less accumulated depreciation	70,000	60,000
	235,000	190,000
Other assets	20,000	40,000
Total assets	$255,000	$230,000

LIABILITIES AND STOCKHOLDERS' EQUITY		
Current liabilities:		
Notes payable	$ 16,000	2,000
Accounts payable	59,000	81,000
Income taxes	75,000	35,000
Other accrued liabilities	21,000	14,000
Total current liabilities	171,000	132,000
Loan payable at 12% interest, due June 30, 1996	10,000	—
Stockholders' equity:		
Common stock, $10 par value: 5,000 shares authorized, issued, and outstanding	50,000	30,000
Additional paid-in capital	10,000	16,000
Retained earnings	14,000	52,000
	74,000	98,000
Total stockholders' equity	$255,000	$230,000

BALANCE SHEET: COMPARATIVE FORM

```
                    THE HART COMPANY
                     Balance Sheet
                   December 31, 199-


                         ASSETS

Current assets:
  Cash and short-term investments              $ 12,000
  Account receivable                             98,000
  Inventories                                    77,000
  Prepaid expenses                               13,000
    Total current assets                       $200,000

Fixed assets, at cost:
  Land                            $ 30,000
  Buildings                        190,000
  Machinery and equipment           75,000
                                  $295,000
  Less accumulated depreciation     60,000
    Total fixed assets                          235,000

Other assets                                     50,000
    Total assets                               $485,000


         LIABILITIES AND SHAREHOLDERS' EQUITY

Current liabilities:
  Accounts payable                             $129,000
  Income taxes                                   75,000
  Other accrued liabilities                     106,000
    Total current liabilities                  $310,000

Long-term debt                                   70,000

Shareholders' equity:
  Common stock, $1 par value: 100,000 shares
    issued and outstanding        $ 50,000
  Additional paid-in capital        10,000
  Retained earnings                 45,000
    Total shareholder's equity                 $105,000
    Total liabilities and
      shareholder's equity                     $485,000
```

BALANCE SHEET: ACCOUNT FORM

```
                     INMAN JANITORIAL PRODUCTS
                   Statement of Financial Condition
                          December 31, 199-


                                ASSETS

Current assets:
   Cash on hand and in banks                           $ 10,000
   Receivable                                            99,000
   Inventories                                          101,000
   Prepaid expenses                                       32,000
      Total current assets                             $242,000

Plant and equipment less accumulated depr.             $225,000

Other assets                                             50,000

   Total assets                                        $517,000


                             LIABILITIES

Current liabilities:
   Accounts payable                                    $108,000
   Income taxes payable                                  45,000
   Other costs and accrued expenses                      16,000
      Total current liabilities                         169,000

Long-term debt                                            85,000

   Total liabilities                                     254,000

Excess of assets over liabilities                      $263,000

Stockholders' equity:
   Common stock, 100,000 shares in stock
      issued, $1 par value:                            $100,000
   Additional paid-in capital                            24,000
   Retained earnings                                     139,000

      Total shareholder's equity                       $263,000
```

BALANCE SHEET: SIMPLIFIED FORM

Chapter 19

MEETINGS

The type of material prepared for a meeting will vary depending on the kind of meeting. Stockholders' meetings, for instance, require more formality in notices, agendas, minutes, and other documents than does an office staff meeting. An informal staff meeting, in fact, might not use any of these items.

When meeting materials such as official notices and published minutes are required, an organization should follow the style prescribed by its bylaws or other rules and regulations. Perhaps the bylaws state that all special meeting notices must contain certain facts (time, date, place, purpose of meeting) and must be signed by the secretary or president or both. If such requirements do not exist, the individuals or organizations arranging the meeting should adopt a standard format for documents such as agendas, notices, proxies, resolutions, and indexes.

The models in this chapter include both formal and informal rules for common meeting materials.

COUNTRYWIDE INNS SOCIETY
Directors' Meeting
February 16, 199–
(9:00–11:30 a.m.)

1. Call to order   9:00 a.m.

2. Announcements   9:05

    a. Quorum

    b. Guests

3. Minutes: reading and approval of previous

    minutes   9:10

4. Reports of officers   9:15

5. Reports of committees   9:30

6. Old business   9:45

    a. Road–repair status

    b. Insurance review

7. New business   10:15

    a. Appointment of Budget Committee

    b. Proposal for bylaws revision

8. Nomination and election of officers   10:45

9. Other announcements   11:15

10. Adjournment   11:30

AGENDA: SHORT FORM

COUNTRYWIDE INNS SOCIETY
Directors' Meeting
February 16, 199-

Regular Meeting   9:00-11:30 a.m.
Place: CIS Headquarters, 1301 Center Road, Dallas, TX 75262
Presiding: Dale Kingsley, President (tele. 817-344-6200)

1. Call to order (D. Kingsley)   9:00 a.m.

2. Roll call (voice call of directors)   9:01

3. Announcements   9:05

   a. Quorum (verify)

   b. Guests (introduction and welcome by

      D. Kingsley)

4. Minutes (reading of previous minutes by   9:10

   secretary; motion to approve as read or

   corrected)

5. Reports of officers   9:15

   a. Treasurer's report (Jane Shearer—

      quarterly report, discussion, and

      approval)

   b. Vice president, chapter coordinator

      (Bill Jennings—report on chapter

      speaker-roster update)

1

AGENDA: LONG FORM

Agenda   2

6. Reports of committees   9:30

   a. Publications Committee (Mark Douglas,

      chair—report on renovation guide-

      lines booklet proposal)

   b. Membership Committee (Nancy Goldman,

      chair—report on October membership

      drive)

7. Old business   9:45

   a. Road-repair status (D. Kingsley to

      present bids from three firms)

   b. Insurance review (D. Kingsley to

      report on changes in deductible

      options)

8. New business   10:15

   a. Appointment of Budget Committee

      (nominations and election of new

      committee)

   b. Bylaws revision (proposal to amend

      bylaws to transfer limited member-

      recruitment duties from directors to

      chapter presidents)

9. Nomination and election of officers   10:45

   (select president, vice president,

   secretary, and treasurer for 199- term)

AGENDA: LONG FORM

Agenda   3

10. Other announcements   11:15

   a. Annual chapter presidents' meeting

     (scheduled: March 1, 199-,

     10:00 a.m., CIS headquarters)

   b. Goodwill tour, Vice President Nora

     Schoenberg (visit to twelve inns,

     northern region, April 199-)

11. Adjournment (call for motion to adjourn)   11:30

AGENDA: LONG FORM

COUNTRYWIDE INNS SOCIETY
Directors' Meeting
February 16, 199-

Regular Meeting   9:00-11:30 a.m.
Place: CIS Headquarters, 1301 Center Road, Dallas, TX 75262
Presiding: Dale Kingsley, President (tele. 817-344-6200)

1. Call to order (D. Kingsley)   9:00 a.m.
2. Roll call (voice call of directors)   9:01
3. Announcements   9:05
   a. Quorum (verify)
   b. Guests (introduction and welcome by
      D. Kingsley)
4. Minutes (reading of previous minutes by   9:10
   secretary; motion to approve as read or
   corrected)
5. Reports of officers   9:15
   a. Treasurer's report (Jane Shearer—quarterly
      report, discussion, and approval)
   b. Vice president, chapter coordinator
      (Bill Jennings—report on chapter
      speaker-roster update)
6. Reports of committees   9:30
   a. Publications Committee (Mark Douglas,
      chair—report on renovation guide-
      lines booklet proposal)
   b. Membership Committee (Nancy Goldman,
      chair—report on October membership
      drive)
7. Old business   9:45
   a. Road-repair status (D. Kingsley to
      present bids from three firms)
   b. Insurance review (D. Kingsley to
      report on changes in deductible
      options)
8. New business   10:15
   a. Appointment of Budget Committee
      (nominations and election of new
      committee)

                                                                    *

                              1

AGENDA: LONG FORM

Agenda   2

      b. Bylaws revision (proposal to amend
         bylaws to transfer limited member-
         recruitment duties from directors to
         chapter presidents)
  9. Nomination and election of officers   10:45
     (select president, vice president,
     secretary, and treasurer for 199- term)
10. Other announcements   11:15
      a. Annual chapter presidents' meeting
         (scheduled: March 1, 199-,
         10:00 a.m., CIS headquarters)
      b. Goodwill tour, Vice President Nora
         Schoenberg (visit to twelve inns,
         northern region, April 199-)
11. Adjournment (call for motion to adjourn)   11:30

AGENDA: LONG FORM

SULLIVAN ENGINEERING
101 Wright Street
Portland, ME 04102
207-632-7778

DATE: October 11, 199-

TO: Design Staff

FROM: Joe Lopez

SUBJECT: Staff Meeting

A meeting of the design staff is scheduled for 9:00 a.m.,
Monday, October 20, 199-, in my office (Room 1600), to review
the schedule and make staff assignments for our new Industrial
Park contract.

I hope you'll make every effort to be present, but if you are
unable to attend, please leave a message with my secretary by
Friday, October 17 (ext. 2106).

Thanks very much.

MEETING NOTICE: INFORMAL

ASSOCIATION OF INDEPENDENT RESEARCHERS
413 Division Street
Ames, IA 50011
515-822-3411

NOTICE

OF THE ANNUAL MEETING

OF THE ASSOCIATION OF INDEPENDENT RESEARCHERS

The Sixth Annual Meeting of the active members of the
Association of Independent Researchers will be held on
Thursday, February 6, 199-, in the Convention Center, 2100
Parkway Drive, Detroit, Michigan 48226. The meeting will begin
at 1:30 p.m. Following the meeting, there will be an informal
reception in the Mezzanine.

The purposes of the meeting are to vote for directors to serve
during the 199- term and to conduct other business that may
properly come before the meeting.

If you cannot be present at the meeting, please sign the
accompanying proxy and return it in the enclosed envelope.

                                        Mary Seymour
                                        Secretary

Ames, Iowa
January 10, 199-

MEETING NOTICE: FORMAL

BURNHILL MANUFACTURING COMPANY, INC.
One Olson Drive
New York, NY 10017
212-666-5050

    We, the undersigned, duly elected directors of Burnhill
Manufacturing Company, Inc., do hereby severally waive notice
of time, place, and purpose of the regular November meeting of
directors of said corporation and consent that the meeting be
held at the Hightop Motor Hotel in the city of Philadelphia,
state of Pennsylvania, on the 14th day of December, 199-, at
1:30 o'clock in the afternoon. We do further consent to the
transaction of any business that may properly come before the
meeting.

Dated _____, 19____ Signed _____
                                   President and Director

                                   _____
                                   Vice President and Director

                                   _____
                                   Secretary and Director

                                   _____
                                   Treasurer and Director

                                   _____
                                   Director

                                   _____
                                   Director

                                   _____
                                   Director

WAIVER OF NOTICE

STATEWIDE INSURANCE ASSOCIATES
P.O. Box 10179
Wichita, KS 67208
316-202-2111

NOTICE

You are hereby notified that the Annual Meeting of the policy-holders of Statewide Insurance Associates, Inc., will be held in the Home Office, 99 Treetop Tower, Wichita, Kansas, on February 17, 199–, at 10:30 o'clock in the morning. If you are unable to attend, please sign this proxy form and mail it promptly in the enclosed envelope. No postage is required.

PROXY

I hereby constitute Gerald Dania, Bette Drew, Timothy Hardin, and James Stowe, or a majority of such of them as actually are present, to act for me in my stead and as my proxy at the Annual Meeting of the policyholders of Statewide Insurance Associates, to be held in Wichita, Kansas, on February 17, 199–, at 10:30 o'clock in the morning, and at any adjournment or adjournments thereof, with full power and authority to act for me in my behalf, with all powers that I, the undersigned, would possess if I were personally present.

Signed _____
        Policyholder

_____   _____
    City   State

PLEASE SIGN AND PROVIDE YOUR CITY AND STATE OF RESIDENCE ABOVE BEFORE MAILING. NO POSTAGE IS REQUIRED.

NATIONAL DOCUMENTARY EDITORS SOCIETY
416 New Jersey Boulevard
Newark, NJ 07102
201-847-7272

ANNUAL MEETING—FEBRUARY 5, 199–

PROXY

I hereby appoint Penny Craft, Dominic Luigi, Kathryn Osage, and Donald Hexman, or any one of them, my proxies, with full power of substitution in each, to attend and vote for me in my name at the Annual Meeting of active members of the National Documentary Editors Society, on Monday, February 5, 199–, and at any adjournments thereof, for directors of the Society, by casting the ballot enclosed in this proxy envelope.

On other matters at the meeting: My appointment

( ) does   ( ) does not

include authorization to vote on other matters that may properly come before the meeting.

Signed _____ Date _____

PROXY-BALLOT

[logo]

BALLOT

National Documentary Editors Society
Election of Directors
For the Term 199– - 199–

Please check the boxes of your choice, sign and enclose the ballot in the proxy envelope, and return it to the Documentary Editors Society.

Yes No   **Yes No**

( ) ( ) Edna K. Trummell   ( ) ( ) Barry O. Tolleston

( ) ( ) Harold P. Fratt   ( ) ( ) Miriam J. Warner

( ) ( ) Susan Lichtner   ( ) ( ) Keith L. Edison II

I vote for the following persons for election to the Board of Directors in place of the above nominees for whom I have cast a negative vote:

_____   _____

_____   _____

_____   _____

Signature _____ Date _____

PLEASE RETURN YOUR BALLOT SO THAT IT WILL BE RECEIVED NO LATER THAN JANUARY 30, 199–. THANK YOU.

PROXY-BALLOT

WHEREAS the directors of Mackenzie & Associates wish to record their deep sorrow upon the death on May 23, 199–, of their friend and colleague Paul E. Bashford, who since 1984 had served as a director of this Company, be it

RESOLVED That the directors of Mackenzie & Associates do hereby express their grievous loss in the death of Paul E. Bashford and do hereby record their sadness upon the loss of an associate who was loved and respected by all.

RESOLVED FURTHER That a copy of this resolution be sent to Mrs. Paul E. Bashford and her family as a humble expression of the Board of Directors' heartfelt sympathy.

WHEREAS the directors of Mackenzie & Associate wish to record their deep sorrow upon the death on May 23, 199–, of their friend and colleague Paul E. Bashford, who since 1984 had served as a director of this Company, be it

RESOLVED That the directors of Mackenzie & Associates do hereby express their grievous loss in the death of Paul E. Bashford and do hereby record their sadness upon the loss of an associate who was loved and respected by all.

RESOLVED FURTHER That a copy of this resolution be sent to Mrs. Paul E. Bashford and her family as a humble expression of the Board of Directors' heartfelt sympathy.

RESOLUTION

NATIONAL HEATING AND COOLING COMPANY, INC.

Special Meeting of Stockholders
August 16, 199-

TIME AND PLACE

A special meeting of the stockholders of National Heating and Cooling Company, Inc., was held at the home office of the Corporation at 1902 Third Avenue, Columbia, South Carolina, 29208 on the sixteenth day of August 199-, at two o'clock in the afternoon.

PRESIDING OFFICER; SECRETARY

Walter Hudgill, president of the Corporation, presided at the meeting, and Alice Druxell, secretary of the Corporation, acted as secretary of the meeting, as provided by the Bylaws.

ROLL CALL

The secretary called the roll of stockholders, and all stockholders were present either in person or by proxy.

NOTICE OF MEETING

The following notice of the meeting was read by the secretary and ordered to be entered into the minutes of this meeting.

You are hereby notified that a Special Meeting of the stockholders of National Heating and Cooling

MINUTES: FORMAL

August 16, 199–

Company, Inc., will be held at the Home Office, 1902 Third Avenue, Columbia, South Carolina, on August 16, 199–, at two o'clock in the afternoon. If you are unable to attend, please sign this proxy card and mail it promptly. No postage is required.

PROOF OF NOTICE   The secretary presented an affidavit showing that the aforesaid notice of meeting had been duly mailed to each stockholder at his or her last known address, more than thirty days preceding this meeting.

INSPECTORS OF ELECTION   The president stated that the Board of Directors had selected two inspectors, Jennifer Craighill and Leon Thurber, and had requested that their appointment be confirmed at this meeting.

Upon motion duly made and seconded, the appointment of Jennifer Craighill and Leon Thurber as inspectors was unanimously confirmed, and they and each of them took and subscribed to the prescribed oath.

The inspectors thereupon took charge of the proxies and, upon examination thereof and of the stock books,

MINUTES: FORMAL

RESOLUTIONS   On motion duly made and seconded, and
                           after due deliberation, the following
                           resolution was voted on:

                               RESOLVED That the minutes of the
                               meeting of stockholders held on the
                               tenth day of January 199- are hereby
                               adopted and approved in their
                               entirety.

                           Upon canvassing the votes, the
                           inspectors reported that the above
                           resolution had been adopted by
                           affirmative vote of all stockholders of
                           the Corporation.

ADJOURNMENT   No other business coming before the
                           meeting, the meeting was thereupon
                           adjourned.

                           _____
                           President

                           _____
                           Secretary

NATIONAL HEATING AND COOLING COMPANY, INC.

Special Meeting of Stockholders
August 16, 199-

TIME AND PLACE

A special meeting of the stockholders of National Heating and Cooling Company, Inc., was held at the home office of the Corporation, at 1902 Third Avenue, Columbia, South Carolina 29208, on the sixteenth day of August, 199-, at two o'clock in the afternoon.

PRESIDING OFFICER; SECRETARY

Walter Hudgill, president of the Corporation, presided at the meeting, and Alice Druxell, secretary of the Corporation, acted as secretary of the meeting, as provided by the Bylaws.

ROLL CALL

The secretary called the roll of stockholders, and all stockholders were present either in person or by proxy.

NOTICE OF MEETING

The following notice of the meeting was read by the secretary and ordered to be entered into the minutes of this meeting.

> You are hereby notified that a Special Meeting of the stockholders of National Heating and Cooling Company, Inc., will be held at the Home Office, 1902 Third Avenue, Columbia, South Carolina, on August 16, 199-, at two o'clock in the afternoon. If you are unable to attend, please sign this proxy card and mail it promptly. No postage is required.

PROOF OF NOTICE

The secretary presented an affidavit showing that the aforesaid notice of meeting had been duly mailed to each stockholder at his or her last known address, more than thirty days preceding this meeting.

INSPECTORS OF ELECTION

The president stated that the Board of Directors had selected two inspectors, Jennifer Craighill and Leon Thurber, and had requested that their appointment be confirmed at this meeting.

MINUTES: FORMAL

RESOLUTIONS   On motion duly made and seconded, and
                          after due deliberation, the following
                          resolution was voted on:

                              RESOLVED That the minutes of the
                              meeting of stockholders held on the
                              tenth day of January 199- are hereby
                              adopted and approved in their
                              entirety.

                          Upon canvassing the votes, the
                          inspectors reported that the above
                          resolution had been adopted by
                          affirmative vote of all stockholders of
                          the Corporation.

ADJOURNMENT   No other business coming before the
                          meeting, the meeting was thereupon
                          adjourned.

                          _____
                          President

                          _____
                          Secretary

THE BUSINESS CLUB OF ARLINGTON

Board of Directors
Regular Meeting
November 17, 199-

CALL TO ORDER
A regular meeting of the Board of Directors of The Business
Club of Arlington was called to order at 1:30 p.m., November
17, 199-, at the Wayside Restaurant and Conference Center, 900
Old Virginia Highway, Arlington, Virginia 22209. The presiding
officer was Alan Gavin. A quorum was present including the
following (alphabetically): Nora Brummell, Alan Gavin, Sally
Lee Hudson, Beverly Inscore, and Martin O. Kimball, Jr.

MINUTES
The secretary, Martin Kimball, read the minutes of the October
15, 199-, meeting, and they were approved as read.

FINANCES
The treasurer, Sally Lee Hudson, presented a financial
statement showing a bank balance on September 30, 199-, of
$2,101.56 (copy attached).

RETAILERS' HOLIDAY FAIR
It was moved, seconded, and unanimously voted to appoint
Beverly Inscore as coordinator of the Retailers' Holiday Fair
program scheduled for December 20-24, 199-. She will follow the
general program used in 199- and issue updated guidelines to
participating retailers. Details will be available at the
December 15 meeting of the Club. Members who have suggestions

MINUTES: INFORMAL

November 17, 199-   2

for the Retailer's Holiday Fair program should contact
Beverly Inscore at 792-8000 or 792-8010, 9 to 5,
Monday-Friday.

ADJOURNMENT
There being no further business, the meeting was adjourned at
2:15 p.m.

_____   _____
Secretary   President

THE BUSINESS CLUB OF ARLINGTON

Board of Directors
Regular Meeting
November 17, 199-

CALL TO ORDER

A regular meeting of the Board of Directors of The Business
Club of Arlington was called to order at 1:30 p.m., November
17, 199-, at the Wayside Restaurant and Conference Center, 900
Old Virginia Highway, Arlington, Virginia 22209. The presiding
officer was Alan Gavin. A quorum was present including the
following (alphabetically): Nora Brummell, Alan Gavin, Sally
Lee Hudson, Beverly Inscore, and Martin O. Kimball, Jr.

MINUTES

The secretary, Martin Kimball, read the minutes of the October
15, 199-, meeting, and they were approved as read.

FINANCES

The treasurer, Sally Lee Hudson, presented a financial
statement showing a bank balance on September 30, 199-, of
$2,101.56 (copy attached).

RETAILERS' HOLIDAY FAIR

It was moved, seconded, and unanimously voted to appoint
Beverly Inscore as coordinator of the Retailers' Holiday Fair
program scheduled for December 20-24, 199-. She will follow the
general program used in 199- and issue updated guidelines to
participating retailers. Details will be available at the
December 15 meeting of the Club. Members who have suggestions
for the Retailer's Holiday Fair program should contact Beverly
Inscore at 792-8000 or 792-8010, 9-5, Monday-Friday.

ADJOURNMENT

There being no further business, the meeting was adjourned at
2:15 p.m.

_____   _____
Secretary   President

MINUTES: INFORMAL

```
    Sales


        August 5, 1989, Book 3, page 6
        October 1, 1990, Book 4, page 30
        June 12, 1991, Book 5, page 8
```

```
    Winter Campaign


        November 1, 1990, Book 4, page 12
        December 10, 1990, Book 4, page 10
        January 17, 1991, Book 5, page 2
```

INDEX TO MINUTES: CARD ENTRIES

```
Sales:                   August 5, 1989, Book 3, page 6
                         October 1, 1990, Book 4, page 30
                         June 12, 1991, Book 5, page 8

Winter Campaign:         November 1, 1990, Book 4, page 12
                         December 7, 1990, Book 4, page 20
                         January 17, 1991, Book 5, page 2
```

INDEX TO MINUTES: COMPUTER-LIST ENTRIES

Chapter 20

RECORD KEEPING

A variety of printed forms and books for record-keeping purposes are available in office-supply stores. These forms include sales slips, service-call forms, expense-report forms, payment journals, and receiving records. Companies also design and print record-keeping forms especially tailored to their own needs.

The specific forms used in an office will depend on the nature of work performed in the office. A mail room will keep different records than a purchasing department. Companies in general have different needs as well. A retail gift store uses different record-keeping forms than a precision-tool manufacturer uses.

Certain types of record-keeping forms, however, are useful in almost any office in a wide variety of industries and professions. The models in this chapter illustrate easy-to-prepare in-house forms that can be adapted to the specific requirements of a particular office or business. They can quickly be set up by typewriter and photocopied, or they can be formatted by computer, stored in memory, and printed out as needed. Data can be entered on the forms by hand, typewriter, or computer.

PHIPPS DENTAL PRODUCTS
202 Bryce Place
Santa Maria, CA 93455

Appointment Schedule
March 16, 199–

For: _____   Department: _____

Time	With Whom	Nature of Appointment	Comments
9:00 a.m.			
9:30			
10:00			
10:30			
11:00			
11:30			
12:00 Noon			
12:30			
1:00			
1:30			
2:00			
2:30			
3:00			
3:30			
4:00			
4:30			
5:00			

APPOINTMENT SCHEDULE: DAILY

PHIPPS DENTAL PRODUCTS
202 Bryce Place
Santa Maria, CA 93455

Appointment Schedule
March 8-14, 199–

For: _____   Department: _____

Day	With Whom	Nature of Appointment	Comments
8			
9			
10			
11			
12			
13			
14			

APPOINTMENT SCHEDULE: WEEKLY

PHIPPS DENTAL PRODUCTS
202 Bryce Place
Santa Maria, CA 93455

Appointment Schedule
March 199–

For: ———————————————— Department: ————————————————

Day	With Whom	Nature of Appointment	Comments
1			
2			
3			
4			
5			
6			
7			
8			
9			
10			
11			
12			
13			
14			
15			
16			
17			
18			
19			
20			
21			
22			
23			
24			
25			
26			
27			
28			
29			
30			
31			

APPOINTMENT SCHEDULE: MONTHLY

PHIPPS DENTAL PRODUCTS
202 Bryce Place
Santa Maria, CA 93455

Appointment Schedule
August 5–9, 199–

For: _____ Department: _____

Day	Time	Contact (Name-Address)	Telephone	Comments
Aug. 5				
Aug. 6				
Aug. 7				
Aug. 8				
Aug. 9				

APPOINTMENT SCHEDULE: TRAVEL

WEBSTER & WORONOCO, INC.
907 Spruce Street
Warren, MI 48091

Travel Itinerary

For: _____   Department: _____

Period: _____   Purpose: _____

From City	To City	Via Flight & Train	Depart. Date & Time	Arrive. Date & Time	Type Accom.	Meals	Car Rental	Hotel Accom.	Reminder

ITINERARY: TRAVEL

PHIPPS DENTAL PRODUCTS
202 Bryce Place
Santa Maria, CA 93455

Activity Schedule

Employee Name _____ Period Covered _____

Position _____ Department _____

Day of Month	Time Spent per Activity					Total Hrs. per Day
	Activity 1	Activity 2	Activity 3	Activity 4	Activity 5	
1						
2						
3						
4						
5						
6						
7						
8						
9						
10						
11						
12						
13						
14						
15						
16						
17						
18						
19						
20						
21						
22						
23						
24						
25						
26						
27						
28						
29						
30						
31						
Totals						

ACTIVITY SCHEDULE: MONTHLY

WHARTON MACHINERY COMPANY
701 Whites Road
Kalamazoo, MI 49008

Long-Range Activity Schedule

Month	Activity	Project Director	Date Planned	Preparation Deadline	Comments
Jan					
Feb					
Mar					
Apr					
May					
Jun					
Jul					
Aug					
Sept					
Oct					
Nov					
Dec					

ACTIVITY SCHEDULE: LONG RANGE

SNOWLAND EQUIPMENT DISTRIBUTORS
200–25 Street
Philadelphia, PA 19103

Meeting-Dates Record, 199–

Type of Meeting	Dates Scheduled											
	Jan	Feb	Mar	Apr	May	Jun	Jul	Aug	Sept	Oct	Nov	Dec

MEETING-DATES RECORD: ANNUAL

SAMUELS & FEINSTEIN, INC.
180 Lexington Avenue
New York, NY 10016

Special Assignments, October 199–

Employee	Department	Supervisor	Assignment	Date Assigned	Due Date

ACTIVITY-ASSIGNMENT LIST: MONTHLY

GABRIEL'S INVESTMENT ADVISORY SERVICE
16 Pine Tree Road
Cleveland, OH 44124

Merit-Rating Record

Employee: _____ Date: _____

Position: _____ Length of Employment: _____

Performance Factor	Rating				
	Well Above Av.	Above Av.	Average	Below Av.	Well Below Av.

MERIT-RATING RECORD

ABBOTT CATERING
4900 Apple Lane
Memphis, TN 38109

Reminder

Subject _____

Action Requested _____

Date Requested _____

Requested by _____

Action Taken _____

By _____   Date _____

REMINDER-CARD RECORD

LAKE SHORE RETAILERS ASSOCIATION
299 Lake Shore Drive
Chicago, IL, 60603

Petty Cash Transactions Record
January 1 – 31, 199–

Date	Voucher No.	To/From	Amount Received	Amount Paid	For

PETTY CASH TRANSACTIONS RECORD

BRETTON-KEITH, INC.
1800 Hart Street
Honolulu, HI 96819

Contributions 199–

Date	Contributed to	Amount

CONTRIBUTIONS RECORD

VICKERS COMPUTING
1006 Roosevelt Avenue
Melbourne, FL 32937

Documents-Receipt Record

Document _____ Release Date _____

Released to _____ Due Date _____

_____ Phone _____

For _____

Comments _____

_____

Approved by _____ Dept. _____

DOCUMENTS-RECEIPT RECORD

LENO, PETERS & WYATT
20 Vernon Drive
Arlington, TX 76015

Records-Retention Schedule

Record Name	Record No.	Period to Be Retained	Special Requirements	Special Instructions

RECORDS-RETENTION SCHEDULE

HORTON REALTY ASSOCIATES
6908 – 44 Avenue, NE
Puyallup, WA 98372

Supplies-Inventory Record

Date	Item	Beginning Quantity	Quantity Used	Remaining Quantity

SUPPLIES-INVENTORY RECORD

RIVIERA WHOLESALERS
1392 Upton Road
Minneapolis, MN 55431

Travel-Supplies Checklist

For: _____   Department: _____

Period: _____   Purpose: _____

( ) Letter stationery	( ) Cash
( ) Memo stationery	( ) Personal checkbook
( ) Envelopes, plain	( ) Credit cards
( ) Envelopes, addressed to company	( ) Business checkbook
( ) Large mailing envelopes	( ) Business credit cards
( ) Legal/letter pads	( ) Travel guides and maps
( ) Postage stamps	( ) Catalogs, brochures, etc.
( ) Address book/list	( ) Itinerary
( ) File folders	( ) Appointment schedule
( ) Business cards	( ) Timetables and flight schedules
( ) Mailing schedule	( ) Reservation confirmations
( ) Calendar	( ) Tickets
( ) Mailing boxes or folders for dicta-tion and computer disks, tapes, etc.	( ) Passports, visas, etc.
	( ) First-aid kit
( ) Dictation equipment	( ) Pens, pencils, erasers
( ) Dictation belts, tapes, disks, etc.	( ) Paper clips
( ) Computer equipment	( ) Scissors
( ) Expense forms	( ) Rubber bands
( ) Other forms	( ) Stamp pad and rubber stamp
_____	( ) Cellophane tape
_____	( ) Pins
_____	( ) Bottle opener
( ) Files	( ) Ruler
_____	( ) Other
_____	_____
_____	_____
_____	_____

TRAVEL-SUPPLIES CHECKLIST

Chapter 21

REPORTS

Reports range in size and complexity from brief, informal notes or memos to formal, book-length works. The format differs accordingly. An informal report might be prepared in a letter or memo format (see chapter 15). A long, formal report would have many more parts to it, including many or all of the following items.

Cover

Flyleaf

Title page

Letter of transmittal or preface

Table of contents

List of figures or tables

Abstract or summary

Introduction

Body

Conclusion

References or Bibliography

Appendixes

Glossary

Index

The manuscript of a report should be prepared double-spaced. The printed version is often single-spaced in the case of a long report. Some organizations have a required format that writers must follow. Although various formats are acceptable, the models in this chapter represent an appropriate style for the major elements in a report (for an example of an index format, refer to the index of this book). All of the following items can be prepared by typewriter or computer.

RISK MANAGEMENT FOR THE

SMALL-BUSINESS ORGANIZATION

Andrea F. Mundell
Management Research Associates
2123 Evergreen Road
Annapolis, Maryland 21403

August 15, 199–

TITLE PAGE: SHORT FORM

RISK MANAGEMENT FOR THE

SMALL-BUSINESS ORGANIZATION

Prepared for

David A. Collette, Vice President
Management Services, Inc.
1214 Main Street, Annapolis, Maryland 21401

Prepared by

Andrea F. Mundell, Manager, Systems Analysis
Management Research Associates
2123 Evergreen Road, Annapolis, Maryland 21403

August 15, 199-

TITLE PAGE: LONG FORM

```
              MANAGEMENT RESEARCH ASSOCIATES
                    2123 Evergreen Road
                    Annapolis, MD 21403
                      301-678-9104
```

DATE: June 7, 199-

TO: Andrea F. Mundell
          Manager, Systems Analysis

FROM: Edmund Germaine

SUBJECT: Risk-Management Report

This will authorize you to prepare a report for David A.
Collette, vice president, Management Services, Inc. A
copy of the request from Management Services is
enclosed, outlining the parameters of information
desired.

Please evaluate procedures for identifying exposures to
loss and describe the principal types of loss such as
public liability, business-interruption, and key-person
losses. Our library has a copy of a study we recently
undertook involving selected liability loss for
nonprofit firms. You may find useful information in it
and in previous research we conducted pertaining to risk
management.

I will look forward to reviewing a draft of your report
on or before August 1, 199-. Please let me know if you
have any questions concerning this authorization.

LETTER OF AUTHORIZATION

MANAGEMENT RESEARCH ASSOCIATES
2123 Evergreen Road
Annapolis, MD 21403
301-678-9104

August 15, 199–

Mr. David A. Collette
Management Services, Inc.
1214 Main Street
Annapolis, MD 21401

Dear Mr. Collette:

RISK-MANAGEMENT STUDY

I am pleased to send you the enclosed report, <u>Risk Management for the Small-Business Organization</u>. You requested this study in your letter of May 27, 199–, to Edmund Germaine, Director of Management Research Associates.

The report evaluates five key areas of loss exposure: property loss, business-interruption loss, liability loss, public liability loss, and key-person loss. It then offers recommendations for loss control and concludes with a checklist to help your organization strengthen its insurance program.

I hope that the report will be helpful to you and your associates. Please let us know if we can be of any further help.

Sincerely yours,

Andrea F. Mundell
Manager, Systems Analysis

Enc.

LETTER OF TRANSMITTAL

CONTENTS

TABLE OF CONTENTS: SHORT FORM

CONTENTS

TABLE OF CONTENTS: LONG FORM

SUMMARY

Every small business is exposed to risks. Some risks are predictable. Others, beyond the control of a business owner, are not. Risk management identifies and analyzes those factors that cause loss and selects the best ways of dealing with each potential for loss.

This report evaluates five kinds of exposure to loss: property losses, business-interruption losses, liability losses, public-liability losses, and key-person losses. It examines the requirements of an effective benefits program for employees, including legally required employee benefits.

The conclusions of the study are that steps can be taken to limit or prevent exposure to risk and to minimize the impact of a loss that might occur. It is recommended that preventive measures be supplemented by insurance as a risk strategy and that services provided by insurers be used to full advantage.

ABSTRACT/SUMMARY

SUMMARY

Every small business is exposed to risks. Some
risks are predictable. Others, beyond the control of a
business owner, are not. Risk management identifies and
analyzes those factors that cause loss and selects the
best ways of dealing with each potential for loss.

This report evaluates five kinds of exposure to
loss: property losses, business-interruption losses,
liability losses, public-liability losses, and
key-person losses. It examines the requirements of an
effective benefits program for employees, including
legally required employee benefits.

The conclusions of the study are that steps can be
taken to limit or prevent exposure to risk and to
minimize the impact of a loss that might occur. It is
recommended that preventive measures be supplemented by
insurance as a risk strategy and that services provided
by insurers be used to full advantage.

ACKNOWLEDGMENTS

I want to thank the following persons who read a draft of this report and provided constructive comments: Martin Archer, management consultant, Lewis Business Services; Henry Beckman, manager, Insurance Brokers, Inc.; Lois Feiffer, director, Feiffer Insurance Professionals; and Edmund Germaine, director, Management Research Associates. I also want to thank the Small Business Administration for providing useful literature and referrals.

ACKNOWLEDGMENTS

I want to thank the following persons who read a draft of this report and provided constructive comments: Martin Archer, management consultant, Lewis Business Services; Henry Beckman, manager, Insurance Brokers, Inc.; Lois Feiffer, director, Feiffer Insurance Professionals; and Edmund Germaine, director, Management Research Associates. I also want to thank the Small Business Administration for providing useful literature and referrals.

I. INTRODUCTION

A. Risk and the Small Business

Is your business subject to risk? Every small business is. Among the hundreds of things that most business owners worry about, a few are predictable or, at least, are items that one can plan for and perhaps even control to a certain extent:

- Expected sales volume

- Salary costs

- Taxes

- Overhead expenses

- Equipment and supply costs

- The price you charge for the goods or services you offer to your customers

---

Portions of this report were adapted from <u>Small Business Risk Management Guide</u>, Business Development Publication MP28 (Washington, D.C.: Small Business Administration, Office of Business Development, n.d.).

TEXT OPENING PAGE

I. INTRODUCTION

A. Risk and the Small Business

Is your business subject to risk? Every small business is. Among the hundreds of things that most business owners worry about, a few are predictable or, at least, are items that one can plan for and perhaps even control to a certain extent:

- Expected sales volume
- Salary costs
- Taxes
- Overhead expenses
- Equipment and supply costs
- The price you charge for the goods or services you offer to your customers

Others are unpredictable and beyond one's control:

- Actions a competitor may take
- Changing tastes and trends
- The effect they have on the market and one's customers
- The local economy and its impact on the customer base (such as plant closings or unemployment)

Some events can and do happen to small businesses all the time. They may directly affect day-to-day operations, impact profits, and result in unexpected financial losses that may be serious enough to cripple a business or even bankrupt it. Most owners have already considered the most obvious risks and have bought insurance to protect against the financial losses that could result from them. They recognize the loss potential from fire and injury, for example.

Portions of this report were adapted from Small Business Risk Management Guide, Business Development Publication MP28 (Washington, D.C.: Small Business Administration, Office of Business Development, n.d.).

TEXT OPENING PAGE

IV.   CONCLUSIONS AND RECOMMENDATIONS

The next two steps of the risk-management process are similar to those we face in managing our personal finances.

1.   Loss control: What can be done to prevent or limit exposure to risk?

2.   What techniques can be used to insure that funds will be available for losses that cannot be avoided or prevented?

A.   Loss Control

1.   Strategies

<u>Preventing or Limiting Exposure to Loss.</u>   One principle of loss prevention is the same in business as it is in personal life: Avoid activities that are too hazardous. For example:

A merchant may decide not to sell a particular product because it is likely to injure customers; thereby, the firm avoids a product-liability

IV. CONCLUSIONS AND RECOMMENDATIONS

The next two steps of the risk-management process are similar to those we face in managing our personal finances.

1. Loss control: What can be done to prevent or limit exposure to risk?

2. What techniques can be used to insure that funds will be available for losses that cannot be avoided or prevented?

A. Loss Control

1. Strategies

Preventing or Limiting Exposure to Loss. One principle of loss prevention is the same in business as it is in personal life: Avoid activities that are too hazardous. For example:

A merchant may decide not to sell a particular product because it is likely to injure customers; thereby, the firm avoids a product-liability exposure.

If you can't avoid an exposure completely, minimize it.

An apartment owner may decide against constructing a new building on a rural hillside site that has a long history of brush fires. Instead, he builds on suburban, level land, which is supplied by town water and is two minutes from a fire station. Although exposure of loss from fire can seldom be eliminated completely, this owner has reduced the possible severity of loss by choosing a safer site closer to the firefighting services.

Look again to see if the extent of possible loss can be further reduced.

That same apartment owner, for example, may decide

TEXT CONTINUATION PAGE

APPENDIX

Insurance Checklist for the Small Business Organization

In addition to helping a business owner identify, minimize, and in some instances eliminate business risks, this checklist will help to strengthen an insurance program and provide guidelines for discussions that one should have with a qualified insurance professional.

For each of the statements, put a check in the first answer column if you understand the statement and how it affects your insurance program. Then study your policies with these points in mind and discuss with your agent questions you still have.

FIRE INSURANCE

	No Action Needed	Look into This
1. You can add other perils (e.g., windstorm, hail, smoke, explosion, vandalism, and malicious mischief) to your basic fire insurance at a relatively small additional fee.	_____	_____

29

APPENDIX OPENING PAGE

APPENDIX

Insurance Checklist for the Small-Business Organization

In addition to helping a business owner identify, minimize, and in some instances eliminate business risks, this checklist will help to strengthen an insurance program and provide guidelines for discussions that one should have with a qualified insurance professional.

For each of the statements, put a check in the first answer column if you understand the statement and how it affects your insurance program. Then study your policies with these points in mind and discuss with your agent questions you still have.

<u>FIRE INSURANCE</u>

	No Action <u>Needed</u>	Look into <u>This</u>
1. You can add other perils (e.g., windstorm, hail, smoke, explosion, vandalism, and malicious mischief) to your basic fire insurance at a relatively small additional fee.	_____	_____
2. If you need comprehensive coverage, your best buy may be one of the all-risk contracts that offer the broadest available protection for the money.	_____	_____
3. The insurance company may indemnify you — that is, compensate you for your losses — in any one of several ways: (1) It may pay actual cash value of the property at the time of loss. (2) It may repair or replace the property with material of like kind and quality.		

29

APPENDIX OPENING PAGE

6. Even if you have several policies

on your property, you can still collect

only the amount of your actual cash

loss.   All the insurers share the payment

proportionately.   Suppose, for example,

you are carrying two policies—one for

$20,000 and one for $30,000—on a

$40,000 building, and fire causes damage

to the building amounting to $12,000.

The $20,000 policy will pay $4,800.   _____   _____

$$\frac{20,000}{50,000}$$

or 2/5 of $12,000.

The $30,000 policy will pay $7,200; that is,

$$\frac{30,000}{50,000}$$

or 3/5 of $12,000.

7. Special protection other than the

standard fire insurance policy is

needed to cover the loss by fire of

APPENDIX CONTINUATION PAGE

Risk Management   31

6. Even if you have several policies
on your property, you can still collect
only the amount of your actual cash
loss. All the insurers share the payment
proportionately. Suppose, for example,
you are carrying two policies—one for
$20,000 and one for $30,000—on a
$40,000 building, and fire causes damage
to the building amounting to $12,000.
The $20,000 policy will pay $4,800.   _____   _____

      20,000
      50,000

   or 2/5 of $12,000.

The $30,000 policy will pay $7,200; that is,

      30,000
      50,000

   or 3/5 of $12,000.

7. Special protection other than the
standard fire insurance policy is
needed to cover the loss by fire of
accounts, bills, currency, deeds,
evidence of debt, and money and
securities.   _____   _____

8. If an insured building is vacant
or unoccupied for more than sixty
consecutive days, coverage is
suspended unless you have a special
endorsement to your policy canceling
this provision.   _____   _____

9. If, either before or after a loss,
you conceal or misrepresent to the
insurer any material fact or circumstance
concerning your insurance or the interest

APPENDIX CONTINUATION PAGE

GLOSSARY OF INSURANCE TERMS

ADJUSTER. A person who investigates damage, makes
estimates, and settles insurance claims.

ADJUSTMENT. The settlement of a claim; final premium
determination.

AGENT'S AUTHORITY. The authority placed in the agent by
the insurance company; the extent to which the agent may
act on behalf of the company. This authority is defined
by a contract between the agent and the company.

ALL-RISK. A term commonly used to describe broad forms
of property or liability coverage. It is a misleading
term because no property or liability policy is truly an
all-risk coverage. A policy will invariably contain
some exclusions.

APPRAISAL. An estimate of value, loss, or damage.

ASSIGNED RISK. A risk that has been declined by one or

GLOSSARY OF INSURANCE TERMS

ADJUSTER. A person who investigates damage, makes estimates, and settles insurance claims.

ADJUSTMENT. The settlement of a claim; final premium determination.

AGENT'S AUTHORITY. The authority placed in the agent by the insurance company; the extent to which the agent may act on behalf of the company. This authority is defined by a contract between the agent and the company.

ALL-RISK. A term commonly used to describe broad forms of property or liability coverage. It is a misleading term because no property or liability policy is truly an all-risk coverage. A policy will invariably contain some exclusions.

APPRAISAL. An estimate of value, loss, or damage.

ASSIGNED RISK. A risk that has been declined by one or more companies. Such a risk may be assigned to designated companies by a recognized authority. The operation is called an "assigned-risk plan."

ASSURED. The insured; the one for whom insurance is written.

BASIC BENEFITS. Basic benefits, generally, are all the benefits offered by a group health plan except major medical. Basic benefits may include hospital, surgical, and medical expense insurance: supplemental accident, diagnostic lab and X ray, radiation therapy, and dental-expense insurance.

BENEFICIARY. A person who will receive policy benefits.

BENEFIT. That amount payable under an insurance policy because of an accident, injury, or illness.

BENEFIT FORMULA. A formula that defines the amounts of

32

GLOSSARY

AGING OF ACCOUNTS RECEIVABLE

Customer	Amount	Current	Past Due			
			30 Days	60 Days	90 Days	Over 90 Days[a]
010324	$1,965.40	$ 840.00	$1,125.40			
010325	210.00	210.00				
010326	16.00	16.00				
010327	3,105.24	1,420.24	900.00	300.00	273.10	211.90
010328	911.07			911.07		
010329	665.98		325.98	109.00	200.00	31.00
010330	1,002.30					1,002.30[b]
010331	491.86	491.86				
010332	23.11			23.11		
010333	40.49	40.49				
Total	$8,431.45	$3,018.59	$2,351.38	$1,343.18	$473.10	$1,245.20

Source: Based on Robert C. Ragan, Financial Recordkeeping for Small Stores, Small Business Management Series No. 32 (Washington, D.C.: U.S. Small Business Administration, 1976), 82.

Note: Only one of the "Over 90 Days" accounts exceeds 160 days.

a. Covers a period of 91 days to 1 year.

b. In litigation.

TABLE: UNNUMBERED STATISTICAL

AGING OF ACCOUNTS RECEIVABLE

Customer	Amount	Current	Past Due			
			30 Days	60 Days	90 Days	Over 90 Days[a]
010324	$1,965.40	$ 840.00	$1,125.40			
010325	210.00	210.00				
010326	16.00	16.00				
010327	3,105.24	1,420.24	900.00	300.00	273.10	211.90
010328	911.07			911.07		
010329	665.98		325.98	109.00	200.00	31.00
010330	1,002.30					1,002.30[b]
010331	491.86	491.86				
010332	23.11			23.11		
010333	40.49	40.49				
Total	$8,431.45	$3,018.59	$2,351.38	$1,343.18	$473.10	$1,245.20

Source: Based on Robert C. Ragan, *Financial Recordkeeping for Small Stores*, Small Business Management Series No. 32 (Washington, D.C.: U.S. Small Business Administration, 1976), 82.

Note: Only one of the "Over 90 Days" accounts exceeds 160 days.

a. Covers a period of 91 days to 1 year.

b. In litigation.

TABLE: UNNUMBERED STATISTICAL

Table 7.16

Break-Even Analysis

Profit and Loss Factors	Statement A		Statement B	
	Break-Even Amount	Percentage of Sales	Break-Even Amount	Percentage of Sales
Sales	$1,000,000	100	$980,000	100
Cost of sales	500,000	50	420,000	43
Gross profit	500,000	50	560,000	57
Operation expenses				
Fixed	400,000	40	375,000	38
Variable	100,000	10	80,000	8
Total	500,000	50	455,000	46
Operating profit	$ NONE[a]	0	$105,000[b]	11

Note: "Break-even" is the point at which gross profit equals
expenses.

a. In Statement A the sales volume is at the break-even point,
and no profit is made.

b. In Statement B the sales volume exceeds the break-even point,
with a profit of $105,000.

TABLE: NUMBERED STATISTICAL

Table 7.16

Break-Even Analysis

Profit and Loss Factors	Statement A		Statement B	
	Break-Even Amount	Percentage of Sales	Break-Even Amount	Percentage of Sales
Sales	$1,000,000	100	$980,000	100
Cost of sales	500,000	50	420,000	43
Gross profit	500,000	50	560,000	57
Operation expenses				
Fixed	400,000	40	375,000	38
Variable	100,000	10	80,000	8
Total	500,000	50	455,000	46
Operating profit	$ NONE[a]	0	$105,000[b]	11

Note: "Break-even" is the point at which gross profit equals expenses.

a. In Statement A the sales volume is at the break-even point, and no profit is made.

b. In Statement B the sales volume exceeds the break-even point, with a profit of $105,000.

TABLE: NUMBERED STATISTICAL

Table of Debit and Credit Entries

	Type of Entry		
Account	When Transaction Decreases Account	When Transaction Increases Account	Typical Balance*
Asset	credit	debit	debit
Liability	debit	credit	credit
Capital	debit	credit	credit
Income	debit	credit	credit
Expense	credit	debit	debit

<u>Note</u>: One account may have both debit and credit entries.

* When an account has more credit entries than debit entries,

there is a credit balance; and when it has more debit entries

than credit entries, there is a debit balance.

TABLE: UNNUMBERED TEXTUAL

Table of Debit and Credit Entries

Type of Entry

Account	When Transaction Decreases Account	When Transaction Increases Account	Typical Balance*
Asset	credit	debit	debit
Liability	debit	credit	credit
Capital	debit	credit	credit
Income	debit	credit	credit
Expense	credit	debit	debit

Note: One account may have both debit and credit entries.

* When an account has more credit entries than debit entries, there is a credit balance; and when it has more debit entries than credit entries, there is a debit balance.

TABLE: UNNUMBERED TEXTUAL

Table 6

Entries for Recording Disposal of Plant Assets in the Journals

Transaction	Amount to Enter	Account Shown as	Column in Which to Enter Amount
<td colspan="4" align="center">Cash Receipts Journal</td>
Sale of fully depreciated asset	Amount of cash received	Gain or loss on disposal of assets	Total cash deposit, and miscellaneous income and expense (credit)
	Cost of the asset	(Name of asset account)	General ledger (credit)
	Cost of the asset	Allowance for depreciation of (name of asset account)	General ledger (debit)
Sale of asset with book value	Cost of the asset	(Name of asset account)	General ledger (credit)
	Difference between cash received and book value	Gain or loss on disposal of asset	Miscellaneous income and expense (credit if cash received is more than book value; debit if less)
	Amount of cash received		Total cash deposit
	Accumulated allowance for depreciation	Allowance for depreciation of (name of asset account)	General Ledger (debit)

Continued on next page

TABLE: NUMBERED TEXTUAL

Table 6—*Continued*

Transaction	Amount to Enter	Account Shown as	Column in Which to Enter Amount
		Cash Disbursement Journal	
Trade-in of fully depreciated asset	Cash paid for new asset	(Name of payee)	Amount of check
	Difference between cash paid and cost of old asset	(Name of asset account)	General ledger (debit if cash paid is more than cost of old asset; credit if less)
	Cost of old asset	Allowance for depreciation of (name of asset account)	General ledger (debit)
Trade-in of asset with book value	Cash paid for new asset	(Name of payee)	Amount of check
	Difference between cost of new asset (cash paid + book value of old asset) and original cost of old asset	(Name of asset account)	General ledger (debit if cost of new asset is more than cost of old asset; credit if less)
	Accumulated allowance for depreciation	Allowance for depreciation of (name of asset account)	General ledger (debit)

Continued on next page

TABLE: NUMBERED TEXTUAL

Table 6 — *Continued*

Transaction	Amount to Enter	Account Shown as	Column in Which to Enter Amount
Junking of fully depreciated asset	Cost of the asset	Allowance for depreciation of (name of account)	General ledger (debit)
	Cost of the asset	(Name of asset account)	General ledger (credit)
Junking of asset with book value	Book value of the asset	Loss on abandonment of property	Miscellaneous income and expense (debit)
	Cost of the asset	(Name of asset account)	General ledger (credit)
	Accumulated allowance for depreciation	Allowance for depreciation of (name of asset account)	General ledger (debit)

Source: Adapted from Robert C. Regan, <u>Financial Recordkeeping for Small Shops</u>, Small Business Management Series No. 32 (Washington, D.C.: U.S. Small Business Administration, 1976), 108.

TABLE: NUMBERED TEXTUAL

COMPUTER-SELECTION CONSIDERATIONS

I.   Needs

    A. Business operations

        1. Operations to be done

II.   Costs

    A. Comparative cost/capabilities

        1. Comparative cost

        2. Comparative capabilities

III. Memory

    A. Capacity

        1. RAM

        2. ROM

IV.   Disk drives

    A. Bit capacity

    B. Multiple drives

        1. Types

V.   Keyboard

    A. Style

        1. Typewriter

Continued next page

OUTLINES

Computer-Selection Considerations — *Continued*

VI.   Software

    A. Disk and cartridge

    B. Program compatibility

        1. Number and type compatibility

            a. Number

            b. Type

VII. Display

    A. Color/black and white

        1. Color

        2. Black and white

    B. Resolution

        1. Quality

    C. Graphics capability

VIII. Expandability

    A. Connections

        1. Add-ons

        2. Attachments

    B. Equipment compatibility

        1. Other manufacturers

IX.   Supplies

    A. Custom forms

    B. Printer paper

    C. Furniture

Continued next page

OUTLINES

Computer–Selection Considerations — *Continued*

    D.   Accessories

        1.   Disks

        2.   Dust covers

X.   Repair and training

    A.   Service contracts

        1.   Availability

        2.   Coverage

    B.   Training

        1.   Availability

        2.   Cost

OUTLINES

```
COMPUTER-SELECTION CONSIDERATIONS


1.  Needs
     a.  Business operations
          i.  Operations to be done

2.  Costs
     a.  Comparative cost/capabilities
          i.  Comparative cost
          ii. Comparative capabilities

3.  Memory
     a.  Capacity
          i.  RAM
          ii. ROM

4.  Disk drives
     a.  Bit capacity
     b.  Multiple drives
          i.  Types

5.  Keyboard
     a.  Style
          i.  Typewriter

6.  Software
     a.  Disk and cartridge
     b.  Program compatibility
          i.  Number and type compatibility
               (a)  Number
               (b)  Type

7.  Display
     a.  Color/black and white
          i.  Color
          ii. Black and white
     b.  Resolution
          i.  Quality
     c.  Graphics capability
```

Continued next page

OUTLINES

Computer-Selection Considerations—*Continued*

8.   Expandability
     a.   Connections
          i.   Add-ons
          ii. Attachments
     b.   Equipment compatibility
          i.   Other manufacturers

9.   Supplies
     a.   Custom forms
     b.   Printer paper
     c.   Furniture
     d.   Accessories
          i.   Disks
          ii. Dust covers

10. Repair and training
     a.   Service contracts
          i.   Availability
          ii. Coverage
     b.   Training
          i.   Availability
          ii. Cost

COMPUTER-SELECTION CONSIDERATIONS

Needs

    1. Business operations
       a. Operations to be done

Costs

    1. Comparative cost/capabilities
       a. Comparative cost
       b. Comparative capabilities

Memory

    1. Capacity
       a. RAM
       b. ROM

Disk drives

    1. Bit capacity
    2. Multiple drives
       a. Types

Keyboard

    1. Style
       a. Typewriter

Software

    1. Disk and cartridge
    2. Program compatibility
       a. Number and type compatibility
          i. Number
          ii. Type

Continued next page

OUTLINES

Computer-Selection Considerations — *Continued*

Display

    1. Color/black and white
        a. Color
        b. Black and white

    2. Resolution
        a. Quality

    3. Graphics capability

Expandability

    1. Connections
        a. Add-ons
        b. Attachments

    2. Equipment compatibility
        a. Other manufacturers

Supplies

    1. Custom forms

    2. Printer paper

    3. Furniture

    4. Accessories
        a. Disks
        b. Dust covers

Repair and training

    1. Service contracts
        a. Availability
        b. Coverage

    2. Training
        a. Availability
        b. Cost

OUTLINES

STRATEGIC PLANNING SESSION

Time	Topic	Responsibility
8:00	Opening comments	President
8:05–8:15	Review agenda Review procedures for session Review roles of facilitator and scribe	Facilitator
8:15–8:30	Review completed analysis of external environment	Preparer of analysis
8:30–10:00	SWOT analysis—Part I Round table discussion aimed at identifying and documenting on the flip chart all the company's strengths, weaknesses, opportunities and threats	Facilitator and group
10:00–10:15	Coffee break	
10:15–12:00	SWOT analysis—Part II	Facilitator and group
12:00–12:45	Lunch break	
12:45–2:30	Develop or redefine "Mission Statement" for organization (statement of purpose)	Facilitator and group
2:30–2:45	Coffee and soft drink break	

Continued next page

LIST: UNNUMBERED MULTICOLUMN

Strategic Planning Session — Continued

Time	Topic	Responsibility
2:45–3:30	Analysis and identification of <u>key results areas</u> (areas in which the company must achieve significant of revenues and profits desired)	Facilitator and group
3:30–5:00	Establish strategic objectives Within each <u>key results</u> area establish a small number of strategic objectives (objectives that are descriptive of a condition you want to achieve)	Facilitator and group
5:00–6:30	Dinner	

Source: Adapted from Michael L. Policastro, <u>Developing a Strategic Business Plan</u>, Business Development Publication MP 21 (Washington, D.C.: U.S. Small Business Administration, n.d.), 7–8.

Evaluating the Computer System

Use the following criteria, listed in order of importance, to evaluate a minicomputer system.

1. Software developer's past performance record. Software developer should have prior experience with similar applications for the same equipment configuration.

2. Commitment of hardware vendor. Where will your commission sales rep be after the contract is signed? How many systems engineers does the vendor have in your local area?

3. Hardware capacity. Does the hardware have adequate processing capability to meet your requirements within the acceptable time frames?

4. Quality of systems software. The quality of the systems software (the operating systems and utilities) will dramatically affect how difficult the system is to program and use.

5. Systems documentation. What kind of systems documentation does the vendor provide and how is it updated? Can the system be understood at some basic level by the user? Is it designed so that

LIST: NUMBERED SINGLE COLUMN

other experts can understand how things were done
and change them when necessary?

6. Service and maintenance support. When your system
    breaks down, how long will it take to get it fixed?
    Who will fix it? Will the work be subcontracted?
    Are there any provisions for backup during down
    time?

7. Expandability and compatibilities. What are the
    technical limits of your system and how close to
    those limits is your current configuration? Does
    software compatibility exist among the vendor's
    product lines?

8. Security. What security features will your system
    have to prevent unauthorized use of the system or
    unauthorized program modifications?

9. Financial stability of vendors. Satisfy yourself
    about the financial stability of your vendor.

10. Environmental requirements. Most minicomputers and
    microcomputers do not require special environments
    such as raised floors, special wiring, or air
    conditioning. Some may, however, and it pays to
    find out in advance.

LIST: NUMBERED SINGLE COLUMN

11. <u>Price</u>. With computers you generally get what you pay for. A low price alone should not be a prime evaluation criterion.

Source: From Michael M. Stewart and Alan C. Shulman, <u>How to Get Started with a Small Business Computer</u>, Management Aids no. 2.027 (Washington, D.C.: U.S. Small Business Administration, 1987), 6–7.

LIST: NUMBERED SINGLE COLUMN

Evaluating the Computer System

Use the following criteria, listed in order of importance, to evaluate a minicomputer system.

1. Software developer's past performance record. Software developer should have prior experience with similar applications for the same equipment configuration.

2. Commitment of hardware vendor. Where will your commission sales rep be after the contract is signed? How many systems engineers does the vendor have in your local area?

3. Hardware capacity. Does the hardware have adequate processing capability to meet your requirements within the acceptable time frames?

4. Quality of systems software. The quality of the systems software (the operating systems and utilities) will dramatically affect how difficult the system is to program and use.

5. Systems documentation. What kind of systems documentation does the vendor provide and how is it updated? Can the system be understood at some basic level by the user? Is it designed so that other experts can understand how things were done and change them when necessary?

6. Service and maintenance support. When your system breaks down, how long will it take to get it fixed? Who will fix it? Will the work be subcontracted? Are there any provisions for backup during down time?

7. Expandability and compatibilities. What are the technical limits of your system and how close to those limits is your current configuration? Does software compatibility exist among the vendor's product lines?

LIST: NUMBERED SINGLE COLUMN

8. <u>Security</u>. What security features will your system
    have to prevent unauthorized use of the system or
    unauthorized program modifications?

9. <u>Financial stability of vendors</u>. Satisfy yourself
    about the financial stability of your vendor.

10. <u>Environmental requirements</u>. Most minicomputers and
    microcomputers do not require special environments
    such as raised floors, special wiring, or air
    conditioning. Some may, however, and it pays to find
    out in advance.

11. <u>Price</u>. With computers you generally get what you pay
    for. A low price alone should not be a prime
    evaluation criterion.

Source: From Michael M. Stewart and Alan C. Shulman, <u>How
to Get Started with a Small Business Computer</u>, Management Aids
no. 2.027 (Washington, D.C.: U.S. Small Business
Administration, 1987), 6-7.

LIST: NUMBERED SINGLE COLUMN

Where Do You Go for Money?

Planned financing may be a combination of these items:

• Taking out a mortgage on the company's building

• Asking suppliers to extend credit on purchases

• Factoring the company's receivables and inventory
  financing

• Borrowing on a note basis from friends

• Borrowing the cash surrender value of relatives' life
  insurance policies

• Contacting an insurance company for a long-term loan

• Contacting the Small Business Administration for a
  business loan

Source: Robert E. Levinson, Problems in Managing a Family-
Owned Business, Business Development Publication MP 3
(Washington, D.C.: U.S. Small Business Administration, n.d.), 5.

LIST: BULLET SINGLE COLUMN

Where Do You Go for Money?

Planned financing may be a combination of these items:

- Taking out a mortgage on the company's building

- Asking suppliers to extend credit on purchases

- Factoring the company's receivables and inventory financing

- Borrowing on a note basis from friends

- Borrowing the cash surrender value of relatives' life insurance policies

- Contacting an insurance company for a long-term loan

- Contacting the Small Business Administration for a business loan

Source: Robert E. Levinson, <u>Problems in Managing a Family-Owned Business</u>, Business Development Publication MP 3 (Washington, D.C.: U.S. Small Business Administration, n.d.), 5.

LIST: BULLET SINGLE COLUMN

Captions: National Political Conventions, 1970-1980
Corrective Actions Plan for Educators
Inventor Services Disclosure Form
Organization Chart: Small Manufacturing Firm

Legends: Ten key strategy areas for developing objectives,
responsibilities, and targets. (Courtesy F. M.
Wexler & Associates.)

Fig. 4. An operating plan forecast may cover any
number of months desired but should project profit
and loss for at least twelve months.

Petty thievery may not seem like a major crime to
someone who pockets a ball-point pen or a candybar.
But to a small business fighting for survival, it's
the kiss of death.

Fig. 3.2. *Above left,* Roger Salvador; *right,*
Dorothy LeLinz; *below left,* Amos Rowley; *right,*
Lillian Haines.

Combined   **Retail Check Stamp.** Many stores rubber-stamp the
caption   lower reverse side of a check and fill in the
and   appropriate information.
legend:

Fig. 5.3. Republics of the USSR. The United States
recognizes fourteen of the fifteen Soviet
republics. It does not recognize jurisdiction in
Estonia.

High School Drug Use, 1991. The ten categories
listed cover reported use by high school juniors
and seniors nationwide but exclude reports and
estimates involving dropouts and truants. Actual
usage is believed to exceed reported usage since
the rate of abuse is estimated to be highest among
dropouts and truants.

1990 Environmental Quality Index. Of the seven
categories, rated by the National Wildlife
Federation, four were considered "worse" and three
"borderline same or worse."

CAPTIONS AND LEGENDS

NOTES

1. Michael J. Shornley, Jr., Techniques for Improving Productivity, vol. 2 (Southampton, Eng.: Hampshire Press of England, 1988), 101-2, 130-34, 200-206.

2. With modern reduction processes readily available, the paper explosion is appearing less threatening every day. For some timely tips on selecting a reduction process, *see* Records, Records, Records, 3d ed. (Washington, D.C.: Records Management Association, 1991), 5-64.

3. Martin R. Thornberg and Leanne P. Dreighton, eds. and comps., Bibliography of Business Management (Cincinnati: New Business School Press, 1987).

4. Mary Shulman, Frank K. Hildegarde, and Sandra Block, trans., Postwar Industrialism: A Study of Industrialization in Eastern European Countries (1946-1986), Studies in European Economic Culture, no. 5 (Rotterdam: Windmill University Press, 1980), 340-47.

5. Henry Hudson, Autobiography of Henry Hudson, ed. V. M. McCardle (San Francisco: Bay Area Publishers, 1975), 99.

6. Paul E. Renfro III et al., Modern Management Aids, vol. 4 of Understanding the Strategic Business Plan (New York: Business Development Press, 1985).

7. Ibid.

8. Ibid., 7-9.

NOTES: NUMBERED

9. Janet Caldwell, "Business Reorganization Guidelines," Eastern Industries Journal, June 1991.

10. "So now you're the president, and you think that you're going to be running your company. Think again!" Walter B. Holmes, Jr., and Kathryn O. Juneau, "Who Is the Real Manager?" Business Quarterly 32, no. 5 (Fall 1990): 14-21.

11. Renfro et al., Modern Management Aids, 59.

12. Harold Lottimer, "Coming to Terms with a Recession," in Proceedings of the Economic Forecaster Society, ed. Mark V. Brownell and Ellen C. Addison (Houston: Economic Forecasters Society, 1981).

13. Afton Sills-Prottle, Inflation Markers (1969; reprint, Chicago: Business News Publishing Co., 1983).

14. Branley & Associates, High-Tech Planning in Business, by William Joline, 2 vols. (Milwaukee: Business University Press, 1985-86). Microfilm.

15. Edith R. Gregg, review of Go for Broke, by Harley J. Tomkins, Western Review, August 1990, 42.

16. Adam Krieger, "Capitalizing on a Down Market" (paper read at the Twenty-third Annual Meeting and Technical Conference of the Midwest Technological Association, March 9-12, 1989, at Holt Convention Hall, Detroit, Michigan).

17. Edna C. Esterbrook, "The Rural Migration of the 1980s" (Ph.D. diss., University of Benston, 1988).

18. Harriet S. Charlemagne, interview by Henry Nardell, 12 September 1990. Tape recording, County Historical Society, San Antonio, Texas.

NOTES: NUMBERED

19.   Arnold Schwartz, map of Centerville Industrial Complex, MS. 141, J. C. Burger Collection, Centerville Library, Indianapolis, n.d.

20.   U.S. Department of Labor, Industry Statistics Update (Washington, D.C.:   U.S. Government Printing Office, 1988).

21.   Branley & Associates, High-Tech Planning, 1:92.

22.   Congressional Record, 1980-90, Washington, D.C.

23.   U.S. Congress, Senate, Committee on Ways and Means, Hearings on Trade Embargo, 96th Cong., 2d sess., 1978. Committee Print 12.

24.   U.S. Bureau of the Census, Statement on Population Shifts, M8109-0067 (Washington, D.C., January 1981).

25.   Iowa Records Center, Des Moines, Iowa, Records of the State Commission on Business Promotion Policy.   Record Group 61.

26.   Edward Calumet, Erosion in the Great Plains (Lincoln: Visual Publishers, 1979).   Slides.

27.   Editorial, New York Times, 14 June 1989.

28.   Encyclopedia America, 10th ed., s.v. "business planning."

29.   To Work I Go and Go, bk. 1, canto 5, stanza 6.

30.   Wyatt v. Newcastle, 109 U.S. 271 (1956).

NOTES: NUMBERED

NOTES

1. Michael J. Shornley, Jr., *Techniques for Improving Productivity*, vol. 2 (Southampton, Eng.: Hampshire Press of England, 1988), 101-2, 130-34, 200-206.

2. With modern reduction processes readily available, the paper explosion is appearing less threatening every day. For some timely tips on selecting a reduction process, *see Records, Records, Records,* 3d ed. (Washington, D.C.: Records Management Association, 1991), 5-64.

3. Martin R. Thornberg and Leanne P. Dreighton, eds. and comps., *Bibliography of Business Management* (Cincinnati: New Business School Press, 1987).

4. Mary Shulman, Frank K. Hildegarde, and Sandra Block, trans., *Postwar Industrialism: A Study of Industrialization in Eastern European Countries (1946-1986)*, Studies in European Economic Culture, no. 5 (Rotterdam: Windmill University Press, 1980), 340-47.

5. Henry Hudson, *Autobiography of Henry Hudson,* ed. V. M. McCardle (San Francisco: Bay Area Publishers, 1975), 99.

6. Paul E. Renfro III et al., *Modern Management Aids*, vol. 4 of *Understanding the Strategic Business Plan* (New York: Business Development Press, 1985).

7. Ibid.

8. Ibid., 7-9.

9. Janet Caldwell, "Business Reorganization Guidelines," *Eastern Industries Journal*, June 1991.

10. "So now you're the president, and you think that you're going to be running your company. Think again!" Walter B. Holmes, Jr., and Kathryn O. Juneau, "Who Is the Real Manager?" *Business Quarterly* 32, no. 5 (Fall 1990): 14-21.

11. Renfro et al., *Modern Management Aids,* 59.

12. Harold Lottimer, "Coming to Terms with a Recession," in *Proceedings of the Economic Forecaster Society*, ed. Mark V. Brownell and Ellen C. Addison (Houston: Economic Forecasters Society, 1981).

NOTES: NUMBERED

Notes (continued)

13. Afton Sills-Prottle, *Inflation Markers* (1969; reprint, Chicago: Business News Publishing Co., 1983).

14. Branley & Associates, *High-Tech Planning in Business*, by William Joline, 2 vols. (Milwaukee: Business University Press, 1985-86). Microfilm.

15. Edith R. Gregg, review of *Go for Broke,* by Harley J. Tomkins, *Western Review*, August 1990, 42.

16. Adam Krieger, "Capitalizing on a Down Market" (paper read at the Twenty-third Annual Meeting and Technical Conference of the Midwest Technological Association, March 9-12, 1989, at Holt Convention Hall, Detroit, Michigan).

17. Edna C. Esterbrook, "The Rural Migration of the 1980s" (Ph.D. diss., University of Benston, 1988).

18. Harriet S. Charlemagne, interview by Henry Nardell, 12 September 1990. Tape recording, County Historical Society, San Antonio, Texas.

19. Arnold Schwartz, map of Centerville Industrial Complex, MS. 141, J. C. Burger Collection, Centerville Library, Indianapolis, n.d.

20. U.S. Department of Labor, *Industry Statistics Update* (Washington, D.C.: U.S. Government Printing Office, 1988).

21. Branley & Associates, *High-Tech Planning,* 1:92.

22. *Congressional Record*, 1980-90, Washington, D.C.

23. U.S. Congress, Senate, Committee on Ways and Means, *Hearings on Trade Embargo,* 96th Cong., 2d sess., 1978. Committee Print 12.

24. U.S. Bureau of the Census, *Statement on Population Shifts,* M8109-0067 (Washington, D.C., January 1981).

25. Iowa Records Center, Des Moines, Iowa, Records of the State Commission on Business Promotion Policy. Record Group 61.

26. Edward Calumet, *Erosion in the Great Plains* (Lincoln: Visual Publishers, 1979). Slides.

27. Editorial, *New York Times*, 14 June 1989.

28. *Encyclopedia America*, 10th ed., s.v. "business planning."

NOTES: NUMBERED

Notes (continued)

29.   *To Work I Go and Go*, bk. 1, canto 5, stanza 6.

30.   *Wyatt v. Newcastle*, 109 U.S. 271 (1956).

REFERENCES

Branley & Associates. 1985-86. High-Tech Planning in Business, by William Joline. 2 vols. Milwaukee: Business University Press. Microfilm.

Caldwell, Janet. 1991. "Business Reorganization Guidelines." Eastern Industries Journal, June.

Calumet, Edward. 1979. Erosion in the Great Plains. Lincoln: Visual Publishers. Slides.

Charlemagne, Harriet S. 1990. Interview by Henry Nardell, 12 September. Tape recording, County Historical Society, San Antonio, Texas.

Congressional Record. 1980-90. Washington, D.C.

Editorial. 1989. New York Times, 14 June.

Encyclopedia America. 10th ed.

Esterbrook, Edna C. 1988. "The Rural Migration of the 1980s." Ph.D. diss., University of Benston.

Gregg, Edith R. 1990. Review of Go for Broke, by Harley J. Tomkins. Western Review, August, 42.

Holmes, Walter B., Jr., and Kathryn O. Juneau. 1990. "Who Is the Real Manager?" Business Quarterly 32, no. 5 (Fall): 14-21.

Hudson, Henry. 1975. Autobiography of Henry Hudson. Edited by V. M. McCardle. San Francisco: Bay Area Publishers.

REFERENCE LIST: NAME-DATE

Iowa Records Center, Des Moines, Iowa. n.d. Records of the
    State Commission on Business Promotion Policy. Record
    Group 61.

Krieger, Adam. 1989. "Capitalizing on a Down Market." Paper
    read at the Twenty-third Annual Meeting and Technical
    Conference of the Midwest Technological Association, March
    9-12, at Holt Convention Hall, Detroit, Michigan.

Lottimer, Harold. 1981. "Coming to Terms with a Recession."
    In Proceedings of the Economic Forecaster Society. Edited
    by Mark V. Brownell and Ellen C. Addison. Houston:
    Economic Forecasters Society, 439-51.

Records, Records, Records. 1991. 3d ed. Washington, D.C.:
    Records Management Association.

Renfro, Paul E., III, Martha Miika, Jean Vendes, and Jonathan
    Kosta. 1985. Modern Management Aids. Vol. 4,
    Understanding the Strategic Business Plan. New York:
    Business Development Press.

Schwartz, Arnold. n.d. Map of Centerville Industrial Complex.
    MS. 141, J. C. Burger Collection, Centerville Library,
    Indianapolis.

Shornley, Michael J., Jr. 1988. Techniques for Improving
    Productivity. Vol. 2. Southampton, Eng.: Hampshire
    Press of England.

Shulman, Mary, Frank K. Hildegarde, and Sandra Block, trans.
    1980. Postwar Industrialism: A Study of Industrialization

REFERENCE LIST: NAME-DATE

in <u>Eastern European Countries (1946-1986)</u>. Studies in

European Economic Culture, no. 5. Rotterdam: Windmill

University Press.

Sills-Prottle, Afton. 1983. <u>Inflation Markers</u>. 1969.

Reprint. Chicago: Business News Publishing Co.

Thornberg, Martin R., and Leanne P. Dreighton, eds. and comps.

1987. <u>Bibliography of Business Management</u>. Cincinnati:

New Business School Press.

<u>To Work I Go and Go</u>. Book 1, canto 5, stanza 6.

U.S. Bureau of the Census. 1981. <u>Statement on Population

Shifts</u>. M8109-0067. Washington, D.C., January.

U.S. Congress, Senate, Committee on Ways and Means. 1978.

<u>Hearings on Trade Embargo</u>. 96th Cong., 2d sess.

Committee Print 12.

U.S. Department of Labor. 1988. <u>Industry Statistics Update</u>.

Washington, D.C.: U.S. Government Printing Office.

<u>Wyatt</u> v. <u>Newcastle</u>, 109 U.S. 271 (1956).

REFERENCE LIST: NAME-DATE

REFERENCES

Branley & Associates. 1985-86. *High-Tech Planning in Business,* by William Joline. 2 vols. Milwaukee: Business University Press. Microfilm.

Caldwell, Janet. 1991. "Business Reorganization Guidelines." *Eastern Industries Journal,* June.

Calumet, Edward. 1979. *Erosion in the Great Plains.* Lincoln: Visual Publishers. Slides.

Charlemagne, Harriet S. 1990. Interview by Henry Nardell, 12 September. Tape recording, County Historical Society, San Antonio, Texas.

Congressional Record. 1980-90. Washington, D.C.

Editorial. 1989. *New York Times,* 14 June.

Encyclopedia America. 10th ed.

Esterbrook, Edna C. 1988. "The Rural Migration of the 1980s." Ph.D. diss., University of Benston.

Gregg, Edith R. 1990. Review of *Go for Broke,* by Harley J. Tomkins. *Western Review,* August, 42.

Holmes, Walter B., Jr., and Kathryn O. Juneau. 1990. "Who Is the Real Manager?" *Business Quarterly* 32, no. 5 (Fall): 14-21.

Hudson, Henry. 1975. *Autobiography of Henry Hudson.* Edited by V. M. McCardle. San Francisco: Bay Area Publishers.

Iowa Records Center, Des Moines, Iowa. n.d. Records of the State Commission on Business Promotion Policy. Record Group 61.

Krieger, Adam. 1989. "Capitalizing on a Down Market." Paper read at the Twenty-third Annual Meeting and Technical Conference of the Midwest Technological Association, March 9-12, at Holt Convention Hall, Detroit, Michigan.

Lottimer, Harold. 1981. "Coming to Terms with a Recession." In *Proceedings of the Economic Forecaster Society.* Edited by Mark V. Brownell and Ellen C. Addison. Houston: Economic Forecasters Society, 439-51.

REFERENCE LIST: NAME-DATE

Records, Records, Records. 1991. 3d ed. Washington, D.C.:
    Records Management Association.

Renfro, Paul E., III, Martha Miika, Jean Vendes, and Jonathan
    Kosta. 1985. *Modern Management Aids.* Vol. 4,
    Understanding the Strategic Business Plan. New York:
    Business Development Press.

Schwartz, Arnold. n.d. Map of Centerville Industrial Complex.
    MS. 141, J. C. Burger Collection, Centerville Library,
    Indianapolis.

Shornley, Michael, Jr. 1988. *Techniques for Improving
    Productivity.* Vol. 2. Southampton, Eng.: Hampshire Press
    of England.

Shulman, Mary, Frank K. Hildegarde, and Sandra Block, trans.
    1980. *Postwar Industrialism: A Study of Industrialization
    in Eastern European Countries (1946-1986).* Studies in
    European Economic Culture, no. 5. Rotterdam: Windmill
    University Press.

Sills-Prottle, Afton. 1983. *Inflation Markers.* 1969.
    Reprint. Chicago: Business News Publishing Co.

Thornberg, Martin R., and Leanne P. Dreighton, eds. and comps.
    1987. *Bibliography of Business Management.* Cincinnati:
    New Business School Press.

To Work I Go and Go. Book 1, canto 5, stanza 6.

U.S. Bureau of the Census. 1981. *Statement on Population
    Shifts.* M8109-0067. Washington, D.C., January.

U.S. Congress, Senate, Committee on Ways and Means. 1978.
    Hearings on Trade Embargo. 96th Cong., 2d sess.
    Committee Print 12.

U.S. Department of Labor. 1988. *Industry Statistics Update.*
    Washington, D.C.: U.S. Government Printing Office.

Wyatt v. Newcastle, 109 U.S. 271 (1956).

REFERENCE LIST: NAME-DATE

SELECT BIBLIOGRAPHY

Branley & Associates. High-Tech Planning in Business, by

    William Joline. 2 vols. Milwaukee: Business University

    Press, 1985-86. Microfilm.

Caldwell, Janet. "Business Reorganization Guidelines."

    Eastern Industries Journal, June 1991.

Calumet, Edward. Erosion in the Great Plains. Lincoln:

    Visual Publishers, 1979. Slides.

Charlemagne, Harriet S. Interview by Henry Nardell, 12

    September 1990. Tape recording, County Historical

    Society, San Antonio, Texas.

Congressional Record. Washington, D.C., 1980-90.

Editorial. New York Times, 14 June 1989.

Encyclopedia America. 10th ed.

Esterbrook, Edna C. "The Rural Migration of the 1980s." Ph.D.

    diss., University of Benston, 1988.

Gregg, Edith R. Review of Go for Broke, by Harley J. Tomkins.

    Western Review, August 1990, 42.

Holmes, Walter B., Jr., and Kathryn O. Juneau. "Who Is the

    Real Manager?" Business Quarterly 32, no. 5 (Fall 1990):

    14-21.

Hudson, Henry. Autobiography of Henry Hudson. Edited by V. M.

    McCardle. San Francisco: Bay Area Publishers, 1975.

BIBLIOGRAPHY

Iowa Records Center, Des Moines, Iowa. Records of the State
    Commission on Business Promotion Policy. Record Group 61.

Krieger, Adam. "Capitalizing on a Down Market." Paper read at
    the Twenty-third Annual Meeting and Technical Conference
    of the Midwest Technological Association, March 9-12,
    1989, at Holt Convention Hall, Detroit, Michigan.

Lottimer, Harold. "Coming to Terms with a Recession." In
    Proceedings of the Economic Forecaster Society. Edited by
    Mark V. Brownell and Ellen C. Addison. Houston: Economic
    Forecasters Society, 1981, 439-51.

Records, Records, Records. 3d ed. Washington, D.C.: Records
    Management Association, 1991.

Renfro, Paul E., III, Martha Miika, Jean Vendes, and Jonathan
    Kosta. Modern Management Aids. Vol. 4, Understanding the
    Strategic Business Plan. New York: Business Development
    Press, 1985.

Schwartz, Arnold. Map of Centerville Industrial Complex. MS.
    141, J. C. Burger Collection, Centerville Library,
    Indianapolis.

Shornley, Michael J., Jr. Techniques for Improving
    Productivity. Vol. 2. Southampton, Eng.: Hampshire
    Press of England, 1988.

Shulman, Mary, Frank K. Hildegarde, and Sandra Block, trans.
    Postwar Industrialism: A Study of Industrialization in
    Eastern European Countries (1946-1986). Studies in

European Economic Culture, no. 5. Rotterdam: Windmill
University Press, 1980.

Sills-Prottle, Afton. <u>Inflation Markers</u>. 1969. Reprint.
Chicago: Business News Publishing Co., 1983.

Thornberg, Martin R., and Leanne P. Dreighton, eds. and comps.
<u>Bibliography of Business Management</u>. Cincinnati: New
Business School Press, 1987.

<u>To Work I Go and Go</u>. Book 1, canto 5, stanza 6.

U.S. Bureau of the Census. <u>Statement on Population Shifts</u>.
M8109-0067. Washington, D.C., January 1981.

U.S. Congress, Senate, Committee on Ways and Means. <u>Hearings on
Trade Embargo</u>. 96th Cong., 2d sess., 1978. Committee
Print 12.

U.S. Department of Labor. <u>Industry Statistics Update</u>.
Washington, D.C.: U.S. Government Printing Office, 1988.

<u>Wyatt</u> v. <u>Newcastle</u>, 109 U.S. 271 (1956).

BIBLIOGRAPHY

SELECT BIBILOGRAPHY

Branley & Associates. *High-Tech Planning in Business*, by
    William Joline. 2 vols. Milwaukee: Business University
    Press, 1985-86. Microfilm.

Caldwell, Janet. "Business Reorganization Guidelines."
    Eastern Industries Journal, June 1991.

Calumet, Edward. *Erosion in the Great Plains.* Lincoln:
    Visual Publishers, 1979. Slides.

Charlemagne, Harriet S. Interview by Henry Nardell, 12
    September 1990. Tape recording, County Historical Society,
    San Antonio, Texas.

Congressional Record. Washington, D.C., 1980-90.

Editorial. *New York Times*, 14 June 1989.

Encyclopedia America. 10th ed.

Esterbrook, Edna C. "The Rural Migration of the 1980s." Ph.D.
    diss., University of Benston, 1988.

Gregg, Edith R. Review of *Go for Broke*, by Harley J. Tomkins.
    Western Review, August 1990, 42.

Holmes, Walter B., Jr., and Kathryn O. Juneau. "Who Is the
    Real Manager?" *Business Quarterly* 32, no. 5 (Fall 1990):
    14-21.

Hudson, Henry. *Autobiography of Henry Hudson.* Edited by V. M.
    McCardle. San Francisco: Bay Area Publishers, 1975.

Iowa Records Center, Des Moines, Iowa. Records of the State
    Commission on Business Promotion Policy. Record Group 61.

Krieger, Adam. "Capitalizing on a Down Market." Paper read at
    the Twenty-third Annual Meeting and Technical Conference
    of the Midwest Technological Association, March 9-12,
    1989, at Holt Convention Hall, Detroit, Michigan.

Lottimer, Harold. "Coming to Terms with a Recession." In
    Proceedings of the Economic Forecaster Society. Edited by
    Mark V. Brownell and Ellen C. Addison. Houston: Economic
    Forecasters Society, 1981, 439-51.

BIBLIOGRAPHY

Records, Records, Records. 3d ed. Washington, D.C.: Records Management Association, 1991.

Renfro, Paul E., III, Martha Miika, Jean Vendes, and Jonathan Kosta. *Modern Management Aids.* Vol. 4, *Understanding the Strategic Business Plan.* New York: Business Development Press, 1985.

Schwartz, Arnold. Map of Centerville Industrial Complex. MS. 141, J. C. Burger Collection, Centerville Library, Indianapolis, n.d.

Shornley, Michael, Jr. *Techniques for Improving Productivity.* Vol. 2. Southampton, Eng.: Hampshire Press of England, 1988.

Shulman, Mary, Frank K. Hildegarde, and Sandra Block, trans. *Postwar Industrialism: A Study of Industrialization in Eastern European Countries (1946-1986).* Studies in European Economic Culture, no. 5. Rotterdam: Windmill University Press, 1980.

Sills-Prottle, Afton. *Inflation Markers.* 1969. Reprint. Chicago: Business News Publishing Co., 1983.

Thornberg, Martin R., and Leanne P. Dreighton, eds. and comps. *Bibliography of Business Management.* Cincinnati: New Business School Press, 1987.

To Work I Go and Go. Book 1, canto 5, stanza 6.

U.S. Bureau of the Census. *Statement on Population Shifts.* M8109-0067. Washington, D.C., January 1981.

U.S. Congress, Senate, Committee on Ways and Means. *Hearings on Trade Embargo.* 96th Cong., 2d sess., 1978. Committee Print 12.

U.S. Department of Labor. *Industry Statistics Update.* Washington, D.C.: U.S. Government Printing Office, 1988.

Wyatt v. Newcastle, 109 U.S. 271 (1956).

BIBLIOGRAPHY

Reprinted, by permission, from Evan K. Matsui, <u>Hidden</u> <u>Mines</u>
      (Boston: The Mining Press, 1990), 63.

From a drawing by Denise Shurtell for Wyatt Kingsley, <u>The Last</u>
      <u>Soldier</u> (New York, 1901).

Photography courtesy of the Museum of Artifacts.

Adapted from Porter 1988, fig. 2.9.

Reprinted, by permission, from Evan K. Matsui, *Hidden Mines*
      (Boston: The Mining Press, 1990), 63.

From a drawing by Denise Shurtell for Wyatt Kingsley, *The Last*
      Soldier (New York, 1901).

Photography courtesy of the Museum of Artifacts.

Adapted from Porter 1988, fig. 2.9.

CREDIT LINES

Precise, simple language is the mark of better business
writing. Pompous language is especially offensive.

    Cold and pompous writing affects readers in
    several ways. Some [cannot believe] that a writer
    could be such a stuffed shirt; others bristle because
    the writer sounds like an unfriendly, uncaring snob;
    ... some wonder if anything worth comprehending is
    hidden behind the cumbersome parade of cold and
    pompous ... words. ... many business people [are]
    unaware that they are creating a counterproductive,
    negative image of themselves and the organizations they
    represent. (De Vries 1981, 29; emphasis mine)

    If a cold and pompous style has become a habit, it may
    take some serious work for you to develop a more
    pleasing and successful style. . . . The first step is
    to recognize that vogue words, jargon, euphemisms,
    unnecessary prefixes and suffixes, and roundabout
    gobbledygook are all signs of a weak and ineffective
    style.   (p. 30)

Readers are not impressed with a writer's pomposity; they are
disgusted that the writer doesn't use plain, understandable
English.

EXTRACT

Precise, simple language is the mark of better business writing. Pompous language is especially offensive.

> Cold and pompous writing affects readers in several ways. Some readers shake their heads in disbelief to think that a writer could be such a stuffed shirt; others bristle because the writer sounds like an unfriendly, uncaring snob; . . . some wonder if anything worth comprehending is hidden behind the cumbersome parade of cold and pompous words and expressions. . . . many business people persistently cling to their cold and pompous writing style, unaware that they are creating a counterproductive, *negative* image of themselves and the organizations they represent. (De Vries 1981, 29; emphasis mine)

> If a cold and pompous style has become a habit, it may take some serious work for you to develop a more pleasing and successful style. . . . The first step is to recognize that vogue words, jargon, euphemisms, unnecessary prefixes and suffixes, and roundabout gobbledygook are all signs of a weak and ineffective style. (p. 30)

Readers are not impressed with a writer's pomposity; they are disgusted that the writer doesn't use plain, understandable English.

EXTRACT

COPYRIGHT NOTICE

MOUNTAIN MANUFACTURING, INC.
101 Hudson Street
Round Rock, TX 78664
512-611-0987

TO:	Roger Kettering General Manager	**DATE:**	October 1, 199-
		COPIES:	Evan Scholey
FROM:	Drake Colter Office Manager		Cecilia Bronte Donald Henderson II Barry Skelton
SUBJECT:	Records Retention		Lillian Grumbel-Fay

Last year our firm purchased additional storage space to house inactive records. Since then, two things have been called to my attention: (1) the increasing paper volume is again straining our storage capacity and (2) changes in certain state statutes may affect our retention requirements. Therefore, I believe someone should be appointed to review state and federal statutes to determine whether we are still in compliance and also to determine whether the changes affect our storage-capacity needs.

The requirements of the following authorities must be considered in records-retention decisions:

- Administrative Decision
- Armed Services Procurement Regulations
- Code of Federal Regulation
- Fair Labor Standards Act
- Industrial Security Manual, Attachment to DD Form 441
- Insurance Company Regulation
- Interstate Commerce Commission

The following records must be evaluated for retention purposes:

- Accounting and fiscal
- Administrative records
- Communications
- Contract administration
- Corporate
- Legal
- Library
- Manufacturing
- Office supplies and service
- Personnel
- Plant and property records
- Printing and duplicating

PROPOSAL: MEMO

Roger Kettering
October 1, 199-
page two

   -Products and services marketing
   -Public relations and advertising
   -Purchasing and procurement
   -Security
   -Taxation
   -Traffic and transportation

The two prime reasons for reviewing our records-retention
policy are (1) to insure that we meet all current federal and
state requirements and (2) to determine whether we must expand
our storage capacity. If it is determined that we must
increase our storage capacity, we may wish to conduct a second
study on the advantages and disadvantages of various types of
storage (full-sized paper containers, reduction media such as
microfilm, and so on).

I hope that we can begin the proposed records-retention review
by November 1, 199-. I'll be happy to assist whomever you
appoint to conduct the evaluation.

PROPOSAL: MEMO

GOVERNMENT ASSISTANCE IN OVERSEAS MARKETING

submitted to

Ruth B. Shaw
President
Creative Plastics, Inc.

submitted by

Carl Walgren, Jr.
Director of Marketing
Creative Plastics, Inc.

March 1, 199-

PROPOSAL: TITLE PAGE

I. Overview

The marketing staff of Creative Plastics has completed its review of governmental assistance to small firms that wish to market their products and services overseas. This proposal contains the results of that review and makes specific recommendations about federal assistance that would benefit Creative Plastics, Inc.

II. Export Fundamentals

The same basic strategy that a firm has used successfully in the U.S. market can be used successfully in entering overseas markets. Selling abroad requires time, personnel, planning, market research, attention to detail, and hard work. It may even require some changes such as voltage, packaging, or metric conversion. Yet, exporting is not difficult if the fundamental elements of the export process are understood and followed:

Portions of this proposal are based on material contained in "Market Overseas with U.S. Government Help," Business Development Publications MT 10 (Washington, D.C.: U.S. Small Business Administration, n.d.).

PROPOSAL: REPORT OPENING PAGE

I. Overview

The marketing staff of Creative Plastics has completed its review of governmental assistance to small firms that wish to market their products and services overseas. This proposal contains the results of that review and makes specific recommendations about federal assistance that would benefit Creative Plastics, Inc.

II. Export Fundamentals

The same basic strategy that a firm has used successfully in the U.S. market can be used successfully in entering overseas markets. Selling abroad requires time, personnel, planning, market research, attention to detail, and hard work. It may even require some changes such as voltage, packaging, or metric conversion. Yet exporting is not difficult if the fundamental elements of the export process are understood and followed:

1. Making the commitment
2. Analyzing the firm's capabilities
3. Determining the export potential of the product or service
4. Locating foreign markets
5. Developing market-entry strategies
6. Learning export procedures
7. Processing an export order

Becoming a successful exporter depends on the determination and commitment the entire company is willing to give to the endeavor. The company has to make things happen. It will involve changes, and those changes must be established and understood by the entire management team and work force.

Portions of this proposal are based on material contained in "Market Overseas with U.S. Government Help," Business Development Publications MT 10 (Washington, D.C.: U.S. Small Business Administration, n.d.).

PROPOSAL: REPORT OPENING PAGE

Government Assistance in Overseas Marketing   q

Specific information about these services that interest you may
be obtained from your local Small Business Administration
District Office. (See the telephone directory under "U.S.
Government.")

X. Export Counseling Services

Various types of export counseling can be obtained through
SBA field offices. These services are available at no cost to
eligible recipients and may include export assistance from
these sources:

• Members of Service Corps of Retired Executives (SCORE)

• Members of Active Corps of Executives (ACE)

• Senior- and graduate-level students of the Small Business
  Institute program, established at nearly 500 colleges and
  universities

• Universities and colleges in the Small Business
  Development Center program

• Initial consultation with an international trade attorney

• Professional international trade management and
  consulting firms provided to eligible businesses under
  the Call Contracting Program

PROPOSAL: REPORT CONTINUATION PAGE

Government Assistance in Overseas Marketing ¶

Specific information about these services that interest you may
be obtained from your local Small Business Administration
District Office. (See the telephone directory under "U.S.
Government.")

X. Export Counseling Services

Various types of export counseling can be obtained through
SBA field offices. These services are available at no cost to
eligible recipients and may include export assistance from
these sources:

- Members of Service Corps of Retired Executives (SCORE)

- Members of Active Corps of Executives (ACE)

- Senior- and graduate-level students of the Small Business
  Institute program, established at nearly 500 colleges and
  universities

- Universities and colleges in the Small Business
  Development Center program

- Initial consultation with an international trade attorney

- Professional international trade management and
  consulting firms provided to eligible businesses under
  the Call Contracting Program

XI. Export Workshops and Training Programs

SBA District Offices across the country cosponsor export
workshops with the Department of Commerce and other
organizations in the public and private sectors concerned with
developing U.S. international trade. Interested parties should
contact the local SBA office for times and places.

XII. Financial Assistance for Small Exporters

The SBA's financial assistance programs are administered by
the financing staff in each SBA District Office. The SBA can
provide financial assistance through loans and loan guarantees
for equipment, facilities, materials, working capital, and
specified export market development activities. Of particular
interest might be the Export Revolving Line of Credit program.
Through this program the SBA can guarantee up to 90 percent of
a bank line of credit to a small business exporter. To be
eligible you must have been in business one year. This twelve-

PROPOSAL: REPORT CONTINUATION PAGE

WRITING:

A PRACTICAL ART OR AN ENIGMA?

Sally Perlman

Writing is a problem for many business people. To them,
Winston Churchill could have been talking about business
writing when he referred to "a riddle wrapped in a mystery
inside an enigma."[1] They know that the quality of their
writing reflects directly on themselves. But the art of
written communication eludes them nevertheless, and the more
they worry about it, the more difficult it becomes.

A PRACTICAL ART

Successful business writing is a <u>practical</u> art, and
successful business people approach each writing task much as
they would any other business activity—step by step. Such a
practical, step-by-step approach to business-writing projects
includes four essential stages: getting organized, conducting
research, preparing drafts, and revising rough copy.[2]
Following these steps will not make writing easy or enjoyable
for everyone. But it will strip away much of the mystery and
help you treat your business writing projects systematically
and routinely, the same way you would handle other business
assignments.

ARTICLE OPENING PAGE

objective <u>never</u> is to show off and try to overwhelm the reader
with your great intellect and wit.

The quality of your business writing depends not only on
your mastery of grammatical and stylistic matters but on
the overall standards you set for yourself. If you have
doubts about your ability to complete a writing project
carefully and thoughtfully, you might want to have an
editor or some other qualified person criticize your final
draft or even rework it for you.[3]

Finally, writers need to recognize that the fourth step —
revising rough copy — is essential, no matter who does it. Only
by adopting a systematic, thorough, and businesslike approach
to this <u>practical</u> art can you fully experience and enjoy the
fruits of better business writing.

NOTES

1. Sir Winston Spencer Churchill, Broadcast, October 1,
1939.

2. Mary A. De Vries, <u>Guide to Better Business Writing</u>
(Piscataway, N.J.: New Century Publishers, 1981), 1.

3. Ibid., 8.

END

ARTICLE CLOSING PAGE

LAKELAND BUSINESS CONSULTANTS
2001 North Avenue
Kansas City, MO 64112
816-274-8515

For further information:

John M. Clarke
816-274-8515, X3351

FOR IMMEDIATE RELEASE

Kansas City, July 9, 199-. A free 18-page "Checklist for
Going into Business" is now available on request from Lakeland
Business Consultants, 2001 North Avenue, Kansas City, Missouri
64112. The checklist is a guide to help prospective owner-
operators prepare a business plan to determine if a proposed
business enterprise is feasible.

The booklet has a checklist-style series of questions· in 15
key operational areas such as "market analysis." It also
provides copies of essential financial statements and cost-
estimate forms.

The questions are grouped according to function, beginning
with a self-analysis series (such as personal skills) and
concluding with an operational series (such as business
records). All questions are designed to help the prospective
owner-operator develop a guide to managing a successful
business.

-MORE-

NEWS RELEASE OPENING PAGE

The checklist is based on a study prepared by the Service Corps of Retired Executives (SCORE). It covers four factors that are described by SCORE as necessary to put the successful operation of a business enterprise: (1) a practical plan with a solid foundation, (2) dedication and willingness to sacrifice to reach your goals, (3) technical skills, and (4) a basic knowledge of management, finance, record keeping, and market analyses.

-30-

NEWS RELEASE CLOSING PAGE

Index